TURN IT AND TURN IT AGAIN

Studies in the Teaching and Learning
of Classical Jewish Texts

Jewish Identity in Post-Modern Society

Series Editor: Roberta Rosenberg Farber – Yeshiva University

Editorial Board:

Sara Abosch – University of Memphis
Geoffrey Alderman – University of Buckingham
Yoram Bilu – Hebrew University
Steven M. Cohen – Hebrew Union College – Jewish Institute of Religion
Bryan Daves – Yeshiva University
Sergio Della Pergola – Hebrew University
Simcha Fishbane – Touro College
Deborah Dash Moore – University of Michigan
Uzi Rebhun – Hebrew University
Reeva Simon – Yeshiva University
Chaim I. Waxman – Rutgers University

TURN IT AND TURN IT AGAIN

Studies in the Teaching and Learning
of Classical Jewish Texts

Edited by JON A. LEVISOHN
and SUSAN P. FENDRICK

BOSTON
2013

Library of Congress Cataloging-in-Publication Data:
The bibliographic data for this title is available from the Library of Congress.

Copyright © 2013 Academic Studies Press
All rights reserved
ISBN 978-1-936235-63-6 (cloth)
ISBN 978-1-61811-081-7 (electronic)
ISBN 978-1-61811-309-2 (paper)

Cover design by Ivan Grave

Published by Academic Studies Press in 2013
28 Montfern Avenue
Brighton, MA 02135, USA
press@academicstudiespress.com
www.academicstudiespress.com

For our parents
Steve and Sybil Levisohn
Camille Munz Fendrick and David Fendrick

And for our children
Ariella, Maya, and Jesse
Meira, Shoshana, Adina, Matan, and Elianna

Contents

Acknowledgements — 8

Foreword
    Sharon Feiman-Nemser — 11

1 Cultivating Curiosity about the Teaching of Classical Jewish Texts
    Jon A. Levisohn and Susan P. Fendrick — 13

PART 1: Focus on Subject Matter

2 A Map of Orientations to the Teaching of Bible
    Barry W. Holtz — 26

3 What Are the Orientations to the Teaching of Rabbinic Literature?
    Jon A. Levisohn — 52

4 Teaching Talmudic Hermeneutics Using a Semiotic Model of Law
    Daniel Reifman — 81

5 Neusner, Brisk, and the *Stam*: Significant Methodologies for Meaningful Talmud Teaching and Study
    Michael Chernick — 105

PART 2: Focus on Teaching and Teachers

6 The Pedagogy of Slowing Down: Teaching Talmud in a Summer Kollel
    Jane Kanarek — 128

7 Serendipity and Pedagogy: Presenting the Weekly *Parashah* through Rabbinic Eyes
    Carl M. Perkins — 158

8 Introducing the Bible: The Contextual Orientation in Practice
    Jon A. Levisohn — 186

PART 3: Focus on Learning and Learners

9 Teaching Ancient Jewish History:
An Experiment in Engaged Learning
Michael Satlow 212

10 "A Judaism That Does Not Hide":
Curricular Warrants for the Teaching of the Documentary
Hypothesis in Community Jewish High Schools
Susan E. Tanchel 236

11 Developing Student Awareness of the Talmud as an Edited
Document: A Pedagogy for the Pluralistic Jewish Day School
Jeffrey Spitzer 264

12 A Theory of *Havruta* Learning
Orit Kent 286

PART 4: Focus on Context

13 "Torah Talk": Teaching *Parashat Ha-shavua* to Young Children
Shira Horowitz 324

14 Using the Contextual Orientation to Facilitate the Study of Bible
with Generation X
Beth Cousens, Susan P. Fendrick, and Jeremy S. Morrison 352

15 Academic Study of the Talmud as a Spiritual Endeavor
in Rabbinic Training: Delights and Dangers
Jonah Chanan Steinberg 377

16 Teaching Rabbinics as an Ethical Endeavor and Teaching Ethics
as a Rabbinic Endeavor
Sarra Lev 388

List of Contributors 415

Index of Biblical and Rabbinic Sources 416

General Index 418

Acknowledgements

This book emerges from the Initiative on Bridging Scholarship and Pedagogy in Jewish Studies, a research project at the Mandel Center for Studies in Jewish Education at Brandeis University. We owe a debt of gratitude, first, to Sharon Feiman-Nemser, director of the Mandel Center, for her enthusiastic support of the project from its inception, and her wise and experienced contributions to making it both exploratory and productive.

We are grateful to the participants in the two Bridging Initiative research seminars in 2003-04 and 2006-07, who responded eagerly to our invitation to explore together what the serious study of the teaching and learning of classical Jewish texts could look like. The enthusiastic engagement of the participants in the Bridging Initiative conferences in 2005 and 2008 reaffirmed the importance of this work and contributed depth and texture to our understanding of the teaching and learning of classical Jewish texts. The work of the project could not have proceeded without the assistance of the staff of the Mandel Center over the last several years, as it progressed from seminars and conferences, to working papers and online videos, to, now, this book: Nora Abrahamer, Janna Dorfman, Liz DiNolfo, Sarah Feinberg, Galit Higgins, Kimberly Hirsh, Valorie Kopp-Aharonov, Deb Laufer, Stacie Martinez, Crystal Massuda, Gevelyn McCaskill, Marcie Quaroni, Susanne Shavelson, Emmajoy Shulman-Kumin, Angela Viehland and David Weinstein. In particular, we want to acknowledge Belina Mizrahi and Beth Polasky for their assistance with the conferences in 2005 and 2008.

At Brandeis, we appreciate the support and counsel of Marc Brettler, David Wright and Sylvia Barack Fishman, in their capacity as chairs of the Department of Near Eastern and Judaic Studies, and of Sylvia Fuks Fried. At Academic Studies Press, we appreciate the patience and diligence of Sharona Vedol, Kira Nemirovsky, and Danielle Padula.

Acknowledgements

We would be remiss if we did not particularly mention Lee Shulman. Throughout the evolution of the project, over and over again, we called upon both his scholarship and his friendship, and neither one ever failed us.

We also express our gratitude to the Mandel Foundation for its partnership with Brandeis University in creating and supporting the Mandel Center and its work.

The conference on Teaching Rabbinic Literature in 2008 was graciously and generously supported by a grant from the Wabash Center for Teaching and Learning in Theology and Religion, as well as a grant from Combined Jewish Philanthropies (CJP). Another grant, from an anonymous source, enabled the videorecording of the conference and the publication of the video footage on the web. Finally, we are grateful to Targum Shlishi, a Raquel and Aryeh Rubin Foundation, for supporting the publication of this book.

A number of the chapters of the book have been revised and condensed from articles first published elsewhere. Chapter 2 is adapted from the third chapter in Barry Holtz, *Textual Knowledge: Teaching the Bible in Theory and Practice* (JTSA Press, 2003) and is reprinted by permission of JTS Press. Chapter 3 is adapted from Jon A. Levisohn, "A Menu of Orientations to the Teaching of Rabbinic Literature," *Journal of Jewish Education* 76:1 (2010), and is reprinted by permission of the publisher (Taylor & Francis Ltd.). Chapter 6 is adapted from Jane Kanarek, "The Pedagogy of Slowing Down: Teaching Talmud in a Summer Kollel," *Teaching Theology and Religion* 13:1 (2010), and is reprinted by permission of the publisher (John Wiley and Sons, Inc.). Chapter 8 is adapted from Jon A. Levisohn, "Introducing the Contextual Orientation to the Bible: A Comparative Study," *Journal of Jewish Education* 74:1 (2008), and is reprinted by permission of the publisher (Taylor & Francis Ltd.). Chapter 9 is adapted from Michael Satlow, "Narratives or Sources? Active Learning and the Teaching of Ancient Jewish History and Texts," *Teaching Theology and Religion* 15:1 (2012), and is reprinted by permission of the publisher (John Wiley and Sons, Inc.). Chapter 10 is adapted from Susan E. Tanchel, "'A Judaism That Does Not Hide': Teaching the Documentary

Acknowledgments

Hypothesis in a Pluralistic Jewish High School," *Journal of Jewish Education* 74:1 (2008), and is reprinted by permission of the publisher (Taylor & Francis Ltd.). Chapter 12 is adapted from Orit Kent, "A Theory of *Havruta* Learning," *Journal of Jewish Education* 76:3 (2010), and is reprinted by permission of the publisher (Taylor & Francis Ltd.). Chapter 14 is adapted from Beth Cousens et al., "Using the Contextual Orientation to Facilitate the Study of Bible with Generation X," *Journal of Jewish Education* 74:1 (2008), and is reprinted by permission of the publisher (Taylor & Francis Ltd.).

Foreword

Sharon Feiman-Nemser

> *Kiddushin 40b:* Rabbi Tarfon and the Elders were once reclining in the upper story of Nitza's house in Lod, when this question was raised before them: "Is study greater, or practice?" Rabbi Tarfon answered, saying: "Practice is greater." Rabbi Akiba answered, saying: "Study is greater." Then they all answered and said: "Study is greater, for study leads to practice."

Writing this Foreword is a particularly pleasurable task because *Turn It and Turn It Again*, the first book from the Mandel Center for Studies in Jewish Education at Brandeis University, captures so much of what the Center is about. Since its founding in 2002, the Mandel Center has become the address for serious research on teaching and learning in Jewish education. This collection of studies by thoughtful teachers of Bible and rabbinic literature exemplifies a new tradition of scholarship in Jewish education and demonstrates how the study of practice can lead to improved practice.

An early project of the Mandel Center, the Initiative on Bridging Scholarship and Pedagogy in Jewish Studies was established to give teachers of Jewish studies—wherever and whomever they teach—the opportunity to explore how to create transformative learning experiences for their students. Led by Jon Levisohn, it brought together scholars and Jewish educators in seminars and conferences to work on questions of pedagogy and to understand better how research can strengthen practice. Besides introducing participants to research on the teaching and learning of specific subjects, the project supported teachers from diverse institutional settings and educational levels in studying some aspect of their teaching and/or their students' learning. This book is the culmination of that effort.

Many people assume that teaching is a highly individualistic practice, that each teacher must find his or her own style, that what works for one teacher probably won't work for another. These assumptions ignore significant advances in our understanding of teaching as a complex intellectual and moral practice. They also undermine the power of serious conversation based in records of practice to encourage more purposeful, meaningful and effective teaching and learning.

This book provides a rare glimpse into the hidden world of teacher thinking—how teachers of Bible and rabbinic literature decide what and how to teach and how they justify their decisions. It offers images of the possible—vivid cases of teaching and learning to nourish the pedagogical imagination. It contributes a shared language for analyzing the teaching and learning of classical Jewish texts by presenting useful concepts and frameworks. Finally, it models an investigative stance toward teaching and learning.

Following Rabbi Akiva, the rabbis taught us that study—inquiry, patient and careful investigation—can and should lead to improved practice. If *Turn It and Turn It Again* serves as a catalyst for thoughtful exchange among teachers of classical Jewish texts, *dayenu*. If it stimulates them to try something new in their teaching, *dayenu*. If it encourages serious reflection on the relationship between what teachers do and what students learn, *dayenu*. If it inspires others to examine their own practice, *dayenu*. I believe it will accomplish all this and more.

1 Introduction: Cultivating Curiosity about the Teaching of Classical Jewish Texts

Jon A. Levisohn and Susan P. Fendrick

> *Ben Bag Bag said: Turn it and turn it again, for all is contained within it.*
> Pirkei Avot (Ethics of the Fathers), 5:22

In some contexts, the teaching of Ben Bag Bag in Pirkei Avot may have already become a cliché. Of course he would say this! What else would we expect from a participant in the rabbinic project, a project that makes sense only if we assume that the Torah contains endless depths of wisdom? But a closer reading reveals that the aphorism is not only about Torah, but also about how one ought to relate to Torah. That is, Ben Bag Bag's teaching is actively promoting an inquiring attitude toward the classical texts of the Jewish tradition, towards Torah in the broader sense—what came to be known as the dual Torahs, the Oral Torah alongside the Written, the inherited teachings alongside the fixed text. Ben Bag Bag's aphorism is not merely a comment about the status of Torah, but an encouragement—even a directive—to "turn it" endlessly, to investigate it, to adopt a stance of inquiry towards text and tradition.

For those immersed in the classical texts of the Jewish tradition—Tanakh, midrashic collections, Mishnah and Talmud, and their commentaries—this stance is second nature. Jews ask questions about these texts. They pursue their meanings, often celebrating the questions more than the answers, and the process of inquiry more than the product. Texts are transmitted; texts are revered; but most of all, texts are studied. For outsiders to the tradition, this inquiry stance is frequently quite surprising.

In adopting Ben Bag Bag's words for the title of this book, we hope to indicate a very simple point: the *teaching* of classical Jewish texts deserves disciplined and focused investigation no less than do the texts themselves. We can transfer the inquiry stance that we are accustomed to take from one domain, the realm of the texts themselves, to another domain, the realm of teaching those texts. We can take our teaching or that of others, or the learning of students, or our conceptual models for teaching, and turn them into texts—to be studied, to generate insight and wisdom, to foster new questions, and to contribute to a culture of inquiry.

And just as the study of Torah is pursued for intellectual purposes rather than immediately practical purposes—classical Jewish texts are rarely studied to determine a halakhic ruling, except by specialists in Jewish law—so too the study of the teaching of Torah can be pursued for intellectual and scholarly purposes rather than immediately practical purposes. We can pursue a study of pedagogy *lishma*, for its own sake. We can discover ideas that shape how we think about teaching and learning as much as or more than they directly shape how we teach.

More than anything else, a fascination with the endlessly intriguing, endlessly surprising work of teaching is the common thread among the contributors to this volume. They refrain from promoting particular teaching techniques. They do not make claims about "best practices" based on general desirable outcomes; even where they are committed to particular approaches in specific contexts, their stance in this book is one of exploration rather than merely advocacy. In other words, to the extent that they share their approach to a particular pedagogic problem, they are exploring that approach with their readers, trying to understand it better, in the hope that what they learn in the process will be interesting to others as well. They pursue arguments, to be sure, but they refrain from "proofs." They prefer close description to categorical prescription. They analyze, and they wonder. They do not intend to tell their readers how to teach—although their work will help all of us who teach classical Jewish texts become better and more thoughtful teachers. They expose the complexity of the practice of teaching complicated texts, rather than concealing that complexity behind assertions about "what works." And so the purpose of this book, we might say, is to cultivate curiosity about the teaching and learning of classical Jewish texts, to question and wonder, to help all of us to think about this work with greater depth and creativity.

Beyond this point, the studies collected here draw on three interwoven intellectual traditions in educational research: a focus within educational research on subject-specific pedagogical knowledge, the movement in academia known as the Scholarship of Teaching and Learning (often abbreviated as "SoTL"), and the broader trend (particularly in K-12 education) of teacher research. All three of those traditions were influential in the design and execution of our original research project—the Initiative on Bridging Scholarship and Pedagogy in Jewish Studies—at the Mandel Center for Studies in Jewish Education at Brandeis University, which gathered together teachers and scholars in a set of seminars and conferences over a number of years, and which generated a large set of working papers on a variety of issues in the teaching of Tanakh and rabbinic literature. Versions of many of those papers appear in this volume.

The first of these three intellectual traditions emerged in the early 1980s, when Lee Shulman called attention to what he called a "missing paradigm" in educational research,[1] a problem that he was pursuing and continued to pursue with colleagues and numerous students at Stanford.[2] The missing paradigm to which Shulman called attention was an approach that places subject matter at the heart of pedagogic inquiry, that recognizes the complexity of subject-specific pedagogic challenges, and that takes the question of teachers' subject matter knowledge (and what they do with that knowledge) seriously. Along the way, he rejected the sharp bifurcation of teacher knowledge into general pedagogical knowledge, on the one hand, and content knowledge, on the other. It is important that teachers know their subjects, and it is important that they possess certain kinds of generic knowledge about teaching. But the most important things that they know fall into a category that he called "pedagogical content knowledge" or PCK—the knowledge of how to guide students into and through a particular content area, of how to take the fundamental concepts within that content area and represent them in multiple ways, of how to frame the overarching intellectual structures within that area, of what is particularly challenging within that area and how to work around those challenges. In terms of research, then, the most interesting questions about teaching—and the most significant questions to pursue, to serve the practical purposes of

---

[1] Lee Shulman, "Those Who Understand: Knowledge Growth in Teaching," *Educational Researcher* (1986): 4-14.

[2] The following draws on material previously published by one of the editors: Jon A. Levisohn, "Strengthening Research on the Pedagogy of Jewish Studies: Introduction to a Suite of Articles on Teaching Bible," *Journal of Jewish Education* 74:1 (2008), and Jon A. Levisohn, "Building Bridges to Overcome Breaches: School and Academy, Content and Pedagogy, Scholarship and Teaching," *South Atlantic Philosophy of Education Society (SAPES) 2008 Yearbook*, 2009.

teacher education and professional development—are questions about how teachers actually approach a particular subject-specific pedagogical challenge, and how they might do so.

The second tradition to which we referred above is the Scholarship of Teaching and Learning. The term "scholarship of teaching" was first coined by Ernest Boyer in an effort to elevate the work of teaching to a more prominent status within academia.[3] Since that time, thanks again to the work of Lee Shulman among others, it has developed the more specific meaning of scholarly inquiry by academics in particular disciplines into the practice of teaching those disciplines. Academics who pursue the Scholarship of Teaching and Learning expand their research agendas in order to make teaching and/or learning the focus of disciplined research and writing, knowing that specialists with a deep and rich knowledge of the subject matter can conduct research on the nuances of teaching their particular subject that outsiders to the field will be hard pressed to pursue. Like other forms of scholarship, the scholarship of teaching must become publicly accessible, and it must be subject to peer review and critique, turning teaching from private property into communal property.[4] Paradigmatically, SoTL is a product of inquiry into the teaching that one knows best—namely, one's own.

The scholarship of teaching is not oriented towards the *evaluation* of teaching, nor does it focus on remediation, the diagnosis and correction of problems. It is not simply synonymous with reflection on teaching or "reflective practice," but is characterized by a qualitatively deeper level of inquiry facilitated by close attention to records of practice such as lesson plans, videotapes, students' work, or teacher journals.[5] Scholars

---

[3] Ernest Boyer, *Scholarship Reconsidered: Priorities of the Professoriate* (San Francisco: Jossey-Bass, 1990).

[4] Lee Shulman, "Teaching as Community Poperty: Putting an End to Pedagogical Solitude," *Change* 25 (1993): 6-7.

[5] Barry Holtz, "Across the Divide: What Might Jewish Educators Learn from Jewish Scholars?," *Journal of Jewish Education* 72 (2006): 5-28, quotes Chris Argyris and Donald Schon, *Theory in Practice: Increasing Professional Effectiveness* (San Francisco: Jossey-Bass, 1974), who argue that practitioners are not the best theorists of their own practice, at least not without help: "We cannot learn what someone's theory-in-use is simply by asking him. We must construct his theory-in-use from observations of his behavior" (9). This is one reason why SoTL thrives when it has access to artifacts of teaching that can serve as data for analysis, as many of the chapters in this volume do.

pursuing SoTL do not just muse about how their teaching went that day; ideally, they ask specific, researchable questions, and gather data that can illuminate those questions. Most basically, the scholarship of teaching can pursue a deeper understanding of a particular aspect of teaching or of student learning about which a professor is simply curious, holding normative questions (about whether this is a good practice, much less the *best* practice) in abeyance.

While SoTL is an emerging research tradition within higher education, there is also a third research tradition known as teacher research, or (somewhat more broadly) practitioner inquiry, found primarily within K-12 education. Where SoTL tends to use the language of academic research and to be oriented toward the development of a field of scholarship (in which studies refer to each other, build on each other, and accumulate into a scholarly tradition), teacher research tends to be focused more on the contribution that an inquiry stance can make towards the professional development of the practitioner. Indeed, the phrase "inquiry as stance," coined by Marilyn Cochran Smith and Susan Lytle,[6] signals this focus: the purpose of teacher research is not primarily to develop new knowledge but to cultivate a stance by teachers toward their work characterized by inquisitiveness and curiosity—about their own teaching, about student learning, and about the conditions within which they work. There is also an important political thrust here, empowering teachers as agents of change rather than as subjects of the research of others and of policies dictated to them.

Consistent with Shulman's call for attention to the "missing paradigm" of subject-specific pedagogical research (sometimes framed in terms of research on PCK), this book focuses on the teaching of specific subjects, the classical texts of the Jewish tradition. As in the Scholarship of Teaching and Learning, these studies pursue and promote the development of a relatively new research tradition, making pedagogy the focus of scholarly inquiry. And in the tradition and spirit of practitioner research, most of the chapters are written by instructors of classical Jewish texts investigating or exploring their own practice.

It is worth noting that all three of these traditions—and this book—reject the idea of a sharp and distinct division of labor between scholars

---

[6] See most recently Marilyn Cochran-Smith and Susan L. Lytle, *Inquiry as Stance: Practitioner Research for the Next Generation* (New York: Teachers College Press, 2009).

and teachers, and likewise reject a sharp conceptual distinction between scholarship and pedagogy. What does this mean? According to a fairly well-entrenched model of education, one group of people, the scholars, produce knowledge; they generate the material to be taught, the "what" of teaching. Then another group of people, the teachers, transmit the knowledge; they are experts on the "how" of teaching. (In addition to the producers and the transmitters, there is a third group of people in the model—the students—who are conceived as consumers.) The division-of-labor model and its corollary conceptual distinction are pervasive. History teachers go to the Holocaust Museum and study history with historians, on the one hand, or they sit with their colleagues and learn about writing across the curriculum, on the other. Teachers of Tanakh go to hear lectures from masterful scholars of Bible, or they learn about multiple intelligences. Doctoral students on their way to the professoriate become expert in their specialties, and grab a few ideas along the way about leading discussions or grading exams. And most fundamentally, teacher education programs are often divided quite literally between "content" courses and "pedagogy" courses, where the former contain intellectual substance and the latter, too frequently, are "practical," in the sense of providing training in techniques rather than exploration of ideas.

But thinking this way about pedagogy is neither useful nor perceptive. It is not useful because, as Deborah Ball writes, it "tends to fragment practice and leaves to individual teachers the challenge of integrating subject matter knowledge and pedagogy in the context of their work."[7] If the real work of teaching requires this integration, then treating the subject in a fragmented way avoids all the hard problems, and encourages idiosyncratic solutions rather than principled ones. And it is not perceptive because, just as there is no pure pedagogy without content, so too there is no pure scholarship without audience. Pedagogy is always the teaching of particular students about *something*, and scholarship is always the communication of ideas about a particular topic to *someone*, some intended audience with anticipated understandings and misunderstandings. Once the scholar formulates her ideas in some way in order to present them to others—colleagues at a conference, students in a lecture hall or a lab, or some dimly perceived readership of the par-

---

[7] Deborah Ball, "Bridging Practices: Intertwining Content and Pedagogy in Teaching and Learning to Teach," *Journal of Teacher Education*, 51:3 (2000): 242.

ticular scholarly journal to which she is submitting her article—she is already, we might say, engaged in the work of pedagogy. So the work of scholarship and the work of teaching are much more similar than they are often understood to be.

What the reader will find in this book, then, are substantive investigations of teaching, often grounded in records of practice, and always attuned to the specific questions that arise about the teaching of Tanakh and rabbinic literature in particular contexts. The authors are smart and thoughtful, and passionate about their work as instructors in the many and varied settings in which they teach. But most of all, they are *curious*. And this, as noted above, is the agenda of the book as a whole. Beyond particular insights into teaching classical Jewish texts, beyond conceptual frameworks and new language about this work, beyond advancing the field of research into subject-specific pedagogy and building up the traditions of the scholarship of teaching and teacher research, our aim in this volume is to foster in the reader the shared conviction that teaching is deserving of close attention, and that such close attention is rewarded with greater insight and understanding. It aims, in other words, to cultivate professional curiosity.

* * *

The book is organized in four sections with four foci: subject matter, teaching and teachers, learning and learners, and context. For many readers, this division will be familiar from Joseph Schwab's four educational commonplaces,[8] or from the instructional triangle of teacher-student-content situated within a circle representing the particular context or milieu.[9] But astute readers will note that the adoption of Schwab's commonplaces for this structural purpose is inevitably problematic. After all, Schwab's point is that all of these elements are at play in instruction. In any given setting, all four of them deserve consideration. Likewise, the power of the instructional triangle as a model of teaching

---

[8] See Joseph Schwab, "The Practical 3: Translation into Curriculum," *School Review* 81:4 (1973): 501-522.

[9] David Cohen and Deborah Loewenberg Ball, *Instruction, Capacity, and Improvement (CPRE Research Report No. RR-43)* (Philadelphia: University of Pennsylvania, Consortium for Policy Research in Education, 1999), and David Hawkins, "I, Thou, and It," in his *The Informed Vision: Essays on Learning and Human Nature* (New York: Agathon Press, 1974), 48-62.

is that it replaces a more simplistic model of teaching as the transmission of content from teacher to student. Instead, the instructional triangle conceptualizes teaching as always involving a set of ongoing, dynamic relationships: the (evolving) relationship between the teacher and the student, the (evolving) relationship between the teacher and the content, and the (evolving) relationship between the student and the content, which the teacher is working to facilitate.

What this means, then, is that the organization of the book into these four foci is unavoidably artificial. None of these chapters is *only* about teaching, or *only* about subject matter. Every time we talk about teaching, we are inevitably also talking about students. Every time we talk about a particular subject, we are inevitably also talking about the context in which that subject is being pursued. If we have nevertheless decided to organize the book as we have done, it is because certain chapters focus *relatively* more on one element and less on the other commonplaces; in each chapter, we can usefully view one as the figure, and the others the ground.

Beyond this organizational scheme for the book, there are other connections and relationships between chapters and across sections that are worth highlighting. First, this volume presents a very wide range of settings in which classical Jewish texts are taught. These include day schools, universities, and rabbinical seminaries, of course, but also include summer camp (Chapter 6, Kanarek), the synagogue pulpit (Chapter 7, Perkins), kindergarten and first-grade classrooms (Chapter 13, Horowitz), and adult education programs (Chapter 14, Cousens et al.). This is intentional. It challenges the presumption that there is one paradigm—one place (the yeshiva or the university) where the subject is *really* pursued. Moreover, this diversity is designed to promote the idea that we can often learn more than we might have expected from diversity. It is entirely natural for readers to look, first, to those chapters that focus on teaching that looks like their own. But we encourage our readers to explore more broadly, and to be open to both unexpected similarities and instructive differences.

Second, there are interesting and important questions to be asked about the similarities and differences between the pedagogic issues in the teaching of Tanakh and the teaching of rabbinic literature. For example, in recent years some Jewish day schools have moved towards a sharper differentiation of the teaching of Tanakh and rabbinic literature, in accordance with the professional norms of the academy, where the study of Bible (and other texts of the Ancient Near East) is distinct from the study of rabbinic texts (and other texts of the Greco-Roman, Sassanian Persian, and Arabic cultures). But other Jewish day schools have moved in the opposite direction, intentionally blurring the line between biblical and rabbinic literature, precisely in order to focus on the interpretive skills required to approach and understand classical texts in general. In this volume, most chapters focus exclusively on one or the other, and in fact, there are two pairs of chapters that highlight that specialization: Chapter 2 (Holtz) develops a set of orientations to the teaching of Tanakh, while Chapter 3 (Levisohn) develops a set of orientations to the teaching of rabbinic literature, and Chapter 10 (Tanchel) explores the teaching of Tanakh at a particular pluralistic Jewish high school while Chapter 11 (Spitzer) explores the teaching of rabbinic literature at that same high school. On the other hand, Chapter 7 (Perkins) blurs the categories in its focus on the development of *derashot,* sermons or study sessions in the synagogue that typically draw on both biblical and rabbinic texts, and Chapter 12 (Kent) likewise blurs the categories in its focus on the practice of *havruta,* paired study of classical texts, both biblical and rabbinic. Chapter 9 (Satlow) does not engage directly with the teaching of texts so much as with the teaching of the historical culture in which those texts are situated.

Third and finally, most (although not all) of the chapters in this book present studies of practice, grounded in records of practice, often records of the author's own practice. Earlier in this introduction, we discussed the traditions of inquiry on which the book draws, but it is worth emphasizing that many of the authors have set about studying their teaching, formulating research questions, gathering relevant data (everything from student work to videotapes of classrooms to teaching journals), and analyzing that data in order to arrive at conclusions that are more than just impressions, and insights that are more than just reflections. This is not familiar work; even those authors who have been trained as researchers in their respective fields have had to learn a new way of thinking about research in order to study their practice. For this they deserve our admiration. On the other hand, none of the authors expect that their work is beyond critique. Indeed, their hope, and our hope as the editors of this book, is that these studies—individually and collectively—will serve as the basis for new explorations, for inquiries that are well-grounded conceptually and empirically, for the kind of ongoing conversation that is the hallmark of a tradition of scholarship.

* * *

But why? What do we hope to accomplish? Earlier, we wrote that the purpose of this book, at the most abstract level, is to cultivate curiosity about the teaching and learning of classical Jewish texts. Hopefully, this introduction has helped to make it clear how the teaching and learning of classical Jewish texts is the kind of thing that one might be curious about. What remains to be said is why that curiosity is important.

The study of Jewish texts, we believe, remains hidebound and parochial. Not everywhere, of course; there are many wonderful examples of talented and inspirational teaching at every level and setting. But as a field, for the most part, we do things because (we believe that) this is how they've always been done, or because we lack the imagination to do things differently, or because we're not quite sure why we're studying these texts to begin with. This occurs in traditionalist environments and liberal ones, in formal settings and informal ones. We cover ground (biblical *parashiot*, chapters of Mishnah, folios of Talmud) in sequential fashion rather than carefully identifying our learning goals and creating the appropriate opportunities to help students meet those goals. We confuse knowledge of plot or *peshat,* the plain sense of the text, with substantive progress in the subject. We celebrate whimsical personal connections to the text, rather than the development of students' knowledge and ability to engage in meaningful textual interpretation. We prize the delivery of new insights by the teacher over the shared, disciplined investigation of the topic, and our assessments focus on the (momentary) retention of those insights. We get derailed by ideological disputes, mistaking them for pedagogical ones. And most of all, we tolerate a culture of idiosyncrasy, a pedagogic culture in which whatever lesson we come up with is good enough, so long as the students are at least minimally engaged.

Consider the following two anecdotes.[10] The first one is about "Rabbi Kaufman," a senior rebbe in an Orthodox day school. After teaching his class the interpretation of the *S'fas Emes* (Yehudah Aryeh Leib of Ger, nineteenth-century Poland) of a passage in Leviticus, he noted that

---

[10] The following paragraphs draw on Jon A. Levisohn, "A Plea for Purposes," *Jewish Educational Leadership* 4:1 (2005).

he chose this particular interpretation of this particular verse at least in part because he happened to encounter the *S'fas Emes* the previous night, while preparing, and thought it might be interesting. In other words, his choice of the *S'fas Emes* emerged from a kind of browsing, an unfocused exploration with no clear conception of or stance toward the purposes of studying Jewish texts in general or this text specifically. For Rabbi Kaufman, preparing to teach means preparing to *tell*, preparing to transmit information that the teacher has discovered. As he candidly admitted about his own pedagogic choice, "I knew I wanted to tell them the new interpretation." Ironically, Rabbi Kaufman apparently lived his entire life without knowing this information—but suddenly, literally overnight, the interpretation of the *S'fas Emes* had become so important that the primary goal of the lesson was that the information should now reside, at least temporarily, in the students' heads.

In a second anecdote, from a very different point on the ideological spectrum, consider the case of "Carol," an experienced Reform supplementary school teacher, who encountered a source-critical analysis of the interwoven strands of the Korach narrative (Numbers chapters 16-18). She found the study session intriguing, stimulating, even compelling—yet opined that she would never teach this material to the pre-teens in her classes. Is this a principled pedagogic position? Hardly. Carol does not, herself, believe in the Sinaitic origin of the text. Her students' parents do not, their rabbi does not, and it is almost certain that the students themselves will not as they grow into adolescence. Why, then, does she reject the teaching of human authorship—or more precisely, the exploration of the text through a critical lens—to her students? What purpose does the temporary preservation of a relic of traditionalism serve? What does Carol think about why she is teaching Torah in the first place?

The point of these anecdotes is that these teachers of Jewish texts lack a sense that curricular choices ought to be responsible to some larger framework of purposes. In Rabbi Kaufman's case, there seems to be nothing other than the instinctive inclusion of something that feels right. In Carol's case, there is nothing other than an instinctive exclusion of something that feels wrong. To these two anecdotes we might add the familiar phenomenon of novice teachers of Jewish texts casting about for curricular materials, via online networks or well-intentioned websites, to help them teach a particular topic or chapter that they find themselves assigned to teach. We should be sympathetic to these teachers, who find themselves adrift with little guidance, but the assembly of a random assortment of worksheets and activities cannot be the answer. This phenomenon, too, testifies to the state of the field. In all these cases, idiosyncrasy triumphs.

Some might argue that the appropriate response to idiosyncrasy is central planning, a coordinated effort to create a consensual curriculum. And indeed, some efforts to develop shared standards and to develop coherent curricula have shown promise. But to actually replace idiosyncrasy with uniformity is both highly improbable and almost certainly unwise. What is needed, alongside the development of proposed standards and thoughtful materials, is the development of the capacities of educators to use materials critically and well. And beyond this, what is needed is a culture of curiosity in this field, a way of talking and thinking about the teaching of classical Jewish texts that makes the familiar strange, that is not afraid to ask challenging questions or to experiment, that finds the work of teaching intellectually engaging and thought-provoking.

If teachers of classical Jewish texts were more consistently curious about their craft, and if they shared their curiosity with their colleagues in environments that supported that type of exploration, we might bootstrap our way out of our epidemic of idiosyncrasy. Curiosity, of course, is not the kind of thing that one can command. It may, however, be the kind of thing that one can spark.

PART 1

**FOCUS ON
SUBJECT MATTER**

2 A Map of Orientations to the Teaching of the Bible[1]

Barry W. Holtz

If we were to ask any educated person to name the qualities most associated with being "a good teacher," one of the first things mentioned would be that a good teacher needs to know the subject matter. But in that simple phrase rests a great deal of complexity. What does it really mean to "know the subject matter"? And how does knowing the subject matter help the individual be a good teacher? Over the past twenty-five years, education researchers have been grappling with these questions, trying to make sense of the relationship between subject matter knowledge and good teaching.

Pamela Grossman, one of the scholars in general education whose work is most relevant to Jewish education, has looked carefully at the importance of a teacher's knowledge of subject matter for the teaching of English literary texts, and her work can be usefully applied to understanding the teaching of classical Jewish texts as well. Her approach to teacher knowledge, focusing as it does on "pedagogical content knowledge,"[2] goes beyond the approach to subject-matter knowledge that characterized earlier research on teachers and teaching, which "found little or no relationship between teachers' subject-matter knowledge and either pupil achievement or general teaching performance."[3] As Grossman points

---

[1] This chapter is a condensed and revised version of chapter three of Barry W. Holtz, *Textual Knowledge: Teaching the Bible in Theory and in Practice* (New York: JTS, 2003).

[2] This term is most associated with Lee Shulman and his former students, one of whom is Pamela Grossman. See Shulman's "Those Who Understand: Knowledge Growth in Teaching," *Educational Researcher* 15, no. 2 (1986): 4–14. Also see Pamela Grossman, "What Are We Talking About Anyhow? Subject-Matter Knowledge of English Teachers," in *Advances in Research on Teaching*, ed. J. Brophy (JAI: Bingley, UK, 1991), 2:245–64; Pamela L. Grossman, Suzanne M. Wilson, and Lee S. Shulman, "Teachers of Substance: Subject-Matter Knowledge for Teaching," in *Knowledge Base for the Beginning Teacher*, ed. M. Reynolds (New York: Pergamon, 1989), 23–36.

[3] Grossman, "What Are We Talking About Anyhow?" 258.

out, these findings may "tell us as much about our difficulties in conceptualizing the role of subject-matter knowledge in teaching as about the relationship between knowledge and teaching itself."[4]

Far more significant for teaching than how many courses in the subject one took in college, or how much information one knows about the subject matter, is what Grossman calls a teacher's "orientation" to the subject matter being taught. Grossman uses "orientation" as an inclusive term that encompasses Joseph Schwab's notions of the "substantive" and "syntactic" structures of a discipline, referring respectively to the interpretive frames or lenses through which the entire field is understood,[5] and the tools that scholars use to introduce new knowledge to a field and the canons by which evidence is viewed as acceptable or not.[6] Grossman, however, adds an important dimension to Schwab's emphasis on knowledge by recognizing the importance of teachers' beliefs about the subject matter as well, "since it is frequently the case that teachers treat their beliefs as knowledge."[7] Unlike knowledge, "beliefs rely heavily on affective and personal evaluations"[8] of teachers, and include matters such as teachers' deep, underlying commitments and their sense of how students learn best and why the subject matter itself is important to study.

"Orientation," as a term, then, encompasses aspects of both the knowledge and belief sides of a teacher's relationship to the subject matter. An orientation represents teachers' "interpretive stance … toward literature [and] becomes important in understanding their goals for instruction, curricular choices, instructional assignments, and classroom questions."[9] "More than a casual attitude towards the subject matter, an orientation towards literature represents a basic organizing framework for knowledge about literature"[10]—and, Grossman further explains, for teaching it. And while teachers who have not explored the structures

---

[4] Ibid.
[5] Joseph J. Schwab, "Education and the Structure of the Disciplines" (1961), in his collected essays, *Science, Curriculum, and Liberal Education*, ed. Ian Westbury and Neil J. Wilkof (Chicago: University of Chicago Press, 1978), 246.
[6] Ibid.
[7] Grossman et al., "Teachers of Substance," 31.
[8] Ibid.
[9] Grossman, "What Are We Talking About Anyhow?" 247.
[10] Ibid., 248.

of their discipline are at a great disadvantage in thinking about how to teach that discipline to others—as Schwab puts it, "To know what structures underlie a given body of knowledge is to know what problems we shall face in imparting this knowledge"[11]—a teacher who has not confronted his or her underlying assumptions, prejudices, emotions, and aims about the subject matter will also teach much less effectively.

Orientations for Teaching Bible

An orientation, then, is no less than a real-life actualization of a teacher's underlying beliefs and pedagogic goals. How might we begin to apply in a specific way the idea of orientations to the teaching of Bible? If we begin in the world of the university, we find no simple answer to the question, "What are the appropriate orientations for Bible teaching?" Such orientations need to be rooted in the approaches to the study of Bible evidenced in the university, and the contemporary academic landscape is dotted with various methods of biblical scholarship, each of which might serve as a starting point for a pedagogy of Bible. In the words of one scholar,

> As recently as two decades ago, there was a consensus among scholars about using a fairly limited number of critical methods for the study of Bible, but today the spectrum of methods employed has enlarged dramatically.... How these different methods of biblical inquiry are to be related logically and procedurally has become a major intellectual challenge that will require a comprehensive frame of reference not readily at hand.[12]

These words, written by Gottwald in 1985, are even more true today, when the modes of biblical criticism encompass a variety of approaches even more varied than those of twenty-five years ago.

Certainly, it is not my intention here to attempt the synthesis of methods advocated by Gottwald above, or even to present a compre-

---

[11] Joseph J. Schwab, "Structure of the Disciplines: Meanings and Significances," in *The Structure of Knowledge and the Curriculum*, ed. G. W. Ford and Lawrence Pugno (Chicago: Rand McNally, 1964), 13.
[12] Norman K. Gottwald, *The Hebrew Bible: A Socio-Literary Introduction* (Philadelphia: Fortress, 1985), 7.

hensive catalog of such methods. Whether one would use Gottwald's own "angles of vision," Edward L. Greenstein's contrast of "synchronic" and "diachronic"[13] approaches to text, or the various attempts to organize contemporary literary approaches,[14] such a task is large and well beyond the scope of this chapter. By way of illustration, one need only consider that even within the "literary" mode alone, we could begin with examples of classic "source criticism" and "form criticism," and continue all the way through present-day feminist, psychoanalytic, or political criticism, and many others as well. "Historical" approaches to the Bible also vary widely. In this area, for example, feminist works such as Meyers's *Discovering Eve* stand side by side with older approaches such as Noth's *The Old Testament World*,[15] with a great range in between.

What I wish to do here instead is to take a stance appropriate to an educational perspective: namely, to consider which methods of biblical research often serve as a basis for pedagogy. Following upon that discussion, I will turn to other approaches to the teaching of Bible, orientations that are less likely to be associated with the university and have their roots in the "wisdom of practice" of teachers and in various ideological or philosophical stances unrelated to the "scientific" study of the Bible. Ultimately, a map of various orientations to teaching Bible will emerge.

Two Bible Teachers:
The Contextual and Literary Orientation

Let us first imagine two different teachers of Bible. How might they orient themselves vis-à-vis their subject matter? How might they prepare lessons for students—either adults or children? What grounds their educational thinking and pedagogic approaches?

---

13 Ibid.; see, in particular, 32–38.
14 Such as those offered in *The New Literary Criticism and the Hebrew Bible*, ed. J. Cheryl Exum and David J. A. Clines (Sheffield, England: Sheffield Academic Press, 1993). For an overview of various approaches, see Steven L. McKenzie and Stephen R. Haynes, eds., *To Each Its Own Meaning* (Louisville: Westminster John Knox, 1999). Also, Walter C. Kaiser and Moises Silva, *An Introduction to Biblical Hermeneutics: The Search for Meaning* (Grand Rapids, MI: Zondervan, 1994).
15 Carol Meyers, *Discovering Eve* (Oxford: Oxford University Press, 1988); Martin Noth, *The Old Testament World* (Philadelphia: Fortress, 1966).

David became interested in the Bible while spending his junior year of college in Israel. He was profoundly touched by the connection of the landscape of the Bible to the land he was literally walking on. He delighted in visiting archaeological sites, began reading books about the Ancient Near East, and started to view the Bible as a living repository of the history of his people. The *realia*, the ancient cultures and languages, and the laws of ancient Israel and their comparison with neighboring laws and practices fascinated him. When David returned from Israel, he began to take religion courses at his university, and found that most of his professors were similarly oriented in their approach to Bible. He pored over copies of the magazine *Biblical Archaeology Review* and even began to study Ugaritic, one of the ancient Semitic languages so important in biblical research.

In preparing his teaching, David found commentaries such as the *Anchor Bible* and the *Jewish Publication Society Commentary on the Torah* to be very useful.[16] For a class he was teaching at his local synagogue, David turned to one of the most popular and influential works about the Bible, Nahum Sarna's *Understanding Genesis*. Originally published by the Jewish Theological Seminary's Melton Research Center in 1966, Sarna's book was one of the first to bring "to the general reader a body of essential knowledge, the distillation and integration of the results of specialized research in many varied disciplines that shed light upon the biblical text."[17]

David wishes to show his students the world of biblical people, what they believed and felt, how they lived, and what they valued. He admires Sarna's emphasis on "the importance of difference [and] those areas in which Israel parted company with its neighbors."[18] David brings to his students lessons that compare the Bible's creation story with the creation myths of other ancient cultures.

---

[16] The Anchor Bible series comprises many volumes, all published by Doubleday in New York, over the course of over three decades. The JPS (of Philadelphia) Torah Commentary appears in five volumes: Nahum M. Sarna on Genesis (1989), Sarna on Exodus (1991), Baruch A. Levine on Leviticus (1989), Jacob Milgrom on Numbers (1990), and Jeffrey H. Tigay on Deuteronomy (1996).

[17] Nahum M. Sarna, *Understanding Genesis* (New York: Melton Research Center and Schocken Books, 1966), xxxiii.

[18] Ibid., xxvii.

A Map of Orientations to the Teaching of the Bible

David is preparing to teach the Joseph story. Looking in *Understanding Genesis*, he notes Sarna's explanations of the text: the "coat of many colors," David learns, was "a token of special favor and perhaps, too, of luxury and lordship";[19] David sees the meaning of Joseph's dreams "against the background of the times";[20] he reads about the situation of slavery in ancient Egypt;[21] and he explores the comparison of the attempted seduction of Joseph in Genesis 39 to the "Tale of Two Brothers" (an ancient story).[22] All the data that David draws from Sarna's book allow David to focus and enrich the lessons he prepares.

Let us imagine, now, a different teacher. Sarah was a literature major in college. She cares about the close reading of literary works and sees her role as helping to guide students along the path of careful textual analysis. The literary critical approaches to fiction and poetry that she learned in college have influenced her thinking and beliefs about being a Bible teacher. But when she began to examine "literary" approaches to the study of Bible, she was astonished to find that most of the works she consulted took a completely different view of the word "literary"—in essence, taking the biblical work apart through a variety of scholarly methods rather than reading it as a whole and appreciating it as literature and a source of meaning. In the words of Kenneth Gros Louis, "What has been called 'literary criticism' of the Bible is not the kind of literary criticism teachers of literature do. In fact, the biblical scholar's definition of 'literary criticism' is virtually the opposite of the literary critic's."[23] Sarah, however, has come upon Robert Alter's *The Art of Biblical Narrative*, and his approach is exactly what she was looking for: an approach of literary analysis of the Bible, which the author describes as

> the manifold varieties of minutely discriminating attention to the artful use of language, to the shifting play of ideas, conventions, tone, sound, imagery, syntax, narrative viewpoint, compositional units, and much else; the kind of disciplined attention, in other

---

19 Ibid., 212.
20 Ibid.
21 Ibid., 213.
22 Ibid., 214–15.
23 Kenneth R. R. Gros Louis, "Some Methodological Considerations," in *Literary Interpretations of Biblical Narratives*, ed. Kenneth R. R. Gros Louis with James S. Ackerman (Nashville: Abingdon, 1982), 2:14.

words, which through a whole spectrum of critical approaches has illuminated, for example, the poetry of Dante, the plays of Shakespeare, the novels of Tolstoy.[24]

Sarah has also read an article by Gros Louis and finds his set of "questions a literary critic considers in approaching a work of literature"[25] very much what she wants her students to consider in her classes: questions about the literary structure, style, tone, and characters' motivations, among others. An article by Joel Rosenberg[26] helps her understand the particular features of *biblical* narrative, and she wants to help her students recognize these features and how they function in conveying the story's meaning.

Unlike David, Sarah is not particularly interested in the Ancient Near East and the historical background to the Bible. Using a term from Alter, Sarah characterizes the approach that her fellow teacher David admires as being "excavative" (she would say "merely excavative!"); that is, "either literally, with the archaeologist's spade and reference to its findings, or with a variety of analytic tools intended to uncover the original meanings of biblical words, the life situations in which specific texts were used, the sundry sources from which longer texts were assembled."[27] She, in contrast, wants her students to primarily "read the text as it is," as she likes to put it, not as it may have been understood in ancient times. In the mode of the New Critics, Sarah wants the text "treated as a privileged object that should be considered predominantly in its own terms with contextual factors being assigned a minor role."[28]

Like David, Sarah is preparing to teach a unit on the Joseph stories in Genesis, and she finds Alter's reading of the text particularly helpful. His suggestion about the literary artistry of the tale will help guide the way Sarah structures her lessons. In his reading of Genesis 42, Alter points out the following, for example:

---

[24] Robert Alter, *The Art of Biblical Narrative* (New York: Basic Books, 1982), 12–13.
[25] Gros Louis, "Some Methodological Considerations," 17. His "questions" appear on 17–20.
[26] Joel Rosenberg, "Biblical Narrative," in *Back to the Sources: Reading the Classic Jewish Texts*, ed. Barry W. Holtz (New York: Simon and Schuster/Summit, 1984), particularly 37–62.
[27] Alter, *The Art of Biblical Narrative*, 13.
[28] K. M. Newton, *Interpreting the Text* (New York and London: Harvester Wheatsheaf, 1990), 174.

> The narrator, as we have noted, began the episode by emphatically and symmetrically stating Joseph's knowledge and the brothers' ignorance. Now, through all this dialogue, he studiously refrains from comment, allowing the dynamics of the relationship between Joseph and his brothers to be revealed solely through their words, and leaving us to wonder in particular about Joseph's precise motives. Whatever those may be, the alertness to analogy to which biblical narrative should have accustomed us ought to make us see that Joseph perpetrates on the brothers first a reversal, then a repetition, of what they did to him.[29]

This passage from Alter's analysis helps Sarah envision what she wants to concentrate on, what worksheets she might design for individualized learning, and what focusing questions she will ask in the whole-class discussions. Her goal is to prepare readers of the Bible as literature, in the spirit of Alter and the other, newer, interpreters of Bible whom she has subsequently discovered.[30]

In David and Sarah, we have paradigms of teachers with two different academic approaches to Bible: what we might call the historical or contextual orientation, and the classic modernist literary analysis. The contextual approach aims at uncovering the meaning of the biblical texts by viewing the Bible *within the context of its own times*, as best as we can determine it. It views the Bible as a record of an ancient civilization, and it hopes to make that world intelligible to students of today. This is the mode of Bible study that has most characterized the modern university,

---

[29] Alter, *The Art of Biblical Narrative*, 165–66.
[30] There are many works that a teacher like Sarah could turn to for help. Aside from the writers already mentioned in this article and just limiting the list to books in English, she would find the readings in the following of great pedagogic assistance: Michael Fishbane's discussion of both narrative and poetry in *Text and Texture* (New York: Schocken, 1979); Meir Sternberg's *The Poetics of Biblical Narrative* (Bloomington: University of Indiana Press, 1985); George Savran's *Telling and Retelling* (Bloomington: University of Indiana Press, 1988); Mieke Bal's *Lethal Love* (Bloomington: University of Indiana Press, 1987); and Herbert Levine's readings of Psalms in his *Sing Unto God a New Song* (Bloomington: University of Indiana Press, 1995). In addition, there is the marvelous translation of the Pentateuch in English, based on the Buber-Rosenzweig German version, done by the American scholar Everett Fox, with its excellent commentaries, *The Five Books of Moses* (New York: Schocken, 1995).

at least until quite recently. This orientation to teaching Bible has also been very influential in the secular school system in Israel, though much less so in the Diaspora.[31] It should be noted that the contextual approach includes a variety of dimensions, including the use of various tools that help locate the Bible in its historical setting. These might include source criticism (looking at the strands of tradition that come together to form the biblical text as we know it, that is, the "documentary hypothesis"), form criticism (looking at all the formal patterns within and among texts), comparative linguistics (understanding the language of the Bible through looking at other languages that are linguistically related), and archaeology, among others.

Sarah's orientation, which we will call the literary criticism orientation, aims at literary readings of biblical texts, using the tools of modern literary analysis. There is a wide range of approaches within this domain, but most pay careful attention to the style, language, characters, themes, and forms of the biblical text. Such approaches are far more commonly used with biblical narratives and poetry than legal, prophetic, or wisdom-literature sections of the Bible. This orientation includes "post-modern" approaches to hermeneutics, most specifically in its use of "reader-response" criticism. What characterizes reader-response reading is that it focuses on the experience of the reader in encountering the text—what happens to the reader, and how the text itself is structured to affect the reader. Post-modern approaches to literary theory includes a wide range of other ways to read texts; perhaps the best-known is feminist criticism, which in its various manifestations focuses on the representations of female characters and on legal passages related to women in the Bible, reads the biblical text through a feminist lens, and places gender at the center of one's reading (and teaching). It includes the work of such scholars as Carol Meyers (see note 15), Mieke Bal (see note 30), Alice Bach, J. Cheryl Exum, Phyllis Trible, and Tikvah Frymer-Kensky, among many others.[32]

---

[31] See Barry W. Holtz, "Teaching the Bible in Our Times," in *International Handbook of Jewish Education*, ed. Helena Miller, Lisa Grant, and Alex Pomson (New York: Springer, 2012).

[32] See Alice Bach, *Women in the Hebrew Bible: A Reader* (New York: Routledge, 1998) and her *Women, Seduction, and Betrayal in Biblical Narrative* (Cambridge: Cambridge University Press, 1997); J. Cheryl Exum, *Fragmented Women: Feminist Subversions of Biblical Narratives* (Harrisburg, PA: Trinity Press Interna-

Parshanut:
Traditional Bible Commentaries

Of course, contextual and literary approaches to the Bible do not exhaust the ways that the Bible is both studied and taught. One obvious next approach is the study of Bible in the light of its classical Jewish commentaries. The use of traditional commentaries in Jewish education emanates from a deep assumption embedded in the tradition that this literature of commentary is part of Torah;[33] for centuries, the interpretations of the traditional commentaries were understood as the authoritative Jewish understanding of the Bible.

Of course, one of the features of the Jewish interpretive literature from its beginnings to the present day is that there is no one authoritative understanding of the text, but rather a range of views. As one scholar has put it, "the characteristic of early rabbinic commentary that is most distinctive … [is] its multiplicity of interpretations."[34] Educationally, it is possible for the teacher to view this range of interpretations as something to be embraced or something to be avoided. That is, a teacher may choose to limit the students' access to this range by presenting the tradition as if there is only one authoritative view (this is typical of the way Rashi, the great medieval commentator, is used in some Orthodox schools), but others see presenting divergent views within the tradition as one of the goals of learning itself. Perhaps the most well-known exponent of the latter approach is the late professor Nehama Leibowitz, who,

---

tional, 1993); Phyllis Trible, *Texts of Terror: Literary-Feminist Readings of Biblical Narratives* (Philadelphia: Fortress Press, 1984); Tikvah Frymer-Kensky, *Studies in Bible and Feminist Criticism* (Philadelphia: Jewish Publication Society, 2006). More popular representations of feminist approaches to reading the Bible include: Elyse M. Goldstein, *The Women's Torah Commentary: New Insights from Women Rabbis on the 54 Weekly Torah Portions* (Woodstock, VT: Jewish Lights Publishing, 2008); and Tamara Cohn Eskenazi and Andrea Weiss, eds.,*The Torah: A Women's Commentary* (New York: URJ Press, 2007).

[33] This idea is discussed in numerous places in the religious and scholarly literature. See, for one example, the well-known essay by Gershom Scholem "Revelation and Tradition as Religious Categories in Judaism," in his *The Messianic Idea in Judaism* (New York: Schocken, 1971), 282–304. Or Jacob Neusner, *The Oral Torah* (Atlanta: Scholars Press, 1991).

[34] Steven D. Fraade, *From Tradition to Commentary* (Albany: State University of New York Press, 1991), 15. See also his interesting notion of a "circulatory view" of rabbinic commentary, on pp. 19–20.

over the course of decades, focused on classic biblical commentaries in both her classes and her numerous writings.[35]

The basis for Leibowitz's approach was much less the academy's method of biblical research than it was a classic Jewish religious perspective to approaching the text through its commentaries. Leibowitz was not a historian who focused on the historical or intellectual context of the commentator, as university scholars might; she was interested in the commentator as a window onto the Bible itself, or onto the way we should understand the Bible.[36] She was committed to a "close reading" of the biblical text—in a sense, occupying the place where traditional reading and modern literary criticism meet. Her approach emanates directly out of the oldest notions of Jewish Bible interpretation, something that James Kugel has characterized as "the doctrine of 'omnisignificance,' whereby nothing in Scripture is said in vain or for rhetorical flourish: every detail is important, everything is intended to impart some teaching."[37] Yet despite the shared use of close reading, modern literary criticism and traditional biblical interpretation are at heart quite different enterprises, based on different foundational assumptions and beliefs about the text.[38]

A typical example of Leibowitz's method is found in her approach to the early part of the Joseph story. (Leibowitz offers a number of different "studies" for this story; I am only choosing one.) She explores the puz-

---

[35] For an analysis of Leibowitz's work, see Marla L. Frankel, *Teaching the Bible: The Philosophy of Nechama Leibowitz* (Tel Aviv: Miskal-Yedioth Ahronoth Books and Chemed Books, 2007) [in Hebrew]. Also: Howard Deitcher, "Between Angels and Mere Mortals: Nehama Leibowitz's Approach to the Study of Biblical Characters," *Journal of Jewish Education* 66, 1–2 (Spring/Summer 2000): 8–22; and Joy Rochwarger, "Words on Fire: Then and Now—In Memory of Nechama Leibowitz," in *Torah of the Mothers*, ed. Ora Wiskind Elper and Susan Handelman (New York and Jerusalem: Urim, 2000), 57–80.

[36] A good example is the scholarly study by Jeremy Cohen, *Be Fertile and Increase, Fill the Earth and Master It: The Ancient and Medieval Career of a Biblical Text* (Ithaca, NY: Cornell University Press, 1989).

[37] James L. Kugel, *The Bible as It Was* (Cambridge, MA: Belknap Press of Harvard University Press, 1997), 21. Also see my discussion in Holtz, *Back to the Sources*, 177–212.

[38] See the excellent discussion of this issue by Robert Alter in "Old Rabbis, New Critics," *The New Republic*, 5 & 12 (January 1987): 27–33. Also my "Midrash and Modernity: Can Midrash Serve a Contemporary Religious Discourse?" in *The Uses of Tradition*, ed. Jack Wertheimer (New York: Jewish Theological Seminary, 1992).

A Map of Orientations to the Teaching of the Bible

zling section in Genesis 37:28 in which Joseph is sold into slavery either by "Midianites" or "Ishmaelites," or, as the text says later, by "Medanites." Her method is to look at the understandings of this confusing narrative by a variety of medieval commentators, with reference back to the midrashic literature and forward to more modern, though nonetheless traditional, commentators such as Samson Raphael Hirsch and Benno Jacob. Whereas Sarna, using a historical/contextual approach, will point out that the "variation may well be due to an interweaving of different traditions"[39] and Greenstein (in the article discussed above) will look at the effect on the reader of the textual ambiguity, Leibowitz is interested in the way traditional commentators dealt with the problem and what they expressed about the Bible through their respective solutions.

With a careful eye to the implications of each of the commentator's views, Leibowitz asks, in typical fashion: "But the main question is how does this new interpretation affect the significance of the story as a whole?"[40] This question stands behind much of her work and explains a good deal of why her writing is so attractive to educators[41]—Leibowitz aims immediately for the significance of the text. We will term this orientation, typified by Leibowitz, the *parshanut* or Jewish interpretive approach, and with this example we have moved outside the warrant of the academy into other educational justifications for teaching practice.

For teachers (and scholars) in general education, the overarching criterion of authority is the world of the university and its culture, rules, and modes of discourse, but in Jewish education, the authority of the discipline resides in multiple locations, not all of which are within the university. For the traditionalist yeshiva teacher, for example, the meaning of the text is what the classical commentators reveal it to be. And the Bible is God's word, not a human document, and the way university scholars might talk about the genres and subgenres of the Bible—narrative, law, prophecy, and so on—is unimaginable; the Bible is not a collection of different types of literature but a seamless whole. In the

---

[39] Sarna, *Understanding Genesis*, 214.
[40] Leibowitz, *Studies in Bereshit*, 407.
[41] Her written materials are also eminently usable. One can easily imagine a teacher taking Leibowitz's chapter, photocopying the various excerpts from the commentators, and basing his or her lesson around an exploration of these texts. Even the questions that Leibowitz appends to each "study," written originally for the students themselves, are well suited for a teacher's use.

realm of Jewish religious education, then, we see the reality of multiple approaches to the discipline, some of which are governed by the rules of university discourse and others of which are quite different[42]—so different, in fact, that even the word "discipline" is outside the realm of their discourse. We might refer here to the notion of "interpretive communities" of textual interpretation, as it appears in the work of the literary critic Stanley Fish. That is, the way we read texts—and, in our case, the way we teach texts—is deeply connected to the community to which we belong. Fish claims that the "interpretive strategies" employed by individual readers "exist prior to the act of reading and therefore determine the shape of what is read rather than, as is usually assumed, the other way around."[43] We live in communities that help us understand texts, what we want to accomplish when we teach them, where we see ourselves, and where we see our students and their futures.

Any particular teacher's orientation toward teaching a text (or indeed, toward any pedagogic situation, such as teaching mathematics) emanates, it appears, from a combination of at least three sources: a) the particular personality and temperament of the teacher him- or herself;[44] b) the available authoritative models of one's milieu or culture (i.e., one's "interpretive community"); and c) the "wisdom of practice,"[45] as it

---

[42] For a related issue, see Jonathan Cohen's discussion of the problem of defining Jewish philosophy as a discipline in his "Enacting the Eclectic: The Case of Jewish Philosophy," *Journal of Curriculum Studies* 30, no. 2 (1998): 207–31.

[43] Stanley Fish, *Is There a Text in This Class?:The Authority of Interpretive Communities* (Cambridge, MA: Harvard University Press, 1980), 171.

[44] There is a good deal of research currently available on the relationship of a teacher's biography and his or her way of teaching. See, for example, Freema Elbaz, *Teaching Thinking: A Study of Practical Knowledge* (London: Croom Helm, 1983); P. S. Millies, "The Relationship between a Teacher's Life and Teaching," in *Teacher Lore: Learning from Our Experience*, ed. William H. Schubert and William Ayers (White Plains, NY: Longman, 1992); F. Michael Connelly and D. Jean Clandinin, "Personal Practical Knowledge and the Modes of Knowing," in *Learning and Teaching the Ways of Knowing*, ed. Eliot Eisner, *84th Yearbook of the National Society for the Study of Education* (Chicago: University of Chicago Press, 1985), 174–98; Marilyn Cochran-Smith and Susan L. Lytle, eds., *Inside/Outside: Teacher Research and Knowledge* (New York: Teachers College Press, 1992); and Rosetta Marantz Cohen, *A Lifetime of Teaching: Portraits of Five Veteran High School Teachers* (New York: Teachers College Press, 1991).

[45] Shulman, "Those Who Understand."

has been experienced by the teacher, either in his or her own career or in knowing about the practices of other teachers. (Some of those models may be colleagues, the teachers of one's own youth,[46] and/or those who transmit their "wisdom" through books and articles.) The teacher in this view "is not only a master of procedure but also of content and rationale ... capable of explaining why something is done."[47] Teachers, then, have their own views about what should be done in the classroom, based on their sense not merely of what works but also of what is worth doing.

Looking for a Moral

But how might wisdom of practice be investigated? Aside from observing teachers at work in classrooms or interviewing them, perhaps the best way to understand wisdom of practice is to look at the curriculum materials actually used by teachers as an indication of the way they may approach their particular subjects. Certainly it is true that decisions about the books that a class uses are not in the hands of teachers alone. But the popularity of certain books—and the way that those books attempt to reflect the actual practices of teachers—makes looking at textbooks a valuable and instructive exercise.[48]

If we turn to one popular example, an orientation to the teaching of Bible different from what we have seen up to now becomes apparent. *A Child's Bible*, by Seymour Rossel, aims to look at the narratives in the Bible as a means of instructing us today in the way we should behave. "The people in the stories," we read in the introduction for the student, "are always a lot like us. So the stories help us learn how we should live, what we should do, and how we should behave."[49] The aim is to see "what

---

[46] Through the "apprenticeship of observation" that all teachers experience—by having been students themselves. See Dan Lortie, *Schoolteacher* (Chicago: University of Chicago Press, 1975).
[47] Shulman, "Those Who Understand," 13.
[48] See Miriam Ben-Peretz, *The Teacher-Curriculum Encounter: Freeing Teachers from the Tyranny of Texts* (Albany: State University of New York Press, 1990), on the potential of curriculum and its limitations; and for some of the difficulties, Sharon Feiman-Nemser and Deborah Loewenberg Ball, "Using Textbooks and Teachers' Guides: A Dilemma for Beginning Teachers and Teacher Educators," *Curriculum Inquiry* 18 (1988): 401–23.
[49] Seymour Rossel, *A Child's Bible* (West Orange, NJ: Behrman House, 1988), 7.

[the stories] mean to us today," and in order to do so, students should ask themselves: "'What truth is this story teaching me?' 'What does this story say that I should do?' 'How does this story say that I should behave?'"⁵⁰

We see this method exemplified in the textbook's explanation of the Joseph story, in a discussion that includes, under "What does it mean": "Your dreams teach you things you need to know. Even a bad dream can help you grow stronger."⁵¹ And under "What does it teach" (the distinction between this and "What does it mean" is not entirely clear to me):

> Joseph heard Pharaoh say that there were two dreams. But he listened very carefully. And that is how he discovered that both were really one and the same dream. If you want to help people by listening to them, you must first listen to their words. But then you must also try to hear what their words mean. Joseph was a good listener.⁵²

The biblical stories, according to this view, are important for the moral lessons that they communicate. Unlike the academic literary method—and the pedagogic approach that emanates from it—which aims at opening up the complexity, indeed, the ambiguity, of the biblical narrative, *A Child's Bible* is oriented toward simplifying the biblical tale into a specific "teaching," as Rossel puts it in his introduction. Contrast this with Alter's comment that "an essential aim of the innovative technique of fiction worked out by the ancient Hebrew writers was to produce a certain indeterminacy of meaning, especially in regard to motive, moral character, and psychology."⁵³ Perhaps for this reason, *A Child's Bible* does not use the actual biblical text itself (filled with the many ambiguities that contemporary Bible scholars delight in pointing out), but rather retells the stories, leaving out the inconvenient complexities of the original and adding clarifying points on its own.

The underlying assumption of this approach is that the Bible communicates clear lessons, and the details of the narratives are to be understood as pointing us in the way of good moral behavior. Educationally,

---

50 Ibid.
51 Ibid., 118.
52 Ibid.
53 Alter, *The Art of Biblical Narrative*, 12.

A Map of Orientations to the Teaching of the Bible

A Child's Bible has the advantage of being accessible to children and clear about its outcomes. The Bible, in these lessons, has something to tell us, and in each case we will be able to define what that something is (or what those somethings are). Children can take home these messages and feel that the Bible speaks to them.[54]

We might characterize the orientation of *A Child's Bible* as a "didactic" or "moralistic" approach to Bible. Although *A Child's Bible* is aimed at the more liberal sector within Jewish religious practice, it ironically resembles approaches seen in more traditional communities, such as that found in the series of textbooks called *Gateway to Torah*.[55]

Although the moralistic approach focuses on finding the meanings of the biblical text, it differs from the literary orientation in at least two ways. First, as I mentioned above, the didactic orientation eschews the literary orientation's close reading of the text with its consequent emphasis on the nuance and specific vocabulary and tone of the biblical text, replacing close reading with an expanded retelling of the narrative. Second, it aims to extract a specific kind of message from the text. A literary method is never about uncovering a message to learn, though people may certainly learn such messages from their reading of texts. We don't expect a person to read *Hamlet* and say that the moral of the story is "don't be wishy-washy about making decisions," or "don't listen to ghosts when they give you missions." Indeed, these comical attempts to sum up the play indicate exactly the nature of the problem: great literary works are admired for their complexity, their ability to mirror the complexity of life itself, perhaps, and not because we can learn a simple lesson from them. Hence, no one puts *Oedipus Rex* and Aesop's fable of "The Fox and Grapes" at the same level of literary accomplishment. In the same spirit, Rosenberg speaks about the nature of the biblical narrative:

> [I]t is impossible to distill *the* message of biblical narrative. Attempts to generalize yield only moral and theological truisms that do violence to the Bible's special way of talking. Biblical narrative rarely moralizes. It explores moral questions, to be sure, but it is in the wit and nuance of the specific moment that one is to find

---

54 Alter and others would no doubt argue that such an educational approach sends a not-so-hidden message that the Bible is simple, perhaps even simplistic. The Bible becomes a kind of Jewish Aesop's Fables.
55 Miriam Lorber and Judith Shamir, *Gateway to Torah* (New York: Ktav, 1991).

the narrative's intelligence most concentrated. This intelligence steadfastly withholds itself from stating "messages." It allows its messages to arise from silences in the narrative. In a sense, it is *weighing* messages, in that discordant voices in the tradition are allowed silently to clash, even as the narrative plunges inexorably forward.[56]

Neither this approach nor a didactic or moralistic approach aims at confronting the issue of the personal meaning of the text in the life of the reader. The teacher who uses the didactic orientation attempts to teach moral messages applicable to all students. The teacher who uses a literary orientation understands that although the student may uncover many meanings in the biblical text, none need address his or her own experience or life. A teacher operating strictly within either orientation will not ask the student, "Well, what does this mean to you?" For that, we need to turn to another orientation, what I call "personalization."

Personalization and Bible Teaching

In the twentieth century, perhaps the most powerful representation of the personalization orientation to the Bible comes from Martin Buber. In his essay "The Man of Today and the Jewish Bible," Buber tries to articulate a way for us to encounter the Bible directly in our lives.[57] Too often, Buber says, people today view the Bible in a distant, "abstract" way with "an interest connected with the history of religion or civilization, or an aesthetic interest, or the like—at any rate it is an interest that springs from the detached spirit"[58] of contemporary life. We picture Buber watching our friend David teach, as he uses his "contextual" orientation; we imagine Buber observing Sarah's lessons as she explores the literary "aesthetic" of the biblical text. Neither satisfies

---

[56] Rosenberg, "Biblical Narrative," 62–63.
[57] In Martin Buber, *On the Bible: Eighteen Studies,* ed. Nahum N. Glatzer (New York: Schocken, 1968). Note Buber's influence on a more recent book, Gabriel Josipovici's *The Book of God: A Response to the Bible* (New Haven: Yale University Press, 1988), in which the author says that we should look at the Bible not "as a book to be deciphered, or a story to be told," but rather, "we should think of it as a person. We do not decipher people, we encounter them" (307).
[58] Buber, "Man of Today," 4.

A Map of Orientations to the Teaching of the Bible

Buber; both seem too safe, neither "confronts … life with the Word."[59] Instead, Buber argues for another course. The "man of today," Buber says,

> can open up to this book and let its rays strike him where they will.… He can absorb the Bible with all his strength, and wait to see what will happen to him.…
> He must yield to it, withhold nothing of his being, and let whatever will occur between himself and it. He does not know which of its sayings and images will overwhelm him and mold him, from where the spirit will ferment and enter into him.… But he holds himself open.[60]

This remarkable passage could well serve as the defining motto of personalization in regard to reading and teaching the Bible. Certainly, it is not easy to picture exactly what it means to translate it to an educational orientation, a way of *teaching*. But attempts to read the Bible in this way might offer a teacher some guidance (or a picture of how she herself already approaches teaching, even if in some inchoate fashion), in the same way that Sarna helps a teacher using a historical approach and Leibowitz is an aid to teachers using a Jewish interpretive approach.

Even within personalization we can delineate a variety of approaches. One might be called "personalization with a psychological perspective." As one recent writer has put it, "with every story we study, we learn not only about what we are reading, but also about ourselves. In deciphering a text, we bring to the fore elements of our own being of which we may not always be conscious. We respond to our own questions and dilemmas."[61] Reading biblical narratives "can serve as vehicles of insight into our own personalities as well as the dynamic tensions within our own families."[62] The study of these texts serves a healing function—they can help our own "search for wholeness."[63] Other personalization approaches suggest more of a political agenda; still others take a more

---

[59] Ibid.
[60] Ibid., 5.
[61] Norman Cohen, *Self, Struggle and Change* (Woodstock, VT: Jewish Lights, 1997), 13.
[62] Ibid., 14–15.
[63] Ibid.

religious/spiritual approach. All, however, share a common goal: to find the links between an individual person's life and the biblical text.[64]

The "Big Ideas" of the Bible

Looking again at various curriculum materials produced for the teaching of Bible, we see another orientation that also ultimately tries to find it own way into the issue of personal meaning and the Bible. This is seen, for example, in the Bible curriculum of the Melton Research Center, which we mentioned earlier in this article. We can see that the Melton materials were influenced by the contextual orientation as well as by the literary approach. Indeed, a comparison between Sarna's *Understanding Genesis* (which, as we noted earlier, was originally written for Melton) and the original Melton teacher's guide by Leonard Gardner[65] shows the way that Gardner's work—very early on in Melton's history—introduced literary approaches and reduced the amount of Ancient Near Eastern comparisons drawn from Sarna's work.[66]

Gardner's writing is clearly aimed at the classroom teacher, and it appears that he (or perhaps better, he and the leadership of the Melton Center at that time) believed that a literary approach was more appropriate for classroom use. One need only compare Sarna's approach to the Joseph story with Gardner's to see the difference. In later years, the revised Melton curriculum materials written by Ruth Zielenziger lean even more heavily toward a literary orientation.[67]

But it would be inaccurate to term the Melton orientation as only or even primarily "literary." Instead of a concern for the literary features

---

[64] For political readings, one might turn to Arthur Waskow's *Godwrestling* (New York: Schocken, 1978); or Judith Plaskow's feminist readings in *Standing Again at Sinai* (New York: Harper and Row, 1990). For a more "spiritual" approach, one could turn to Lawrence Kushner's *God Was in This Place and I, I Did Not Know* (Woodstock, VT: Jewish Lights, 1993).

[65] Leonard Gardner, *Genesis: The Teacher's Guide* (New York: Melton Research Center, 1966).

[66] See the discussion of the early years of the Melton Bible curriculum in Ruth Zielenziger, "A History of the Bible Program of the Melton Research Center with Special Reference to the Curricular Principles on Which It Is Based" (Ph.D. diss., Jewish Theological Seminary, 1989).

[67] Ruth Zielenziger, *Genesis: A New Teacher's Guide* (New York: Melton Research Center, 1979).

of the text alone, the curriculum might be characterized as having an "ideational" approach; that is, with a primary focus on answering the question, "What are the 'big ideas' that the Bible is expressing?" Or perhaps better, "What are the values of the Bible?" As Gardner put it:

> There are two kinds of activities at which the lesson plans aim. The first is an analysis of the structure of the text. This requires a close reading of the text and a search for the particular devices which are employed: repetition, opening and closing statements; turning points or reversals....
> The second kind of classroom activity at which we aim is to take each of the Bible stories as a metaphor which communicates an important idea. Thus in our analysis of the text, we search for the idea in its metaphorical expression. Once discovered, we work to make the idea clear in a more literal mode and to apply it to our own experience.[68]

From this passage, we see that although there is interest in the literary features of the text, the primary goal is to uncover the "idea in its metaphorical expression," to see the major moral and theological insights or ideas of the Bible.[69] Examples of "big ideas" and values found in the curriculum are "the basic belief in the essential goodness of the universe" that we learn from the Creation story and "the endowment of man with moral autonomy and the stress upon the human aspect of evil" that we learn from the Cain and Abel story.[70] Though it uses close reading of the text, this approach differs from the literary approach of Robert Alter and others because it seeks explicitly to extract a message from the text;[71]

---

[68] Gardner, *Genesis*, 210.
[69] Ibid., 211.
[70] I've taken both examples from Sarna's *Understanding Genesis*, the original basis of the curriculum, which, despite its emphasis on a contextual framework and comparisons with the ancient Near Eastern sources, still asserts these basic ideas and values. The first example is found on p. 18, the second on p. 28. Looking at Gardner or Zielenziger, *Genesis: A New Teacher's Guide*, makes the case even more clearly.
[71] There is, however, an interesting convergence between the Melton approach and that advocated by Zvi Adar, an influential Israeli educator of the same period. See Adar's *Humanistic Values in the Bible* (New York: Reconstructionist, 1967), and his article "The Teaching of the Bible in Israel and the Problem of Religious Education," in *Scripta Hierosolymitana* 13 (Jerusalem: Magnes, 1963). See Zielenziger, "A History of the Bible Program," 33–35.

it is not framed moralistically or didactically, but rather represents an account of the various philosophical underpinnings of the biblical text.

A Call to Action

In the Melton materials we can discern another pedagogic orientation as well: the idea that learning Torah is intended to move people toward *action*—in this case, toward character development. How was character education supposed to occur? The most serious attempt to answer that question was by Burton Cohen and Joseph Schwab, in an article called "Practical Logic: Problems of Ethical Decision."[72] The authors argue that although "emotional factors may play a primary role in the development of character it seems likely that the role of intellect will not be an insignificant one."[73] By arguing for the role of "advancing the student's character development through his intellect,"[74] the authors saw an opportunity to relate the normal work of schools (learning of subject matter) to questions of character and ethical development of individuals, a match that made a great deal of sense in the realm of Jewish education, where intellectual activities are framed by a larger religious agenda.

The method for accomplishing this was a set of exercises that related the ethical principles learned in studying Genesis to "life situations" through an approach that the authors called "practical logic,"[75] a sophisticated method of ethical reasoning based on the notion that applying an ethical precept to a particular life situation is not a simple matter of learning a moral aphorism or idea and then behaving in the manner expected by this principle. Rather, the application of biblical

---

[72] Burton Cohen and Joseph Schwab, "Practical Logic: Problems of Ethical Decision." The article originally appeared in *The American Behavioral Scientist* 8, no. 8 (April 1965) and was subsequently reprinted as an appendix to Gardner's *Teacher's Guide*. The page numbers in the references below refer to the reprint in Gardner.

[73] Ibid., 493.

[74] Ibid.

[75] Ibid., 494. Also see Burton Cohen, "The Teaching of Deliberation in the Jewish School," in *Studies in Jewish Education*, ed. Michael Rosenak (Jerusalem: Magnes, 1984), 2:122–35. For an interesting perspective on this type of approach to moral decision making, see Michael Oakeshott's "The Tower of Babel," in *Rationalism in Politics and Other Essays* (London: Methuen, 1962), 59–79.

"lessons" to life involves a host of challenges to the individual, including (among the five "problems" discussed in the article): "the difficulty of identifying which ethical principle is applicable to a particular set of circumstances"[76] and the fact that "a given concrete situation evokes from … [a person's] catalogue of ethical precepts not one, but two or more apparently equally valid but apparently irreconcilable principles."[77] Practical logic was an approach to dealing with the "relevance" of the Bible arguably more subtle and thoughtful than the way that that term has come to be used in educational parlance.

We can see this as related to a much older understanding within Judaism of studying Torah as a means to shaping action. Classical Jewish sources portray the purpose of study as leading a person toward observing the *mitzvot*, the commandments.[78] Of course, within Jewish tradition there is a great deal of debate about the ultimate purposes of studying Torah—is the activity an end in itself? Does it have a purely intellectual purpose, a spiritual purpose, or is it intended to lead us to performing the commandments? There is a great deal of debate about these questions within the sources, but there is no doubt that one significant tradition—perhaps the dominant view—holds that there is a direct relationship between study and action.[79] When we learn Torah, we are moved toward doing; study is not merely an intellectual activity.

Another more contemporary reflection of the Call to Action orientation is seen when teachers (in educational settings and in publication) focus on the call for social justice and social action reflected in the biblical text. What all these approaches share is the belief that one of the most important purposes of studying (and thus teaching) the biblical text is to shape the character and actions of its student, not just to

---

[76] Cohen, "The Teaching of Deliberation," 494.
[77] Ibid.
[78] See, for example, Eliot Dorff, "Study Leads to Action," *Religious Education*, 75, no. 2 (March/April 1980): 171-192.
[79] See the excellent discussion of these issues in Norman Lamm, *Torah Lishmah: Torah for Torah's Sake in the Works of Rabbi Hayyim of Volozhin and His Contemporaries* (Hoboken, NJ: Ktav, 1989). For the educational implications of the question, see the sophisticated analysis by Michael Rosenak, *Roads to the Palace: Jewish Texts and Teaching* (Providence: Berghahn, 1995), esp. 231-34; see also my discussion in Barry Holtz, *Finding Our Way* (New York: Schocken, 1990), 212-30.

highlight for them the text's meanings over the ages and in their own time (whether historical, literary, traditional, personal, philosophical, or moralistic).

Decoding and Translation

One final orientation to teaching Bible is so elementary that it is easy to overlook, but so widespread that it is important not to ignore; we might call this the Decoding and Translation Orientation. This is simply the basic comprehension of the text—decoding (i.e., pronouncing) the Hebrew, translating from Hebrew, understanding the "facts," the characters' names, the plot details of stories, the nature of the laws, and the plain meaning of the words. Sometimes, it includes memorizing sections of the text or learning to sing the verses according to traditional cantillation notes. At its best, such an approach leads to the assimilation of vast comprehensive knowledge; at its worst, it can be mind-numbing and tedious.

For example, in Ruth Zielenziger's study of the early years of the Melton Bible curriculum, she describes the approach to teaching the Bible most commonly found in synagogue schools in the early 1950s,[80] one that had long been the main approach to Bible teaching dating from the days of the *cheder*. In the early part of the twentieth century, students would read the biblical text in Hebrew and translate it into Yiddish; later, under the influence of Samson Benderly's advocacy of the "natural method" (*ivrit b'ivrit*) for teaching Hebrew, students would read the text in biblical Hebrew and then (at least in theory) translate the text into modern Hebrew. The goal of using the natural method for learning Hebrew to improve biblical studies was never fully realized for most students,[81] and for many the exercise of translating from biblical Hebrew to modern Hebrew only increased confusion. Furthermore, virtually no discussion of the *meaning* of the text occurred.

We might argue that the Decoding and Translation Orientation at its best is a temporary stage or tool in the service of other orientations.

---

[80] See Zielenziger, "A History of the Bible Program," 38–43.
[81] See the excellent discussion of Benderly and the natural method in Jonathan B. Krasner's recent *The Benderly Boys and American Jewish Education* (Waltham, MA: Brandeis University Press, 2011). Also my discussion of Bible teaching in the article referenced in note 31 above.

A "Map" of the Teaching of Bible

Let me now summarize the discussion above with a conceptual map of our orientations for teaching Bible—that is, some of the core pedagogic stances toward the biblical text that teachers may hold or choose to hold.

Conceptual Map for Teaching the Bible

Orientation	Key Element	Examples	Questions to Explore
1. The Contextual Orientation	Bible in the context of its own times.	Academic research on Bible—historically-oriented studies (Sarna, *Understanding Genesis*; Brettler, *How to Read the Jewish Bible*).	How would people in biblical times have understood these texts? What can the Ancient Near Eastern context teach us about understanding the Bible, and what, in turn, can the Bible teach us about that world? How can the discoveries of archeology, geography, and the knowledge of other ancient Semitic languages uncover the meaning of the Bible in its own time?
2. The Literary Criticism Orientation	Tools of modern and postmodern literary criticism applied to the Bible.	Academic research on Bible—literary critical studies (e.g. Alter; Greenstein; sometimes in textbooks such as *Being Torah, Melton Bible Curriculum*).	How can we apply the skills of literary criticism to the Bible, reading the Bible the way we would read any great work of literature? How do the general tools of literary criticism—such as close reading of the text, attention to detail, shifts of language and tone, metaphors, etc.—help us understand the Bible? How do the specific literary features of the Bible—such as repeating words and roots, "type scenes," repeated dialogue, etc.—reveal the meaning of biblical texts?

Orientation	Key Element	Examples	Questions to Explore
3. *Parshanut*: The Jewish Interpretive Orientation	Exploration of classical commentators' understanding of Bible.	Nehama Leibowitz.	How do our rabbinic ancestors interpret the gaps and "difficulties" in biblical texts? How do we make sense of the conflicts among the interpreters?
4. Moralistic-Didactic Orientation	Exploring the Bible as a source of moral lessons.	Textbooks (e.g. *A Child's Bible*).	What is the moral lesson that the Bible teaches us? What's the "message" of the text? How do I sum up a text's message and meaning?
5. Personalization	The Bible as a source of personal meaning in people's lives.	Some curricular materials; found in contemporary popular works on the Bible (Visotzsky; Norman Cohen; Waskow; Pitzele).	How can the Bible speak to us, psychologically and spiritually? What does it mean to "make meaning" of biblical texts for our personal lives? How do we make the Bible "relevant" for our students?
6. The Ideational Orientation	The Bible as a repository of core ideas and values.	Melton Bible curriculum.	How do we help students become intellectual readers and interpreters? What are the complex ideas embedded in the Bible?
7. The Bible Leads to Action Orientation	Study leads us to performing commandments, ethical behavior, *tikkun olam*.	Textbooks of various sorts, e.g. *Sefer HaHinukh*, modern books on the Bible's relevance for practice.	What mitzvot do we learn about from the Bible? How do we take the Bible and apply it to issues of contemporary life? How does the Bible help guide our ethical behavior?
8. The Decoding and Translation Orientation	Decoding the Hebrew and comprehending the basics.	Older textbooks.	How do we read aloud (decode) and translate biblical Hebrew? What tools do students need to learn to facilitate these skills (grammar, vocabulary, etc.)?

Conclusion

In the end, of course, our "map" is only partially complete. It should be viewed not as a theoretical construct of pedagogical approaches based on philosophical positions, but rather as a kind of "middle range" representation of current Bible teaching approaches, covering some of the most commonly found examples of the way teachers think about—and practice—contemporary Bible pedagogy. This map is meant to be a heuristic device; it has the advantage of being compact and the disadvantage of being inattentive to some of the subtle distinctions that might be adumbrated.

Outlining the map is not the end of our task, for many questions remain about the use of this theoretical construct in practice. What are the practical implications of having such a map? In what way might it guide or influence Bible teachers or those responsible for working with teachers? How does the map of orientations relate to the question of a teacher's goals? In helping to organize teachers' thinking, the map may let teachers have a better sense of why they are doing what they are doing.

Finally, understanding orientations to the Bible also invites teachers to see the perspectives of the particular students in their classes and the characteristics of particular texts. Not every orientation will speak to every student. And not every text will be served equally well by any given orientation. Having this conceptual tool allows us to think harder about the particulars of our work, make sense of what we are already doing, and focus on the practices that best illuminate the Bible for a variety of students and using a wide range of biblical texts.

3 What Are the Orientations to the Teaching of Rabbinic Literature?[1]

Jon A. Levisohn

A. Introduction

We use the language of "subjects" in education all the time. We talk about the subject of math, or English, or indeed rabbinic literature. In higher education, we typically talk about "disciplines," but we mostly mean the same thing. We have departments of history, composed of people who call themselves historians, who practice something that we call the discipline of history. But what do we mean when we talk about a subject or a discipline? What holds a discipline together? What makes a subject a subject? What is any particular subject about?

We might be tempted to say that an academic discipline shares a particular methodology. But as we get closer to any particular discipline—chemistry or sociology or philosophy—and notice the multiple procedures of inquiry in use, any initial confidence in that formulation evaporates. In fact, getting clear about what constitutes a subject or a discipline is quite difficult. Instead, "subjects should be taken to represent ... centers of intellectual capacity and interest radiating outward without assignable limit."[2]

Subjects and disciplines are also fields of *teaching*, not just fields of inquiry. And when we turn to the teaching of a subject, we likewise find deep internal diversity. The teaching of history, for example, is carried out very differently in different contexts. Sam Wineburg and Suzanne

---

[1] This chapter is a condensed and revised version of a longer article: Jon Levisohn, "A Menu of Orientations to the Teaching of Rabbinic Literature," *Journal of Jewish Education* 76:1 (2010): 4-51.

[2] Israel Scheffler, "University Scholarship and the Education of Teachers," in his *Reason and Teaching* (Indianapolis: Hackett Publishing Company, 1989), 89. First published in *Teachers College Record* 70:1 (1968): 1-12.

What Are the Orientations to the Teaching of Rabbinic Literature?

Wilson[3] demonstrate this point in a simple and elegant way: they show the reader not one but two teachers of history, both skilled and knowledgeable, both generating intense engagement, and both contributing to deep and meaningful learning. But the two teachers approach the teaching of their subject in fundamentally different ways. The contrast dramatically illustrates that just as the study of history is not one thing, so too the teaching of history is not one thing.

Similarly, Pamela Grossman documents the diversity among novice teachers of English, who approach their subject with fundamentally distinct understandings of the subject and hence with distinct pedagogic practices.[4] To make sense of that diversity, Grossman superimposes a taxonomy, borrowed from literary theory, of three approaches to literary interpretation. She emphasizes the seriousness and depth of these orientations. "More than a casual attitude towards the subject matter, an orientation towards literature represents a basic organizing framework for knowledge about literature."[5] Grossman does not claim that her three orientations cover the full range of possibilities, and observes, moreover, that they can be combined in the practices of particular teachers.

About ten years later, Barry Holtz[6] applies Grossman's idea of teaching orientations to the teaching of Tanakh. While freely acknowledging his debt to Grossman, Holtz expands her three orientations to teaching English to eight orientations to the teaching of Bible. The following chart compares these orientations.[7]

---

[3] Sam Wineburg and Suzanne Wilson, "Models of Wisdom in the Teaching of History [1988]," in, *Historical Thinking and Other Unnatural Acts: Charting the Future of Teaching the Past*, ed. Sam Wineburg (Philadelphia: Temple University Press, 2001).

[4] Pamela Grossman, "What Are We Talking About Anyway? Subject-Matter Knowledge of Secondary English Teachers," in *Advances in Research on Teaching, Vol. 2*, ed. Jere Brophy (Greenwich, CT: JAI Press, 1991), 245-264.

[5] Grossman, "What are We Talking About Anyway?," 248.

[6] Barry Holtz, *Textual Knowledge: Teaching the Bible in Theory and Practice* (New York: JTS Press, 2003), chapter 3, revised and republished as chapter 2 in this volume. Note that, through his thought experiment about two different teachers of Torah (David and Sarah), Holtz accomplishes something similar to Wineburg and Wilson in their more comprehensive empirical analysis, showing the reader how the subject can be approached in fundamentally different ways.

[7] Among his revisions to his 2003 text, Holtz reduces the number of orientations from nine (in his original chapter) to eight (in the present version).

Pam Grossman: Orientations to the Teaching of English	Barry Holtz: Orientations to the Teaching of Bible
Reader Orientation Text Orientation Context Orientation	1. Contextual Orientation 2. Literary Criticism Orientation 3. *Parshanut*, the Jewish Interpretive Orientation 4. Moralistic-Didactic Orientation 5. Personalization Orientation 6. Ideational Orientation 7. Bible Leads to Action Orientation 8. Decoding and Translation Orientation

B. The Concept of a Teaching Orientation

Building on Grossman and Holtz, this chapter will lay out a taxonomy of orientations to the teaching of rabbinic literature.

Before proceeding further, however, the concept of an orientation needs closer attention. Grossman writes that an orientation is "more than a casual attitude towards the subject matter."[8] For his part, Holtz defines an orientation as

> a description not of a teacher's "method" in some technical meaning of the word, but in a deeper sense, of a teacher's most powerful conceptions and beliefs about the field he or she is teaching. It is the living expression of the philosophical questions.... What is my view of the aims of education [in this subject], and how as a teacher do I attain those aims?[9]

First, then, a negative definition: an orientation is not a casual attitude, and it is not a pedagogic method or technique. For example, "studying a Talmudic tractate sequentially" is a technique, not an orientation. (Whether to study a *masekhet* sequentially or whether to select topics—teaching "thematically"—is certainly an important pedagogic choice, but that choice itself is not comprehensive enough to be an orien-

---

[8] Grossman, "What Are We Talking About Anyway?," 248.
[9] Holtz, *Textual Knowledge*, 48-49.

tation and is compatible with multiple orientations.[10]) Other techniques, such as using computer applications or graphic organizers to display the logic of a *sugya*, are also not orientations. (There may well be certain orientations—those that emphasize technical halakhic discussions—for which graphic organizers are more helpful, and others for which they are not.) Instead, an orientation is broader and deeper than the techniques a teacher employs. Even *havruta*, paired study, which should be understood as a practice[11] rather than a technique, is not an orientation, because it can be associated with a range of conceptions of the purposes of studying rabbinic literature—and in fact, can be pursued outside of rabbinic literature as well.

The teachers' conceptions to which Holtz refers are conceptions about what a subject is all about, its boundaries, its central challenges, and especially its purposes—why it is worth teaching and learning. However, an orientation is not a conception of *ultimate* purposes, nor does it flow directly or necessarily from an ideological or religious stance towards the subject. This may seem counter-intuitive, because many assume that the most significant pedagogical fault line lies between those who treat classical texts as sacred (in some sense) and those who do not, between devotional readings and critical ones, between a hermeneutics of trust and a hermeneutics of suspicion.[12] This assumption is incorrect. In the study of Jewish texts, an abstract conception of sacredness, even a stance on divine origins, may be theologically meaningful but pedagogically inert. The affirmation that one is encountering the word of God (in some sense) provides little pedagogic guidance. Likewise, the

---

10 Anecdotally, this issue receives a great deal of time and energy among practitioners, but arguments for or against teaching a tractate sequentially or teaching thematically ought to be pursued in terms of a larger conceptual model of teaching rabbinic literature, rather than being pursued as a question of technique outside of any orientational context.

11 See Orit Kent, "A Theory of Havruta Learning," chapter 12 below. Also see Elie Holzer and Orit Kent, "Havruta: What do we know and what can we hope to learn from Studying in Havruta?," in *International Handbook of Jewish Education*, ed. Helena Miller, Lisa D. Grant, and Alex Pomson (Springer, 2011), 407-418, and earlier work cited there.

12 The phrase "hermeneutics of suspicion" first appears in Paul Ricoeur, *Freud and Philosophy*, trans. Denis Savage (New Haven: Yale University Press, 1970), 32, to refer to a mode of interpretation in which the interpreter assumes that the surface or naïve meaning of a text masks a deeper (especially political or sexual) meaning.

idea that one is encountering a text that is *not* the word of God is also compatible with a very wide range of pedagogic practices.

Something similar is the case regarding the teaching of other subjects, too. A passionate instructor of mathematics might wax poetic about the astonishing beauty of mathematics; she might defend its role as a fundamental language of the universe; she might expound on the centrality of a sophisticated understanding of number systems to her conception of human flourishing. But none of these convictions alone will help us understand how such a teacher teaches, what she emphasizes, what mathematical capacities she tries to nurture in students and how she tries to do so—and why. I do not mean to denigrate the pursuit of abstract conceptions of the disciplines, including theological conceptions, but it is inevitable that the more abstract, the loftier, the more ultimate one's conception, the less it will guide pedagogy.

Thus, an orientation combines a set of teachers' (a) conceptions and goals and (b) characteristic practices, which hang together in a coherent way. The former is essential, because an orientation is not merely technique. The latter is essential, because an orientation is not a theory of the subject but a *theory of practice*. Moreover, while some orientations are associated with certain pedagogic practices, they are not reducible to those practices. Orientations are also subject-specific in a way that method or technique, which can be employed in multiple subjects, is not. We might say that an orientation to the teaching of a subject is like a conceptual model of (at least some instances of) the teaching and learning of that particular subject for a particular context.

So the first definitional point is to distinguish an orientation from a technique, on the one hand, and from an ideology on the other. The second definitional point is to distinguish an orientation from a research methodology. This is an important point to emphasize, because of a tendency to multiply orientations by making finer and finer distinctions. We ought to resist that temptation: not every methodological distinction makes a pedagogical difference.

A third definitional point about orientations is that there is no hierarchy of orientations, and as Grossman notes about her orientations to literature, "one could find examples of both excellent and mediocre teaching within each."[13] Some instructors, when they first encounter a

---

[13] Grossman, "What Are We Talking About Anyway?," 263.

range of orientations, immediately approve of some and disapprove of others, but the theory of orientations emerges from a pluralistic stance: there are multiple responsible ways of teaching a particular subject at any level—not good ways and bad, not educative ways and miseducative, but representatives of a genuine diversity of purposes.

This does not mean that we cannot debate those purposes. We certainly can do so, and should do so. (Indeed, one benefit of articulating orientations is precisely to focus on the range of possible purposes, and thus to provide nuanced and responsible language for that debate.) But we ought to debate them in terms of particular settings and particular sets of students, and we ought to think carefully, when we are debating, about whether we are imagining the best possible version of the orientation.

Fourth, and most fundamentally, there is a basic conceptual question about orientations. Are they mutually exclusive and immutable categories (let us call this the "strong" view of orientations)? Or are they instead a rough approximation of a collection of ideas about the purposes and practices of teaching the subject that typically, but do not necessarily, hang together (the "weak" view)? According to the strong view, each orientation should have some essential quality distinct from every other; each orientation should offer distinct answers to basic questions of purpose and methodology. Holtz's rhetoric of a "map" of orientations (see chapter 2 above) implicitly endorses the strong view. On a map, a clear border marks each country as separate from every other. According to the weak view, on the other hand, orientations are historically contingent rather than fixed and eternal, and the relationship between orientations need not be one of mutual exclusivity.[14]

The weak view is more compelling. Despite his use of the metaphor of a map, Holtz himself inclines toward the weak view: "the concept of orientation is in essence a heuristic device, not a definitional surety."[15] Thus, Holtz's work on orientations is not the discovery of natural kinds or of some deep structure of the discipline. Instead, when we think about identifying orientations, we ought to think about identifying a cultural practice, along with the knowledge and beliefs that support that practice.

---

[14] The issue here is *conceptual* mutual exclusivity, not practical. After all, even on the strong view, particular teachers might usefully combine orientations in their practice. I return to this point at the end of the chapter.

[15] Barry Holtz, "Response to the Suite of Articles on Teaching the Bible," *Journal of Jewish Education* 74:2 (2008): 233.

Instead of the metaphor of a map, orientations are more like cuisines: each cuisine uses a set of common ingredients, culinary techniques, and tastes, but none of these is necessarily exclusive to that cuisine.[16] Orientations, too, can overlap in the teacher's beliefs about the purpose of the subject, about the kinds of questions that are worth asking, and about what constitutes a compelling answer, as well as in terms of pedagogic and interpretive practices. None of these is exclusive to a particular orientation. Nevertheless, we still know what we mean when we talk about Chinese or Mexican cuisine. So, too, we know what we mean, roughly, when we talk about a teaching orientation. Instead of a "map" of orientations, let us instead talk about a "menu."

To summarize: what is an orientation to teaching? An orientation is not a technique or method of teaching, and not merely an attitude held by the teacher, and not an approach to *studying* a subject. Instead, a teaching orientation is a conceptual model of teaching that subject. It is a teacher's fundamental stance toward a particular subject that encompasses the teacher's conception of the purposes of teaching that subject and a set of paradigmatic teaching practices. These purposes and practices hang together; an orientation has internal coherence. An orientation can be pursued well or it can be pursued poorly; an orientation is not, itself, good or bad. As part of our understanding of an orientation, we assume that any subject can have multiple orientations—but we do not assume that these orientations are mutually exclusive (in either their purposes or their practices). Nor do we assume that orientations are fixed and eternal. On the contrary, our menu below represents the range of pedagogic stances to the subject that we have identified as currently in use.[17]

D. The Orientations to Teaching Rabbinic Literature

What, then, are the orientations to teaching rabbinic literature? The following menu of ten orientations represents our best current understanding, informed by hundreds of colleagues in dozens of institutions.

---

[16] I owe this idea to Susan P. Fendrick (personal communication, October 2007).
[17] I discuss the methodology that leads to the development of the orientations in the longer version of this chapter, Jon Levisohn, "A Menu of Orientations Towards the Teaching of Rabbinic Literature," Journal of Jewish Education 76:1 (2010): 4-51. That article also contains more complete discussions of each of the ten orientations than the brief treatments that I provide in the next section of this chapter.

What Are the Orientations to the Teaching of Rabbinic Literature?

1. Torah/Instruction Orientation

Rabbinic literature generates the forms of Judaism that we know today. In this sense, rabbinic literature is prescriptive of behavior and sometimes belief too—or at least, it tries to be. But more generally, rabbinic literature is also a kind of sacred literature, which is to say it has been treated as sacred by Jews for centuries. It is Torah, not only in the sense of being an "oral Torah" that, in the traditional conception, accompanies the written Torah, but in the more specific, etymological sense of being a source of teaching. The encounter with this sacred literature has the potential to be illuminating, or inspirational, or instructive.

Instruction, in the sense in which it is being used here, is not the same as direct prescription of behavior (which is why the Torah Orientation is compatible with a wide range of ideological stances, from extremely traditionalist through extremely liberal[18]). Some rabbinic texts, of course, do prescribe behavior, but much of rabbinic literature is not prescriptive in this way. Nevertheless, both aggadic and halakhic texts can function as a source for instruction or a location of inspiration. Classical liturgical texts can function in this way as well. Passages from the Talmud or midrashic literature or the Siddur are taught because the instructor believes that, under the right conditions, a patient encounter with this material can promote increased awareness of truths about the world, human nature, or the divine, leading to inspiration, guidance, or enlightenment.

An instructor working within the Torah Orientation will typically select texts—often aggadic material but sometimes halakhic material as well, or as noted above liturgical material—that have the potential to illuminate, to inspire, or to guide, often in indirect ways that emerge only through a patient encounter under the right conditions. The instructor thus assumes responsibility for creating those conditions. Sometimes this means a certain kind of preliminary discussion, prior to encounter-

---

18 This parenthetical remark is intended to emphasize the point made above about the inadequacy of ideology as an analytical lens through which to understand pedagogy. The standard dichotomies (traditional versus liberal, or academic versus devotional, or historical-critical versus religious) do not get us very far. I do not mean to suggest that religious ideology is irrelevant to pedagogy. However, each one of the ten orientations is compatible with a range of ideological commitments.

ing the text. Sometimes it means employing a text as a trigger, a means to the end of discussing an emotionally or ideologically weighty topic. Sometimes instructors will create the conditions for students neither to accept a text nor to reject it, but to engage it in meaningful and generative dialogue. Teaching within this orientation aims to help Jews to understand, or at least slow down enough to explore, the potential significance of rabbinic literature in their lives.

Teachers may wish to inspire greater commitment to certain ideals: service, perhaps, or justice, or compassion. Alternatively, teachers may wish to inspire greater commitment to Judaism in general. The Torah Orientation can be a prominent mode used in adult education classes, especially in one-off sessions that do not aspire to develop textual-analytic abilities but do hope to foster meaningful engagement.[19] It may also be used with K-12 students, particularly in informal settings[20] but also through what Scot Berman calls "value analysis."[21] Analogously, teaching that focuses on the purported philosophical ideas behind the rabbinic text (often associated with the Shalom Hartman Institute in Jerusalem or the approach to Talmudic interpretation offered by the philosopher Emmanuel Levinas) may be thought of as part of this orientation, since the purpose of developing those ideas is to propose them as powerful guides for the lives and moral choices of students. Often, teaching within this orientation will focus on one particular text or a small number of texts, although topically- or thematically-organized courses can also fit this orientation (for example, a course that focuses on rabbinic texts on relationships).

---

[19] Adult education does not usually focus on cultivating textual-analytic skills, but may sometimes have a different skill in mind—namely, the skill of responsibly mining texts for meaning. See the discussion of the Skills Orientation below.

[20] One educator writes: "We have found ... that much of our informal teaching centers around rabbinic texts.... We are developing a curriculum of concepts, morals, messages we want to get across over a four-year high school experience."

[21] Scot Berman, "So What!?!: Talmud Study Through Values Analysis," *Ten Da'at; A Journal of Jewish Education* X:1 (1997). Some consider aggadic material to be particularly suited to the promotion of values, ideals, or philosophical insights. However, one can also argue for other orientations to teaching aggada as well (most obviously, the Literary Orientation and the Cultural Orientation, but others too).

What Are the Orientations to the Teaching of Rabbinic Literature?

Now, if asked about the ultimate purposes of teaching and learning their subject, many or most instructors might endorse the characterization used above for the Torah Orientation, the idea that "a patient encounter with this material can promote increased awareness of truths about the world and human nature." What is uniquely characteristic of the Torah Orientation, however, is the way in which that purpose becomes the dominant and guiding principle for pedagogic decisions. A teacher within this orientation is focused on and holds herself responsible for the students' experience, primarily. She may use literary analysis or historical context or jurisprudential categories, but her primary focus is creating the moment of encounter. By way of contrast, a teacher of a semester-long Talmud class in a yeshiva may likewise hope to foster "increased awareness of truths about the world or about human nature," but on a daily or weekly basis, pedagogic decisions are driven more by a concern for exploring the themes of the particular tractate being studied, or for developing the students' skills.

2. Contextual Orientation

The Contextual Orientation lies at the opposite end of the spectrum from the Torah Orientation—not necessarily in terms of their purposes (which, as noted, are not mutually exclusive) but in terms of setting. Where the Torah Orientation is typically (although not exclusively) pursued in one-off adult Jewish educational sessions, the Contextual Orientation is more typical of semester-long university courses. In fact, references to "academic" or "modern" Talmud study usually refer to the Contextual Orientation. Within this orientation, teachers are primarily interested in understanding the original contexts of rabbinic texts, including how the texts came to assume their final form, and how understanding that context illuminates their meaning. This is because they possess an overriding concern for *peshat*, for discerning the plain sense of the text as they see it.[22] Typically, teachers within this orientation will employ comparisons of parallel texts within the traditional

---

[22] I owe this point to Barry Wimpfheimer (personal communication, February 2009); see also Yaakov Elman, "Progressive *Derash* and Retrospective *Peshat*: Nonhalakhic Considerations in Talmud Torah," in *Modern Scholarship in the Study of Torah: Contributions and Limitations*, ed. Shalom Carmy (New York: Jason Aronson, 1996), 251 ff.

canon (e.g., comparing the Mishnah or the Babylonian Talmud with the Tosefta or Jerusalem Talmud, or using variant manuscripts) and without (using Greek or Latin texts). In some settings and with certain texts, archeological or other material sources may also be introduced into the classroom as teaching resources.[23] In other settings and with other texts, it will be particularly important to compare rabbinic literature to early Christian literature.

As noted, teaching within this orientation is compatible with extended learning opportunities, such as semester-long courses in high schools or universities. Even outside the university, the motivation behind the Contextual Orientation is often linked to a belief that academic scholarship reveals significant truths about the text. Teachers within the Contextual Orientation are concerned that students understand the complexity and multivocality of the texts. They may emphasize the strata of the texts, as well as other "academic" issues, such as problems of attribution, the work of redactors to construct the received text, and the presence of competing traditions within the text. In terms of student learning, they focus on the students' capacities to discern those strata and those issues on their own as important learning outcomes, and may construct learning opportunities to develop those capacities.

Clearly, there are many traditionalist settings in which the Contextual Orientation is considered anathema or at least inappropriate, because of what some would call an implied "lack of respect" for the text and its transmitters, particularly the amoraic interpreters of earlier traditions. Nonetheless, a number of traditionalist educational theorists argue on behalf of the Contextual Orientation.[24] In any case, it seems clear that

---

[23] See, e.g., Daniel Sperber, "On the Legitimacy, or Indeed, Necessity, of Scientific Disciplines for True 'Learning' of the Talmud," in *Modern Scholarship in the Study of Torah: Contributions and Limitations,* ed. Shalom Carmy (New York: Jason Aronson, 1996), and Yaron Eliav, "Archeology and the Study of Rabbinic Literature" (unpublished).

[24] See, e.g., Beverly Gribetz, "Historical Perspectives in Teaching Talmud," in *Wisdom From All My Teachers: Challenges and Initiatives in Contemporary Torah Education,* ed. Jeffrey Saks and Susan Handelman (Jerusalem: Urim Publications, 2003); David Bigman, "Finding a Home for Critical Talmud Study," *The Edah Journal* 2:1 (2002); and Pinchas Hayman, "Methodology and Method in the Teaching of Tannaitic Literature," in *Teaching Classical Rabbinic Texts: Studies in Jewish Education, Vol. 8,* ed. Asher Shkedi and Marc Hirshman (Jerusa-

the more specific concerns—familiar to us from the teaching of the Bible—about internal contradictions within the text are less relevant. The motivation to harmonize disparate texts certainly does exist in the field of rabbinic literature, but on the other hand *mahloket*, the principled dispute between rabbis, is present on every page of the Talmud! So it seems fair to say that the Contextual Orientation to the teaching of rabbinic literature is less ideologically fraught than its counterpart in Bible. Moreover, teachers within the Contextual Orientation may pursue the historical-critical investigation of rabbinic texts not in order to challenge the authority of the rabbis but to explore their remarkable legal and cultural creativity.

3. Jurisprudential Orientation

Within this orientation, rabbinic literature is treated as the product of a legal system, rather than as a literary text, a historical text, or even (primarily) a text that ought to trigger a wide-ranging exploration of truths about human nature or the world. Legal argument, *shaqla ve-tarya* ("give and take"), debates about legal concepts and rulings—these are the heart of the subject. As the manifestation of a legal system, rabbinic literature is appropriately examined through categories of legal analysis, sometimes (in some settings) in comparison with other legal systems (e.g., Roman law) and sometimes with categories developed internally within the Jewish tradition of talmudic interpretation. This Jurisprudential Orientation shares some aspects with the Halakhic Orientation, to follow, but is not primarily concerned with practical legal implications.

This is the case whether the Jurisprudential Orientation is carried out by scholars of comparative law, teaching students of law, or traditionalists in the yeshiva, mediating among apparently contradictory texts and encouraging students in the exercise of *hiddush*, innovative insight. In either situation, academic or traditional, the intellectual experience of exploring the legal system takes precedence over the determination of

---

lem: Magnes Press, 2002). By way of contrast, Sperber, "On the Legitimacy," argues for the indispensability of historical-critical scholarship to the pursuit of traditionalist goals of discerning halakhic implications. In other words, in his case, historical study is in support of teaching and learning within the Halakhic Orientation (see below), rather than representing the Contextual Orientation.

any actual legal ruling. Rabbinic law obeys its own logic and employs its own concepts; the Jurisprudential Orientation seeks to understand that logic and to immerse the students in that conceptual universe.

The Jurisprudential Orientation may be found in law schools, where texts are selected in order to explore a certain legal issue or jurisprudential theme, and where teachers and students are accustomed to the exploration of legal concepts and arguments, often without regard for final legal rulings (sometimes called "black letter law"). The field of *Mishpat Ivri*, the label used for the academic study of Jewish law, is also quite obviously concerned with rabbinic texts as products of a jurisprudential system, so courses in *Mishpat Ivri* are also located within this orientation. But beyond these settings, almost all study in traditional Ashkenazi (especially Lithuanian-style) yeshivot in North America and in Israel seems to fit within this orientation.[25]

Naturally, the characterization offered here does not do justice to the diversity of traditionalist interpretive strategies, *darkei ha-limmud*. But this is one of the occasions when it is important to remember that not every interpretive distinction makes an orientational difference; as significant as those distinctions among interpretive strategies may be (in terms of determining what constitutes a good answer to a question and, even more importantly, what constitutes a good question), they are not manifest as dramatic differences in pedagogic purposes and practices.[26] In general, teachers within the Jurisprudential Orientation

---

[25] Michael Rosenzweig, focusing not on pedagogy but on "methodology," emphasizes that contemporary *yeshivot* conform to the pattern established over the last century and a half. "This is noteworthy," he adds, "given the fact that access to a plethora of historical material ... might conceivably have challenged the continuity in *yeshivah* study by redirecting the focus away from the classical, ahistorical emphasis that has long prevailed"—*might* have, but in fact did not (Michael Rosenzweig, "The Study of the Talmud in Contemporary Yeshivot," in *Printing the Talmud: From Bomberg to Schottenstein*, ed. Sharon Liberman Mintz and Gabriel M. Goldstein (New York: Yeshiva University, 2005), 113.

[26] This assessment is based on an understanding that, differences among *darkei ha-limmud* notwithstanding, traditionalists teaching within the Jurisprudential Orientation share important features: they tend to select tractates (rather than specific texts) and follow the order of the tractate or the chapter within it; the tractates tend to be the "yeshivish" ones that are heavy on jurisprudential concepts and debates; they bracket or avoid altogether both the practical-halakhic implications of the texts and the personal-spiritual implications; to

What Are the Orientations to the Teaching of Rabbinic Literature?

may aspire to help students understand the legal complexity of the system for its own sake, or to achieve other pedagogical goals relating to the understanding of law across cultures. In traditionalist settings, the Jurisprudential Orientation may be motivated by the need to do a kind of conceptual "basic research"; like basic research in the physical sciences, there is no expectation of immediate payoff, and the pursuit of the truths of nature are their own reward.

The pursuit of the Jurisprudential Orientation may be motivated by the sense that this orientation places debate and argument at its center—and that an emphasis on (engaging in, understanding, and appreciating) debate and argument is culturally healthy, distinctively Jewish, and perhaps even theologically significant.[27] But for some, the motivation is even more fundamental: they believe that the Jurisprudential Orientation is not merely the preferred pedagogic option but rather the *only* real or authentic way to engage with these texts.[28] That is, accurately or not, some believe that the Jurisprudential Orientation—and more specifically, a sequential exposure to only certain selected tractates rich in jurisprudential material—reflects the way that Talmud has always been studied at the highest level.

But instructors committed to the Jurisprudential Orientation may in fact instead select a legal topic, a *sugya*, which is discussed in multiple texts across a diverse set of tractates. Alternatively, they may select

---

the extent that they are focused on the development of the skills of textual analysis, those skills are heavily jurisprudential (understanding Talmudic argument rather than, for example, understanding literary tropes); and, as mentioned above, teaching and learning is conceptualized not just as an occasion for understanding the text and its difficulties but especially as an occasion for *hiddush*, innovation in the resolution of textual difficulties. At the same time, the differences among *darkei ha-limmud* are surely deep and significant. As Elman notes in "Progressive *derash* and retrospective *peshat*," 253, the field would benefit greatly from straightforward, non-polemical comparative analyses of the various approaches.

[27] See Yehuda Brandes and Aharon Lichenstein, "From Discipline to Meaning: More on Teaching Gemara: A Response," in their *Talmud Study in Yeshiva High Schools* (ATID, 2007), for a contemporary expression of this view.

[28] See Aliza Segal and Zvi Bekerman, "What is Taught in Talmud Class: Is it Class or is it Talmud?," *Journal of Jewish Education* 75:1 (2009): 27, who quote a teacher asserting that Tractate Sanhedrin, with its complicated jurisprudential discussions, is "actual real classic gemara."

multiple legal topics to explore a particular jurisprudential phenomenon, what Schreiber calls a "meta-sugya."[29] Within this orientation, the boundaries between the text and its later commentators may be blurred—not that the opinion of a medieval *rishon* (early commentator) is conflated with the Talmudic text, but that they are regarded, in some sense, as part of one ahistorical conversation. After all, the commentaries are, for the most part, efforts to elucidate legal concepts, so drawing upon them is entirely consistent with the Jurisprudential Orientation. Indeed, one of the motivations for teaching within the Jurisprudential Orientation—for traditionalists—is to immerse the students (not only within the rabbinic legal world but also) within that tradition of interpretation. For non-traditionalists, on the other hand, the motivation may be less focused on the tradition of interpretation, and more focused on a principled conception of the subject: at its heart, some will argue, Talmud is a diverse set of complex, constructed legal debates.

4. Halakhic Orientation

Rabbinic texts—especially the legal texts, of course, but in some cases non-legal texts as well—are the primary sources for understanding the development of halakha, the Jewish legal tradition. Teachers within this orientation aspire to help students understand halakha in its complexity as a legal tradition and system. Typically, the emphasis will be on Mishnah and Talmud, although in some contexts this orientation will be served by a focus on midrash halakha. Rabbinic material may or may not be juxtaposed with pre-rabbinic (biblical) material, but it will often be juxtaposed with later legal layers, i.e., the commentators, responsa literature, and legal codes that build on the classical rabbinic texts as the legal tradition develops over time.

We can imagine an investigation into topics such as the laws of cooking on Shabbat, or the laws relating to the payment of workers, or the laws of marriage and divorce. Such an investigation would begin with the biblical sources and proceed through the development of the halakhic

---

[29] Doniel Schreiber, "The Brisker Derech Today: Are We Pursuing the 'Path' Envisioned by Reb Hayyim?" in *Wisdom from All My Teachers: Challenges and Initiatives in Contemporary Torah Education*, eds. Jeffrey Saks and Susan Handelman (Jerusalem: Urim Publications, 2003), 234.

What Are the Orientations to the Teaching of Rabbinic Literature?

tradition in the Talmud, codes, and commentators, perhaps including contemporary responsa on the topic. There is a variety of criteria of selection for appropriate topics. Some topics might be chosen as appropriately representative of some principles of halakhic argumentation. Others might be chosen to explore the way in which the halakhic tradition adheres to the rulings of earlier sages, who are granted greater authority than later sages while room is also left for logical argumentation about the application of those precedents and rulings. Others might be chosen as case studies that represent points on an ideological spectrum between halakha as an enterprise that seeks to preserve a prior way of life and halakha as a location of cultural innovation.

Thus, teaching within this orientation need not entail a dry transmission of facts about legal rulings (although perhaps that is the particular pathology of the Halakhic Orientation at its worst). Instead, the Halakhic Orientation can be as challenging and intellectual engaging as any other nuanced, complex study of intellectual history, and the thoughtful instructor can surely identify an aspirational set of subject- and orientation-specific goals for her students. Those goals may be as relevant in a liberal setting as they are in a traditional one.

Whatever the topics chosen, however, what is distinctive here is the focus on halakhic topics in a way that is different from the Jurisprudential Orientation. This is not to say that the Jurisprudential Orientation never focuses on halakhic matters, of course. But when the Jurisprudential Orientation focuses on halakha, it is interested in the logic or the concepts more than in the ruling itself. And the Jurisprudential Orientation will rarely trace the development of a *sugya* into the contemporary period, as the Halakhic Orientation might.

This is an appropriate occasion, therefore, to mention the ambiguity of the category of "rabbinic literature." Central texts such as the Mishnah and the Babylonian Talmud elicit little controversy, but what else is included? We have already had occasion to mention midrashic collections, texts such as Tosefta and the Jerusalem Talmud, and the Siddur, and to note that within the Jurisprudential Orientation there is a natural tendency to extend forward to the commentaries on Talmud. So where are the boundaries? Are geonic texts included in "rabbinic literature" as well? What about medieval commentaries, or early modern halakhic texts, or contemporary responsa? The malleability of the boundaries is another indication of the diversity of orientations; in one teaching context, the relevant material includes early Christian texts, while in another, recent Jewish ones. There is little point in trying to determine what "counts" as rabbinic literature, in the abstract, because there are no available criteria that are neutral across orientations.

5. Literary Orientation

In addition to whatever else it is, rabbinic literature (both legal and non-legal) is also *literature,* consciously crafted compositions that employ their own literary forms, structures, and patterns in the service of their literary objectives. Where the Contextual Orientation focuses on diachronic analysis, the Literary Orientation focuses on synchronic analysis, taking the text as a (redacted) unified whole and attending to the literary features and devices embedded within that whole. Teachers within this orientation will typically choose texts (again, both legal and non-legal) upon which literary analysis can be performed to great effect, and will aspire to foster their students' capacities to do so as well. It is easy to think about treating rabbinic narratives in this way—searching for word play or character development—but legal passages or larger textual units (e.g., whole chapters of Mishnah) can also serve as rich teaching material within this orientation.[30]

Of course, if literary analysis presumes to generate insight into the meaning of a text on the basis of literary features, then potentially it has a role to play wherever one engages in textual interpretation. This may make it hard to see the distinction between the Literary Orientation and others, and raises again the way in which orientations function like cuisines. There are two ways to think about this. One way is to say that when one uses literary analysis while also pursuing, say, Torah as instruction, one is blending two different orientations, the Literary Orientation and the Torah Orientation. There are surely occasions where this occurs. However, just as we said above that instructors may endorse the idea that the encounter with rabbinic texts should lead to illumination or instruction without necessarily participating in the Torah Orientation, we may need to say something similar here: instructors may use literary analysis as one of the tools in their interpretational toolkits without necessarily participating in the Literary Orientation.

---

[30] Elman, "Progressive *Derash* and Retrospective *Peshat*," 261-276.

What Are the Orientations to the Teaching of Rabbinic Literature?

The Literary Orientation, instead, comprises not only the interpretational tool—that is, not just the use of literary analysis by the instructor—but a cluster of other characteristic practices as well. In this orientation, literary analysis is foregrounded and made the explicit focus of discussion or inquiry. The instructor may select texts that are literarily rich and generative (or, conversely, may determine that the Literary Orientation is called for when she encounters a particular text). She may devote time and attention to developing the students' own capacity to interpret with a literary lens. However, we need not go so far as to say that the Literary Orientation cares about literary analysis "for its own sake," in the manner of New Criticism in literary theory; after all, we can easily imagine a teacher who focuses on the literary structures of the Mishnah not because they are beautiful or elegant in themselves but because they reveal important insights into the thinking of the editors of the Mishnah. Or consider Walfish's argument for the Literary Orientation to the teaching of Mishnah, as a pedagogic solution to the problem of Mishnah as a text that is both terse and hence difficult and yet not difficult enough (as compared to Talmud) and hence undervalued.[31] For Walfish, the Literary Orientation is not a matter of studying Mishnah as literature "for its own sake"; there are other reasons for employing literary analysis. But for Walfish or others who advocate or employ a Literary Orientation, the attention given to literary analysis is sufficiently prominent, in terms of instructional time and priorities that it tends to crowd out explicit attention to other purposes.

6. Cultural Orientation

Studying rabbinic literature provides a window into rabbinic culture, the wellspring of Judaism as it developed over time. The tools used to understand that culture are the analytical and conceptual tools of the cultural anthropologist, reading texts as products and markers of culture. The questions that we ought to ask of the texts, from this perspective, are questions such as the following. What cultural assumptions lie behind the text (whether or not we ascribe those assumptions to the author of the text)? What cultural dynamics are described or enacted

---

[31] Avraham Walfish, "Teaching the Mishnah as a Literary Text" [Hebrew], in *Teaching Classical Rabbinic Texts: Studies in Jewish Education, Vol. 8*, eds. Asher Shkedi and Marc Hirshman (Jerusalem: Magnes Press, 2002).

in the text? What cultural values are defended or promoted? Teachers within this orientation will typically select texts that are particularly significant in the understanding of rabbinic culture or of Judaism more generally from aggadic texts or halakhic texts. (Liturgical texts may find a place here too.) Some will teach in an effort to raise an awareness of the ways in which rabbinic culture is historically situated in its time and place, in which case the Cultural Orientation may share certain assumptions with the Contextual Orientation. Others, however, will construct a trans-historical conception of the rabbinic culture that they want their students to encounter and, perhaps, the norms of which they want their students to adopt. Within this orientation, certain kinds of feminist readings of texts raise awareness of the dynamics of gender as they are expressed in rabbinic culture and in Judaism more generally. As Charlotte Fonrobert writes, in one particular example, "The goal of reading gender in talmudic aggadah here is first and foremost to understand in all its complexity the cultural imagination of the talmudic editors who carefully weave the fabric of the talmudic *sugyot*."[32]

The Cultural Orientation is usually more text-focused than student-focused, but not in all cases. For example, Gidon Rothstein imagines an instructional approach that aspires to overcome the gap between the cultural norms and assumptions of the students and the cultural norms and assumptions of the rabbis, in an effort to make the strange familiar.[33] Lehman echoes this in her study of her own teaching in rabbinical school: "My goal each semester is to find a means of connecting the world in which my students live with that of the rabbis."[34] On the other hand, it may be more common to find instructors leaning in the opposite direction, committed to helping students understand the ways in which the rabbis, constructing Judaism in their time and place, are very different than we are—in other words, making the familiar strange. David Kraemer argues that instructors ought to acknowledge

---

[32] Charlotte Elisheva Fonrobert, "When the Rabbi Weeps: On Reading Gender in Talmudic Aggadah," *Journal of Jewish Women's Studies and Gender Issues* 4 (2001): 57.

[33] Gidon Rothstein, "Helping Students Get a Foot in the Door: Geertz's 'Thick Description' and the Use of Academic Scholarship in the Teaching of Rabbinic Texts" (unpublished).

[34] Marjorie Lehman, "For the Love of Talmud: Reflections on the Teaching of Bava Metzia, Perek 2," *Journal of Jewish Education* 68:1 (2002), 89.

the strangeness of rabbinic culture as a first step to overcoming it: "noticing, naming, describing the strangeness of the rabbinic text will allow the student to affirm what he or she experiences and begin the task of cultural translation."[35] Each of these stances assumes that rabbinic culture should be located historically, rather than construed as trans-historical. Moreover, each reflects an implicit claim about the way that the Cultural Orientation can contribute to the intellectual-spiritual perspective of the student.

As already noted, in situations where rabbinic culture is understood primarily as an historical category (rather than, for example, as a trans-historical category), there may be a close connection between the Cultural Orientation and the Contextual Orientation. Both tend to establish a certain critical distance from rabbinic texts, and both are focused on the meaning of the texts in their original context. Some instructors may well blend both orientations. Still, the questions that they ask are distinct. The Contextual Orientation asks questions that begin in the text, seeking answers in its cultural context(s), but with a primary desire to hear and understand the different historical voices in the text. The Cultural Orientation asks questions about culture, seeking answers in the texts (texts that are taken to reveal central aspects of culture), but also implicitly or explicitly facilitating an encounter between the culture of the rabbis and the culture of the students. Furthermore, unlike the Contextual Orientation—but in this respect like the Literary Orientation—the Cultural Orientation is more concerned with the rabbinic texts, as we find them, rather than their component parts and the process of their redaction, only turning to other materials as background or supplements to contribute to our understanding of the rabbis' cultural project.

7. Historical Orientation

Rabbinic literature provides evidence for the social, intellectual and political history of the Jewish communities of late antiquity. Who were these people—not just the rabbis but the whole set of communities—and what did they do with their lives? How were they affected by empires, armies, political movements, material conditions, and cultural

---

[35] David Kraemer, 'Welcoming the Strange in Rabbinic Literature" (unpublished).

developments? In some settings, these questions are considered to be irrelevant or even distracting; consider the derisive quip that "some people care about what Abaye and Rava *said* and some people care about what they *wore*."[36] But in other settings instructors are committed to exploring that history, and the texts are means to that end. They are windows into the past, and like real windows, they work best when they are transparent and when they do not obstruct our view of the landscape.

There is always the thorny question of whether we can take rabbinic texts at face value (and contemporary academic historiography tends to assume that we cannot). So the window is never truly transparent; the glass always distorts our view of what lies beyond it, even as it enables that view. How can we compensate for the inevitable bias of the authors of these texts, the rabbis, who (like any author) had their own ideological purposes—either as leaders of a community or as a self-appointed elite that aspired to leadership—in writing about historical events and the world around them? Yet, even if we adopt a hermeneutics of suspicion rather than a hermeneutics of trust, these texts are often the only window into the past that we have.

The preceding sentences suggest that the Historical Orientation shares a kind of skeptical stance with the Contextual Orientation (as well as with some versions of the Cultural Orientation). But their focus is different. In the Contextual Orientation, the goal is understanding the text—the window itself, as it were—in its original context. In the Historical Orientation, on the other hand, the goal is to peer *through* the window at some aspect of the historical landscape beyond, either the historical setting depicted in the text or, more skeptically, the historical setting of the redaction of the text.

Thus, the goal of teaching within the Historical Orientation is the development of an appropriate understanding of some aspect of the history of the Jews in late antiquity, or the development within students of historiographical sensibilities appropriate to the study of that history. Instructors will select texts and construct learning opportunities that illuminate that history or central interpretive questions about it.

---

[36] Sperber, "On the Legitimacy," and Barry Wimpfheimer, "The Shiva," in *Why Study Talmud in the Twenty-First Century?*, ed. Paul Socken (Lanham, MD: Lexington Books, 2009).

8. Bekiut Orientation

In certain settings, rabbinic literature is taught and learned in order to foster students' encounter with a maximum quantity of material, in a sequential fashion, with as little pre-arranged focus as possible. This is sometimes called *"bekiut"* or *"bekius,"* which translates literally as "mastery," but is more accurately translated in this context as "coverage." The purpose of studying Talmud or Mishnah *biv'kiut* (in a *bekiut* way) or *liv'kiut* (for the purpose of *bekiut*) is to cover ground. Like coverage goals elsewhere in education, here too the demand for coverage often crowds out competing concerns for depth of understanding or perhaps even longevity of retention. Nevertheless, there is a certain educational logic to the enterprise. We can imagine the argument: just as students will absorb the literary norms associated with the modern novel even if they forget the details of the novels that they read, so here too a sequential, immersive exposure to the texts may foster an apprehension of rabbinic norms, a facility with rabbinic logic, and a familiarity with rabbinic concepts, even as the details quickly slip from the mind.

One paradigm of the Bekiut Orientation is a kind of anti-theoretical reaction against the sometimes fanciful pursuit of conceptual explanations for textual difficulties (within the Jurisprudential Orientation, as practiced in some Ashkenazi yeshivot). Knowledge of the texts is the primary goal, not understanding, not *hiddush*, and certainly not personal growth or spiritual development. A familiar paradigm of *bekiut* is the program known as Daf Yomi, the "daily page," the standardized schedule of study of one folio of Talmud per day, around which has grown a cottage industry of classes, study guides, and audio-recorded lessons.[37] The breakneck pace of Daf Yomi highlights an additional component to the Bekiut Orientation, namely, the ritualization of teaching and learning. This is obviously present in Daf Yomi, where the required speed blurs the line between study as intellectual engagement and study as liturgical recitation. But it is often present in other *bekiut* study as well, which may be a ritualized performance as much as it is an intellectual pursuit.

So the claim advanced above, that the purpose of studying Talmud *biv'kiut* is to cover ground, is only partially accurate; one might also say that, at a deeper level, the purpose of study within the Bekiut Orien-

---

[37] The Day Yomi program was publicly initiated in 1923 by Meir Shapira, at the Agudas Yisroel convention in Vienna.

tation is simply *torah lishma*, Torah for its own sake. Setting aside any mastery of content, setting aside the benefits of immersion in a particular body of literature, simply occupying oneself in the study of Talmud is, for some, an activity with religious purpose and intrinsic value.[38] One aspect of that religious attitude is a kind of submission to the text—not in the sense of a suspension of critical evaluation of arguments, and not necessarily in terms of a commitment to carry out the text's prescriptions, but rather in the sense of a commitment to listen patiently and non-selectively to what the text has to say. Thus, the instructor within the Bekiut Orientation emphasizes the students' face-to-face encounter with the text as it presents itself, with little editorial selection, "interesting" and "relevant" passages studied along with those that are less so.

9. Interpretive Orientation

In contrast to other classical literature, much of rabbinic literature is constructed as interpretation of other texts, both biblical texts and texts from earlier in the rabbinic period. These interpretations proceed according to their own norms, sometimes playful and pluralistic, sometimes rigidly argumentative. The Interpretive Orientation takes this quality of the text to be its defining characteristic, the (or at least a

---

[38] Teasing apart the concept of *torah lish'ma* is notoriously difficult. We can easily identify the opposite of *torah lish'ma*, namely, study for extrinsic purposes such as career advancement or practical guidance or scholarly reputation. But what does it mean to study something for its own sake? What if one studies for the sake of becoming a more adept student—is that *torah lish'ma*? Or for the sake of heightened self-consciousness or moral attunement? In some views, even study for the purpose of religious enlightenment—"cleaving to God"—violates the strict standard of *torah lish'ma* (although, according to other views, that is precisely the correct meaning of *torah lish'ma*). The classic study of *torah lish'ma* is Norman Lamm, *Torah Lishmah: Study of Torah for Torah's Sake in the Work of Rabbi Hayyim Volozhin and His Contemporaries* (New York: Ktav, 1989); see also Michael Rosenak, *Roads to the Palace: Jewish Texts and Teaching* (Providence, RI: Bergahn Books, 1995), 231-234. Note, here, that while the Bekiut Orientation is often pursued in the context of an ideological commitment to *torah lish'ma*, the latter commitment is not by any means *limited* to the Bekiut Orientation. The adult students who arrive at a synagogue for a text study session in which the teacher is committed to the Torah Orientation, are surely engaged in *torah lish'ma*, and would be no less committed to that ideal if the instructor decided to adopt the Literary Orientation or any other.

primary) answer to the question of what the subject of rabbinic literature is about.

The interpretational strategies of rabbinic texts are sometimes (or often) the source of pedagogic dissonance. Within the Interpretive Orientation, then, teachers will focus in particular on the interpretive moves that are made in particular texts or by particular rabbis within those texts, or perhaps on the rabbis' assumptions about the prior texts that are interpreted and the rabbis' beliefs about the nature of interpretation itself. Once we adopt the Interpretive Orientation, we can avoid the implicit or even explicit devaluation of midrashic literature as secondary to, and poorly derived from, biblical literature. However, an instructor might also employ the Interpretive Orientation with an eye toward the way in which later strata of rabbinic literature employ earlier teachings, sometimes in radically new ways. In that case, they may teach a tractate sequentially and work on the interpretive issues as they emerge.

In either case, the instructor will frame an inquiry into the interpretive process represented by the text—asking how that interpretive process works—in order to help students understand and appreciate the generative interpretive culture of the rabbis. (So in this respect, there is a close connection between the Interpretive Orientation and the Cultural Orientation.[39]) But instructors may also choose this orientation in an effort to help students become more aware of their *own* interpretive processes, and perhaps to open up the cultural space for students to carry out the creative work of interpretation themselves.

10. Skills Orientation

In certain settings and certain conditions, teachers of rabbinic literature are primarily focused on helping students acquire the textual-analytic and linguistic skills to master rabbinic literature, or at least access it independently. Initially, this may seem unworthy of the label of "orientation"; after all, nearly all of the orientations can be said to be (potentially) concerned with helping students acquire skills of one sort or another. The Literary Orientation typically intends to foster appreciation

---

[39] See Lehman, "For the Love of Talmud," for an example of a conscious combination (what I call, in the conclusion to this chapter, a "principled eclecticism") of the Cultural Orientation, the Contextual Orientation, and the Interpretive Orientation.

of and capacity for literary analysis. The Cultural Orientation intends to promote a kind of anthropological sensibility, in which students learn to ask certain kinds of questions about why the rabbis would say what they say and believe what they believe. The Historical Orientation intends to cultivate a set of historiographical capacities, specifically focused on the issues and problems of the history of the Jews in late antiquity. Even the Torah Orientation, which is often pursued in adult education settings that we do not normally associate with the acquisition of skills, can be pursued toward an increasingly expanded capacity (on the part of students) to appreciate the instructional potential of the texts or to discern that instruction for themselves. These are all skills or capacities or subject-specific habits of mind, and we may assume that most thoughtful teachers who have the opportunity to construct an extended learning experience are concerned with the development of such skills. So why should we identify a Skills Orientation distinct from other orientations?[40]

Nevertheless, just as we noted above in the case of the Literary Orientation that there are times and settings where the focus on literary analysis dominates the pedagogic space, so too here we may note that the Skills Orientation emerges because there are times and settings where the focus on skills dominates the pedagogic space. There are times and settings where this focus on skills is not, significantly, a focus on the kinds of orientation-specific skills identified in the previous paragraph, but rather on what we might call "basic skills" or "foundational skills," skills of access to the basic meaning of the text in its original language. And there are times and settings where this focus crowds out other purposes and practices to a significant extent, where teachers teach and students learn with the express purpose of mastering the secret code.

This happens, in part, due to the nature of the texts themselves, which are terse and obscure, and which regularly employ technical terms that assume a great deal of background knowledge. But in addition, the focus on skills also occurs for a culturally specific reason, namely the enor-

---

[40] This issue is taken up by several of the respondents in a symposium on the longer version of this chapter, published in the *Journal of Jewish Education* 76:2 (2010). My further discussion is published as "Do We Know an Orientation When We See It? Continuing the Conversation about the Teaching of Rabbinic Literature," *Journal of Jewish Education* 76:3 (2010): 272-283.

mous cultural capital that accrues (in certain environments) to those who are able to access these texts. We may think, first, of the Orthodox world, where the ability to decipher—not to insightfully interpret but just to decipher—these obscure texts is a kind of rite of passage among boys and men.

This is not to say, however, that the teaching and learning among men in the Orthodox community is carried out within the Skills Orientation. Typically, it is not. In the male Orthodox world, the acquisition of skills happens (if it does) as a by-product of teaching within other orientations, especially within the Jurisprudential Orientation. Instead, good examples of the Skills Orientation are to be found elsewhere—among liberal Jewish educational programs (where facility with classical rabbinic texts also imparts significant cultural capital) and especially among Orthodox women's yeshivot (where students and teachers are acutely aware that access to the texts is a tool of empowerment, a key that opens up many doors). Teachers committed to the Skills Orientation place an emphasis on teaching technical terminology, providing direct instruction on standard forms of talmudic argumentation, making explicit the cultural assumptions and the historical background, even employing a developed sequential curriculum,[41] all in order to accelerate the acquisition of the desired skills. Teaching and learning within this orientation sometimes has a certain impatient quality, especially when young adults imagine themselves making up for lost time and when teachers try to help them do so. Orientations, I claimed above, are sets of purposes and practices that hang together in the actual teaching and learning of a particular subject. In identifying this orientation, we are calling to mind images of real educational environments, real teachers and real students engaged in an aspirational endeavor, where the challenge of learning to access the texts of rabbinic literature is sometimes wearisome and sometimes frustrating but also, ultimately, empowering.

---

41   Pam Grossman and Susan Stodolsky, "Content as Context: The Role of School Subjects in Secondary School Teaching," *Educational Researcher* 24:8 (1995): 5-11, 23, call attention to the way that teachers of some subjects (e.g., languages and math) believe that one must first study *a* followed by *b* and then *c*, but teachers of other subjects (e.g., social studies) seem to place less importance on sequentiality. Talmud typically has little sequentiality—except for some instructors within the Skills Orientation.

E. Conclusion: How To Use a Menu

These ten orientations to the teaching of rabbinic literature, then, constitute the menu. (See the chart below.) They certainly do not encompass every instance of the teaching of these texts. They do not encompass, for example, the use of rabbinic texts in the teaching of *other* subjects (e.g., comparative religion or the history of Jewish thought), the intentional integration of rabbinic literature with other literatures, or more casual uses of rabbinic texts for reflective or devotional purposes.[42] It may be that they do not appropriately represent the teaching of rabbinic literature in the ultra-Orthodox world, especially in Israel. But they represent ten coherent, developed conceptions of what the subject of rabbinic literature is all about, as a subject of teaching and learning, each with its associated, characteristic pedagogical practices.

Orientations to Teaching English	*Orientations to Teaching Bible*	*Orientations to Teaching Rabbinic Literature*
Reader Orientation Text Orientation Context Orientation	1. Contextual Orientation 2. Literary Criticism Orientation 3. *Parshanut*, the Jewish Interpretive Orientation 4. Moralistic-Didactic Orientation 5. Personalization Orientation 6. Ideational Orientation 7. Bible Leads to Action Orientation 8. Decoding and Translation Orientation	1. Torah/Instruction Orientation 2. Contextual Orientation 3. Jurisprudential Orientation 4. Halakhic Orientation 5. Literary Orientation 6. Cultural Orientation 7. Historical Orientation 8. *Beki'ut* Orientation 9. Interpretive Orientation 10. Skills Orientation

---

[42] I have in mind, here, instances wherein instructors choose a rabbinic text to teach, but the choice might have been otherwise. The instructor might have chosen a text from Maimonides, or from Yehuda Amichai, or something else entirely. I do not mean to denigrate the teaching or learning that occurs under these conditions, but it seems unavoidable that these are not instances of

What Are the Orientations to the Teaching of Rabbinic Literature?

Readers who have persevered to this point might now wonder why this exercise is worth pursuing: the "so what?" question. There are three good answers, and one poor one.

First, the menu of orientations provides a kind of theoretical framework for the field of rabbinic literature, as a field of teaching and learning. Second, the specificity of the menu of orientations enables new questions and new inquiries, across orientations or within a particular orientation. And third, there may be a more practical benefit for instructors of rabbinic literature, for whom encountering the menu of orientations is like holding up a mirror to their practice. Is this what I do? Is this what I believe? Relatedly, the metaphor of a menu of orientations implies *choices:* practitioners may come to see more options in the teaching of rabbinic literature, a greater range of purposes and practices, than they had previously recognized.

Here, however, we come to the poor answer to the "so what" question. There is a way in which the metaphor of a menu is potentially misleading. When we are faced with a menu, we usually choose one option (or, one main option). We might imagine therefore that our purpose, in thinking about orientations to the teaching of rabbinic literature, is to make sure that we are firmly embedded in one and only one orientation. But this would be a mistake. In the case of orientations, there is no particular reason to think that teaching within one orientation is always preferable to employing multiple orientations.

In some circumstances, we can imagine that orientational purity is indeed beneficial. A teacher who restricts herself to one orientation imposes a kind of discipline on her teaching, focusing consistent attention on the desired pedagogic goals, continually reinforcing them while avoiding idiosyncratic distractions. However, in other circumstances, the pedagogic goals of an institution (or even an individual teacher) may not be well served by specialization or orientational purity. Instead, a school might benefit from a principled eclecticism in the teaching of rabbinic literature—consciously choosing to employ not one but multiple specific orientations in order to provide a broader perspective on

---

teaching the subject of rabbinic literature. So while these instances of teaching may well appear, in some respects, like the Torah Orientation, the absence of pedagogic commitment to rabbinic literature *as a subject* is significant. Jon Spira-Savett helped me clarify this point.

the field.[43] Principled eclecticism is not the same as indefensible idiosyncrasy.

Careful and critical attention to the orientations can nurture the former and help avoid the latter. As a heuristic device, the menu of orientations can open up new possibilities. It can enable teachers to ask questions about what kinds of knowledge are important in this field, and enable teacher educators, too, to ask questions about what kinds of knowledge are important for teachers to have. It can even serve as a framework for discussion *among* teachers about the practices of teaching rabbinic literature—discussion that is more nuanced and more specific, that is less ideological and more pedagogical, than it might otherwise have been. Indeed, in my experience exploring the orientations with teachers over the last several years, it has already played these roles.

---

[43] Barry Holtz, *Textual Knowledge*, 52 ff, suggests that it is the mark of a good teacher to combine multiple orientations, and cites Gail Dorph in favor of this claim as well (see Gail Zaiman Dorph, "Conceptions and Preconceptions: A Study of Prospective Jewish Educators' Knowledge and Beliefs about Torah," Ph.D. diss., Jewish Theological Seminary, 1993). Thus, they endorse what I am calling here "principled eclecticism" as a form of flexibility that is desirable in all teachers. But why should it be the case that the instructor who employs multiple orientations is necessarily a better teacher than the one who employs a single orientation well? In other words, while the importance of flexible subject matter knowledge is clear (see G. Williamson McDiarmid, Deborah Loewenberg Ball, and Charles W. Anderson, "Why Staying One Chapter Ahead Doesn't Really Work: Subject-Specific Pedagogy," in *The Knowledge Base for Beginning Teachers*, ed. Maynard Reynolds (Elmsford, NY: Pergamon Press, 1989), it is not clear to me whether and why flexibility must necessarily entail, specifically, *orientational* flexibility.

4 Teaching Talmudic Hermeneutics Using a Semiotic Model of Law

Daniel Reifman

A major difficulty students face in mastering Talmud study—beyond developing the requisite textual skills to make sense of the Talmud text[1]—is acclimating to the Talmud's mode of reasoning. Students' assumptions regarding logic and common sense are stymied by the Talmud's tendency to juxtapose laws from disparate areas of halakha, make strained inferences from earlier sources, and construct hair-splitting distinctions. Such phenomena occur so often as to be unavoidable, and when students come across them they are usually encouraged to "suspend disbelief" as they work through the give-and-take of the debate. Practical though it may be, this approach only postpones addressing the underlying problem: students' frustration with a thought process that seems very foreign to their own.

Essentially, what students of Talmud have difficulty with is thinking about law. Although some of the seemingly illogical aspects of Talmudic reasoning are unique to halakhic discourse, most of the analytical practices described above are—in one form or another—endemic to any highly developed legal system. What is required to help students make sense of the Talmud's mode of thinking, then, is a model of how law functions.

The usefulness of thinking about halakha as a typical legal system is not limited to beginning Talmud students. As students advance to more complex sugyot, a host of questions about the nature of the halakhic system invariably arises: Why do some areas of halakha exhibit greater

---

[1] I would group these skills into three general categories: 1) language: non-Hebrew speakers need to master the basics of both mishnaic Hebrew and the Aramaic of the Babylonian Talmud; 2) syntax: the traditional printings of the Talmud do not contain punctuation, so students must learn how to parse the text; 3) terminology: the text of the Bavli is structured primarily by means of a few dozen key terms and phrases, whose literal meanings are less significant than the functions they serve within the text.

degrees of flexibility than others? What are the functional limits on what a text can be interpreted to mean? How does halakha incorporate data from other disciplines, such as ethics, sociology, and the sciences? These, too, are issues that legal theorists must grapple with in analyzing any legal system, and the approaches they have developed within other legal systems can provide useful models for halakha, as well.

The issue of how law functions is, of course, the subject of a long-standing debate within the field of legal theory. Although the precise positions on each side shift from generation to generation, the basic tension remains between those who perceive law as a system based on a fixed set of principles and those who challenge the coherence of any such system. In recent years, some legal scholars have sought a middle ground, describing the way law functions as a cohesive system despite its fundamental indeterminacy.

This paper will propose that a semiotic model has significant advantages in explaining how law functions, and as such is useful in helping students make sense of many aspects of Talmudic reasoning. This model is based on the premise that law is most fundamentally a system of signs, and follows the same basic rules as other sign systems, such as language. By using the same methodology that semioticians use in analyzing other sign systems to analyze the way legal texts generate meaning, we can give students a framework for making sense of the seemingly illogical aspects of Talmudic reasoning, as well as addressing higher-order questions about the nature of halakhic development.

Obviously many students will not find explicit use of semiotics helpful. However, even if the term "semiotics" is never mentioned in the classroom, many of the basic principles that emerge from a semiotic model of law can be translated into simple didactic techniques that can help in achieving the aforementioned goals. Indeed, the techniques that teachers (and students) find most effective for teaching Talmud and halakha usually reflect these principles, and greater awareness on the part of the teacher of how these principles operate can help her fine-tune her use of these techniques. Moreover, there are some students who are ready for a more sophisticated understanding of how halakha functions as a system, and for whom explicit exposure to semiotic theory within the context of a Talmud or halakha class can be extremely beneficial.

In exploring how this methodology can be used in a classroom setting, this paper will present examples drawn from two of my classes during the 2006-7 academic year, when I first began testing this methodology with my students. Most of the texts presented were covered in my class on the third chapter of Kiddushin at Yeshivat Chovevei Torah, geared toward students with 2-3 years of experience studying Talmud. The class's goal was simply to increase the students' facility with the Talmud text and basic commentaries. I have also drawn on texts from one of my classes at the Drisha Institute for Jewish Education, an advanced halakha class on the laws of kashrut. During that year, I also used this approach in a continuing education course at Drisha examining the "Shabbes goy," looking at Jacob Katz's seminal work in the field of history of halakha[2] from a legal-theory standpoint (as a complement to Katz's historical-critical analysis). Despite the varying skill levels of the students and the different focuses of the courses, I found that a semiotic approach lent itself equally well to all three classes, and students almost uniformly confirmed that it enhanced their understanding of the material.[3]

In the interest of clarity, all the examples I have chosen relate to a single phenomenon in Talmudic hermeneutics—the statutory interpretation of mishnayot. It should become clear, however, that this methodology has implications for a broad range of issues in rabbinic hermeneutics and general philosophy of law.

Developing a Semiotic Model of Law

In order to clarify what is meant by a semiotic model of law, let us first review how the field of semiotics analyzes other sign-systems, such as language, highlighting several features that will be relevant to our analysis of law. One of the foundational principles of semiotics is Ferdinand de Saussure's tenet that signs are composed of two distinct elements:

---

[2] Jacob Katz, *The "Shabbes Goy": A Study in Halakhic Flexibility*, trans. Yoel Lerner (Philadelphia: Jewish Publication Society, 1989).

[3] A previous version of this chapter, which also explores the texts I used in the continuing education course, appears under the same title as Working Paper No. 17 in the series produced by the Initiative on Bridging Scholarship and Pedagogy in Jewish Studies at the Mandel Center for Studies in Jewish Education at Brandeis University (April 2010). See http://www.brandeis.edu/mandel/pdfs/Bridging_working_papers/ReifmanPaper_rev51810.pdf

the *signifier* or sign-vehicle—the aural or written form of the word—and the *signified* or sign-meaning—the mental concept it evokes. (For the sake of convenience, I will follow Umberto Eco's use of the notations /X/ to denote the vehicle of sign X and "X" to denote its meaning.[4]) Although within a given context the signifier and signified function as a unit, like two sides of a piece of paper, it is crucial to Saussure's theory that the two are not inextricably bound, because their distinctness is what allows for polysemy—a given form signifying more than one concept—and synonymy—a given concept being represented by more than one form. For example, the English language pairs the sign-vehicle /plane/ with a number of sign-meanings, among them "aircraft", "level", or "carpentry tool"; conversely, the concept "flying vehicle" can be represented either as /plane/ or /aircraft/.[5]

A corollary of the fact that the signifier and signified are discrete entities is that the relationship between them is arbitrary and therefore completely dependent on context: expression and content enter into mutual correlation under established coded circumstances. An observer who isn't familiar with the code being used (e.g., someone reading or hearing a foreign language) can't attach any meaning to the signifiers she observes because she lacks the necessary context for decoding them. And because a given signifier can encode for multiple meanings even within a given semiotic system, even those familiar with that system can be confounded by ambiguity if the context doesn't rule out all but one meaning. In such circumstances, signs can be disambiguated only by invoking a second signifier, which we will refer to as the *interpretant*,[6]

---

[4] Umberto Eco, *A Theory of Semiotics* (Bloomington: Indiana University Press, 1976), xi.

[5] Ibid., 49.

[6] Ibid., 68-70. The use of the term "interpretant" in this context traces back to the nineteenth-century American semiotician Charles Sanders Peirce, who conceived of a triadic model of semiotics (object-representamen-interpretant), wherein the interpretant is the effect that the representamen (the equivalent of Saussure's "signified") has on the interpreter that allows him to associate the representamen with its object. Peirce added, however, that the interpretant itself then becomes a representamen, which triggers another interpretant, in an endless process of semiosis. The relevance of this last notion for legal semiotics will be evident later in the paper. However, in the interest of simplicity, I have chosen to use the more straightforward terminology of Saussure's binary model.

whose significance is that it has an overlapping—but not completely identical—semantic range with that of the first signifier: the intersection between the semantic ranges of the first signifier and the interpretant defines which aspects of the first signifier's meaning are relevant in this context. For example, if /plane/ appeared in a context where its meaning was not evident, then /aircraft/ (or /level/ or /carpentry tool/) could serve as the interpretant to clarify what was meant. /Aircraft/ doesn't replace the original signifier, since it can be used to refer to things that couldn't be called /plane/, such as a helicopter; rather, the interpreter would now understand that the semantic range of the original signifier is limited to those objects that can be referred to both as /plane/ and as /aircraft/, that is to say, objects that fall within the semantic ranges of both the original signifier and the interpretant.

The above example is a fairly simple case of disambiguation, since the various possible sign-meanings of /plane/ are mutually exclusive: there is no object that could be referred to both as /aircraft/ and as /carpentry tool/. However, even when the general sign-meaning being referred to is clear, what is often ambiguous is which aspects of that sign-meaning are pertinent. In such cases, it is helpful to think of the sign-meaning as a bundle of *semes*—isolable units of meaning—only some of which may be relevant in a given context. Consider the following perfectly banal exchange:

> A: "Please bring me a chair."
> B: "What do you need it for?"
> A: "I'd like something to sit on."

In this case, the primary signifier being analyzed is /chair/, and the interpretant that clarifies its meaning is /something to sit on/. When B asks, "What do you need it for?" he is essentially inquiring what part of the semantic range of /chair/ is relevant in this situation. For although the meaning of A's request may seem straightforward, that is only because we subconsciously impose a particular context on the situation, namely that A is standing and would like to sit down. Were A's request made in a cold room with a dying fire, it would be clear that A intended to use the chair as fuel, and the pertinent semes would be ones that relate to the chair's material construction, not its function. In this context, the semantic range of /chair/ might include "table", "broomstick"—meanings that we ordinarily would never associate with /chair/, because we reflexively translate /chair/ into /something to sit on/.

Moreover, even once it's been established that A wants the chair to sit on, the interpretant /something to sit on/ clarifies only that the general function of the chair is relevant, but doesn't tell us if more specific design features that relate to the chair's function—such as a back or firm seat—are also significant. If a stool or sofa would also fulfill A's request, then it would emerge that these other features are not relevant semes of /chair/ in the context of A's request, and that /something to sit on/, rather than /chair/, is a more precise expression of A's desire.

What this example makes clear is that on one level, semiotics simply creates a framework for precise analytical reasoning: in distinguishing between signifier and signified, and then between discrete semes, it forces the interpreter to identify as precisely as possible what information a signifier means to convey. Once the relevant set of semes has been identified, an interpreter can test the semantic range of the signifier by creating oppositional signifiers corresponding to each of those semes, then asking test questions to determine the semantic boundary between that signifier and its opposites. In the example above, if it emerged that a back is a relevant aspect of A's /chair/, the signifier /stool/ would function as an oppositional signifier—the semantic equivalent of /not a chair/. B could then pose a series of test questions to define the precise boundary between the semantic range of /chair/ and /stool/; for example, whether a stool with a low back would be considered a /chair/ or a /stool/.

What this example further demonstrates is that the semantic boundaries of a given signifier can never be defined with complete precision. The distinction between /chair/ and /stool/ is not simply the presence or absence of a back, since a low back would presumably not qualify something as a chair, just as a slightly-lower-than–normal back wouldn't disqualify it. Presumably there is some height at which the back renders a "something to sit on" a chair, but it would potentially require an infinite number of test questions to determine that height absolutely precisely. One could then repeat the same process with a host of other factors that might influence whether or not the back rendered the object a /chair/, such as its width, thickness, stability, shape, etc. In other words, /back/ itself becomes the subject of semantic analysis, and hence becomes vulnerable to what is known as the Sorites paradox, or the paradox of the heap: given that one grain of sand doesn't constitute a heap, and that no one grain added to something that's not a heap will make it a heap, it follows that no number of grains of sand will constitute a heap! Scholars often "solve" this paradox by acknowledging that some terms are inherently vague, but a semiotic model shows that *any* signifier is subject to this fundamental vagueness to a greater or lesser degree, the degree dependent only on the extent to which the context in which the signifier appears helps clarify its meaning; that is to say, there are no signifiers that are inherently vague any more than there are signifiers that have inherent meaning. Ultimately the functionality of semiotic systems relies on our being able to make clear distinctions between different signifiers, but as those distinctions get finer and finer, they will necessarily begin to seem arbitrary and absurd,[7] just as it seems arbitrary and absurd to determine that the boundary between /not a heap/ and /heap/ should be drawn between, say, 242 and 243 grains. Because absolute semantic boundaries cannot be established, there can be no hard-and-fast rules for how a given signifier is to be used.

The simple model we have developed to describe the way individual words or phrases generate meaning may not seem relevant to much longer and more complex texts. However, any unitary text can be summarized according to the general meaning that a particular society attaches to it. Thus *Othello* might be referred to as "a tragedy of love and jealousy," and the book of Jonah may be called "a discourse on repentance." Obviously these works can be dissected much further by analyzing the significance of specific lines or passages in each, but if they are to function as units within a system of meaning (in this case, a literary or religious canon), one must be able to speak of their unitary, overall significance. If so, these texts too, despite their length and complexity, can be said to have one-to-one correspondence with specific ideas, and

---

[7] The following passage from the Babylonian Talmud, Bava Batra (23b), illustrates this idea nicely:

> Mishnah: If a young pigeon is found within fifty cubits [of a dovecote]—it belongs to the owner of the dovecote; [if it is found] beyond fifty cubits—it belongs to the finder....
>
> R. Jeremiah inquired: If one foot is within fifty cubits and the other beyond fifty cubits, what is the ruling? It was for this that they expelled R. Jeremiah from the study hall.

the relationship between each text and its corresponding meaning follows the same fundamental principle that Saussure laid down for much smaller text units, namely that the two are fundamentally distinct entities that associate with one another only contextually. This is precisely the power of a broad-based semiotic model: it establishes a universal set of principles for any form that communicates information.

This underlying identity of all sign systems has vital implications for hermeneutics in general. To put it plainly, semiotics rejects what we might refer to as a formalist position, that the meaning of a text is somehow fixed by the intent of the author, the historical context of its creation, etc. Rather, the meaning of a text is a function of the process of interpretation, and is circumscribed only insofar as the context of that interpretation is circumscribed (e.g., by what the literary scholar Stanley Fish refers to as an "interpretive community"). This position has been expressed, in one form or another, by numerous schools of literary criticism and legal scholarship over the past few decades. What a semiotic model contributes is a more rigorously methodological perspective on the issue, and with it a sense of conclusiveness: if Saussure's fundamental thesis is correct, then the formalist position is simply untenable. As much as literary or legal texts may seem to present their own meaning, at least in a general sense, they can be no more self-interpreting than any other signifier.

However, a semiotic model of law would also reject the most extreme version of anti-formalist legal theory, the position known as legal shamanism: legal terms are, like a shaman's incantations, fundamentally meaningless expressions that judges invoke to convince their audiences that they are doing something substantive. Rather, it shifts the focus from what legal rules cannot do—determine their own range of application—to what they can: communicate legal meaning in a context-dependent fashion—that is to say, tell people something (though never everything) about how the law expects them to act in a particular set of circumstances. This shift in emphasis allows us to articulate why inconsistencies in the application of legal concepts don't undermine the validity of law as a system—or more precisely, to articulate what we mean when we speak of law as a coherent system. Law coheres in the same sense that every other semiotic system coheres: it constitutes a network of signifiers and signifieds that associate with one another in a way that conveys information. In eschewing both of these extreme positions—that legal texts have either a single, straightforward meaning or no meaning at all—a semiotic model suggests a deeply intuitive approach to legal hermeneutics. This is the message we want to convey to students who struggle with Talmudic logic—that what seems like an arcane system of inferences, comparisons, and distinctions shares fundamental features with all other sign systems and can be approached using the same tools used to analyze those systems.

Interpreting Legal Terms and Concepts

A simple instance of how semiotic analysis can be applied to law comes to us in one of the basic notions in Anglo-American property law, the idea that ownership is comparable to a "bundle of sticks." What jurists mean by this is that ownership is not a uniform legal entity, but rather an assemblage of specific rights and responsibilities, the components of which can vary from case to case. Whether an individual is considered the owner of an object or property will therefore vary based on the context, depending on whether her particular "bundle" of rights and responsibilities includes the "stick" relevant to that context. For example, one may be considered the owner of a property when it comes to the right to exclude others from that property (considered one of the most basic rights to property) but be restricted in one's ability to transfer it to others (for instance, by a lien). Likewise, there can be discrepancies between the standards for ownership imposed by different jurisdictions even with reference to a single feature.

The metaphor of the bundle has thrived in legal circles largely because of the ease it affords jurists and lawyers when dissecting legal issues concerning property. Normally the notion that a bedrock legal concept such as ownership has no fixed definition would be immensely disconcerting. There is—let it be said—something deeply appealing about the sort of absolutist vision of legal hermeneutics according to which legal texts simply "mean what they say," if only because the (presumed) purpose of legal texts is to communicate law clearly and unambiguously. As a result, even those with no interest in the scholarly debate find themselves drawn toward the formalists' position. The simple, concrete image of the bundle anchors a concept that is both highly abstract and potentially destabilizing.

The bundle image is, of course, merely another way of articulating the semiotic model of law that we have developed. The various rights and responsibilities related to property are the semes which, alone or in combination, constitute the sign-meaning of /ownership/. Just as the semantic range of a linguistic signifier such as /chair/ can be determined only by studying the specific attributes people use it to communicate (e.g., "something to sit on", "wooden object"), so, too, the semantic range of /ownership/ can be established only by knowing which specific rights and responsibilities the law applies to one considered an /owner/. But /ownership/ is merely one example; any legal signifier is comparable to a "bundle of sticks," its definition wholly dependent on the specific contexts in which it is applied.

As we turn to examples of statutory interpretation of mishnayot, let us first examine instances where the indeterminacy of the text centers on a single term. Consider Mishnah Kiddushin 3:5:

> [If a man states:] "I betrothed my daughter, but I don't know to whom I betrothed her," and another individual comes and states, "I betrothed her"—he is believed....

What does the mishnah mean when it rules that this individual is /believed/? When I ask my students to paraphrase the mishnah's ruling, they usually see no basis for ambiguity: it means simply that we accept his words as truth. Certainly nothing in the mishnah prepares them for the amoraic debate that follows:

> Rav stated: He is believed in order to give her a get, but he is not believed in order to marry her.... R. Assi stated: He is believed even in order to marry her.... (B. Kiddushin [63a])

Based on my students' instinctive reading of the mishnah, R. Assi's position emerges naturally from the mishnah text while Rav's distinction seems groundless. Simply put, if we accept this man's self-identification as the betrother (i.e., the one who already completed the legal act of *kiddushin*, the first stage of the legal act of marriage), why would we forbid him to "marry her"—that is, to proceed with the act of *nissuin* (the domestic and sexual consummation of marriage)? Once again, the formalist impulse—the reflexive search for a single, unequivocal meaning—shapes the way students process the mishnah's language. In this case, that impulse makes it difficult for them to understand the dynamics of a debate when one side seems to violate that unified meaning.

A semiotic model can help students understand how multiple meanings can be constructed from an apparently straightforward text. Once we understand that all signifiers are equally indeterminate, we realize that the meaning of /believed/—no less than /ownership/ or /chair/—is context dependent. Without articulating with regard to what this individual is believed—that is to say, what the practical ramifications of believing him will be—the mishnah's ruling has no meaning in a legal sense. Any interpretation must, therefore, begin with an assessment—conscious or unconscious—of the purpose for believing this would-be husband. If R. Assi's interpretation seems the simpler of the two, that may be because we take for granted that betrothal naturally concludes in marriage, and that the purpose of believing this individual is to allow the betrothal to follow its natural course. But sometimes chairs need to be used for fuel rather than furniture, and marriages need to be dissolved rather than consummated, and so Rav contends that the mishnah is interested in identifying the mystery suitor only because he holds the key to freeing the daughter from her status as an *agunah*—a woman inexorably "bound" to a marriage and consequently unable to marry another.

A similar analysis could be applied to the term /betrothed/ in Mishnah Kiddushin 3:1:

> [If a man] says to his friend, "Go betroth such-and-such woman for me," and [his friend] went and betrothed her for himself—she is betrothed to the second; and so, too, [if a man] says to a woman, "Behold, you are betrothed to me after thirty days," and another came and betrothed her during the thirty days—she is betrothed to the second: [if she is] the daughter if a non-priest [marrying] a priest, she may eat *terumah*.
>
> [However, if a man says, "You are betrothed to me] from today and after thirty days," and another came and betrothed her during the thirty days—she is betrothed and not betrothed: [if she is] the daughter of a non-priest [marrying] a priest or the daughter of a priest [marrying] a non-priest, she may not eat *terumah*.

The first time I taught this mishnah, I was surprised to find that the aspect my students found most puzzling was the repeated allusion to the woman's status vis-à-vis the consumption of *terumah*. Those with experience studying Talmud take this sort of "status marker" for granted, and the ability to eat *terumah* is a common marker in cases involving priestly status. But to the uninitiated student, the issue of *terumah* consumption seems to have little relevance for the issue at hand.

Rather than dismiss the reference as a common rhetorical device, I used a semiotic approach to address why the author of the mishnah would feel a need to use this status marker. From a semiotic perspective, these allusions function as interpretants that clarify the mishnah's ruling—/betrothed/ or /betrothed and not betrothed/. But an interpretant seems utterly extraneous in the context of the first set of cases, where, like /believed/ in the previous example, /betrothed/ appears to be self-defining: the reader implicitly understands the ramifications of the woman's status as "betrothed", including its impact on her ability to eat terumah. In order to explain how /betrothed/ is not self-defining, I employed the "bundle of sticks" metaphor, explicitly drawing a parallel between the legal concepts of betrothal and ownership.

Like ownership, betrothal can be reduced to an assemblage of legal rights and responsibilities (as well as non-legal aspects, of course, such as love or fidelity), so that ultimately its legal import can be measured only in terms of its specific practical ramifications. And just as the sticks in the ownership bundle can be "unbundled" to correlate with the many different permutations of ownership, so, too, the various rights and responsibilities of marriage can combine in different ways, so that not every instance of betrothal will have exactly the same set of legal ramifications. We could ask for no better illustration of this than the mishnah's ruling in the second set of cases, where /betrothed/ is bizarrely paired with its polar opposite—/not betrothed/. In truth, the construct "X and not X" is not as strange as it at first sounds. Similar phrases appear elsewhere in rabbinic literature with the sense of "partially X," [8] and parallels exist even in modern parlance (English speakers understand exactly what is meant by the response "yes and no"). In this instance, this construct denotes the inconclusive nature of the betrothal, what

---

[8] For example, *bashel ve'lo bashel* (lit., "cooked and not cooked") is used in Sabbath (18b) in the Babylonian Talmud to mean "partially cooked."

the Mishnah elsewhere (Yebamot 3:8) refers to as *kiddushei safek* (lit., "dubious betrothal"). But in terms of expressing the nature of this woman's legal status, /betrothed and not betrothed/ is exactly correct: because the betrothal is inconclusive, she is neither fully "betrothed" nor fully "not betrothed"; rather, her status combines aspects of both.

This synthesis requires explanation, however, and so the mishnah invokes an interpretant—/*bat yisrael le'kohein o bat kohein le'yisrael lo tokhal bi'terumah*/—to explain that her status combines only the restrictive elements of each: she is "betrothed" as far as losing her right to eat terumah if marrying out of a priestly family, and *also* "not betrothed" as far as not gaining such a right if marrying into a priestly family. The combination of two terms that are normally mutually exclusive demonstrates the inherent instability of each; that is to say, it demonstrates that no term necessarily signifies the full set of semes normally associated with it. Based on this, we can better understand what the interpretant /*bat yisrael le'kohein tokhal bi'terumah*/ adds to our understanding of /betrothed/ in the first half of the mishnah: despite the involvement of the first suitor, there is no lingering doubt about the woman's betrothal to the second. She is "betrothed" in the full normative sense of the term.

Interpreting Composite Legal Texts

The sort of analysis engendered by /betrothed and not betrothed/ brings us to the next stage of our study: the analysis of composite legal signifiers—that is, legal texts longer than a single word or phrase. Fundamentally, semiotic analysis of composite signifiers involves the same basic principles we outlined regarding the analysis of simple signifiers. First, the interpreter must deconstruct the sign-meaning into its potential component semes, though now those semes are themselves signifiers—individual terms and phrases—whose semantic range must be established in order to understand the meaning of the text as a whole. Then the interpreter must decide the relative importance of those semes within the text's overall meaning, including—as will invariably be the case—those which aren't relevant at all.

This hermeneutic approach obviously shares much with poststructuralist literary theory. Literary scholars such as Roland Barthes and Jacques Derrida demonstrate the ways in which texts are necessarily fragmentary, and then use this idea to destabilize the meaning of the text and to demonstrate that no interpretation can claim singular authority. The point of drawing on post-structuralism, however, is not to adopt a nihilistic position on legal hermeneutics, whereby the indeterminacy of legal texts undermines their ability to dictate law. Unlike literary critics, jurists do not have the luxury of merely pondering the open-endedness of meaning. The role of the jurist is to bring clarity and consistency to the workings of the legal code. As such, her interpretation—singular or not—must be regarded as authoritative in order for the system to function. What an appreciation of indeterminacy yields, however, is an understanding of the process of interpretation, and—as with simple legal signifiers—a more accurate account of what happens when jurists disagree about the meaning of a legal text.

In introducing my students to this form of analysis, I have found it extremely beneficial to begin with the following example from contemporary law, which they find familiar and accessible. One of the most contentious hermeneutic issues in contemporary American law is the interpretation of the Second Amendment to the Constitution: "A well regulated Militia, being necessary to the security of a free State, the right of the people to keep and bear Arms, shall not be infringed." On one level, the debate over what this text signifies revolves around the meaning of the individual terms within it. What constitutes /infringement/? What is meant by /keep and bear/, and should they be understood as two separate terms or as a single phrase? For the most part, each of these terms can be defined—and thereby shape the meaning of the overall text—independently from one another. On another level, however, the debate concerns how to resolve the contradictory implications of these terms with one another. For instance, the preamble's reference to a /Militia/ seems to limit the semantic range of the text to militia-related arms, but the subsequent reference to /the people/ seems to broaden its scope to arms possessed by individual citizens. Since in their fullest form these implications are mutually exclusive, neither term's meaning can be assessed without considering its impact on the other's.

Once the conflict between these terms has been established, there is no unwritten rule that an interpreter must find the compromise meaning that best balances the implications of both terms.[9] At this second level of analysis, the question is not merely what each of these terms means, but to what extent that meaning functionally impacts the semantic range of the law—indeed, whether it affects it at all. If a jurist is convinced that "the people" necessarily encompasses all citizens, irrespective of their participation in the militia, then the reference to /Militia/ (and with it the entire preamble) has little or no impact on how she would apply the law. The same is true of the phrase /the people/ for a jurist who understands "Militia" as referring exclusively to a formal military body.[10] Hermeneutic purists will surely object to interpreting such a carefully

---

[9] Ronald Dworkin famously makes the case that the task of legal interpretation is to do precisely this—to construct the "best" possible meaning of the law.

[10] Adam Freeman's analysis of the current debate over the implications of the commas (!) in the Second Amendment ("Clause and Effect," *New York Times* Op-Ed page, Dec. 16, 2007) is a case in point:

> The decision invalidating [Washington, DC]'s gun ban, written by Judge Laurence H. Silberman of the United States Court of Appeals for the District of Columbia Circuit, cites the second comma (the one after "state") as proof that the Second Amendment does not merely protect the "collective" right of states to maintain their militias, but endows each citizen with an "individual" right to carry a gun, regardless of membership in the local militia.
>
> How does a mere comma do that? According to the court, the second comma divides the amendment into two clauses: one "prefatory" and the other "operative." On this reading, the bit about a well-regulated militia is just preliminary throat clearing; the framers don't really get down to business until they start talking about "the right of the people ... shall not be infringed."
>
> The circuit court's opinion is only the latest volley in a long-simmering comma war. In a 2001 Fifth Circuit case, a group of anti-gun academics submitted an amicus curiae (friend of the court) brief arguing that the "unusual" commas of the Second Amendment support the collective rights interpretation. According to these amici, the founders' use of commas reveals that what they really meant to say was "a well-regulated militia ... shall not be infringed."
>
> Now that the issue is heading to the Supreme Court, the pro-gun American Civil Rights Union is firing back with its own punctuation-packing brief. Nelson Lund, a professor of law at George Mason University, argues that everything before the second comma is an "absolute phrase" and, therefore, does not modify anything in the main clause. Professor Lund states that the Second Amendment "has exactly the same meaning that it would have if the preamble had been omitted."

worded document (the final draft of the Second Amendment—like virtually all constitutional texts—was the product of lengthy and heated debate) without taking every word and phrase into account. After all, doesn't the text of the law explicitly mention both /Militia/ and /the people/? But the fact that the text functions as a semiotic unit—the fact that the law can mean only one thing within a given context—says that its overall meaning is fundamentally indeterminate and isn't limited by the sum of its parts. This is not to say that the conflicting implications are irrelevant to one's understanding of the text. Quite the opposite: a jurist will necessarily have confronted the internal tension in the text before deciding what it means. But having completed that analysis to her own satisfaction—having decided on the subset of semes that will determine the semantic range of the text—the jurist can now conceive of that text as expressing a single concept: "what the Second Amendment means." Those semes that conflict with the jurist's interpretation cease to have any legal significance for her.

Given these inevitable textual sacrifices,[11] however, not to mention the highly politicized nature of this debate, one could be excused for suggesting that all this hermeneutic analysis is beside the point. It often seems as though the legal positions have nothing to do with interpretation at all, the textual arguments being no more than windowdressing for distinctly non-legal considerations. Such ruminations are characteristic of contemporary legal theorists who take a thoroughly agnostic view of judicial interpretation. But again, denying that a text determines its own meaning is different than denying that a text means anything at all. The very fact that textual arguments can be articulated at all means that the words carry some weight in the way we make sense of the Amendment as a whole. If it still seems that both of the above interpretations violate the simple sense of the text—or to put it differently, if the text doesn't seem to generate any obvious meaning that is relevant to the current debate—that may be because the context in which the Second Amendment was drafted was significantly different than our own. In an era when state militia were composed of ordinary citizens who provided their own weapons, /Militia/ and /the people/ posed fewer conflicting

---

[11] That is, the need to reject some inferences that *could* be made from the text, essentially declaring that certain aspects or portions of the text are irrelevant to the meaning of the text as a whole.

implications. But the binding nature of law means that the Amendment must still be made relevant even though times have changed, forcing jurists into the awkward position of having to decide which of these terms reflects the "real" scope of the law.

Using this model, we can analyze a more complex instance of Talmudic interpretation than those cited above. Mishnah Kiddushin 3:7 states:

> [If a man] has two groups of daughters by two wives and says, "I married off my elder daughter, and I don't know whether [the betrothal referred to] the elder daughter of the seniors, or the elder daughter of the juniors, or the younger daughter of the elders who is older than the elder daughter of the juniors"—they are all prohibited [to marry another] except the younger daughter of the juniors; this is R. Meir's position. R. Yose says: They are all permitted [to marry another] except the elder daughter of the seniors.

The mishnah presents a highly unusual case in a somewhat unusual fashion. Normally mishnayot include only two components—a concise explanation of the case(s) or issue(s) at hand, and an even shorter record of the ruling (or the debate over the ruling) associated therewith. In this mishnah, however, the brief introduction that sets up the background of the case is followed by a relatively lengthy record of the father's thought process, which not only introduces the complicating factor in the case (he can't recall which daughter he intended to betroth) but also explains the rationale for implicating multiple daughters as the one who was betrothed (any of them might conceivably be referred to as "elder"). The Mishnah then presents R. Meir and R. Yose's rulings in typically succinct fashion, with no account of their reasoning or how it might relate to the logic of the father's internal monologue.

Its peculiar style notwithstanding, the mishnah reads fairly coherently. A cursory reading gives no evidence of the tension that emerges in the Talmud (Babylonian Talmud, Kiddushin 64b-65a), as the amoraim investigate the parameters of the tannaitic debate:

> Abaye said: The controversy refers [only] to two groups of daughters; but in the case of one group, all agree that "elder" [refers to the eldest daughter], "younger" [refers to the youngest daughter], and the middle daughter is referred to as such.

> R. Ada b. Matna said to Abaye: If so, the middle daughter of the [junior] group [within a family with two groups of daughters] should be permitted [according to all]![12]
> What case are we dealing with here? Where there are only [two daughters in the junior group],[13] and this is a logical [assumption], for if there is a middle daughter [in the mishnah's case], let her be mentioned!
> But even in your view, the middle one of the first [senior] group, who is certainly [implicated in the ambiguous betrothal] and forbidden[14]— is she mentioned?[15]
> How can you compare? [Regarding the middle daughter of the senior group, even] the one younger than her is mentioned as being forbidden, and the same applies to this [middle] one, who is older than her; but [regarding the junior group], if it is so that there is [a middle one], let her be mentioned!

Abaye states that R. Meir's stringent position—that all but the youngest daughter must receive a *get* before marrying another—applies only to a case where the father has two groups of daughters from two wives. However, in a case where all the daughters are from a single wife, the ambiguity that triggers R. Meir's stringency disappears: Abaye insists that in such a family, the middle daughter would be referred to by her exact sibling position, and therefore wouldn't be implicated in the father's betrothal of his "elder daughter." R. Ada bar Matna challenges Abaye's position regarding the middle daughter by drawing a comparison to (what he assumes is) a known quantity: the

---

[12] She, too, should be referred to simply as the "middle daughter," since she has no more seniority than the middle daughter in a family with only one group of daughters; both are older only than the youngest daughter in their family. Clearly R. Ada bar Matna assumes that R. Meir would prohibit the middle daughter of the junior group, thereby contradicting Abaye's understanding of his position.

[13] Therefore the mishnah tells us nothing about R. Meir's position regarding the middle daughter of the junior group, and it's possible that even R. Meir would permit her to marry without first receiving a *get*.

[14] As explained in the next line: The middle daughter of the senior group is obviously forbidden, since she is older than the youngest daughter of the senior group, who is herself explicitly implicated.

[15] So the fact that a given daughter isn't explicitly mentioned doesn't mean that her status is uncertain.

status of the middle daughter within the younger of the two groups of daughters. If R. Meir would implicate this daughter as possibly being the betrothed "elder daughter" even though she has only one younger sister, then surely he would say the same regarding the middle daughter of a single group, even though she, too, has only one younger sister. The Talmud then debates what evidence the mishnah provides regarding the middle daughter of the junior group, and whether it supports R. Ada bar Matna's assumption that R. Meir would prohibit her. In the process, the Talmud weighs the possibility that the case addressed in the mishnah has no middle daughters at all, but rather two groups of only two daughters each.

This is a short but difficult passage. With each new daughter who is introduced to the discussion and each minute shift in the understanding of R. Meir's position, the reader is forced to double back and re-examine her previous assumptions. It can be helpful, even at the initial stages of negotiating the Talmud's give-and-take, for students to see how the positions of the amoraim positions are—at least implicitly—grounded in inferences from the mishnah text. This allows students to link each stage of the argument to a line in the mishnah, transforming what might have been seen as an abstruse conceptual debate into a more concrete interpretive one. For instance, Abaye may defend his distinction between one group of daughters and two groups of daughters on logical rather than textual grounds ("... the middle daughter is referred to as such"), but it's clear that what enables his interpretation is the mishnah's reference to a man who "has two groups of daughters from two wives," implying that a similar case involving a man with only one group of daughters wouldn't evoke the same tannaitic debate. Similarly, R. Ada bar Matna's rejoinder—"If so, the middle daughter of the second [junior] group should be permitted [according to all]!"—makes no sense without textual evidence that R. Meir would, in fact, prohibit the middle daughter of the junior group, something implied only by the wording of his ruling, "They are *all* prohibited." Finally, the Talmud defends Abaye's position by explicitly citing the fact that no middle daughter is mentioned in the father's speech. Though on one level this analysis is simply to help the students grasp the various amoraim's positions, by the end I have succeeded in making a more subtle hermeneutic point—that the amoraic debate reflects the tension inherent within the mishnah text itself.

Nonetheless, even once they have mastered the intricacies of the debate, students often harbor a sense of discomfort about the Talmud's excessive scrutiny to textual detail. It may be granted that each of the amoraim's positions can be linked to an inference in the mishnah text, but aren't these inferences rather strained? There is a hint of anti-formalist sentiment at work here, a sense that judicial interpretation is detached from the text of the law. This sentiment is usually so subconscious that it goes unexpressed. When students do articulate it, a teacher's reaction is often simply to invoke the peculiar nature of the rabbinic hermeneutics: like midrashic exegesis of the Bible, which extracts the maximum possible meaning from every word, the Talmud reads the Mishnah text with the assumption that it is articulated in highly deliberate fashion. From a purely pedagogic standpoint, this is a less-than-ideal response, for the simple reason that it asks the student to suspend his critical faculties, thereby reinforcing his sense of distance from the text. But it is also not altogether accurate, for the assumption that texts are articulated in highly deliberate fashion—far from being particular to rabbinic hermeneutics—is intrinsic to virtually all legal systems. The gravity of law demands that it be so: in everyday conversation it may not matter whether an object falls within the semantic range of /chair/, but in a legal context, such determinations—for example, whether private ownership of a handgun is covered by the Second Amendment—can have significant and wide-ranging consequences. In considering whether the mishnah's ruling does or doesn't apply to a particular case and does or doesn't restrict the marriageability of a particular daughter, the amoraim are merely exploring its precise semantic parameters, defining "what Mishnah Kiddushin 3:7 means," as they would need to do with any legal pronouncement.

The debate over Mishnah Kiddushin 3:7 illustrates particularly clearly the way interpretation becomes an act of reading a text against itself, as jurists are forced to choose between the conflicting implications that emerge from the text, sometimes from a single word. A simple exercise I have used in teaching this mishnah is to ask students to consider the implications of the opening line—"[If a man] has two groups of daughters by two wives...." A straightforward reading would suggest that, a) the mishnah's ruling would apply to *all* families with two groups of daughters (otherwise wouldn't it mention the exceptional cases?), but also, b) that the mishnah's ruling wouldn't apply to *any* families with only one group of daughters (otherwise why mention specifically "two groups"?). Now I ask the students to consider how these inferences stand up to the Talmud's analysis. Abaye clearly articulates the second inference, but then R. Ada bar Matna uses the first inference to challenge him: since there is no logical distinction to be made between the middle daughter of a single group of daughters and the middle daughter of the junior of two groups of daughters (each is next-to-youngest in her family), Abaye's exclusion of all one-group families would also end up excluding some two-group families, something not indicated by the mishnah's language. What the amoraic debate demonstrates, then, is that these two inferences—each perfectly reasonable on its own—are mutually exclusive. Abaye and R. Ada bar Matna each define the meaning of the mishnah in concert with one of these inferences, thereby excluding the other from having legal significance.

Understanding Legal Evolution

As we mentioned above, a semiotic model of law can also be used to help students understand the way law develops over time. This is helpful when approaching a text such as Mishnah Avodah Zarah 5:2, which is formulated in a way that suggests something about its composition history:

> If [idolatrous] libation wine fell on grapes, one should rinse them and they are permitted, but if they were split [when the wine fell on them], they are prohibited.[16] If [libation wine] fell on figs or dates, if there is [sufficient wine] in them to impart flavor, it is prohibited.
> There was an incident involving Boethus ben Zunin that he brought dried figs on a ship, and a cask of libation wine broke and fell on them, and he consulted the Sages who permitted them.
> This is the general principle: Whatever benefits [from the libation wine's] imparting a flavor [to it] is prohibited, but whatever doesn't benefit [from the libation wine's] imparting a flavor [to it] is permitted, such as vinegar that fell upon split beans.

---

16 The Talmud (Babylonian Talmud, Avodah Zarah 66a) debates whether this applies regardless of the ratio of wine to grapes, or only if there was sufficient wine to impart taste to the grapes (as is the case with dates and figs). Our analysis, however, will address only the law regarding figs and dates.

The mishnah progresses in four distinct stages: 1) the initial case-specific rulings regarding libation wine that fell on grapes, dates, or figs; 2) the case involving Boethus ben Zunin's dried figs, which the Sages permit for unspecified reasons; 3) the general distinction between foods that benefit from the flavor of the wine and foods affected adversely by its flavor; 4) application of this principle to the case of vinegar (presumably made from libation wine) that falls into a dish of split beans. While the mishnah doesn't articulate the connection between the stages, their sequence suggests that the historical event is what precipitated the general formulation of the law: the conceptual distinction between complementary and uncomplementary flavors seems to have been tacked on to the earlier part of the mishnah in order to resolve the Sages' lenient ruling in the Boethus ben Zunin incident with the existing law.[17]

If this assessment is correct, we can use the model we developed above to analyze the diachronic shift in the law's perceived semantic range. Before the conceptual formulation, the semantic range of the law was defined only by /figs or dates/; there was no basis for determining what the relevant semes of /figs and dates/ should be, and therefore no additional guidance for determining the semantic range of the law. Here, then, is an opening to stretch students' interpretive skills: what principle might we have formulated from this specific case had one not already been provided for us? Should it apply to all foods? Only sweet foods? Only raw foods? Only fruit? At the very least, students will typically insist—based on an intuitively formalist reading of the text—that the law applies to all /figs and dates/, regardless of whether they are fresh or dried. For the rabbis, however, the relevant seme of /figs and dates/ is none of the above, but rather that the wine complements their flavor. /Whatever benefits [from the libation wine's] imparting a flavor [to it]/ serves as an interpretant for /figs and dates/, the same way /something to sit on/ serves as an interpretant for /chair/. As counterintuitive as it may seem, /dried figs/ now becomes an oppositional signifier to /figs/, since only fresh figs fall within the semantic range of

---

[17] Text-critical scholars have long noted the frequency of mishnayot that exhibit this basic pattern—a list of specific cases followed by a *zeh ha-k'lal* ("this is the principle") clause, and suggest that even when the ontological or chronological development isn't as blatant as in this case, this form points to the diachronic development of the Mishnah text.

the interpretant.[18] But students will appreciate the significance of this interpretive move much more if they have spent time formulating their own general principle before considering that of the rabbis.

At this point the students' instinct may shift to an anti-formalist perspective: isn't the sages' ruling merely a ruse to save Boethus ben Zunin's figs, and not a justifiable interpretation of the original law? Without additional information about the event, we have no way to assess the sages' motives, but there's no reason to assume that wanting to save Boethus ben Zunin's figs did *not* play a role in their decision. What I want to convey to my students is that while we can question the wisdom of a judicial system that allows such factors to influence legal rulings, a semiotic model shows that partiality per se doesn't invalidate an interpretation. Even the most neutral reading of the law has to emphasize some semes at the expense of others, and a corollary of the fact that signifiers aren't self-defining is that all semes have equal potential to determine a signifier's semantic range. The validity of this process of picking and choosing semes is established by its very necessity: a functioning semiotic system depends on the ability of its users (both speakers and listeners) to assign meaning to signifiers as they see fit, regardless of the generally perceived prominence of the semes they choose to ignore.

---

18 In presenting this *sugya* in translation, I have chosen to simplify the analysis somewhat. When I presented this paper at the Mandel Center Conference on Teaching Rabbinic Literature, Lawrence Kaplan noted that the mishnaic Hebrew term for dried figs is *grogerot*, not *te'einim*, so that the rabbis' lenient ruling in the Boethus ben Zunin case may not have been perceived as conflicting with the existing law regarding figs (just as English speakers might not consider a reference to /plums/ as also referring to prunes). Nonetheless, I maintain that the mishnah's deliberate juxtaposition of the rabbis' ruling with the original law shows that the author of the mishnah did perceive a conflict between them.

However, even if the rabbis' ruling doesn't directly conflict with the dictum regarding figs and dates, it still marks a major break with the general principle—stated several times in the Mishnah and clearly operating here—that *kol she'yeish bahem benotein ta'am asur* (a forbidden substance that imparts taste to permitted foods renders those foods forbidden). Against the background of this principle, the rabbis' permitting of Boethus ben Zunin's figs is clearly highly innovative. Indeed, the principle of *notein ta'am lifgam, mutar* (if the taste that is imparted is a spoiled taste, then it is permitted) eventually becomes a major exception to the general principle of *kol she'yeish bahem benotein ta'am asur*.

Conclusion

The methodology I have presented here represents only one of many possible perspectives on talmudic reasoning, one that emphasizes the similarities between Talmudic law and other legal systems. In doing so, it implicitly downplays the many distinctive features of talmudic law, as well as the differences between religious and secular legal systems, all of which are important to a well-rounded understanding of how the Talmud and halakha function. However, given that students tend to already appreciate the distinctiveness of Talmudic and halakhic reasoning and distinguish between all things secular and religious, I feel that it is important to underscore the basic elements that all legal systems share. More fundamentally, a semiotic model does more than draw parallels between different legal systems; it speaks to the very essence of hermeneutics. When we give our students the tools to analyze how text generates meaning, every aspect of Talmud and halakha—both the generic and the idiosyncratic—becomes more comprehensible.

5 Neusner, Brisk, and the *Stam*: Significant Methodologies for Meaningful Talmud Teaching and Study

Michael Chernick

The following challenges face those who teach students in a required Talmud course:

1. Rationalizing and justifying the study of the Talmud, which is complicated by the difficulty for Western students of the Talmud's form of expression;
2. Identifying specific pedagogical methods that help to create a sense of connection between students and the Talmud;
3. Creating enough of a positive attitude toward Talmud study so that students are likely to continue to study it in the future (or at very least, are genuinely interested in doing so).

This chapter does not consider those students whose religious commitment to studying classical Jewish texts or whose cultural habituation regarding Talmud study make it familiar and compelling. These students tend not to require attention to these challenges, but they are clearly in the minority among academic students of Talmud in Judaic studies programs, adult education programs, and even non-Orthodox rabbinical seminaries.

The Rationalization of Talmud Study

The rationalization of Talmud study must answer the question, "Why is it necessary or important to study the Talmud at all?" In my experience, from my early teaching in yeshiva high schools and from 34 years of teaching Talmud at Hebrew Union College-Jewish Institute of Religion (HUC-JIR) in New York, most students who must take a required Talmud course explicitly or implicitly want to know why they must. The "why?" usually proceeds from the (correct) sense that the Talmud is an ancient and frequently arcane document. Indeed, in its own formative moment, the Talmud was the text of an elite, and it largely remains so today. Why then do those who do not seek to be members of that elite need to engage with this text?[1]

Talmud study is difficult at two levels: 1) form (both language and argumentation), and 2) content:

1) The language of the Talmud is a mixture of Hebrew and Aramaic. This language challenges even those who have full command of modern or even mishnaic Hebrew. If one studies the Talmud in translation, technical terms—even when translated into English—often remain mysterious. This is due to the general failure of translators to explain these terms fully, often giving primacy to brevity over clarity.

    Subsumed under the issue of form is the Talmud's distinct style of argumentation. The fact that its argument is not linear, but is, rather, filled with questions, retorts, and rhetorical thrusts and parries, makes it confusing to Western readers. Even if language was not a barrier to comprehending the Talmud, its form of presenting issues is sufficiently foreign to almost all students of whatever nationality or cultural background that it makes them wonder whether the effort needed to grasp this work is worth expending.

2) At the level of content, the Talmud's concerns are often (usually?) distant from those of the students. For most students, what connection is there between them and the ritual purity of pots and

---

[1] Many students studying for the pulpit rabbinate, whether in seminaries of movements that do not see themselves bound by halakha or in the *batei midrash* (study halls) of movements that have a stake in halakha, often do not feel the need to join the elite circle of those who can study the Talmud. This seems counterintuitive: wouldn't a rabbi want to be the master of the quintessential rabbinic document? Here we need to recall that the pulpit rabbinate calls for a host of skills unrelated to Talmud study, and it is not surprising that for reasons discussed below even future rabbis might wonder why Talmud study should take away precious time from learning how to counsel, administer a synagogue's programs, craft a sermon, or create an uplifting worship service.

pans, animal sacrifices, or taking tithes? Even matters with which (Jewish) students may have some familiarity, such as Shabbat or *tzedakah*, are rarely discussed and analyzed in contemporary circles in the kind of depth found in a talmudic passage or *sugya*. It is this that often causes students of Talmud to wonder, "Why so much detail?"

The beginning of making the case for the study of Talmud as a necessary component in a broader Jewish studies curriculum is the recognition that rabbinic Judaism is the historical victor in the narrative of the Jewish people. While Second Commonwealth Judaism(s) may have been a story of sects, by the gaonic period one of these "sects"—namely, rabbinic (talmudic) Judaism—became the Judaism of the majority, despite challenges from groups like the Karaites. This development set the stage for further advances in Judaism and Jewish life from the early Middle Ages on. Therefore, the Talmud is the key to in-depth understanding of most of the disciplines that now constitute Jewish studies, because the culture it created is the foundation on which they are built. Even the Bible, as crucial as it is for the understanding of the Jewish experience, is significant for later Judaism only as it is interpreted by the rabbis.

The Role of Traditional and Contemporary Scholarship in Talmudic Pedagogy

How, then, do we make this singly important work accessible to Jewish students in high school, college, and institutions of advanced learning?

This chapter outlines the development of a pedagogical praxis based on three traditional and academic methods of interpreting the Talmud: first, Jacob Neusner's approach to rabbinic literatures; second, the so-called "Brisker *derekh*" (or method); and third, the reigning academic theory that the anonymous voice (the *stam*) of the Talmud is that of post-amoraic redactors. I have developed and used this three-fold approach to create a successful encounter between student and text. Once this encounter occurs, students understand the need for knowing something about the Talmud, get more enjoyment out of Talmud study, and acquire an appreciation of the Talmud as a literature that helps one to understand Jewish culture in general.

Neusner's Analysis of Mishnaic and Talmudic Literature

Jacob Neusner (1932–) is the author of numerous provocative studies of formative rabbinic texts. His work has revolutionized the study of early rabbinic literature. Its main thrust is to view rabbinic literature, whether halakhic or aggadic, as statements of theology or philosophy. In order to accomplish this, Neusner and his students bring an interdisciplinary approach to the text. That is, they analyze rabbinic literature using methods like form criticism, history of religion methodologies, anthropology, economics, and the like. In a certain way, Neusner's contribution and that of his circle is a form of conceptualization similar to that of the Brisker *derekh* (see below), but one that conceptualizes issues differently from the way the latter's purely legal analysis does.

The Brisker Derekh

R. Hayyim Soloveitchik (1853-1918), who eventually became the Orthodox rabbi of Brest-Litovsk in Poland (called Brisk in Yiddish), initiated a new trend in Talmud study. Possessed of remarkable analytic powers, he would carefully scrutinize a halakhic (Jewish legal) subject under discussion in the Talmud and divide it into what he felt were its component legal conceptual parts. Concomitantly, he developed terminology usually based on existent talmudic rubrics with which to describe these legal concepts. For him, the evidence of the correctness of his hypotheses about these concepts was that they could explain what underlay the debates found in the Talmud, and between its early commentators (*rishonim*), in a clear and orderly fashion. His approach to the Talmud spread, and was adopted as the method par excellence of Talmud study in the Lithuanian yeshivot.

The "Stam": Recognition of the Talmud's Significant Redactional Stratum

Among the most important developments in twentieth-century academic talmudic scholarship has been the recognition of an anonymous stratum of the Talmud which shapes the characteristic talmudic argument out of individual units of tannaitic and amoraic traditions. Though this later stratum of redaction had already been recognized by medieval and Wissenschaft scholars, the sense of its pervasiveness until recently had not.[2] The idea that the talmudic text is primarily the result of the work of anonymous, post-amoraic redactors is relatively recent, and it has significant implications for approaching the talmudic text.

The most important of these implications for a methodology of textual analysis is the separation of the original units of tannaitica and amoraica from their redactional matrix. This makes understanding the structure of the talmudic argument easier, and also allows teachers and students to consider what might have been the original meanings of these teachings independently of the meanings that their anonymous interpreters assigned to them. By separating strata, students can see how early rabbinic ideas were transformed as time and place necessitated. This became the template for use of the Talmud as time went on. Because of this tradition of interpretation and development, post-talmudic interpreters felt licensed to offer novel interpretations (*hiddushim*) of a talmudic passage's original and plain meaning. This allowed them to use the Talmud to address the contemporary concerns of the Jewish community. Consequently, the Talmud remained Judaism's basic constitutional document for a millennium and a half. It remains that for some Jews even today.

The Pedagogical Impact of the Use of These Methods

Neusner

The immediate benefit of using Neusner's approach to rabbinic literature is that it reduces the sense of disconnection between the student and the Talmud. This is because Neusner dealt with rabbinic literature in a Western philosophical/theological and interdisciplinary way. Therefore, a teacher can help students understand issues dealt with in the Talmud using a Western prism. What is likely to be viewed by a student as an odd and irrelevant discussion can be presented as a reasonable one if one uses Neusner's approach. For example, the talmu-

---

[2] Shamma Friedman, "A Critical Study of Yevamot X with a Methodological Introduction" (Hebrew), *Texts and Studies, Analecta Judaica* I, ed. H. Z. Dimitrovsky (New York: Jewish Theological Seminary of America, 1977), 283-300.

dic discussion about the time for reciting the Shema in the evening—"much ado about nothing" on the surface—can be viewed, according to a Neusnerian approach, as a discussion about a philosophical point of some significance.

Let us analyze a snippet of the very first passage in the Talmud (Babylonian Talmud, Berakhot 2a) that discusses this issue. Analyzing the text as Neusner might, we can generate an approach that neither skirts the technical issues in the passage nor leaves the student disconnected from it.

The mishnah provides three answers to the question, "When do we recite the Shema in the evening?":

1. R. Eliezer: From when the priests enter to eat the food dedicated to them by the populace (*terumah*) until the end of the first night watch in the Temple (approximately 1/3 of the hours of darkness);
2. The Sages: Until midnight (1/2 of the hours of darkness);
3. Rabban Gamliel: Until dawn.

The continuation of the mishnah informs us that the sages actually agree with Rabban Gamliel. However, they enacted a requirement that any mitzvah that according to Torah law one may perform until dawn should be performed only until midnight. This was to prevent people from deferring the performance of the mitzvah, falling asleep, and thereby missing the opportunity to observe a Torah-based obligation by sleeping past dawn.

How many actual debates are there in this mishnah? According to the Talmud, only two: Eliezer and Gamliel actually debate what is the temporal end point for the fulfillment of the recitation of the evening Shema. The sages merely enact a "fence around the Law," but actually agree with Gamliel.

The Gemara raises the following questions:
1. What is the biblical source for reciting the Shema at night? (Implicitly: How do we even know it's an obligation?)
2. Why do we discuss the evening Shema before the morning one?

A biblical source is cited—"... When you lie down and when you arise" (Deut. 6:7)—and it answers both questions that the Gemara raises:

it explains the source of the obligation of the evening and morning Shema recitations; and why we begin with the evening Shema first ("when you lie down ... when you arise")—i.e., we begin with the Shema recited at the time when people are going to sleep.

The Gemara continues:

> I might also say that the biblical source is derived from the Creation, as its says, "It was evening, it was morning...." (Gen. 1:5).

This second prooftext gives a different explanation for why the mishnah discusses the evening Shema first. After all, the "Jewish day" begins at night, as we can see from the Creation narrative. But this Genesis passage does not provide a source for the recitation of the evening Shema, since it is not about the Shema at all. Why would the Talmud provide us with a verse that answered its two questions well, and then provide us with a verse that answered only its second question?

A Neusnerian approach to the problematic order of the sugya's argument and to the mishnah on which it comments would be to suggest that both the Mishnah and the Talmud present two schools of philosophical thought about the nature of time. Is time imbedded in the cosmos and determined solely by Nature, or put more theologically, by God? Or is time defined by human conventions like eating, lying down to sleep, or arising for work, or by human determination that a certain thing should occur, for example, guarding the Temple or reciting the Shema?

Philosophically, is time independent of us (Rabban Gamliel), or do we have a role in shaping time's meaning even if in the long term it is independent of us (Rabbi Eliezer)? If we have such a role, how do we exercise our meaning-making dominion over time? That is, to what extent does human consciousness and intention shape temporal reality for the individual and the community? (E.g., are the first Tuesday and last Thursday of November any different from other days in November? If so, is their significance inherent or an act of intention and will? In Jewish terms, why is the seventh day of the week any different from the fifth or the sixth?)

In terms of Jewish religious thought, the power of humanity to shape reality by using our intentional ability to define situations—for example, to define sacred time—makes us partners with God in the ongoing creation of the world. From the standpoint of Judaism, this confers infinite worth on humanity created in God's image and with some of God's power. These questions and thoughts are not beyond a Western student's horizon of thinking. They reflect classical philosophical concerns and some of the concerns of Jewish theology and ethics. As such, they bring what would otherwise be a discussion of the fine points of ritual law in a distant and foreign context (that of priestly practices and Temple observances) into the intellectual and spiritual world of the student. Thereby, the emotional and intellectual distance between *talmid* (student) and Talmud is reduced.

Brisk

The Brisker *derekh* gives the student a conceptual grasp of the debates that appear on every page of the Talmud. This method proposes that every talmudic debate is dependent on each side of the debate being rooted in different halakhic rubrics, or in different facets of a single halakhic framework. This approach is important because the Talmud frequently does not provide rationales for its tradents' opposing positions. This makes these positions less memorable, because they become a jumble of "exempt/obligated" or "permitted/forbidden." Therefore, arguments often get blurred, especially in a particularly detailed and logically complicated *sugya*. When there are clear distinctions between the views of the disputants, and real reasons are offered for the opinions, students have a fighting chance at organizing and remembering what is happening in the talmudic discussion.

In order to show how the Brisker *derekh* works in solving some of the pedagogical problems mentioned above, let us apply it to the following passage in the Babylonian Talmud, Berakhot 17b:

> Mishnah: One whose dead lies before him [i.e., someone whose relative has died and whom s/he is responsible to bury, henceforth referred to by the Hebrew term *onen*] is exempt from reciting the Shema and the *Tefillah* [the Amida], from *tefillin*, and from all the [time-oriented] commandments of the Torah....

> Gemara: [The mishnah implies that when the corpse] is in the *onen*'s presence, he is exempt; and when [the corpse] is not in his presence, [the *onen*] is obliged [to recite the Shema, etc.].

But isn't this mishnah contradicted [by the following baraita]?:

One whose dead lies before him [i.e., one who is an *onen*] should eat in another room. If one has no other room, one should eat in a friend's room. If one does not have a friend's room, one should make a partition and eat. If one cannot make the partition, one should turn one's face away and eat.

And [the *onen*] should not recline and eat or eat meat or drink wine. He should not bless [food], nor recite the invitation to Grace. Nor should others bless on behalf of the *onen*, nor should they count the *onen* to the quorum for Grace after Meals [i.e., according to traditional usage, three or ten men].

[And the *onen*] is exempt from reciting the Shema and the *Tefillah*, from *tefillin*, and from all the [time-oriented] commandments of the Torah)....

In sum, the implication of the mishnah is that when an *onen* is not in the presence of a relative's corpse, he or she is required to observe a variety of mitzvot; in contrast, the baraita exempts the *onen* even from these mitzvot when he or she is not in the corpse's presence. The Gemara's problem is how to resolve the conflict between the mishnah and baraita. This conflict must be resolved since, according to the hierarchy of authoritative texts that the Talmud sets up, a baraita (a source from the same time period as the Mishnah but not part of the Mishnah) cannot usually disagree with a mishnaic dictum.

The Gemara resolves the conflict thus:

R. Papa said, "Explain [that the exemptions mentioned in the baraita] refer only to the *onen* who turns his/her face away [from the corpse in order to eat. Under those circumstances, since s/he remains in the corpse's presence, s/he is exempt from the various mitzvot listed in both the mishnah and baraita.]³

---

3   The reader will recall that the opening gambit in this talmudic discussion was that the mishnah implied that an *onen* was exempt from certain mitzvot only when in a relative's corpse's presence. Having the baraita's exemptions apply only to the case where an *onen* was forced to remain in the corpse's presence squares the baraita with the mishnah.

R. Ashi said, "Since it is incumbent upon the *onen* to bury his/ her [dead relative], it is as if that relative was always in his/her presence.... [Hence, the mishnah and baraita agree: One is exempt from the mitzvot listed in both texts, since as long as one is responsible for the burial of one's dead relative, it is as if that relative is in one's presence.]

The confused reader of this passage should not feel unintelligent. Consider the amount of information that it contains: 1) issues of exemption with a hefty list of commandments attached; 2) issues of the location of a corpse; 3) issues of the location of the relative responsible for the corpse's burial; 4) rules about eating in front of a corpse; 5) a longer list of eating and liturgical restrictions in the baraita than in the mishnah; 6) the positing of a discrepancy between the mishnah and baraita; and 7) the resolution of that discrepancy in two different ways by two different amoraic sages, R. Papa and R. Ashi.

According to the Brisker *derekh*, the key to unpacking the passage lies in identifying the most obvious debate that it contains. Therefore, for the student, the focal point of the passage should be the disparate resolutions of the "conflict" between the mishnah and baraita that R. Papa and R. Ashi suggest.

The Brisker *derekh* would conceptualize the difference between R. Papa and R. Ashi thus: R. Papa rests his view on the halakhic rubric of *kevod ha-met* (the honor due the dead); R. Ashi undergirds his view with the halakhic consideration of *mitzvat kevurah*, the obligation to bury the dead, and its relationship to the talmudic principle that "one engaged in one mitzvah is exempt from another."

For this purpose, *kevod ha-met* is defined by the Talmud in "geographical" terms. That is, one may not carry out the normal activities of a living human being in the presence of a dead person. To do so shows a lack of sensitivity for the dignity of the person who, when alive, could do those things. As the Talmud puts it later in the passage, there is a mocking quality about such behavior, one similar to showing off a physical capability in the presence of a person with a disability. If, however, people entirely remove themselves from the corpse's presence, they may carry out regular life activities because they have demonstrated that they are sensitive to the honor of the dead.

As noted, R. Ashi sees the obligation to bury the dead as the foundation of the exemptions mentioned in the mishnah and baraita. For him, the corpse's locus is a metaphor. That is, whether one removes oneself entirely from the deceased's locale or not, one is exempt from the mitzvot listed in the mishnah and baraita because of the talmudic principle that "one who is involved in one mitzvah is exempt from another." Thus, since there is an obligation to bury the deceased incumbent on his or her relatives, their primary duty is to that obligation. Therefore, they are exempted from all other mitzvah-obligations in order to see the mitzvah of *kevurah* (burial) performed with all due haste. Since this exemption is so thoroughly directed to the person of the deceased, it is as if he or she is always present until burial occurs. Consequently, the mishnah's and baraita's exemptions are informed by a single concept: "One who is involved in one mitzvah [in this case, burial of the dead] is exempt from another."

This reduction of the details of the *sugya* to concepts (*kevod ha-met, mitzvat kevurah*, "one who is involved in one mitzvah is exempt from another") eliminates the need for the student to keep each and every detail of the mishnah and baraita in mind once the analysis of the text has been completed. The student should be able to reconstruct the *sugya* in broad strokes on the basis of the more succinctly stated concepts we have described. The concepts also give a reasoned basis for the otherwise unexplained views of R. Papa and R. Ashi.

The "Stam"

Dividing the *sugya* into its chronological components helps the student see how historical forces may have influenced the development of talmudic law and rabbinic thought, and how talmudic law and rabbinic thought have influenced the history of Jewry and Judaism. The identification of a redactional level in the Talmud also means that we can help the student account for the Talmud's discourse style—and take control of it—by separating the original material from the redactional matrix into which it has been placed—or forced.

While I have referred to the redactional level of the Talmud, I have not yet offered a detailed picture of what its redactors did. There are a number of redaction theories, but for clarity's sake I will present only one. It proposes that originally the "proto-Talmud" consisted of more or less chronological lists of tannaitic and amoraic material closely or loosely connected to the Mishnah. The basic elements of these lists generally had attributions and were formulated in Hebrew. The anonymous redactor(s) (the *stam*) took the elements of these lists and transformed them into a series of running arguments, called in Aramaic *sugyot* (singular, *sugya*). The connectives necessary to create these arguments were in Aramaic, which is one of the identifying marks of stammaitic intervention, and were anonymous.

Once we remove the redactional "glue" holding together the individual pieces of tannaitic and amoraic material in an argument form, we can restore the tannaitic and amoraic dicta in Hebrew to their original state as simple lists of opinions. We can then recognize these dicta as the building blocks that the redactors used to create the *sugya*'s complex give and take. Marking tannaitic, amoraic, and stammaitic elements of the *sugya*, whether translated or untranslated, in different fonts or colors makes the recognition of these separate strata even easier. This has the effect of showing that without its redactional level, the Talmud's discourse was more linear, and therefore more understandable. In turn, this aids the student's comprehension of and control over the talmudic material being studied.

Once we separate the various strata of talmudic teachings, we are also in a position to consider what might have been the original meaning of tannaitic or amoraic teachings, independent of the meaning later anonymous interpreters assigned to them. This contributes to a less mythical, more historical understanding of Jewish law and rabbinic thought. Once students see clearly that halakha and aggadah are developing and changing entities, re-interpreted over and over, teacher and student can consider together the developments in Jewish practice, ethics, and thought that have taken place throughout Jewish history, as well as the paths that Judaism might take today as it tries to navigate between the Jewish past, present, and future.

To illustrate the pedagogic approach that emphasizes how the redactors have created a *sugya* out of elements of earlier talmudic strata, and why this makes a difference, let us turn to the *sugya* in the Babylonian Talmud, Berakhot 26a. The issue here is the set times for prayer, which in talmudic literature is identified as the Eighteen Benedictions (the Amida), or *Tefillah*.

Below, I distinguish between tannaitic, amoraic, and anonymous material as follows: 1) tannaitic material is in plain font, 2) amoraic material is underlined, and 3) anonymous material is in italics. (To avoid confusion, terms that have been italicized elsewhere will not be italicized in this passage.)

Mishnah: The morning Tefillah [may be recited] until midday. R. Judah says: Until the fourth hour [of the morning]. The afternoon Tefillah [may be recited] until evening. R. Judah says: Until "half Minhah".... (i.e., 1 ¾ hours before evening). The evening Tefillah has no set time....

Gemara: [Challenge:] *But this [mishnah] is contradicted by [the following baraita]*: Its proper performance [i.e., the proper recitation of the Shema] is at the first light of the sun in order to attach the [benediction about the Egyptian] Redemption to the Tefillah so that one will be praying [the Tefillah] when it is [fully] day.[4]

[Response:] *That baraita was taught in reference to the especially pious.*

[Documentation for that response (an amoraic source used by the anonymous redactor)]:
As R. Yohanan said: The especially pious would finish it [the recitation of the Shema] with the first light of the sun.

[Continuation of the documentation material by the anonymous redactor, including a new question:] *And everyone else prayed [i.e., the morning Tefillah] until midday. But no further [into the day]?*

[Documentation for the new question (an amoraic tradition used by the anonymous redactor)]: *But didn't R. Mari, the son of R. Huna, the son of R. Jeremiah, the son of Abba citing R. Yohanan say:* "One who forgot the evening Tefillah should repeat it twice in the morning. One who forgot the morning Tefillah, should repeat it twice at [the time of the afternoon Tefillah (minhah)]"?

---

[4] The proper time for the *Tefillah* was when it was fully day, since at least the time aspect of its halakhot followed the times of the sacrificial system.

[Anonymous comment that sharpens the question: *On the basis of this amoraic tradition it appears that*] one can pray continuously all day.

[Anonymous response to the new anonymous question above: *Yes. One can pray all day*], but until midday they give one a reward for prayer [recited] on time; from then on, they reward one for prayer [alone], but not for prayer in its proper time....

[An anonymous question:][5] It was problematic to them [i.e. to those in the bet midrash, or academy, or student circle]: if one erred and did not pray the afternoon Tefillah [minchah], what is the rule in regard to [making it up by] praying the evening Tefillah [arvit] twice?

[Anonymous explanation of the issues that generate the question above:] *If you say that one who errs and does not pray the evening Tefillah can [make it up by] pray[ing] the morning Tefillah [shaharit] twice, that is because [one prays the evening and morning Tefillah within] a single day, as it says, "It was morning; it was evening; one day" (Gen. 1:5). But in this case [of the afternoon Tefillah we might propose that] the Tefillah replaces the daily offering, and once its day has passed its sacrifice is null and void. Or perhaps [we might say], since the Tefillah is a request for mercy, whenever one wishes he may pray it.*[6]

---

[5] This may be an amoraic question known to and introduced by the anonymous redactor. See David Weiss Halivni, *Mekorot u-Mesorot: Eruvin-Pesahim* [Hebrew] (New York-Jerusalem: Jewish Theological Seminary of America, 1982), 249, n. 3***; Idem., *Mekorot u-Mesorot: Yoma-Hagiga* [Hebrew] (New York/Jerusalem: Jewish Theological Seminary of America, 1985), 11, n. 21. There are, however, cases where the question itself is the redactor's. In that case the question forms an introduction, frame, or reconstruction of a question believed to be the generative source of an amoraic tradition. Idem, *Mekorot u-Mesorot: Bava Kamma* [Hebrew] (Jerusalem: Magnes Press-Hebrew University), 117, 337 n. 2.

[6] In this passage, the anonymous redactor tries to explain the basis for the initial, probably amoraic question of whether one may recite a missed evening *Tefillah* with a repeated morning one. According to the *stam*, the reason the amoraim have this question is because they do not know whether the *Tefillah* follows the rules of the daily offerings, which are time-bound, or whether the *Tefillah*'s nature as a request for God's mercy, which is always available, allows one to pray it at any time.

[Answer to the question based on an amoraic source:] Come and hear: <u>R. Huna son of Judah cited R. Yitzchak who cited R. Yohanan: if one erred and did not pray the afternoon Tefillah, he should pray the evening Tefillah twice.</u>

[The anonymous redactor clarifies which principle of the two that undergird the question has been rejected in light of the answer:] *And [the rule that] "once its day has passed, its sacrifice is null and void" does not apply.*

As we can see, the anonymous material shapes the tannaitic and amoraic material into a format of questions and answers. While doing so, however, its discursive form complicates talmudic passages, including this example, by introducing ideas that are not inherent in the earlier strata on which it comments. It is this complex discourse that makes it difficult for students to follow what is going on, and often leaves them wondering whether "talmudic logic" is in fact logical. Removal of the *stam's* contribution usually reveals the basic building blocks of the *sugya*, making grasping its essence more feasible.

How might this work in our present example? Taking away all the elements that are anonymous and in Aramaic, this is what we get starting with the mishnah:

Mishnah: The morning Tefillah [may be recited] until midday. R. Judah says: Until the fourth hour [of the morning]. The afternoon Tefillah [may be recited] until evening. R. Judah says: until the "half Minhah."

[Baraita:] Its proper performance [i.e., the proper recitation of the morning Shema] is at the first light of the sun in order to attach the [benediction about the Egyptian] Redemption to the Tefillah so that one will be praying [the Tefillah] when it is [fully] day.

<u>R. Yohanan said: The especially pious would finish it [the recitation of the Shema] with the first light of the sun.</u>
   <u>R. Mari, the son of R. Huna, the son of R. Jeremiah, the son of Abba cited R. Yohanan [thus]: "If one forgot the evening Tefillah, he</u>

<u>should repeat it twice in the morning. One who forgot the morning Tefillah, should repeat it twice at the [time of the Afternoon Tefillah (Minhah)]."</u>

<u>R. Huna son of Judah cited R. Isaac who cited R. Yohanan: "One who forgot the afternoon Tefillah should repeat it [at the time of the] Evening Tefillah.</u>

The baraita's comment appears here because it shares the mishnah's concern for the proper time for the morning Tefillah. All it adds is that the best way to perform the obligations of reciting the Shema and reciting the Tefillah is to start the Shema at first light. This in no way contradicts the mishnah.

R. Yohanan's comment shows knowledge of the baraita or a source similar to it.[7] All that he says is that the especially pious followed the baraita's view—yet the anonymous stratum of the Talmud views this baraita's remark as a challenge to the mishnah's dictum. This is because the *stam* understood the term meaning "best way" (*mitzvatah*) in this context in its literal sense of "obligatory" (i.e., "its mitzvah is to recite it at first light").[8] The *stam* adds that "everyone else prayed until midday," and propounds a question on the basis of that observation.

What follows are several statements ultimately attributed to R. Yohanan about what to do if one missed one of the required daily prayers. The general principle that emerges is that one may make up the inadvertent omission by repeating the Tefillah again at the set time for the

---

7   See Tosefta Berakhot 1:2 and Jerusalem Talmud Berakhot 1:2 (3a). The latter Jerusalem talmudic source parallels the Babylonian *sugya* in regard to the baraita and the explanation that only the most pious conducted themselves in the way that the baraita suggests. There are no anonymous connectives in the Jerusalem Talmud's presentation of this material, and the explanation of the baraita is in the name of Mar ʿUqba (second generation Palestinian amora) rather than in the name of R. Yohanan. Many Palestinian traditions appear in R. Yohanan's name in the Babylonian Talmud even though he may have not been their author. See Abraham Weiss, *Studies in the Literature of the Amoraim* [Hebrew] (New York: Yeshiva University, 1962), 247-8.

8   See the use of *mitzvatah/mitzvato* in Mishnah Menahot 10:9; Tosefta Hullin 10:7. Other sources indicate that *mitzvatah/mitzvato* means not merely "the best way," but the obligatory way. See Tosefta Bekhorot 1:14; Tosefta Parah 4:6; ibid. 12:12. R. Yohanan clarified that the baraita's use of *mitzvatah* meant the "best way," which was only observed by the particularly pious.

recitation of the next *Tefillah*. This general rule applies to all three *Tefillot* of the day. It is likely that these traditions were brought together here as an addendum to the basic mishnaic agenda about the set time for recitation of the *Tefillah*. These traditions answer the (amoraic?) question, "But what if one inadvertently missed one of the *Tefillot* that the Mishnah requires to be said thrice daily and within a specific time frame?"

This deconstruction of the *sugya* into its tannaitic and amoraic infrastructure produces a well organized passage that proceeds logically from the Mishnah's rules about *Tefillah* times, to the best way of performing the mitzvah of *Tefillah*, the way the most pious performed it. The reverse situation is then addressed: What may one do when instead of punctilious observance of this obligation one fails to carry it out because of forgetfulness? One second generation Palestinian amora, R. Yohanan, cited initially by two different fourth-generation Babylonians, allows some deviation from the mishnah: one may make up the missed *Tefillah* but only during the set time for the next *Tefillah*—not whenever one wishes. Thus, the mishnah's concern for time orientation is partially supported and partially undermined.

If this was the "proto-*sugya*" then it unfolds in a rather orderly fashion: mishnah's rules; most favored way of performing those rules by the pious; least favored ways of performing those rules by the negligent. As stated above, this orderliness coupled with a lack of intricate give-and take make for a more easily grasped piece of Talmud. Students get a chance to "get it" and thereby feel that they are not facing an incomprehensible, opaque text.

But it is unfair to the study of the Talmud and to students to avoid learning it according to its present-day formulation. Hence, those who teach the Talmud by separating one stratum from another are obliged to reconstruct the *sugya* in order to understand the Talmud as we have it. Having gained control over the less discursive, more orderly "proto-*sugya*," we may add the *stam* back into the passage in a fashion that allows students to see what the *stam* has contributed to the original material. Such a summative reconstruction might look like this:

The teacher uses the present day text of the Talmud to point out how the *stam* uses the tannaitic and amoraic elements at its disposal to work its way to a major question and its answer. Its small question (perhaps based on amoraic queries) is, "Are the times set in the mishnah absolute because they follow the set times for the daily sacrifice, or can one pray anytime one wishes because prayer is a request for ever-available Divine mercy?"

Twice, the *stam* answers that one can pray anytime, "all day long." He uses the rulings cited in R. Yohanan's name to prove this. But, of course, R. Yohanan never said that people can pray all day long at any time. He said one can make up a *Tefillah* that one inadvertently forgot to say at the next set time for *Tefillah*.

It is also important for the teacher to help students to understand that, though the *stam* has read meanings into the original elements of the *sugya* that are distant from their *peshat* (plain meaning), this was in order for it to make a statement of great import. Never clearly articulated either in tannaitic or amoraic sources, the *stam*'s argument is this: *Tefillah* is a request for mercy, and Heaven's doors are always open in order to hear that request. This is a great step forward in understanding the nature of prayer, one which apparently the *stam* did not wish to take without trying to root it in the traditions of the great sages of the past, which it used.

In sum, the benefits of separating tannaitic, amoraic, and stammaitic material eases study of the talmudic text. It also shows how the meaning of early material is reshaped by its placement in a redactional matrix. Recognizing the existence of strata within the Talmud and dividing talmudic passages into them allows students to chart the development of rabbinic Jewish ideas from period to period and often from generation to generation within periods.

Impact of These Methods

The three pedagogical approaches described above respond to the student-driven issues with which I started this paper: Neusner bridges the potential "disconnect" between the world of the rabbis and the world of the student; the Brisker *derekh* brings the talmudic debates into sharp focus; and the recognition of the work of the redactors in the formation of the Talmud helps the student unravel the complicated discourse of the Talmud and to perceive it as a repository of a dynamic, multifaceted, and thought-provoking Jewish tradition. Joining these methods into a teaching and learning format places Talmud study within the reach of the average student. Once a basic understanding of the Talmud is in place, there is a greater likelihood of understanding how Talmud study is important intellectually and as a basis for understanding Judaism as we—the descendants of a millennium and a half of rabbinic Jews—know it today.

There is another beneficial by-product of this multi-method approach. I consciously introduce the use of the Brisker *derekh* as a traditional, advanced yeshiva methodology for the study of the Talmud. In the case of some HUC students (and probably some students at other non-Orthodox seminaries), the problem of feeling "authentic" is profound. In those seminaries, many students have not had an intensive Jewish education before coming to the place in which they will study to become clergy. While their sense of lack of authenticity is right to some degree, it is also wrong. Our program is intensive and extensive, and if one puts in the effort, one can emerge with the tools to be a life-long learner—with the core text study skills that a yeshiva student would acquire in the fairly standard 10 years of day school from seventh grade through college graduation. Our students are motivated adult learners, which yeshiva students may not have been throughout their entire Talmud learning careers. With such learners, a lot of "catching up" can be accomplished in a short time.

That is why I let them know that studying Talmud using the Brisker *derekh* catapults them into the *batei midrash* (the study halls) of the best of the Lithuanian yeshivas. When they study this way, they do so as traditional yeshiva Talmudists study. If they succeed at this form of study, they have reason to be proud of themselves, and have no reason to view themselves as inauthentic as long as they preserve and extend their learning.

The major question for students about the methods from which I have carved a teaching practice is whether they are "true." This is a question that students almost always wind up asking at some point in my introductory course. What they mean by this question is this: is the conceptualization of a debate à la Brisk an imposition of "our" thinking on that of the Rabbis, similar to how the anonymous redactors imposed their thinking on that of the tannaim and amoraim? Or has Neusner gotten the Rabbis right when he says that the Mishnah and Talmud are works of philosophy and theology—since they are so apparently works of law? Or, when an amora apparently responds to an anonymous question, why insist that the question is a post-amoraic framing device for the amora's earlier statement? Couldn't it be that an amora is responding to an anonymous question that is actually older than the amora's view?

These are reasonable questions, and my answers tend to run along the following lines: There is no way for us to know whether the rabbis thought what Reb Hayyim or Jacob Neusner say they did. Further, the post-amoraic redaction theory is under attack by excellent contemporary academicians like Robert Brody, Leib Moscovitz, and Richard Kalmin. So, you have asked very good questions. But my interest in this course is not in some scholarly "truth," but in communicating the Talmud—its content and its methods—to my students as best I can, and fostering their connection to it and their ability to study and understand it. I can posit that the rabbis got up each morning and took different sides on various questions for no other reason than that they liked to fight about arcane matters, or I can posit that they had thoughtful theoretical bases for their disputes. These methods may not in fact reflect rabbinic thought as the rabbis understood it, but the pedagogic question I must ask myself is, "Which methods helps students understand and appreciate the Talmud most?"

Specifically regarding the issue of post-amoraic anonymous redaction, it is worth noting that this theory has an estimable foundation built on extensive research by excellent academic scholars. Furthermore, it has its roots in the testimonies of figures who were a lot closer to the Talmud's creation than we are—namely, the *geonim* and early *rishonim*. It is also a wonderful heuristic device and, consequently, a benefit to the good teaching and learning of the Talmud. If and when scholars who question the post-amoraic anonymous redaction theory can produce more than a handful of examples—some of which are debatable—that support their view that the anonymous voice of the Talmud is older than the amoraic or tannaitic tradition, in the name of academic honesty, I would then stop using this method for teaching the Talmud. But not until then.

A note on history: Despite my argument that recognizing stammaitic redaction allows for studying the impact of historical forces on developments in Judaism, in a sense my method is almost completely ahistorical. It does not make the assumption that, or draw students' attention to the ways that, any of the views expressed by talmudic sages are the products of their reactions to historical circumstances that affected their religious, economic, social, and political lives. I generally reserve that kind of study for my advanced and academically sophisticated electives, in which I explicitly think more historically—and urge my students to do likewise. Sometimes, certainly, disputes turn out to be differences of opinion reflecting different life circumstances in the locales in which particular rabbis lived, rather than (only) conceptually-oriented disputes. But in teaching introductory Talmud courses, I want to give my students a feeling for what traditional talmudic learning can be (for the reasons explored above), and history, for better or worse, has played virtually no role in that form of Talmud study.[9] However, as a way of both hinting at and preparing students for a more historically-oriented study of Jewish law and lore, from time to time I do mention that all the conceptual fireworks that go on in class may go up in smoke if a rabbi says directly that he ruled one way or another chiefly because of the conditions under which he lived rather than because of any conceptual framework that he constructed.

---

[9] It might be argued that none of the methods I have described are interested much in history. I would reply that though it is clear that the *stam* itself was clearly uninterested in history and chronology, those of us who use the contemporary academic method of separating the *stam* from its earlier tannaitic and amoraic sources are very much interested in history. We believe that practicing this method we can chart developments that contribute to the history of Jewish ideas. Further, when archeology or external documentation support historical realia or biographical details mentioned in a tannaitic or amoraic statement presented without the mistaken or literary fictional mediation of the *stam*, then we are dealing with history at the highest level of academic rigor.

Regarding Jacob Neusner, he was clearly interested in history in his early work. However, as he became more doubtful about the accuracy of attributions, he became less interested in history. This made sense since it was, in his view, impossible to date any given tradition and thereby to retrieve an accurate history of ideas or a factual biography of any of the talmudic sages. This ultimately led him to hold that the redactors' agenda caused them to co-opt all previous traditions to conform to their viewpoint. This meant they chose whatever fit what Neusner considers to be their single, coherent message and to reject what did not. Accordingly, we can only retrieve the ideas of the redactors' period. This is slim history indeed.

As noted at the outset of this paper, Brisk was concerned only with meta-historical and abstract concepts.

Michael Chernick

The methods that I use to teach Talmud in a Reform rabbinical seminary serve me and my students well in addressing the pedagogic challenges outlined at the beginning of this paper. My approach, using one traditional method and two contemporary academic ones, inspires students to take the Talmud—and the study of it—seriously, and to use it to deepen their understanding of rabbinic Judaism as it developed historically into simply "Judaism." With appropriate modifications, such an approach can foster a similar engagement in students at a variety of levels and in various settings, and provide them with insights useful for understanding the Jewish beliefs and practices of the past, and considering what shape Jewish thought and behavior should take in the future.

PART 2

FOCUS ON TEACHING AND TEACHERS

6 The Pedagogy of Slowing Down: Teaching Talmud in a Summer Kollel

Jane Kanarek

Introduction

This chapter describes a set of practices in Talmud teaching that I have come to call "the pedagogy of slowing down." It reflects an effort to more deeply understand my own practices in teaching Talmud through a close of examination of an intensive Talmud class at the Northwoods Kollel of Camp Ramah in Wisconsin.[1] I wanted to better comprehend my classroom practices—what I do when teaching Talmud, and why. Below, I will describe the techniques of slowing down that emerged from research into and reflection on my own pedagogy in the Kollel, and present some potential effects of the pedagogy of slowing down. My aim is to present another example of a mode of Talmud pedagogy, to contribute to the growing literature on this topic.[2]

---

[1] Camp Ramah in Wisconsin is one of the camps of the National Ramah Commission, the camping arm of Conservative Judaism, and is affiliated with the Jewish Theological Seminary of America.

[2] Other examples from which I have learned include Shamma Friedman, "Benjamin and Minna Revees Chair Lecture," available online at http://www.atranet.co.il/sf/revees_chair.pdf; Pinchas Hayman, "On the Teaching of Talmud: Toward a Methodological Basis for a Curriculum in Oral-Tradition Studies," *Religious Education* 92:1 (1997): 61-76; Jeffrey S. Kress and Marjorie Lehman, "The Babylonian Talmud in Cognitive Perspective: Reflections on the Nature of the Bavli and Its Pedagogical Implications," *Journal of Jewish Education* 69:2 (2003): 58-78; Marjorie Lehman, "For the Love of Talmud: Reflections on the Teaching of Bava Metzia, Perek 2," *Journal of Jewish Education* 68:1 (2002): 87-103; and Marjorie Lehman, "Examining the Role of Gender Studies in the Teaching of Talmudic Literature," *Journal of Jewish Education* 72:2 (2006): 109-21.

Background and Context

The Northwoods Kollel brings four to six college-age students to Camp Ramah in Wisconsin for a nine-week intensive learning program. A Talmud class five mornings a week forms the core of the program. In the afternoons, students have classes in halakha, midrash, hasidic thought, and contemporary religious philosophy. Two nights a week, the students have guided study in which they pursue their own projects. In addition to their studies, Kollel members are responsible for teaching one period of general Judaica to campers five days a week.

The program is not geared toward beginners. Kollel members have had prior experience learning Talmud as well as some knowledge of Modern Hebrew. Previous Talmud exposure ranges from informal study with peers to a year spent in a yeshiva in Israel. Hebrew language ability ranges from a few years of college-level Hebrew to native fluency, so we do not focus on decoding words or understanding the basic structure of talmudic arguments. I seek to reinforce and strengthen students' skills, so they can use them to move toward deeper readings and consider fully the multiple meanings possible in a *sugya*. The Kollel aims to combine intensive study of sacred Jewish texts in an intellectually open and rigorous environment with an explicit commitment to traditional-egalitarian Judaism. Finally, while located in a summer camp, the Kollel is an intellectually rigorous program, close to the type of program one would find in a yeshiva setting.

For three summers (2005, 2006, and 2007), I spent approximately one month each year teaching Talmud in the Kollel. This paper examines my teaching during one summer period, July 2007. In order to analyze my pedagogy, I kept a teaching journal throughout the summer and made audio recordings of each class. While the journal and the audio recordings form the primary data for my analysis, teaching notes as well as notes from conversations with students will provide additional resources.

In 2007, the Kollel was composed of three men and three women, four more-advanced students and two less-advanced students. In Talmud class, we studied selected *sugyot* from the first chapter of Tractate Kiddushin in the Babylonian Talmud. The *sugyot* all center on the topic of marriage, and more specifically the issue of a man's betrothing a woman with money.[3] Talmud study was divided between *havruta* (study with a partner) and class time. Students generally spent one to one-and-a-half hours in *havruta* and one-and-a-quarter to one-and-a-half hours in class. Twice a week, we had an extra half-hour of class before they began *havruta*. This time division was dictated by the camp schedule.

The Language of "Slowing Down"

During our closing conversation at the end of the summer, I asked the students to assess their learning experience in Talmud. One way in which several students described their pedagogical experience was "slowing down." When I examined my teaching journal, I saw that the language of "slowing down" also recurred in my own observations. For example, I wrote: "Another teaching challenge is slowing down some of the students as they read. Fast reading is a knowledge marker in certain parts of the Talmud world, and I need to figure out strategies to get the students to slow down" (teaching journal, 7/17/07). The term "the pedagogy of slowing down" thus emerged as a descriptive term in an after-the-fact analysis of my teaching.

It also became clear that "slowing down" was part of my own learning process as a teacher. After the first class I wrote, "I am not yet sure what the pace of the *shiur* [class] will be and how that will balance with havruta time" (teaching journal, 7/13/07). Almost a week later, I wrote:

> I still misjudge the amount of time it will take to complete material. I had thought we would finish the Tos. [Tosafot] and the Rashba[4] today but we only got through one Tos. And this is with

---

[3] Rabbinic marriage has two main components—betrothal (*erusin* or *kiddushin*) and marriage (*nisu'in* or *huppah*). Mishnah Kiddushin 1:1 legislates that betrothal can be effected by the man through three means: money, document, or sexual intercourse. Once betrothal has taken place, the woman is forbidden to have sexual relations with any man, including her future husband. Should the couple dissolve their relationship at this point, the woman needs a bill of divorce (*get*). The marriage portion of the ceremony permits the couple, *inter alia*, to have sexual intercourse.

[4] Tosafot refers to the Tosafists, twelfth- and thirteenth-century Franco-German Talmudic commentators. Rashba is the acronym for the Spanish commentator Rabbi Solomon the son of Abraham Adret (c. 1235-1310).

students who are good readers. Tomorrow we will start with *shiur* at 9:30. But [after tomorrow]I may want to start making *shiur* longer, definitely starting at 12:30, or maybe even a little earlier. I will see. Timing is still an issue I am working with. I think that part of what surprises me is my ability to get them to slow down in class. (Teaching journal, 7/19/07)

Even after the second-to-last class, I commented: "Again, I am surprised by how long it takes to read through a *sugya*" (teaching journal, 7/30/07). These comments were not reflections on the speed of the students' reading, since as I wrote, these students "are good readers." Instead, I was surprised by "my ability to get them to slow down in class."

Many of the Kollel students had previously studied Talmud in environments where the marker of being a "good learner" is how quickly a person can read the Talmud's text. At the beginning, I found that their translations often elided aspects of a *sugya*, missing the meanings of words as well as stages in the argument. They sacrificed precision for speed of reading the assigned material. Their use of speed as a marker of their own success often had the effect of shutting down opportunities for their own questions—questions both about the content of the text and the intricacies of its structure. Once they had finished reading and translating the text, they believed their analysis was complete.

As I reflected on my teaching and the recurring language of slowing down, I realized that in my teaching, "slowing down" is not only a pedagogic technique but also a cultural move. When I began teaching this class, I knew that I wanted to teach a rigorous course that would help students who already possessed a good grasp of how to translate and explain a *sugya*'s structure identify others markers for success. I wanted to help them move more deeply inside the textual world of the Babylonian Talmud. I came to understand over the course of the summer that one of my larger teaching goals was to provide an alternative cultural model, a model where success in learning was measured more by the content of what was said than the speed in which the answers were reached.

The emphasis on content in the pedagogy of slowing down is similar to the type of in-depth Talmud study known as *iyun*. Like *iyun*, it emphasizes depth over breadth (*bekiut*) and seeks out multiple readings. However, while *iyun* is distinguished by the use of medieval and modern commentaries, the methodology of "slowing down" does not necessitate this practice. When commentaries are utilized, they are chosen to deepen a particular aspect or aspects of a *sugya*, to further elucidate the talmudic text itself. The practice of slowing down emphasizes that no matter what is studied, Mishnah or medieval commentaries, students must read and interpret attentively.

Michael Fishbane speaks powerfully to this notion of attentive reading as enabling people to enter more fully into the ancient textual world:

> Martin Buber once said that the task of the translator is to overcome "the leprosy of fluency"—that disease of the spirit whereby one presumes to know from the outset what one is reading and therefore blithely reads past the text and its distinctive meaning. The effective translator must therefore reformulate the words of the text so as to produce a new encounter with its language and thus facilitate a new hearing and understanding. I would add that the spiritual task of the commentator is likewise to mediate and influence the pace of reading, so that the reader can be addressed anew by the innate power of the text.[5]

Fishbane's description of the tasks of the translator and the commentator is equally apt for the classroom (or summer camp) teacher. Just as the translator and commentator reveal new meanings through their formulations and explications of the text, so too a teacher's methods should aid students in reaching new understandings. As the commentator shifts the pace of reading by the addition of words, so too the teacher can shift the pace of learning by the kinds of questions she asks and the ways in which she asks students to probe a text's distinctive language. The challenge for a teacher—a kind of commentator—lies in encouraging students to articulate the words of the text so that they move beyond the two admittedly essential steps of turning Hebrew and Aramaic words into English and explaining the progression of an argument. The teacher must also help the students to become "translators" of the Babylonian Talmud, people who have learned new ways of hearing and understanding such that they can find new meanings and power in the text. The phrase "the pedagogy of slowing down" is therefore a

---

5 Michael Fishbane, *The JPS Bible Commentary: Haftarot* (Philadelphia: Jewish Publication Society, 2002), xxx.

descriptive title for a practice through which the teacher helps the students to read more closely, to investigate the multiplicity of meanings inherent in a text, and thus to bridge the gap between the ancient text and its contemporary students.

While the requirements of elementary education may appear to be far from those of college students, Chip Wood's writing about elementary and junior-high school is helpful in furthering the conversation about the pedagogy of slowing down.[6] Wood describes the ways in which schedule and curriculum rush teachers and children and contends that this hurriedness often hinders learning. He argues for a cultural shift in the use of time, a change in the pace of school and the pace of teaching, in order "… to improve the pace of learning."[7] He envisions "'3 Rs' as shaping schools for the next generations: "Rigor, Recreation, and Reflection."[8] Rigor connotes not inflexibility but " 'scrupulous accuracy; precision' in classroom practice…." It involves the ways in which students learn, engaging in "thoughtful, respectful, and difficult questions," as well as the ways in which teachers prepare and instruct, rehearsing and elevating "their use of language in the classroom."[9] Recreation and reflection provide generative time, a space in which students can learn how to interact with one another and their environment as well as reconsider the day's experiences. For Wood, these three "Rs" join together in giving students and teachers the ability to slow down and learn in a considered and deep manner. As in Wood's program, as we will see, the pedagogy of slowing down in Talmud instruction engages teacher and students in both rigor and reflection.

What Slowing Down Does Not Entail

As I move to a description of the teaching techniques that I have identified as elements in my pedagogy of slowing down, I begin with a negative description—what slowing down does not entail. First, it does not mean tailoring the class to the weakest students, in this case those who

---

[6] Chip Wood, *Time to Teach, Time to Learn: Changing the Pace of School* (Turner Falls, MA: Northeast Foundation for Children, 1999).
[7] Ibid., 32.
[8] Ibid., 267.
[9] Ibid., 268.

have the hardest time mastering a *sugya*'s structure. Second, it does not necessitate asking students to read more slowly (although at times that may be needed). In listening to recordings of my teaching, I noticed that the tempo of our conversations was quick. I responded to students' answers to my questions quickly, whether by asking another question or by re-stating what they had said. Third, it does not mean teaching only a very limited amount of material. Over the course of this three-and-a-half week period (approximately eighteen hours of classroom time), we studied five different units. While the emphasis remained on a deeper analysis of the selected material, the class still had a sense of progression, of moving forward through material.

To accomplish these dual goals of progression and depth, before I began teaching I had decided which *sugyot* would be studied as well as the ways in which the chosen *sugyot* fit into a larger framework. Questions I considered were: what are the central ideas that I think should emerge from the study of this particular Talmud text? Do these *sugyot* come together into a larger picture and if so, what is it? Are there any threads that unite these *sugyot*? What are they?[10] New ideas, of course, should and will emerge in the course of discussion. However, a teacher's awareness of what she wants to try to illustrate through her choice of material helps prevent discussions from turning to overly marginal issues and supports the students in asking better questions.

The discussion in these shiurim, therefore, was not free ranging. When reading texts, I did not ask for volunteers but instead called on students. Calling on students helped me to control the pacing of the class, to make sure that discussion was not dominated by a particular student, to balance different skill levels, and to focus on specific areas where individual students needed to improve their technical skills. This is different than the approach described by Moshe and Tova Hartman Halbertal, in which "[a] usual class in the Yeshiva will quickly turn from

---

[10] Since this class was not operating under the yeshiva model of a year-long course, choosing relevant *sugyot* from one chapter was central to my teaching. The point was not simply to see what the Talmud says and to progress linearly through as much of a chapter as we could. In addition, I did not want to construct an edited approach to a topic by self-selecting *sugyot* from the whole Babylonian Talmud. Instead, by remaining within a chapter and selecting from it alone, I aimed to give the students *sugyot* that, while reinforcing their textual skills, would also raise interesting ideas that could be joined into a coherent whole.

a well-ordered presentation of the teacher into a lively and sometimes chaotic exchange between a few bright students and their teacher."[11]

These three negative components are central to my approach because they help to balance different students' levels and needs. Stronger students should feel challenged, and weaker students should not feel lost in the material. In the case of the Kollel, I had the advantage of being present for *havruta* study, during which I could also challenge stronger students and support the learning of less advanced students by giving them tailored pointers, extra time, or additional questions. For example, I encouraged one *havruta* to rewrite the *sugya* in their own handwriting, dividing its words into very short phrases. At first they worried that this would "slow [them] down too much." However, three days later one of the students approached me and said that this was the first time she had totally understood a *sugya* and that she understood everything in class (teaching journal, 7/19/07).

Components of Slowing Down

In analyzing the data from my class, the repeated occurrence of the words "slowing down" was striking. The sheer frequency of this term prompted me to look at my data through a new lens, isolating particular teaching strategies and practices that reflect the pedagogy of slowing down. In the following section, I enumerate and describe these strategies and practices, and then provide and analyze examples from class transcripts.

The first component of the pedagogy of slowing down is **precision**. Precision begins with the accurate reading and translation of Hebrew and Aramaic. In students' preparation for class, this entailed use of the Jastrow and Frank dictionaries as well as the Frank grammar.[12] A student's claim that "Well, I know what the argument means; I just can't trans-

---

[11] Moshe Halbertal and Tova Hartman Halbertal, "The Yeshiva," in *Philosophers on Education: Historical Perspectives,* ed. Amelie Oksenberg Rorty (London and New York: Routledge, 1998), 459.

[12] Marcus Jastrow, *A Dictionary of the Targumim, the Talmud Bavli and Yerushalmi, and the Midrashic Literature* (New York: Judaica Press, 1996); Yitzhak Frank, *The Practical Talmud Dictionary,* 2nd Edition (Jerusalem: Ariel United Israel Institutes, 1994); Yitzhak Frank, *Grammar for Gemara: An Introduction to Babylonian Aramaic,* new revised and expanded edition (Jerusalem: Ariel United Israel Institutes, 1995).

late it," was inadequate. My teaching assumption was that if a person could not translate properly, he did not properly understand the *sugya*.

In addition to precision in translation, I required precision in explaining the text's argument. Students had to describe clearly how the argument moved from one stage to the next. This included translating and identifying the function of technical terminology that serves as markers for different types of *sugya* structures (terms like *ibaye lehu, u-reminhu,* etc.).[13] I also asked for as much precision as possible in issues of redaction, such as identifying the different layers of the talmudic text—tannaitic (texts from the period of the tannaim, c. 70–220 CE), amoraic (texts from the period of the amoraim, c. 220–550 CE), and anonymous (texts from the anonymous editorial strata)—and recognizing parallel sources from other rabbinic texts.[14]

The second component of this pedagogical practice is **thinking about meaning**. I asked students to consider how particular words or phrases may open multiple interpretive possibilities, and also to look for ideologies and tensions in a *sugya*, fault lines where the dominant ideology may break down.[15] As students considered these interpretive questions, I insisted that they ground their opinions in the words of the assigned texts. In preparing my teaching notes, I considered where I wanted to ask these interpretive questions. While at times I first had the students translate and parse the entire argument, more often I

---

[13] *Ibaye lehu* means "it was asked of them." It introduces a question about a legal matter. *U-reminhu* means "throw them [against one another]." It introduces a contradiction between two sources, commonly of equal authority. (See Frank, *Dictionary*, 10 and 240.)

[14] Admittedly, identifying the layers of a *sugya* with complete accuracy is a difficult task and one that cannot always be done with complete precision and certainty. However, as the Babylonian Talmud is a redacted text composed of different historical strata, it was important that students have knowledge of basic criteria for separating the layers of a *sugya* and be able to accomplish this task with reasonable accuracy. On criteria for distinguishing these layers, see Shamma Friedman, "Perek Ha-'Ishah Rabbah Ba-Bavli," in *Mehkarim U-Mekorot*, ed. H. Dimitrovsky (New York: Jewish Theological Seminary of America, 1977), 277-441.

[15] In asking these questions, I am influenced by the work of Charlotte Fonrobert, who argues for a methodology of "reading against the grain" when analyzing gender ideologies (Fonrobert, *Menstrual Purity: Rabbinic and Christian Reconstructions of Biblical Gender* [Stanford: Stanford University Press, 2000], 9).

interwove questions on the meaning as we moved through the *sugya*. Although the moments when I asked meaning questions varied, the fact of my asking them did not.

The third component of this practice is the **use of medieval Talmudic commentators**, the *rishonim*.[16] It is important to state that I was not teaching *rishonim* as an independent literary genre. While the interpretive methodologies of *rishonim* vary from one school to another, my goal was not for the students to master these differences. Instead, I aimed to use *rishonim* to help students further open a *sugya*'s interpretive possibilities, as part of the ongoing conversation about the Talmud's meaning. Therefore, when I chose *rishonim* for a particular *sugya*, I was careful to make sure that they revolved primarily around one issue. Although I did not demand the same level of precision here as I did with the Talmud itself, students still had to accurately translate and then summarize the arguments of a particular *rishon*. (Again, "I know what the words mean; I just can't translate them," was considered inadequate.) In reading these medieval commentators, I focused on the ways in which they presented different meanings for one phrase, juxtaposed one *sugya* with another, or re-contextualized a particular issue.[17]

The fourth component involves **putting together the big picture**. At the end of each unit, I circled back to the beginning of the *sugya*, articulating links between the different components we had studied. These links can make more explicit points of thematic continuity, or highlight disagreements and the meanings of those disagreements. In addition, I tied the current unit in with previous units, trying to illustrate a con-

---

[16] The term *rishonim* refers to those scholars living from the mid-eleventh century to the fifteenth century.

[17] Since this paper is based on research into my own teaching practices, I have included *rishonim* as part of the pedagogy of slowing down. However, I can imagine teaching a beginning Talmud class that utilized many of the other techniques described. One would emphasize translation and the mastery of technical terms, and de-emphasize these more advanced skills. Still, it remains important to ask "meaning" questions with beginners. Meaning questions help to keep beginners interested in skill acquisition by showing them how central mastery of the technical aspects of Talmud is to a serious discussion of content. In addition, training students to ask meaning questions from the outset encourages them to train themselves to read deeply and to see skills and meaning as intertwined with one another.

tinuity of the issues investigated. I asked students to see whether any ideological issues or tensions we had uncovered earlier also manifested themselves in this material.

Pedagogical Practices in Practice

In this section, I will concretize the above pedagogical practices and explore them more closely through an examination of selections from class transcripts. Although I have described the four components of slowing down in a linear fashion, more often these components were interwoven with one another, as the teaching transcripts will show. Specifically, I did not necessarily complete stage one (precision) and then continue on to stage two (meaning).

In the very first class, I began introducing students to these practices of precision and multiple reading possibilities. We started our discussion by examining Deuteronomy 24:1-4, verses that lay the legal foundation for much of the rabbinic discussion about marriage and that are central to the opening *sugyot* of Tractate Kiddushin:

> JK: Let's just start with the *pesukim* [verses]. Where I'd like to start is with the general question, what are the different things—let's just list them—that we actually learn from these *pesukim* from *Devarim*, *perek kaf-daled* [Deuteronomy 24]?
>
> Student 1: We learn about getting divorced and how [...] you can't get back together but really nothing about how you actually get married in the first place.
>
> JK: Okay, so be specific about what we learn about divorce.
>
> Student 1: So all we learn about it is part of prompting reasons for divorce if you find *ervat davar* [nakedness of a thing],[18] which is unclear in itself then you write this *sefer keritot* [book of divorce].
>
> JK: Okay, is *ervat davar* the only thing that we find that is the only reason?

---

[18] I have intentionally used a literal translation in order to convey the ambiguity of this phrase.

Student 1: Well, *im lo timtza hen be'einav* [if she does not find favor in his eyes; Deut. 24:1], like so if he finds some sort of problem with her so it's coming from his point of view, um, then he writes her this *sefer keritot*.

JK: *Keritut* [corrects pronunciation].

Student 1: *Keritut*. And that's the majority of like what we have in terms of the basis for divorce.

JK: Okay, and do you read *im lo timtza hen be'einav ki matza bah ervat davar* [if he does not find favor in her eyes because he has found in her nakedness of a thing; Deut. 24:1] as one reason, two separate reasons, how would you read that? Is it a clause that's all linked to each other?

Student 1: I'd see it as *ki matza bah ervat davar* as being part of the *lo timtza hen* so I would see it as being part of it.

JK: Okay.[19]

In this opening discussion, I immediately introduced the students to the requirement of reading precision. When Student 1 mispronounced "keritut" as "keritot," I corrected his pronunciation. When the student answered my first question about what we learn from Deuteronomy 24:1-4 with a general sentence, I quickly asked him to refine his answer, to "… be specific about what we learn about divorce." When he gave a more specific response about *ervat davar*, I again challenged him to refine that statement further. When he gave an answer based on the words, "If she does not find favor in his eyes," I challenged him yet again to give a more precise reading of the verse by breaking it down into its constituent clauses.

This continued sequence of rapid questions that I directed towards the student was an important aspect of teaching the group that they must each, as individuals, be able to support their opinions. By concentrating on one student and not asking questions of anyone else or letting them

---

[19] Class transcript, 7/13/07. Some of the language (here and below) has been smoothed out.

jump into the conversation, I was setting a precedent that each student needs to be able to support his or her answer independently. Therefore, only when I felt I had pushed this student sufficiently did I invite others to join in. I said, "Okay, someone else jump in, continue with the divorce material…. Yeah, [Student 2]." But even in asking another student to give his answer, I continued to direct him to the part of the conversation I wanted him to continue. Focused attention on one student is important in showing the students that they have to have thought about what they say; I will ask them to support their answers.

As the conversation proceeded, I continued to ask students to support their answers. In addition, I started to frame questions that helped link this biblical material to the later rabbinic texts. Because I knew that rabbinic sources would formulate both physical action and verbal statement as elements of the betrothal ritual, I asked students to consider whether they might see any verbal component hinted at in the biblical text. Although at this point in the class I did not make those connections between biblical and rabbinic material explicit, I was trying to encourage the students to extract as much information as they could from these Deuteronomic verses.

> Student 2 continued: With the divorce material, when she is divorced she is sent from his home which means that she is living in his home.
>
> JK: Okay, great. So that tells us something as well about what happens with marriage, right. There is something about [the man as the] center.
>
> Student 2: Right, he takes her. Jumping off from that point, he takes her, *ki yikah ish ishah* [when a man takes a woman]. So, again, the active party here is the *ish* [man], um, and also in short order *vehayetah le-ish aher* [and she will be to another man]. It seems like it is the general course of affairs that she will get married soon after … or at least that is what the text is supposing is a likely possibility of what's happening.
>
> JK: Okay. And in this whole divorce procedure it is also seems like we have a concrete action that's defined here. There's some kind of *sefer keritut* and then there's an action as well, right, so there's a book and

there's also an act that has to go into her hand. So there's a physical action. There's a writing of a document and then a physical action that happens as well. Any verbal actions that you would see here?

Extrapolating from these verses, students started to frame the social context of marriage. In this series of questions and responses, they began to articulate the idea that marriage centers on the man's home, that he is the active party, and that the divorce ritual has different components. As much as I challenged them to read what was present in the text, I also asked them to be attentive to its gaps. After the conversation continued for a few more statements, Student 2 remarked, "It's odd that we're getting so much material, so much general material, out of so specific a case. This is like a really specific casuistic law." While the student framed his comment as one about the nature of casuistic law, he had also commented on the striking amount of information we had been able to infer from a close reading of these verses.

Continuing on, I asked the students to begin a discussion that focused explicitly on the betrothal aspect of these verses. Students named the verbs *lakah* [take][20] and *ba'al* [to have sexual relations][21] as important to understanding betrothal. Using their comments, I then framed a question:

JK: Do you read *lakah*, the verbs *lakah* and *ba'al* as two separate actions or both one action, that they're both part of the process of what's happening?

Student 3: I read it as one, but [Student 6] read it as two.

---

[20] The verbal root *lakah* also has the meaning, "to take in marriage," according to Francis Brown, et al., *The New Brown, Driver, Briggs, Gesenius Hebrew and English Lexicon: With an Appendix Containing the Biblical Aramaic* (Peabody, MA: Hendrickson, 1979), 543.

[21] The verbal root *ba'al* also has the meanings, "to marry, rule over, possess" (*Brown, Driver, Briggs*, 127). Robert Alter, in *The Five Books of Moses: A Translation with Commentary* (New York: W.W. Norton & Co, 2004), translates this phrase from Deuteronomy 24:1 as follows: "When a man takes a wife and cohabits with her..." (996). NJPS (*Tanakh: A New Translation of the Holy Scriptures According to the Traditional Hebrew Text*, Philadelphia: Jewish Publication Society, 1985) translates as: "A man takes a wife and possesses her."

JK: Okay.

Student 2: I read it as two.

Student 6: We're already informed by the mishnah.

Student 2: It seems like one follows.

JK: Wait, wait. I want each of you to argue your sides. So, [Student 3], why did you read it as one?

Student 3: I don't think it was as much a conscious thing as it was just, uh, that was just my *peshat* [simple] reading. That's how I interpreted it.

JK: Okay, how did you get to that as your *peshat* reading?

Student 3: [Pause]. I guess because maybe they [the two verbs] come so close together and it's almost like this is the unit that makes you married and then … what happens you know *"im"* [if] something else [happens afterward]….

JK: Very nice.

Student 3: And then if something else happens, something else happens.

In this instance, I did not direct my question to one student in particular. In answering my question, Student 3 told the class about her opinion and her *havruta*'s (Student 6's) disagreement. Two other students jumped into the discussion, and then I intervened. Once again, I wanted to teach the students that they had to be able to provide a reason for their answers. When Student 3 told me that her reading was not particularly thought out—what she terms a *"peshat* reading"—I challenged her to articulate further what she meant by her statement. Whether she succeeded in defending her answer was almost beside the point. I wanted this student to learn that she needed to be reflective about her readings. Only when Student 3 had answered did I turn to the other student in the *havruta* pair and ask her to state why she thinks they are two separate actions. I did not want the other students' jumping in with their answers to cause Student 6's position to get lost. From the outset of the class, I tried to teach the students that a close and thoughtful reading of even a short text can elicit a range of possibilities.

As the course progressed, I continued to emphasize precise translation. However, I also asked integrative questions, questions that asked the students to link together material we had already studied with the current *sugya*. For example, in Kiddushin 3a-b *(minyana de-reisha le-ma'utei mai—ve-ein davar aher korta)* begins by asking a question about the mishnah's mention of three methods that effect betrothal (money, document, and sexual intercourse) and the two methods that dissolve a marriage (divorce document and death of the husband). The transcript begins after the student has read half of the *sugya* and begun to translate it. It opens with my correction of his mistranslation:

JK: The number of the *reisha* [the opening clause of Mishnah Kiddushin 1:1 concerning marriage]—what does it come to exclude?

Student 2: And the number of the *seifa'* [the final clause of Mishnah Kiddushin 1:1 concerning divorce]—what does it come to exclude?

JK: So why is the Gemara [Talmud] asking this question?

Student 2: Because it's acknowledging the arbitrary, no, the specific nature of the three things listed which means that what is it not going to accept...?

JK: Okay, so in that understanding you're understanding it as asking a question about what characteristic of the mishnah?

Student 2: About its, I mean, the arbitrariness.

JK: Okay, so you're focusing on it could have picked five. Why does it pick three?

Student 2: Sure.[22]

---

[22] Class transcript, 7/20/07.

In this section, I paused the student's translation to ask him to think of reasons why the Talmud might be asking its question. In his initial answer, the student was undecided about what the Talmud addressed, specificity or arbitrariness. I asked the student to refine his answer further, and the student focused on the seeming arbitrariness of the mishnah's language. I then translated the student's answer into my own words: the Gemara assumes that the mishnah did not have to choose three methods for betrothal. It could have chosen five.

Two teaching practices are reflected here. The first is the continued focus on one student; the second is the translation of the student's answer into clearer language. I reformulated the student's answer both to encourage him about his comment and to give other students a specific point to which they could respond. Translation is only the beginning of understanding a *sugya*.

Other students also wanted to respond to my initial question.

JK: I saw a couple of hands. [Student 4]?

Student 4: Um, maybe the fact that why does it *davka* [specifically] take pains to say *be-shalosh derakhim* [in three ways]. It says the number and then it lists them. It could have just said *kesef, shetar,* and *bi'ah* [money, document and intercourse].

JK: Okay, so it could have just said, *kesef, shetar,* and *bi'ah*. It doesn't need to say "three." What would be proof that the "three" is superfluous in addition to the fact that it lists the three things?

Student 4: I'm not sure.

Student 3: In addition to the fact that it lists them?

JK: Yeah, in addition [to the fact] that it lists three things. What might be proof that you're onto something?

Student 4 focused on a seeming redundancy in the mishnah's language as lying behind the Talmud's question. She noticed that the mishnah states, "A woman is acquired in three ways and acquires herself in two ways. She is acquired by money, by document, and by sexual intercourse..." (Mishnah Kiddushin 1:1). The number three, though, is superfluous. If the mishnah had just stated the trio of money, document, and sexual intercourse, we would have been able to infer the number three from this list. This literary observation is not the end of the story. I wanted Student 4 (as well as the other students) to bring additional evidence for the accuracy of this literary observation. Through the practice of continued questioning, I was directing the students to search for support for their assertions. So in response to a student's question about my original question, I restated that I was looking for an answer that moves beyond that of the list in our mishnah.

The students continued:

Student 1: Somewhere else it lists things but it doesn't give a number?

JK: Okay, where else does it list things and not give a number?

[Pause.]

Student 1: I don't remember.

Student 3: The other property?

JK: Okay, so where have seen other property?

Student 3: In the other mishnahs?

JK: Okay.

Class: Oh!!!

Student 1 began by stating the conceptual framework: perhaps I am asking them to think of another example of a place where there is a list without a number. I moved the discussion forward by affirming Student 1's statement and asking for the citation of that source. When Student 1 could not name such a source, another student joined in the discussion with a suggestion: other places where we have seen property discussed. I then prompted her forward with yet another question. She answered, with the intonation of a question, "in the other mishnahs?" Student 3 refers to the mishnayot of the first chapter of Tractate Kiddushin, mishnayot that we had studied in the first two classes. When I affirmed her answer, the class, in unison, makes a sound of recognition.

In this exchange, it would have been quicker for me to simply give them the answer. However, by asking a series of questions that enabled them to make the link between the Gemara's question and the first chapter of the Mishnah, I was modeling a process of inquiry. In their *havrutot*, I wanted them to begin to ask similar questions of the material: questions about the Talmud's literary formulations and the links between one *sugya* and other material they have already studied. In other words, I wanted them to see that *sugyot* are connected with one another, and that they should conceptualize the material as linked.

I had formulated this point about the literary uniqueness of Mishnah Kiddushin 1:1 in advance of the class. I also knew that I wanted the students to arrive at this point through my asking a series of questions. By questioning the students, I could better choose when to integrate different students into the conversation. In addition, because I knew this larger point, I could better integrate student comments into this framework, and refine and modify my original ideas in light of their insights. Prompted by this connection, the students jumped in with further observations. Once they looked at their copies of the Mishnah, they saw that the only mishnah that has a number along with a list is Mishnah Kiddushin 1:1.

> Student 2: *Yevamah*[23] is not listed with a number the way she's acquired and acquires herself.

> JK: Great. Um, so if we go back to our *mekorot* [sources]—right—if we go back to our first sheet we, you had the mishnayot of [Tractate] Kiddushin for example.

> [Pause and rustling of paper].

---

[23] A *yevamah* is a woman whose husband has died without children. She is required to marry her husband's brother and their child is considered to be the husband's. See, for example, Deut. 25:5-20, Ruth 4:1-15, and Maimonides, *Mishneh Torah*, Laws of Yibum and Halitzah 1:1.

Right. So look at your mishnayot.

Student 3: Yeah, [a] case like *eved kena'ani nikneh be-kesef* [a Canaanite slave is acquired by means of money], we don't get the number.

JK: Great. So the only place we actually have a number is in our opening mishnah. Now you could say, okay, that's 'cause it's a literary style. We're opening with that fancy.... It does sharpen the Talmud's ability to ask the question about that three because it's actually, the other mishnayot just list the things and don't give a number.

I pointed out that while one could say that the first mishnah simply provides us with an opening flourish and therefore names the number three, the fact that the rest of the mishnayot do not do so sharpens the Gemara's question. Why does our mishnah state the number three? Again, I have directed the students back toward earlier material we had studied, encouraging them to understand *sugyot* as conceptually linked.

Perhaps prompted by this idea that one *sugya* is linked with another, Student 3 made another observation about the word "three."

Student 3: It's also, we're sort of in the mindset of questioning the *shalosh* [three]. Like, you know, like it's just continuing to question the same number. We're just questioning something else about it.

JK: Okay.

Student 3: Like, why three specifically, as opposed to like why three negative ... why three female? Why three male?

JK: Okay.

Student 3: Why three?

JK: Okay. Great. So it's continuing that kind of trend we've seen already about focusing in closely on small details. [Student 2], if we follow yours up a little bit of why 3, why not 5, um where else could we push that kind of question?

Student 2: Um [pause]. Well, it ... one would think maybe it's not an exhaustive list ... or that the 3 things listed are general categories under which other things fall.

JK: Okay. So one way to frame that is: is the mishnah's list exclusive? Is it only these three methods and no others that can be used?

Student 2: Exhaustive.

Student 3: And they're reading it as yes.

Student 3 remarked on the fact that this *sugya* is continuing a literary trend we saw in the opening *sugya* (2a-b), which interrogates the feminine form of the word "three." She had formulated yet another connection between this *sugya* and the material we had previously studied.

After this discussion, I wanted to return to Student 2's initial observation, to make sure that we did justice to it. I knew that I wanted to use his statement to make a point about lists in the Gemara. I reframed Student 2's answer about the Gemara's choice of the number three. This reframing enabled me to introduce the students to a mode of the Gemara's reading of mishnaic lists. When they see another list, they should ask themselves: is this list inclusive or exclusive? What can we extrapolate from a close examination of its wording? In addition, reframing a student's words enabled me to act as bridge between different opinions, demonstrating how two different students can both have plausible arguments.

On this same *sugya* on Kiddushin 3a-b, we also studied a number of *rishonim*. We focused on the issue of why barter (*halifin*) is not a permissible method of betrothing a woman. As a reason for disqualifying barter, the *sugya* states, "Barter has validity [when performed] with less than the equivalent of a *perutah*[24] and a woman for less than a *perutah* will not cause herself to be acquired (*la makniya nafshah*)." I asked the students to learn specific comments of Rashi[25] (s.v. *la makniya nafshah*), Tosafot (s.v. *ve-ishah be-pahot mi-shaveh perutah la makniya nafshah*), and Ritva[26] (s.v. *salka da'takh amina mah sadeh mikanya be-*

---

[24] A coin of minimal worth.
[25] Rabbi Shlomo the son of Yitzhak, 1040/1-1105.
[26] Rabbi Yom Tov the son of Abraham Ishbili, c. 1250-1330.

halifin af ishah nami mikanya be-halifin). They were instructed to also look at Ramban[27] (s.v. *le-ma'ute halifin ve-khu*) if they have additional time. The assigned *rishonim* focused on three words in the *sugya*: *la makniya nafshah* ([a woman] does not cause herself to be acquired). On the assignment sheet, I asked students to compare the positions of Rashi, Tosafot, and Ritva. Below are my questions:

Rashi
1. What does Rashi say the reason behind the phrase *la makniya nafshah* is?
2. What is the halakhic point he makes in the second part of his comment concerning *halifin*?

Tosafot
1. How does Rabbenu Tam[28] disagree with Rashi and his understanding of *la makniya nafshah*? Why? Break down his reasoning.
2. What is his version of the text of the Gemara?
3. Why, according to Tosafot, doesn't the Gemara ask here about the possibility that *kiddushin* could be done with *shetar* [document] or *hazakah* [legal presumption]?

Once you think you have figured out what Tosafot is saying, try and read his explanation of the Gemara back into the text. This is a good way to test if you have understood his *perush* [interpretation] and if it is a convincing read of the *sugya*.

Ritva
1. What difficulties does the Ritva have with the proposal that *kinyan ishah* [acquiring a woman] also be permitted through *halifin*?
2. How does he explain why *halifin* isn't a method of *kinyan ishah*?
3. How does he explain the (our) version *la makniya nafshah*? How is the explanation the same as or different from that of Rashi?

Finally, try and compare all three of these commentators.

---

[27] Rabbi Moses the son of Nahman (Nahmanides), c. 1194-1270.
[28] Rabbi Yaakov the son of Meir Tam, c. 1100-1171.

I gave the students these questions in order to direct them to specific comparative issues and to guide them in the process of studying *rishonim*. By instructing them to read Tosafot's understanding of the *sugya* back into the Gemara itself, I wanted the students to begin to see how Tosafot engages in close textual explication. An ability to recognize and articulate the multiple reading possibilities that medieval commentators present aids these students' explorations of their own different readings.

As the students studied these medieval commentators, they discovered that Rashi and Tosafot have two different versions of our text. While Rashi reads "*la makniya nafshah*" (feminine singular active causative participle), Rabbenu Tam, one of the tosafists, reads "*la mikanya*" (feminine singular passive/reflexive participle). Focusing on the subjectivity of the word "herself," Rashi explained that barter is not a valid method of betrothal because it is derogatory towards the woman (*gen'ai hu lah*). Rabbenu Tam, however, emended the text and removed the word "herself."[29] In his opinion, the invalidity of barter as a method of betrothal is not dependent on the woman's stringency about her degradation, but rather on barter not being in the category of money.

The next transcript begins after I have told the students how extant manuscript traditions of this *sugya* do not support Rabbenu Tam's reading, but contain the word "herself."

> JK: Well, let's also look at the language here. It says *le-khen nir'eh le-Rabbenu Tam*, not "Rabbenu Tam had the version," but "therefore it seemed, it appeared to Rabbenu Tam" that we should read the text this way.
>
> Students: Ohh.
>
> JK: Which again I think strengthens the point that he's making a reading choice of what the correct reading is of the *girsa* [textual

---

[29] On this textual emendation, see Aryeh Cohen, "This Patriarchy Which Is Not One: The Ideology of Marriage in Rashi and Tosafot," *Hebrew Union College Annual* 70 (1999), 126-27.

version] based on a certain ideological or legal concern he has about wanting to define categories.

Student 3: Oh. Desire to keep the woman as the object.

JK: Well, let's keep that as one possibility, that it may be a desire to keep the woman as the object. Okay, let's keep that as one possibility. [Student 2]?

Student 2: I just, I just, I don't know…. Two things. One is that like we all, we all read superimposing our own values on texts. Fundamentally, you know, we can't even avoid that, so it's not like … that's a special thing per se. But I guess it just makes it more explicit because he's, because Tosafot is telling us to leave out reading a word. Uh, no, but also, you know it's also, it's a totally tricky thing to try to get at the rationales behind the people who are doing something like this.

JK: Great. So we may not be able to get at the rationale, but we could ask, what are the effects of the move that he's making and the move that Rashi's making? So one possible way of looking at the effects is saying, removing the woman's subjectivity. I think there's another way we can also look at the effects of what he's doing as well, um, which we'll kind of circle back to.[30]

I began by pointing to textual support for my contention that Rabbenu Tam actively emends the *sugya*. I was trying to teach the students that they should pay attention to what the text actually says rather than what they want it to say or might assume that it says. Second, I stated the fact that I think this reading choice is ideologically based. I did not hide this assumption I make about reading. Third, when Student 3 stated that behind this reading lies a desire to objectify the woman, I accepted that opinion, but named it as one possibility. I thus affirmed her interpretation while opening the door to other opinions about Rabbenu Tam's reading.

---

30 Class transcript, 7/22/07.

Student 2 returned to the question of ideological reading. While he affirmed the ideological nature of Rabbenu Tam's reading, he also questioned whether we do, in fact, have the ability to understand the rationale behind a particular reading. Student 2's statement resulted in my reformulation of a question and integration of Student 3's statement into that reformulation. While we may not be able with certainty to get at the rationale, we can still ask questions about the effects of various readings. In other words, we can ask, "What's at stake?" in choosing one reading over another.

I took this idea a step further in the continuing discussion about this *sugya*.

> JK: ... Tosafot is moving us away from the idea of *da'at* [intention], um, from the idea of *da'at*, and moving us back to and centering us on the idea of taking *kesef* [money] and putting it at the center. And kind of, what are the pluses and minuses of Rabbenu Tam's move of removing *da'at*, even though there's not really *girsa* proof of that in the Gemara, but making the *girsa* read that. What are the pluses and minuses of putting *kesef* at the center and not *da'at*?

> Student 1: Well, he's avoiding the subjectivity of it. Well, if this woman doesn't feel it as *gen'ai* [degradation] because she's getting this amount or maybe some people would feel *gen'ai* for getting a *perutah*. Like, he's taking away that whole subjective element to put it in with the fixed standard of money and therefore there's no question of like how she feels about it. Like, yeah.

> JK: Okay, great. That's exactly what he does. Plus and minus of doing that?

> Student 1: It creates a universal standard that you don't have rich or poor women, like, feeling different or that there should be any sort of different *gen'ai* between them or something like that. But on the other hand, it reduces it to a monetary standard that is a sort of set amount and focuses it as a more an alliance of *kinyan* [acquiring] than anything else.

> JK: Okay, nice. So those are kind of our two paradigms we're working with. One was also something that [Student 3] brought out earlier—

this idea of it takes away from the subjectivity of the woman and just turns it purely into *kinyan* and monetary transaction. On the other hand, Rabbenu Tam codifies in law this idea that, um, we're not working by a subjective standard and *kinyan* is not to be done with, um, is not to turn on the issue of *gen'ai* or not *gen'ai*. It's one standard. It's *kesef*.

Student 2: It's similar to the rationale behind minimum wage....

As I stated above, Tosafot (and Rabbenu Tam) place money at the center of betrothal. A woman must be betrothed with money, and because *halifin* does not fall into the category of money, it is invalid as a method of betrothal. To them, this, and not Rashi's suggestion of derogation and the women's intention, explains why *halifin* cannot be used. At this point, I asked the students to consider both the positive and negative aspects of Rabbenu Tam's move. Student 1 successfully articulated how Rabbenu Tam's perspective can be viewed as creating a universal standard (positive, from our point of view) or as emphasizing how betrothal is like a monetary purchase (negative). Again, I tied Student 1's articulation into Student 3's earlier statement, validating her perspective, but also illustrating how careful examination reveals that it is not the only way to approach the issue. Student 2 then connected this discussion to the contemporary issue of minimum wage. While I did not generally emphasize drawing parallels between these older discussions and modern politics, Student 2's leap nicely illustrated how nuanced readings can help students connect the world of the Talmud with contemporary issues.

A number of pedagogical values are illustrated in the discussion of these commentators. The first, as always, is the importance of reading precision, learning to read the words themselves carefully and accurately. The second is the simultaneous affirmation of one interpretive perspective while opening the door for other possibilities. The third is a willingness to reformulate my own ideas. Through the combination of these techniques, I challenged the students to examine an issue rigorously and from a number of perspectives. I required them to ground their ideas in the text, listen to each other, and constantly push themselves to delve more deeply into the interpretive possibilities of the Talmud.

Jane Kanarek

Potential of the Pedagogy of Slowing Down

In the section that follows, I will articulate more fully the potential of the pedagogy of slowing down, through reflections that emerge from my investigation of my Kollel teaching. While I knew at the beginning of the summer that I wanted to help my students become stronger, more attentive, and deeper readers of the Gemara, I believe that the process of slowing down—a process I only fully understood after the fact—played a significant role in enabling this to occur. Slowing down not only contributed to the students becoming more attentive readers but also to stronger class dynamics and the ongoing development of their religious voices.

The precision that is possible in slowing down helped students to identify what they were having trouble understanding, and equally important, why they were having difficulty. Students could more readily define whether the stumbling block was a dictionary problem (a word they cannot find) or a logic problem (a construction they have not yet mastered), or whether the text in question holds multiple interpretive possibilities. In addition, the requirement that they be alert to parallel texts and weave in older material with what was currently being studied aided significantly in parsing an argument.

The methods through which *rishonim* sought to ground their readings in the Gemara text reinforced my challenge to the students that they do the same. Students could compare their ideas about the *sugya* with those of later commentators, seeing both similarities and differences in their respective ideas. Through close readings of the *rishonim*, students could see the possibilities that arose from attentive, detailed, and creative reading and thinking. The use of *rishonim* also facilitated the students' abilities to identify tensions in the text, to see places where the dominant ideology may break down. I challenged them to ask, "What is at stake in these different readings?" The fact that many of the *rishonim* were difficult to understand was actually of pedagogic benefit, as it helped facilitate the process of—and foster the value of—slowing down.

Most significant was an increased ability on the part of each student to find a range of interpretive possibilities in the *sugya*. I observed that the marker of success in this class over time became not so much speed of reading and preparation of material, but what a student could articulate about the text. This shift to quality over quantity had some important corollaries.

First was an increased opportunity for me, as a teacher, to better bridge the different class levels.[31] Slowing down enabled me to more clearly see which strategies would best help individual students to acquire necessary skills in reading and interpretation. I could then integrate these observations into class and suggestions for *havruta* preparation.

Second, I observed a striking shift in the ways in which different *havruta* pairs prepared for class. At the beginning of the summer, stronger students completed the assigned material significantly more quickly than the weaker students. However, by the end of the summer this gap had lessened (though not entirely closed). I wrote: "… I am definitely not having a moving too fast issue now. Class has acted to slow down the *havrutot* because they are now interested in seeing how much they can see in the *sugya*" (teaching journal, 7/25/07). I believe that the lessening of the gap can be explained not only because of the weaker students' increasing comfort with the Talmudic texts, but also because the stronger students no longer raced through the material as quickly as possible. Instead, they wanted to extract as much meaning from the text as possible. Marking success by what was generated rather than speed meant more time spent thinking and articulating ideas in *havruta* preparation.

Third, I perceived an increasing patience in reading, even with potentially ethically difficult texts. The chosen material's emphasis on betrothal as a man "acquiring" a woman raises troubling questions about the nature of Jewish marriage and women's status in Jewish law.[32] However, I made explicit to my students throughout the class that I wanted to hear their opinions, reactions, and even anger about this material. However, at the same time as I reinforced my desire to hear them speak

---

[31] If the gaps between student levels are too wide, for example beginners to advanced, slowing down will not help in meeting the different students' needs. I imagine that all the students will be frustrated!

[32] Rachel Adler, *Engendering Judaism: An Inclusive Theology and Ethics* (Philadelphia: Jewish Publication Society, 1998), 169-207, has written a critique of the traditional Jewish marriage ceremony and *kiddushin* in particular.

their minds, I also reinforced my requirement that they ground their opinions about what the text was saying in the words of the text, first demonstrating that they could translate and explain it.

As the students became closer readers of the Gemara, they learned to support their ideas more strongly. In turn, they discovered that this strengthened reading capacity resulted in the ability to better express their opinions. My choice to be explicit about both of these points—reading and opinion—meant that even if I asked a student to momentarily hold back, he trusted that we would circle back to his perspective. I believe that because students knew they would have time to express their opinions, they were less anxious about making sure they said everything at the beginning. Once they trusted that they would have this time, they were willing to build their skills as they explored the ethical tensions in a text. Then, as their skills grew, they found that they not only had permission to but were more capable of inserting their own perspective into the text itself, expressing questions and concerns and offering different readings.

This emphasis on taking time to express grounded opinions was also bound up with the Kollel's larger ideology of supporting and exploring observant-egalitarian Judaism. The process of encouraging students to carefully articulate textual values paralleled the process we wanted them to undertake in their own religious introspection and growth. Just as the students learned to read, analyze, and think about a text, they could learn to read, analyze, and consider their own Jewish lives. They could consider and discuss with one another issues about Jewish practice, including ritual observance and egalitarianism, with the same depth, openness, rigor, and consideration toward one another as they did in Talmud class. Through finding a voice in the study of Talmud, I aimed to help them find a similar voice in Jewish practice.

In sum, I strove to open up a space for reading and thinking characterized simultaneously by intellectual openness and reading rigor. By pushing students to articulate their opinions while grounding those opinions in the specific words of the text, and exposing them to the interpretive tradition of the *rishonim* (demonstrating that the Gemara's meaning is not fixed or static), I wanted to give them tools to become insiders in our tradition. And with their increased abilities, I found, came increased joy in the process of learning Talmud itself.

Conclusion

As cited above, Fishbane conceptualizes the commentator's spiritual task as "… to mediate and influence the pace of reading, so that the reader can be addressed anew by the innate power of the text." In providing a cultural model of Talmud study that slowed down by emphasizing accurate translation and rigor in thinking about meaning, I hoped to give all of my students a sense of accomplishment and an ability to begin to internalize these texts, and so our tradition. Creating a space for conversations based on precise translation and explanation that open into realms of multiple opinions and interpretive possibilities facilitated this process of becoming a translator. One of my students said that the class had given him "[a v]oice in the tradition by learning and mastering the rabbis—then [I can] agree or disagree." It is finding that voice through traditional text study that I found to be central to both the practices and the goals of the pedagogy of slowing down.

7 Serendipity and Pedagogy: Presenting the Weekly *Parashah* Through Rabbinic Eyes

Carl M. Perkins

Introduction

On December 19, 2007, an article about Walter H.G. Lewin, a professor (now emeritus) of physics at MIT, appeared on the front page of the *New York Times*. Professor Lewin, then 71, was described as a distinguished looking, careful pedagogue who spends 25 hours preparing each of his lectures, choreographing every detail. He is a popular lecturer; for a time, his lectures, which appear on the internet at iTunes U, were the most downloaded in the world. To understand why, and to appreciate why he was the subject of the *Times*' attention, all one must do is to take a look at the picture that the *Times* chose to highlight its article. There, on the front page of the paper, is a picture of Professor Lewin hoisted on a 30-pound steel ball, attached to a pendulum, "swinging across the stage, holding himself nearly horizontal as his hair blows in the breeze he created."[1]

Professor Lewin's flair for the dramatic, his devotion to capturing his students' attention—and holding tightly onto it—resonates personally with me. I used to teach chemistry at a college preparatory school in Boston. During my tenure, I was very much aware of the need to engage

---

[1] See http://www.nytimes.com/2007/12/19/education/19physics.html for the web version of the article. The picture of Professor Lewin as a human pendulum to which I refer above, which I believe captures the essence of his appeal, is not as prominent on this webpage as it was in print. In the print edition of the newspaper, it appeared on page 1; here, it appears mid-way through the article on the left side, above the rather flat caption, "Professor Lewin demonstrates physics of pendulums." (The picture that is most prominent on the webpage appeared on p. A21 of the printed edition.)

my students. I took pains to attract their attention and to engage their minds and, ultimately, their hearts. The way I saw it, a typical high school student is willing to give a teacher about a minute—maybe less—before he or she tunes out. During that brief window, the teacher must make a convincing case that the student should pay attention. And that case is often made most effectively through some sort of visual demonstration, a demonstration that has a playful quality to it—yet which is deeper than it may appear.

And so, as a former high school science teacher, I could relate to the antics I saw in Dr. Lewin's lectures. But antics in the classroom are not just a form of entertainment: they create moments of engagement with the subject matter of the course, moments which allow learning to take place. Professor Lewin understands that when the cultural gap between learner and subject matter is huge, unless the learning environment is creative and fun it can be hard for learning to take place. In an area of inquiry that seems distant and unapproachable, if a teacher can "let go," he or she can help his or her students open themselves up for truly insightful learning to take place.

Though I no longer teach science, I follow similar principles every week as I try to teach rabbinic perspectives on the themes of the *parashah* of the week (the weekly Torah portion) in the context of a Shabbat morning service in my synagogue.

There are many pedagogic challenges in teaching this material in the synagogue on a Shabbat morning. One of them is the very limited amount of available time: I barely have a half hour—and that only on days when the service moves along at a brisk pace. I never know precisely whom I will be facing in my "classroom." There may be "regulars"—men and women who come virtually every week, and who have been coming for years. Some of these may remember what I said in a *d'var torah* (a "word of Torah," a lesson illuminating a Jewish text, usually based on the weekly Torah portion, used here interchangeably with *derashah*) ten or fifteen years ago. There may also be visitors, such as out-of-town guests who are at the synagogue to attend a bar or bat mitzvah celebration, who have never come before and may never come again. I may have 50 to 60 seventh graders, sitting in a group by themselves, and looking very wary, or very oblivious. Incidentally, knowing that adolescents and pre-adolescents may be present somewhat restricts my choice of subject matter and manner of presentation: certain topics are best avoided, or approached only very delicately.

There is no such thing as an "average student"; even if there were, I wouldn't be able to assume that he or she knows anything about rabbinic culture. Some of my "students" are Jewish; others, Gentile. I have to think long and hard about whether to use the word, "we," as in the phrase, "we Jews," and if so, how and when. Some students are very literate, articulate, and intellectual. Others don't read much, and may have a simple view of life. Some come to synagogue thinking that they will be interested in hearing what I have to say. Many others are like the teenagers I used to face in my chemistry classes: they're willing to give me a minute or so before they tune out, or fall asleep.[2] It is my duty as the *darshan* (preacher or teacher) to try to reach all of them.

Underlying all of these challenges—many of which are very similar to those I faced as a science teacher—is my responsibility as a *darshan* to present material from and about a foreign culture. Rabbinic Judaism—and the rabbinic way of reading the biblical text, of gleaning moral insights from it, and of organizing one's life around it—is as exotic to many of the Jews who attend services in my synagogue as it is to most Gentiles. The notion that Jewish learning, and specifically the study of rabbinic texts, is at all interesting, insightful, or deserving of being central to one's Jewish identity is foreign to many—especially to visitors, but also to congregants who don't generally come to services, and even some who do. And yet I see it as my mission to suggest just that, each and every Shabbat.

Thus, a significant pedagogic challenge is simply to get people's attention—and to hold it long enough for them to absorb that broad underlying message. I see my challenge, much like the challenge of the science teacher in a world in which many bright people imagine that they could not possibly fully understand science, as making rabbinic

---

[2] Actually, although students occasionally closed their eyes during the chemistry classes I taught several decades ago, I don't recall them falling fully asleep, whereas in synagogue this is not uncommon. Even during scintillating discussions, men and women can fall fast asleep. Until one gets used to it, it can be distracting, if not unnerving.

culture real and relevant, getting it to speak intelligibly to people who might otherwise not consider rabbinic notions at all relevant to the way they lead or think about their lives.

The great modern Jewish philosopher, Franz Rosenzweig, at the opening address of the Lehrhaus in Frankfurt, Germany in 1920, described the contemporary challenge of bridging the gap between Torah and life as follows: when Jews were living in pre-modern Jewish communities, they were at home in the world of Torah. The role of the *darshan* was to help them understand the contemporary world. Since the Enlightenment, Jews have become at home in the contemporary world, and it is the responsibility of the *darshan* to help them understand the world of Torah.[3] I agree with Rosenzweig, but I think we *darshanim* have more in common with our forebears than his words might suggest. For in either case, we *darshanim* are explicators, we are translators, we are seeking to bridge a gap in understanding, and to reveal connections between Torah and life that would otherwise be hidden.

Before determining how to present their material or message, all *darshanim* face a prior challenge: to determine what to talk *about*. How does one make that choice? How do *I* make that choice? There are many themes on which I could speak on a given Shabbat. How do I determine what to focus my attention and that of my congregation on? When and how do I make that decision? Do I ever second-guess myself? How do I know that I've made the "right" decision? My exploration of these questions is what guides this essay.

First, a few general observations: while this might seem obvious, I always seek a topic that resonates within me. That is, I seek a theme, an idea or a concept—suggested by the *parashah* and/or the occasion—that interests or excites me, and possibly even moves me. My reasoning is that if *I* get a buzz from thinking about it, I can make it interesting to others. If I don't, I'm unlikely to succeed.

How do I "make" that happen? It's not really possible for me to control the process. I can set aside time and provide opportunities for inspiration, but I can never know when that magic moment of connection will take place, or what particular result it will produce. I gain solace from

---

[3] Franz Rosenzweig, "Upon Opening the Judisches Lehrhaus," in *On Jewish Learning*, ed. N.N. Glatzer (New York: Schocken Books, 1965), 98-99

another statement by Rosenzweig, who, in discussing the challenge of adult Jewish education in Weimar Germany, said, "The highest things cannot be planned; for them, readiness is everything. Readiness is the one thing we can offer to the Jewish individual within us, the individual we aim at."[4] I try to be ready—to be inspired, and to be motivated to share that inspiration with others. How do I get ready? I open my eyes; I read; I reflect. I constantly try to think about what is going on in my community, in our country, in the world. I consider who is going to be in shul on a particular day. When an idea occurs to me, when a text says to me, "*Darsheini!*"—"Explicate me, preach about me!"—I jot down a few notes, and include enough detail so that I can make sense—and use—of them later.

How much in advance do I do this? A friend of mine who is a Methodist minister sketches out her sermons six to nine months in advance. On the one hand, I envy her; on the other, I don't believe that I could ever do that. I find it hard to become inspired so far in advance. Even when it comes to High Holiday sermons, for which I begin collecting material and ideas soon after the previous Simchat Torah, I don't begin writing my drafts until about six weeks before the holidays.

Sometimes an idea occurs to me that I know will be useful months ahead. I may jot down in my calendar that I want to speak about it on a particular Shabbat, but I rarely sketch out more than a few paragraphs. Years ago, there were occasions when, weeks ahead of time, I decided that I was going to speak about such-and-such on a given Shabbat, only to discover as the time approached that the subject seemed less compelling. Now I generally wait until the week of the *derashah* to formulate precisely what I'm going to say. If an idea hasn't yet occurred to me, I await its occurrence during that week. It generally appears in one moment or in a series of moments of serendipity, when it seems as though everything falls into place. There is a flash of insight, and I know, sometimes vaguely but usually quite specifically, what I'm going to talk about and how I am going to present it.

In this chapter, I focus on that serendipity. How does it happen? How do I know if I'm not there yet, and how do I know when I *am* there?

---

[4] Franz Rosenzweig, "Towards a Renaissance of Jewish Learning," in *On Jewish Learning*, ed. N.N. Glatzer (New York: Schocken Books, 1965), 65.

What are the elements that make it work? What has to be present? To illustrate the process, I will focus on the development of two *derashot* for *Parashat Sh'mot* (the first reading in the book of Exodus, Exod. 1:1-6:1). Both were delivered, coincidentally, in the same calendar year. The first was delivered on January 12, 2007; the second on December 29, 2007. I will review edited diary notes that I took (deliberately collecting data for this study), recording the process of discovering what I was going to discuss and how I was going to present my material, and compare and reflect on those two experiences.

"Barefoot in the Sanctuary": Preparing a Torah Discussion for *Parashat Sh'mot* (January 13, 2007)

Tuesday, January 9, 2007.

Yes. The eureka moment has hit. It's 7:38 am on Tuesday. I've got to be at the shul for a meeting in 7 minutes. But there it is: an essay entitled, "Shoeless in the Sanctuary" in my email in-box. The obvious allusion is to the passage in this coming week's Torah portion in which God speaks to Moses at the site of the burning bush and says, "Remove your shoes, for the ground on which you stand is holy" (Exod. 3:5). I subscribe to about three or four different *d'var torah* email distribution lists. Each week, several essays, articles, or *divrei torah* come across my desk and trigger (or fail to trigger) an interest in a particular topic to talk about on the upcoming Shabbat. Ordinarily, I start thinking about the next Shabbat's *d'var torah* on Monday morning, at the latest. But yesterday, I didn't go to morning minyan at 6:45 a.m., so I didn't get to hear the first few verses of the upcoming week's *parashah*, and therefore didn't get to begin to reflect on what to speak about.

Why does this odd topic (the *absence* of shoes in the sanctuary— i.e., the ancient Temple in Jerusalem—and the *presence* of shoes in the synagogue) grip me? I have no idea. Actually, if pressed to answer the question, I do. I'm energized by the idea of looking through rabbinic eyes at something we ordinarily take for granted, in this case shoes. I want people to think about the role of shoes in our own society—and what they represent. I want them to reflect on the fact that, although Moses was told to *remove* his shoes while standing on holy ground, we ourselves *wear* shoes—generally very nice ones—in shul. I want to help people see the true oddness of Moses removing his shoes, to get them to explore that moment. I want people to see that Rabbinic Judaism is not the same as Biblical Israel. I'm intrigued by the idea of showing how an obvious, often overlooked, feature of daily life may in fact be of significance, may in fact reflect something important about our culture, and how it differs from other cultures, such as rabbinic culture. This topic clearly presents many opportunities for engagement.

Plus, this coming Shabbat is a Shabbat on which we don't have a bar or bat mitzvah, so there's not the same need (within me) to make a strong moral or ethical point. I can have a bit more fun than usual. Instead of talking about "serious" topics, I can talk about shoes in the synagogue—a topic that no one expects to be addressed in shul. This coming Shabbat, because it's a three-day ski weekend here in New England, we'll probably have at most about 80 people in shul. We'll be meeting in our small chapel rather than in the larger sanctuary. It's a more intimate, less formal space—much more conducive to a cozy discussion.

On the other hand, it's Martin Luther King, Jr., Day weekend. How will we acknowledge that? Should the powerful messages of King's life—the need to overcome discrimination, the need to fight for what one believes in, even at the risk of one's own life, the need for our society to be fully inclusive—moral messages rooted in the book of Exodus, from which we are about to begin reading, be somehow contained within this *d'var torah*? They probably can't be. Delivering a *d'var torah* or leading a discussion (on wearing shoes or taking them off) that will ignore those issues, is, at the very least, an issue for me. I take Martin Luther King, Jr., Day very seriously. In previous years, I've given sermons on King's life.[5] Several years ago, I researched and gave a sermon on his relationship with Abraham Joshua Heschel. Last year (2006), I researched Alice Walker's work and spoke about it.[6] Generally, I feel irresistibly drawn

---

[5] See, e.g., http://www.templealiyah.com/uploadedFiles/site/About/Leadership/Rabbi/MLK%202004.pdf.

[6] See http://www.templealiyah.com/uploadedFiles/site/About/Leadership/Rabbi/MLK%202006.pdf.

to acknowledge this day in my *d'var torah*. Can (should, will) I resist the urge, the need, to do that this coming week? We shall see.

Wednesday, January 10, 2007

Last night at 10:00 p.m., before leaving my office, I pulled out my Sh'mot file from my file cabinet. I had vaguely recalled thinking about, reading about, and possibly even speaking about, this odd topic a while ago—perhaps many years ago. I took a quick scan, and, lo and behold, I found a study sheet on this precise topic that I had used in 2002! I quickly put it away without reading it. I did, though, get a glimpse of the acknowledgement at the top of the page. It made reference to an article I had read at the time to prepare for the *d'var torah*. The article was written by a different author from the one who'd written the article I'd just received. Good, I thought. I will learn something new. Let me see what the new article has to teach me, before looking more closely at what I had written five years ago.

A few hours later, before going to bed, I started reading the 2007 article on shoelessness. I was disappointed. As I read it, I became bored. Oy, I thought. This is not working. It's not sounding interesting—how will my own *derashah* be interesting? On the other hand, I thought, it's 12:40 a.m. Maybe it's just that it's too late to get excited about a topic. Let me take another look at it tomorrow.

Thursday, January 11, 2007

I just received a nice midrashic spark (in an Oz Ve-Shalom *d'var torah* that came in the mail today) that reminded me that this topic (shoelessness) can indeed be interesting (which therefore encouraged me not to lose heart):

> Taking off one's shoes expresses giving oneself up entirely to the meaning of a place, to let your personality get its standing and take up its position entirely and directly on it without any intermediary. So the priests in the Temple had always to function barefooted, and nothing was allowed to be *hotzetz*, to intervene between their feet and the ground, or between their hands and the holy vessels during the service, or between the priestly garments and their body. Nothing in the Temple was mere gaudy show, man-designed to impress and have effect on the eye of the

beholder. Everything was to work back on the personality of the ministrant, and if one wished to act in the service of the Temple one had to identify oneself directly with it, and become sanctified by it, and be a part of it. "The floor sanctifies" (Zevahim 24a)—the holy soil sanctifies the priest.

(Rabbi S.R. Hirsch, Exod. 3:5, Levi translation)

Now *this* is the kind of writing that turns me on. This clarified for me what I'd like to explore on Shabbat: *How does clothing contribute to or take away from our ability to experience the holy?* Why is it that in our society, everyone wears fancy clothes on Rosh Hashanah and Yom Kippur? Why is it that the characters in *Sex in the City*—particularly its star, played by Sarah Jessica Parker, were depicted as focusing so much attention, and spending so much money, on shoes? What is it about shoes that they can so delight women—and, apparently, intrigue men? (Are women's attitudes toward shoes different from those of men? How?) Why is it that no adult in a liberal congregation would ever think of taking off their shoes on the *bimah*, yet they'll often wear otherwise revealing clothing in public without a second thought?

Friday, January 12, 2007

Oy. It's already Friday morning, I've had one pastoral encounter in my office and I'm heading off to see two other congregants in their homes, and I still haven't found an hour to clarify precisely what I'm going to say on Shabbat, and how I'm going to say it.

But just this morning, the following email (edited slightly for readability) from a colleague came across my desk:

> Subject: Shvartze
>
> I'm sure that subject line got your attention. I'm working on a sermon about how decades after the civil rights movement (in which Jews were active) many Jews are still racially intolerant. I hear congregants use the Yiddish derogatory term "shvartze" all the time in various contexts, in referring to their cleaning lady, their team's quarterback, or my assistant (!). Was MLK a shvartze? Barack Obama? Bill Cosby? Michael Jordan or Tiger Woods?
>
> How would we feel if Gentiles used "kike" the way some Jews use "shvartze"?

> Is shvartze as bad as the "N-word"?
>
> Do those who use shvartze have the right to be outraged at Michael Richard's racial tirade? Or former Sen. George Allen's Macaca comment?
>
> I plan to talk about King, Heschel, the recent PBS special about antisemitism (which was very well done), and the slavery of our people in Sh'mot.
>
> Any texts you can think of on racial slurs or prejudices?
>
> I've also been thinking about what MLK's feelings would be on the Black community's use (ownership?) of the N-word today.

Now *that's* a topic to speak about! It's enough to make me feel inadequate, or ashamed. It's relevant, timely, and important. Do I go with my original (and, in comparison, seemingly frivolous) topic—or do I switch gears, and try to lead a discussion on racism, exclusion, slavery, the Exodus from Egypt, etc?

I have to go. I'll have to decide later this afternoon.

Friday, January 12, 2007

1:30 p.m. I'm back in the office, several hours after I'd hoped to be. Three things have just happened, which have convinced me to deliver the *d'var torah* on shoelessness as I'd hoped.

First, I was grabbing a quick bite at home before returning to the shul to write up my *d'var torah* when my teenage daughter came in. "What are you talking about tomorrow?" she asked. I told her that I was thinking about speaking about Moses removing his shoes when God spoke to him at the burning bush, but that I was also tempted to say something about the connection between MLK's life and work and the Exodus story.

"Didn't you speak about that once before?" she asked, referring to shoelessness. "I remember you speaking about how, in a holy place, you should dress the way you would if you were approaching to meet royalty. If the practice is to remove your shoes, you remove your shoes, and if the practice is to keep your shoes on, you keep your shoes on."

That was the first thing that happened. And it was fairly important. I realized, through hearing my daughter's recollection of that earlier discussion five years ago, just how interesting that topic really is to talk about. (Incidentally, although I was initially dismayed by how well she remembered my *derashah* from five years ago, I also realized that her memory is exceptional. Moreover, because of the holiday weekend, most likely no one else who had been present at the earlier discussion would be in shul the next day.)

Then, just a moment ago, I heard a story on the news about the practice of removing shoes as part of the security check before getting on an airplane.[7] I suddenly realized that there was an additional element in this topic, one that hadn't been present in January 2002. That was still several months before the famous shoe bomber's attempt to blow up a trans-Atlantic plane had resulted in all of us removing our shoes before getting on planes. If any of us had been told back in 2000 that, by 2007, all Americans—passively, compliantly, and fairly uncomplainingly—would be removing their shoes before getting on planes, would any of us have believed it?

Finally, my administrative assistant, with whom I happened to be discussing the topic of my upcoming *d'var torah* (as I sometimes, but not always, do) reminded me of a recent story in the news regarding the appropriateness—or lack thereof—of going barefoot (or close to it) in the presence of "royalty." The story concerned a group of women's lacrosse players who met with President Bush at the White House. A widely reproduced photograph revealed that several of the women were wearing flip-flops, which generated much discussion regarding whether or not that was appropriate.[8]

---

[7] The story was aired on WBUR at 1:38 pm on Friday, January 12, 2007. The headline for it (copied from the WBUR website) reads as follows:

Scanners Will Let Some Travelers Keep Shoes On
Soon, select airports will feature shoe scanners that can check for explosives while shoes are still on your feet. Fliers who've cleared security checks for "registered traveler" programs will be able to use the scanners. The *Wall Street Journal*'s Laura Meckler talks with Luke Burbank about how that may boost "registered traveler" membership.

The audio and transcript are available at: http://www.npr.org/templates/story/story.php?storyId=6831828 .

[8] For one version of the AP story with accompanying photograph, see http://usatoday30.usatoday.com/news/nation/2005-07-19-flip-flops_x.htm .

OK. So now it is 1:59 p.m. on Friday afternoon. It's too late to fuss around too much with the study sheet. Rather than re-doing it, as I would have preferred to do, were it not for the time constraints—exacerbated by my hesitation to choose my topic—I am going to use the same study sheet that I used in 2002. After all, I put a lot of time and energy into the composition of the sheet back then: the revised translations are all mine, as are the selection, organization, and formatting of the material. The quote from R. Samson Raphael Hirsch, which only came to my attention this week, is something that I can bring with me, and present for people to respond to.

[What follows is the final copy of my study sheet:]

Parashat Sh'mot 5767
January 12, 2007

Barefoot in the Synagogue?
(With thanks to Professor Eliezer Bashan, Department of Jewish History, Bar Ilan University)

Barefoot in the Bible:

"Remove your sandals from your feet, for the place on which you stand is holy ground." (Exodus 3:5) (See also Joshua 5:15)

"David meanwhile went up... weeping as he went; his head was covered and he walked **barefoot**." (II Sam. 15:30)

"Save your **foot** from going **bare**, and your throat from thirst." (Jeremiah 2:25)

"Previously, the LORD had said to Isaiah... 'Go, untie the sackcloth from your loins and take your sandals off your feet,' which he had done, going naked and barefoot. So shall the king of Assyria drive off the captives of Egypt and the exiles of Nubia, young and old, naked and **barefoot**." (Isaiah 20:2-4)

Barefoot in the Talmudic Period

One may not enter the Holy Mount of the Temple with one's staff, or with one's shoes on or with one's money belt or with one's feet dust-stained. One should also not take a short-cut through it, nor, it goes without saying, spit there." (Mishnah Berakhot 9:5)

What about the synagogue? In Babylonia...

Rabba said: The synagogue is similar to a person's home. Just as in a person's home one does not want it to serve as a thoroughfare for strangers, even though one does not mind spitting within the home or wearing footwear, so too, the synagogue must not be used as a thoroughfare, but spitting and wearing shoes are permitted. (Babylonian Talmud: Berakhot 63a)

But in the Land of Israel...

Judah b. Rabbi went into a synagogue and left his sandals outside, and they were stolen. He said, 'Had I not gone into the synagogue, my sandals would not have been stolen.'" (Jerusalem Talmud, Bava Metzia 2, 9)

[Page two begins here]

Barefoot in the Middle Ages: Conflicting Cultural Norms
What happens when Jews move from Christian Spain to Moslem Algeria?

A Teshuvah of Rabbi Solomon b. Simeon b. Tzemah Duran, Algeria (Rashbash, d. 1467):

"**Question**: You wrote concerning a congregation [of immigrants] that wished to reach consensus that one should not enter the synagogue wearing shoes, due to the contempt in which the Ishmaelites (Moslems) held them. Moreover, there is another [pre-existing] synagogue in the very same city in which it is the custom not to enter wearing shoes. A few individuals came forward challenging this idea, arguing that Maimonides permitted entering a synagogue in shoes; and now you ask my opinion on the subject.

"**Response**: "It is well known that a synagogue deserves to be glorified, exalted and respected, keeping any sign of contempt away from it. Respect, however, is anything that people consider as such, ... true respect or contempt are according to the way people think and the mores of the place. For example, in the lands of the Christians, where it is not considered a sign of contempt to enter in one's shoes, or even to appear in shoes before the monarch, if a person enters a synagogue in one of their cities wearing shoes that does not show contempt. But in these lands [Moslem countries], where it is a sign of contempt to come before dignitaries, not to mention before the king, wearing shoes, in their cities one must not enter a synagogue wearing shoes, since if one does not do so before a king of flesh and blood, all the more so before the King of Kings, the Holy One, blessed be He.

"Considering the fact that in Christian countries people wear their shoes until they get into bed, one is permitted to enter a synagogue in a Christian city in one's shoes, but in countries where care is taken [not] to enter the home in shoes ... it is unfitting to sully the house of our Lord.... Thus, in the land of Edom [the Christian world], where one does not stand before important people except in footwear, it is forbidden to stand in the house of prayer barefoot. In the land of Ishmael [the Moslem world], where it is customary to stand before dignitaries barefoot, it is permitted [to remove one's shoes]. The law in this regard varies according to the local custom of what is considered a sign of contempt or of respect ... according to the place and its practices.... It all depends on complying with the custom of the place."

"Therefore it is a good thing which they sought to do, to avoid being held in contempt by the nation that thought us contemptuous."

January 12, 2007

2:20 p.m. Final entry before delivering the *d'var torah*:

I'm ready. I am going to remind people of that moment when God told Moses to remove his shoes, and ask people, Why? Why, in this story, is removing shoes associated with being in the presence of God? Is that an association that makes sense to us? If so, why don't we do the same? If not, why not? Is the purpose of removing shoes to help Moses sense the presence of God, or is it a sign of respect for the holy? What helps *us* be conscious that we are in the presence of God? A head covering? Certain clothing? What are sartorial signs of respect in our culture? Are there ever circumstances when we remove an article of clothing as a sign of respect? (Off hand, I can think of several: we would never keep on an overcoat if we were meeting a dignitary. And the practice of removing hats has long been a sign of respect in our society.)

Once we've had the chance to discuss that, I'm hoping that I can review the phenomenon of shoelessness in the Bible and in the talmudic period (as presented in the study sheet), and then, eventually, get to that marvelous *teshuvah* on the second side of the sheet. I know that I will have to be judicious: I will not have time to review in detail every one of the sources. That's fine. They're there for people to review and to pique people's interest as I'm speaking. They're there to make the additional point that all we're doing is reviewing the highlights of a topic that is far deeper and broader than we'll get the chance to discuss in shul. The underlying message: there's more than what meets the eye—more to learn, more to understand, more to enjoy, more to appreciate.

Sunday, January 14, 2007

My preparation for yesterday's *derashah* did not end until the last few moments before it began, as we were singing "Etz Hayim Hi," and as the ark was closing. What I had been wondering about all during *shaharit* (the morning service) was, how should I begin? What should I use as the "hook"? How could I engage the group to explore the issue I wanted them to explore?

I'm surprised that the obvious way to do that had not occurred to me until then. But this is not the first time this has happened. It is sometimes a source of distress to me that I am generally unable to figure out precisely how to frame a *derashah* until it is about to begin, and I am therefore unable to articulate ahead of time precisely how it will flow. On the one hand, this increases its spontaneity and pizazz; on the other hand, it can be stressful.

During *shaharit*, I came to the conclusion that the best way to spark this discussion would be to do the unexpected: take my shoes off, and lead the discussion in my stocking feet. (The notion of doing so barefoot was too far over the edge for me to consider.) One might think that that would have been obvious. Yet somehow, it hadn't occurred to me until that morning. One might think that this would have ended for me the suspense and the speculation, and would have allowed me to recite *shaharit* with full *kavannah* (attention and focus), but instead I obsessed—as I am wont to do—over the question of whether or not "to frame the frame." In other words, I wondered whether (a) to simply take my shoes off; or (b) to *draw attention to the fact* that I was taking my shoes off. I decided to do the latter. First, the davenning was taking place in a small room. Only the dozen or so folks in the front—if that many—would see what I was doing, and by the time the others would realize that I was shoeless, they would feel as though they had missed something—a feeling that might inspire some irritation, if not hostility, which could chill the discussion. (In my view, a good Torah discussion requires a nice, gentle, mutually supportive feeling in the room. It must never dissolve into a debate—or, if it does, it must be a good-natured one.) Also, I knew that a bold move like this would be appreciated (and even admired) by some, but would be resented by others. Certain people whom I knew (or speculated) would be irritated by such a gesture would, perhaps, be mollified by an initial comment from me.

I decided to introduce the *derashah* by first moving a chair alongside the Torah reading table. This already drew attention and evoked a giggle from one not very inhibited congregant. I then spoke briefly about the notion of *"l'shem hinukh"*—the idea that sometimes one does things differently "for educational purposes."

At this point, I had everyone's attention. So I sat down, and I asked out loud, "How does it feel to observe me doing what I'm doing right now?" I proceeded to carefully unlace my shoes and then to take them off.

There were a few—just a few—startled expressions. Most people had amused expressions on their faces.

At first, the reactions were muted. People weren't sure what to say, because the question had focused on a feeling. I generally don't do this right at the start of a *derashah*—if at all—because people are reluctant to "open up" and talk about feelings in the presence of the community. But I wanted or needed to push this along quickly. (The *haftarah* had taken longer than usual and we were running late.)

After one or two tepid, innocuous, and not very illuminating comments, one person said, "It feels odd."

"Why?" I asked.

"Because you never do that—*we* never do that—in shul," she said. Others quickly chimed in.

"It feels comfortable."

"It's relaxing."

"It's informal."

"It doesn't feel like shul."

"It feels Japanese."

"It reminds one of a house of *shiva*."

"It feels like we're at home, rather than out."

This led very quickly to a discussion among several women concerning how grateful they are when they are able to take off their (generally uncomfortable) shoes.

"Does it evoke holiness?" I asked. Before anyone could respond, I continued, "Sure, in the Bible, as we saw in today's *parashah*, we know that somehow taking off one's shoes is a sign that one is in the presence of holiness, but is that the case today?" We continued discussing this issue. One person said that it seemed as though when someone takes off his shoes it reveals his or her vulnerability and inferiority—but another said that it connoted superiority! No one seemed to associate it with holiness. We got through the notion that, yes, priests did serve barefoot in the ancient Temple, and therefore, when *kohanim* perform the *birkat kohanim* today [not the practice in our congregation] they remove their shoes, but since none of us does that automatically when we enter a synagogue, and we don't do it when we pray, shoelessness doesn't, in general, have that connotation for us.

One mother said, "This is an amazing coincidence. As we were getting ready to go to shul this morning, my son [who was due to become a bar mitzvah three weeks later] resisted putting on his shoes. 'I don't want to wear shoes today,' he said. 'But you *have* to,' I said. 'We go to a Shoe-Wearing Shul!'"

"Wow," I said. "But what if ours were a Shoeless Shul? What then?"

"Then we probably wouldn't be here!" she responded.

After a few minutes of enjoyable, lively comments, with hands rising faster than I could call on them, I said that we were going to examine the appropriateness of shoelessness versus shoe-wearing in holy places in the Jewish tradition. I passed out the study sheets. We went through the first page of the study sheet fairly quickly, with me teaching the texts. Then, since twenty minutes had already flown by, I turned to the *teshuvah* on the second page. "This," I said, "is a *delightful teshuvah*." I don't usually comment like that, but I couldn't help myself. The insight, the understanding contained within this *teshuvah*, I found fascinating. And I also loved the humanity, the compassion of the author: the way in which he empathized with the immigrants who'd come from a place where it was "*pas nisht*" (unseemly) to take off one's shoes in public, and had come to a place where it was "*pas nisht*" to wear them!

I used that as a segue to thinking about today. I brought up the case of the Northwestern University women's lacrosse team, and their appearance in flip-flops before the President of the United States. (I suddenly realized that the parents of a Northwestern freshman were sitting in the room—an odd coincidence of the sort one must always be prepared for.) I talked about what it's like today when people who aren't regular davenners come into shul. Some people, I said, dress in a very revealing manner in shul—and yet within the cultural context in which they live, it is most likely entirely appropriate. I began to suggest that our study could help us be more understanding and accepting of different attitudes toward clothing.

Finally, as I wrapped up our discussion, I said that this should inspire us to think about how our clothing contributes to—or interferes with—our ability to access the holy.

And at that, I said, "Shabbat shalom," and sat down to put my shoes back on. "So now you're putting them back on!" someone cried out. "Yes," I said. "Because we now have the practice, specifically, of *not* davenning in our bare feet."

There were many interesting follow-up conversations during kiddush, the light meal offered after services. One congregant (an Israeli) talked about how, when the army captures prisoners of war, one of the first things they do is have the prisoners remove their shoes. There was also the inevitable: another congregant pulled me aside to tell me that I ought to choose my socks more carefully. (She had noticed a tiny hole in one of my socks during the *derashah*.)[9]

Do I regret not speaking about MLK? We did announce the community-wide service in a local church to take place tomorrow, on Martin Luther King, Jr. Day, in which a number of young people from our congregation will be participating, so I don't feel as bad as I otherwise would have. Had we celebrated a bar or bat mitzvah yesterday, had two hundred people been in the room on that day, then I would have felt compelled to speak on a weightier theme. But neither was the case. In retrospect, I'm glad I did what I did.

The December Dilemma and the Exodus Generation: Preparing a Torah Discussion for *Parashat Sh'mot* (December 29, 2007)

December 24, 2007

It just happened. The moment. The realization that I know what I'm going to talk about this Shabbat. Because I've got a few moments, and I'm alone in front of my computer, I'm going to jot down my sensations at this moment, and my recollections of how this came to be.

Until yesterday, I really hadn't given much thought to [the book of] Exodus. After all, I've been speaking about *Bereishit* (Genesis) for several

---

[9] As Professor Lewin convincingly demonstrates, there are risks whenever teachers seek to use themselves as objects to illustrate their points. For a particularly telling example, see segment #8 of lecture #11, "Work and Mechanical Energy," of Physics 8.01 (Physics 1, Classical Mechanics), recorded on October 4, 1999. (http://ocw.mit.edu/ocwweb/Physics/8-01Physics-ifall1999/videolectures/detail/Video-Segment-Index-for-L-11.htm .) According to the MIT website, the topic of this segment is the following: "A wrecking ball is converting gravitational potential energy into kinetic energy and back and forth. If released with zero speed, the wrecking ball should NOT swing higher than its height when it was released. Professor Lewin puts his life on the line by demonstrating this." (A picture capturing the moment of truth appears at: http://ocw.mit.edu/ocwweb/Physics/8-01Physics-ifall1999/coursehome/index.htm .)

months. I've been teaching a *Parashat Ha-shavua* class on *Sefer B'reishit*, which just came to an end, for almost as long. The last session of the class was last Tuesday night. We don't have a Shabbat *minchah* minyan [at which the beginning of the next week's *parashah* would be read] and so, until yesterday, I hadn't given *Sh'mot* much thought.

Yesterday, as I was going through the Sunday [*New York*] *Times*, a piece caught my attention. On the "Op-Art" page at the end of the Week in Review section of the paper was a comic strip entitled "The Creche." It told the story of a complexly interfaith couple. (The wife is a "non-believing half-Jew with Armenian Christian roots" and the husband is an "Italian, Sicilian, Irish and English" man who experienced a "spiritual awakening" several years ago.) The strip tells the story of the December dilemma in one particular American household. As I read it, I don't recall thinking, "This would be a good thing to share in shul some upcoming Shabbat morning." But I did think, "This would be a neat thing to share at some point with someone."

I routinely receive *divrei torah* from Bar-Ilan University. One, whose title I glanced at yesterday, was on "The Jewishness of the Children of Israel in Egypt."[10] That reminded me that *Sh'mot* is coming, that I will have to be giving *divrei torah* on *Sh'mot*. It also reminded me of that classic midrash on how and why the Children of Israel remained distinctive in Egypt. "They didn't change their language, they didn't change their names," etc. But I didn't give it much thought. I've spoken about that before. No "buzz" occurred in my head this time. Besides, it was a busy and stressful day. I had just learned that a gentle, kindly, older member of the congregation has just been diagnosed with pancreatic cancer. It's very progressed and his prognosis is not good. My mother-in-law has recently moved to a nursing home, and we have had to clear out her apartment. In addition, I was having difficulty scheduling a visit by a cantor applying for a job at our shul, and I learned that we have been having difficulty covering a *shiva* minyan at the shul. Finally, my two kids were home from college, and I wanted to spend at least a little time with them.

In any event, it wasn't until this morning (Monday morning) that the spark occurred. I didn't attend morning minyan. I had to attend to

---

10 Moshe Kaveh, "*Hazehut Ha-yehudit Shel Am Yisrael: Hearot l'farashat 'Shmot'*," Bar-Ilan University *Daf Shevui*, #736.

a few phone calls before going into the office. But then, as I was about to eat breakfast, and my wife was about to leave for work herself, I saw yesterday's paper on the dining room table. It was turned to the Maureen Dowd column on the op-ed page. My kids always like reading Maureen Dowd—as do I—so it occurred to me to cut it out of the paper and stick it onto the refrigerator. I went and got the paper cutter. As I was about to cut the article out, I turned the page over to see if there was anything on the other side worth saving. That's when I, once again, saw the cartoon. It suddenly occurred to me that I shouldn't rip it apart, that my wife, Elana, who works professionally with interfaith couples, might want to see this and to use it in her work. And so I put the paper cutter down. I picked up the paper and went upstairs and showed it to my wife. She was rushing around, and so simply said, "Great. Thanks a lot. Just leave it here." A few minutes later, she came down to breakfast with it, and looked at it. I pointed out how interesting I found the last panel of the strip. We spoke about it, and I realized that we had different understandings of it. I glanced at the cartoon and realized that I had misread the last panel, and so I now had a totally different understanding of the cartoon. We talked about it, about the challenges of working with interfaith families, etc. And then she left.

And then it suddenly occurred to me out of the blue that I could teach this cartoon as a text. This would accomplish several things, one of them being to alert people that the phenomenon of intermarriage is so much more complex than most people think. The old paradigms just aren't as useful as they used to be—certainly not the traditional understanding that one intermarries as a rejection of Judaism.

And then, a connection was suddenly made between this piece and the title of the Bar-Ilan *d'var torah* that I had seen yesterday. Not only was this a useful piece to teach, but it was a piece appropriate to teach *this coming Shabbat*, for it was, literally, on an *inyana d'yoma* (an issue of the day)—given that Christmas is coming this week. (Admittedly, as my daughter reminded me a few minutes ago, Christmas will be behind us by next Shabbat. But my thought was that as long as we're in between Christmas and New Year's Day, as long as we're in December, it's still appropriate and useful to talk about the December dilemma.) And it is also appropriate to teach this text for *Parashat Sh'mot*, as seen through the lens of the rabbinic authors of that famous midrash of the Israelites' retention of their distinctive practices in Egypt.

Serendipity and Pedagogy

For consider the following proposition: isn't one possible contemporary version of "They did not change their names, they did not change their language," the following: "They did not put up a Christmas tree" or "They did not put up a crèche in their living room"? Yes! That's certainly an appropriate proposition, with which one might agree or disagree, a perfect topic for a discussion which would accomplish several goals. First, it would make the point that shul is the place to discuss real issues. The question of how much Christmas interfaith families should bring into their homes is a very real dilemma that affects many members of our congregation. Second, such a discussion would be a reminder that the issues of today are not only the issues of today. They were the issues of the rabbinic period as well—as convincingly demonstrated by that famous midrash. Not only in twenty-first-century America, but also in the Greco-Roman world of late antiquity, Jews have found themselves wondering how far to go in embracing the practices of their environment. This would allow me to teach that wonderful midrash, thereby demonstrating the relevance of studying these ancient texts—which can live and breathe today, if only we let them.

But is this the *best* time to teach this text? After all, there won't be that many people in shul this coming Shabbat. I could get a lot more "mileage" out of teaching these "texts" (by which I mean the comic strip and the midrash) on a Shabbat when we would expect four hundred people, rather than sixty. On what other occasions could I teach this? Well, we're expecting a Keruv Shabbat sometime in March. That's not a bad time. But by then, talking about Christmas will really seem like warmed-over cholent. And a midrash on the Exodus just won't seem appropriate to teach then. Maybe I could put it off until Pesach, but again, who wants to think about Christmas then? All things considered, the excitement of striking while the iron is hot seems irresistible.

Now, what's odd is that the thought processes that I've described above (in the preceding few paragraphs) took place in about a second. That is, long before I had realized how to verbally articulate what I had come to understand, I had had a serendipitous moment of pedagogic insight. I call it serendipity because one never knows whether it is going to happen or not. Readiness, as Rosenzweig would say, is all. This is why I try to give myself some time on Monday mornings to "make it happen"—that is, to allow it to happen, which is the most I can do. In this case, had I gone ahead and attended to pressing matters, had I begun returning emails and responding to phone calls, I might not have allowed the *d'var torah* to develop in quite the way that it did.

[I did not write a diary entry after this d'var torah was delivered.[11]]

Comparing and Contrasting Two Different *Derashot* for *Sh'mot* (A Year Apart)

What did the processes of deciding what to talk about on these two Shabbatot in 2007 have in common with one another? What principles might we derive that could be useful, either to me or to other *darshanim*, in the future?

The "Aha!" Moment

In both cases, there was an "Aha!" moment—or, actually, several "Aha!" moments. In each case, the key serendipitous moment at which I realized what I was going to talk about included an awareness of (a) a connection to the Torah portion of the week; (b) some element, issue or theme in a rabbinic text or texts that (c) mirrors some aspect of American culture that I believe is—or should be—at the forefront of the consciousness of the members of my congregation, and that is itself explored in yet another, modern "text." Simultaneously or eventually came (d) the discovery of an interesting, intriguing, and possibly even fun way to share that with the congregation. When all of those elements are present, as they were in these two cases, a spark goes off.

In the first case, the key moment occurred as I was preparing to go to shul on a Tuesday morning. I wasn't thinking of the need to come up with a topic to address four days later—but it's hard to believe that, after sixteen years of writing *derashot* virtually every week, my brain doesn't start doing that on its own. That particular week I didn't begin thinking consciously about the *parashah* until Tuesday. So it is quite possible that, internally, a certain level of anxiety had already arisen and part of my consciousness was already focused on solving my weekly

---

[11] The obverse side of the study sheet for *Parashat Sh'mot*, December 29, 2007, contained the English and Hebrew text of *Midrash Tehillim* 114:4. For the reverse side, see http://www.nytimes.com/imagepages/2007/12/23/opinion/23opart.ready.html

puzzle. I wish I could remember whether, on January 9, I was putting on my shoes as that moment occurred. Even if I had just done so a few minutes earlier, it's quite possible that that action precipitated this particular "Aha!" moment. The full form that the *derashah* would eventually take unfolded over several days, and I didn't make the final decisions regarding how I would present the material until a few moments before delivery.

Similarly, on that Monday morning in December during the week when we were again reading *Parashat Sh'mot*, I found myself absentmindedly and inadvertently being drawn to that comic strip, that graphic "text" that I had noticed, yet not quite set aside. Was it entirely coincidental that I almost cut it into pieces? Did that somehow trigger an internal investigation into whether it wasn't indeed more worthwhile, more worth saving, than I had thought? The fundamental flash of insight came to me as I somehow connected two unrelated ideas that had crossed my mind during the preceding day. Somehow, as I was reflecting on the comic strip after discussing it with my wife, the national holiday (Christmas) that was about to take place, that familiar midrash on how and why the Jews were redeemed from Egypt, and the next book of the Torah from which we were about to read came into my mind, and the spark flew. Additional insights concerning the precise way in which I would deliver the *derashah* wouldn't be made until days later, and the final decisions wouldn't be made until the day I delivered it.

Could those "Aha!" moments happen on their own? It's hard to say. I don't think I would ever really risk that by, say, ignoring the *parashah* of the week until Shabbat.[12] The fact is, I make myself conducive to being inspired. I begin reviewing the *parashah* early each week; sometimes this is enough to inspire me. Before the age of email, I would deliberately open up my file for the upcoming *parashah*. Now, I subscribe to various *d'var torah* listservs that engage me with germane ideas. By now, I look forward to that feeling—of delight, of joy, of satisfaction—when a curi-

---

12 It's not coincidental that my vacation weeks generally go from Sunday to Sunday. The thought of leaving the office on a Friday—as tempting as it has sometimes been—is accompanied by the dread of returning to it on a Friday. Given the kind of thinking I would likely find myself doing, it would be the functional equivalent of returning on a Tuesday or a Wednesday.

ous, interesting, enlightening connection is made, and by now, I know it when I experience it.

I suppose that I have developed a heightened awareness of the potential for connections among ideas—particularly during the first part of every week! By now, even though it isn't an item on my calendar, I "know" that I must make such a connection during those days—and the sooner the better.

Doubt

Doubt in the wisdom of my choice can arise even when I least expect it. With respect to my two *derashot* on *Parashat Sh'mot* in 2007, there was doubt in both cases. Even though in those cases I ultimately did speak on the topic that occurred to me during the "Aha!" moments, I wasn't sure—until almost the last moment—that I would.

In the first case, my doubt was focused on whether it was appropriate not to speak about Martin Luther King, Jr., on the Shabbat closest to the day commemorating his birth. But doubt plagued me before I delivered my December Sh'mot *derashah* as well. First, I wondered whether it was appropriate to talk about Christmas. Was it appropriate to share in shul the reflections of an intermarried Jew celebrating Christmas with her family? My reservations concerned whether it was appropriate to introduce empathically an interfaith couple's set of conflicts. (That was not difficult for me to resolve, but it did require me to formulate responses in the event that I would be challenged by congregants during kiddush.) Also, I had a practical doubt: I wondered (up to the day of delivery) whether it wouldn't make more sense to refrain from delivering the *derashah*, to hold onto it for another, "better" occasion.

In the days immediately before I delivered that *derashah*, I faced doubts based on an uncanny similarity with the January date on which I had spoken on *Parashat Sh'mot*. On December 27th, 2007, former Pakistani Prime Minister Benazir Bhutto was assassinated in Rawalpindi, two weeks before national elections in which she was a leading opposition candidate were scheduled to take place. I recall being saddened and depressed by the news of her killing. Were she an American or Israeli political leader, there is no doubt that I would have shelved my *derashah* and spoken about her.[13] Perhaps part of the temptation to speak about Bhutto arose from her charm and charisma, and from the fact that she had lived and studied in the Boston area during her youth. There is no question that I could have delivered a sermon about Bhutto's life which could have touched on the question of the challenges and risks inherent in liberation struggles—nicely linked with the themes of the *parashah*.

But Benazir Bhutto was a complicated figure. In the words of an article about her (published in Boston a week after her death), "Like her country, Bhutto is a riddle. Brilliant, beautiful, fearless, she is also ruthlessly ambitious, devious and corrupt."[14] Moreover, as troubling as the news of the assassination might be, I believed that it wasn't as significant for American Jews as the assassinations of, say, Martin Luther King, Jr., or John F. Kennedy, and therefore did not demand a *derashah* focused on the event. I therefore decided to go with my original plan.

In both January and December, it wasn't entirely clear until the last minute how I would address the topic. In both cases, I knew that I had a great discussion topic (so I knew that I wasn't going to deliver a formal sermon), but in both cases I wasn't sure how to frame the discussion. In January, it wasn't until the morning of the *derashah* that I discovered, or determined, that I would be taking my shoes off. In December, I wasn't sure what would be the most effective technique for introducing a cartoon that, through photocopying, had been reduced in size, and was therefore difficult to read. (I eventually decided to have someone read it out loud. I almost decided to have different people read the different

---

[13] That is what I did after the assassination of Israeli Prime Minister Yitzhak Rabin and after the deaths of Israeli diplomat Abba Eban and former U.S. president Ronald Reagan. See, e.g., http://www.templealiyah.com/uploadedFiles/site/About/Leadership/Rabbi/ShlachLcha%202004.pdf and http://www.templealiyah.com/uploadedFiles/site/About/Leadership/Rabbi/Vayishlach%202002.pdf .

An anecdote: My late father-in-law, Rabbi Simcha Kling, z"l, a pulpit rabbi for over forty years, once told me that he always tried to complete his two Shabbat *derashot* by Wednesday, knowing that on Thursday or Friday he might have to officiate at a funeral and be unable to do much writing. He told me that the only time he recalled tearing up his sermon and starting from scratch late in the week was on Friday, November 22, 1963, the day on which President John F. Kennedy was assassinated.

[14] Gail Sheehy, "A Wrong Must Be Righted," *Parade Magazine*, January 6, 2008, 6.

voices in the text, and were I to do it again, I would make that choice.) In the case of the December *derashah*, the appearance of a comic strip alongside a rabbinic midrash was enough of a curiously jarring juxtaposition that I felt additional theatrics were unnecessary.

What Makes for a Successful Choice?

Looking back over both of my *Sh'mot derashot*, and reflecting on many others, what seems to unite them is that the subject matter is "on the edge." I know I have found a suitable topic for a *derashah* when I know that it has the potential to encourage people to look at something familiar in a new way.[15] In the context of a Shabbat morning service, the mode of presentation provides some comfort and security even (or especially) when the topic raises questions that may be either uncomfortable or at least unusual in the synagogue setting. For example, in January we talked about fashion and holy places—neither, ironically, a very common topic to talk about in shul. In December, we talked openly about interfaith relationships—a very hot-button issue for many, and again, something we don't discuss often (enough) in shul.

In the case of both of my *Sh'mot derashot*, it seems to me that the "Aha!" moments occurred because I was ready for them to occur. Both times, I was eager for a moment that would allow me to present yet another juxtaposition of the two cultures of which I feel so much a part, and that I so much want my congregants to see in one unified field of view. I believe that it is essential to consider a variety of approaches to one's pedagogic task. Otherwise, one can be too quick to dismiss a quirky and off-beat idea that might, nonetheless, ultimately prove to be the core of a successful *derashah*.

Finally, in deciding what material to present and how to present it, I think that it is necessary to be willing to be playful. Being playful is not inconsistent with caring deeply about one's educational mission. A good model is Professor Lewin, whose work I described at the beginning of

---

[15] I am reminded of the title of a presentation given by Dr. David Starr at "Teaching Rabbinic Literature: Bridging Scholarship and Pedagogy," a conference at Brandeis University in January 2008: "Making the Strange Familiar, The Familiar Strange: Teaching Rabbinics to Adults in Me'ah." In several respects, I aim to do the same thing when I present rabbinic teachings in synagogue on Shabbat mornings.

this chapter. A more playful teacher—a more enthusiastic teacher, who loves his subject and loves presenting it more than Professor Lewin—is hard to imagine.[16] It is not surprising that Lewin, who creates enchanting moments of engagement in his classroom, is successful at what he does; his enthusiasm, excitement, and playfulness is inviting.

To conclude, let me again quote Rosenzweig, who discusses the vital role that a teacher's enthusiasm and excitement play in his or her teaching. "To begin with," he tells instructors of adult Jewish education,

> [D]on't offer [one's students] anything. Listen. And words will come to the listener, and they will join together and form desires. And desires are the messengers of confidence.... The teacher cannot be a teacher according to a plan. He must be much more and much less, a master and at the same time a pupil. It will not be enough that he himself knows or that he himself can teach. He must be capable of something quite different—he must be able to "desire."[17]

---

[16] One can hear the playfulness in his voice as he invites his students to observe him closely, as he does at the end of lecture 10 (http://ocw.mit.edu/ocwweb/Physics/8-01Physics-ifall1999/videolectures/detail/Video-Segment-Index-for-L-10.htm) and also at the end of lecture 11 (http://ocw.mit.edu/ocwweb/Physics/8-01Physics-ifall1999/videolectures/detail/Video-Segment-Index-for-L-11.htm). In both cases, the camera picks up many signs of amusement on the part of his students.

[17] Franz Rosenzweig, "Toward a Renaissance of Jewish Learning," 69.

8 Introducing the Bible: The Contextual Orientation in Practice

Jon A. Levisohn

Introduction

Much of what we "know" about how Bible is taught is anecdotal, based on our own experiences or limited impressions of the experiences of others. What systematic knowledge do we have about what is important to teachers of Bible in different settings? About the decisions teachers make, and on what basis? About what teaching Bible actually looks like? In his chapter above, Barry Holtz takes an important step forward[1] by establishing an organizational scheme for the variety of approaches or "orientations" to the teaching of Bible.[2] In the short time since its publication, Holtz's language of orientations has become a standard for those who write and teach about teaching Bible.[3]

But beyond providing vocabulary, Holtz's identification of different orientations or approaches to teaching Bible enables us to ask deeper and richer questions *about* those approaches. This paper is an effort to do that kind of exploratory work within one orientation, the Contextual Orientation. In this approach to the teaching of Bible, most common in academic settings, the teacher strives to present the texts

---

[1] Barry Holtz, *Textual Knowledge: Teaching the Bible in Theory and Practice* (New York: JTS Press, 2003).
[2] See chapter 2 in this volume. For further exploration of the concept of an orientation, see chapter 3 above, in which the concept is extended to rabbinic literature.
[3] Holtz deals exclusively with the Hebrew Bible or Tanakh, as will I. It is of course true that "Bible" means different things to different people, itself an important pedagogical topic. But for the purpose of this chapter, I will simply use "Bible" to refer to the Hebrew Bible.

of the Bible in their original context, and to promote the students' understanding of their original meaning through modern, critical scholarship. As Holtz writes, "It views the Bible as a record of an ancient civilization, and it hopes to make that world intelligible to students of today."[4]

This is fine, so far as it goes. The Contextual Orientation, by seeking the meaning that obtained at one particular (distant) time, is not concerned with discerning a trans-historical and eternal meaning.[5] It also rejects the notion of the unity of the text that serves as a cornerstone not only for traditional interpretation (in which discrepancies are midrashically harmonized) but also for contemporary literary critical interpretation.

But what actually happens within the Contextual Orientation? How does a teacher committed to this orientation articulate the premises of the orientation to an audience of students? What are the key pedagogical objectives for a teacher within this orientation, and how does he or she accomplish those objectives? What are the options *within* the orientation, and what choices do teachers have to make? My agenda in this chapter, most broadly, is to argue that the identification of various distinct orientations is only the first step towards a robust exploration of the modes and methods of teaching Bible, a first step that must be followed by further steps that probe pedagogic practices and purposes far more closely. As William James famously wrote in *Varieties of Religious Experience*, "A large acquaintance with particulars often makes us wiser than the possession of abstract formulas."[6]

---

[4] Chapter 2, p. 33, above.

[5] The precise "context" to which the Contextual Orientation refers is actually ambiguous (as we will see, the subject of this study frequently talks about "contexts," in the plural). Is it the original meaning of the original author(s)? Or the meaning as understood by the original audience(s)? Or the meaning as understood by the redactor, or the audience at the time of redaction? For our purposes, however, we need only note the ambiguity without resolving it.

[6] William James, *The Varieties of Religious Experience* [1902] (New York: Penguin, 1982), xxxv.

This kind of inquiry is important not merely for its own sake but because of its potential to contribute to the improvement of practice. But this chapter does not attempt to identify "best practices." It does not endorse or argue for a particular pedagogic method. Instead, the focus is on deepening our understanding, in the conviction that what teachers need, more than tips and techniques, more than practical advice, is thoughtful understanding of the pedagogic choices and challenges that their chosen subject presents. What can we understand about what happens in the teaching of Bible from the Contextual Orientation? If we look at it closely and linger long enough, what will we see?

To begin to gain some insight into the Contextual Orientation in practice, this paper will examine how "Moshe," a university instructor who is committed to teaching within the Contextual Orientation, introduces the study of Bible to his students.[7] His introduction is not merely a prologue to his "actual" teaching; on the contrary, it is the pedagogic moment where he articulates what is most important to him about Bible, the occasion for him to frame his teaching approach and identify its significant features. I will compare how he introduces the Bible in two different contexts: first, in his survey course on Bible ("Bible 101") for undergraduates; and second, in the opening session of

---

[7] The analysis is based on videotapes—and transcripts of those videotapes—of Moshe's teaching of the introductory session in the two settings (in the fall of 2005), triangulated through Moshe's review of the analysis and a discussion of the findings with him in a subsequent interview (on May 17, 2006, which will be quoted occasionally below). For more on the methodology of the study, see the longer version of this chapter, Jon A. Levisohn, "Introducing the Contextual Orientation to the Bible: A Comparative Study," Journal of Jewish Education 74:1 (2008): 56-59. The use of a pseudonym requires some explanation, especially since many readers will easily discern the identity of the subject. If his identity is already known, then what is the purpose of pretending to conceal it? More important than protecting anonymity, and more important than following scholarly conventions for educational research, the pseudonym serves another significant function: to signal that, as I will repeat below, the purpose of this paper is not to discover the truth about this particular teacher but to use him as an example in order to explore certain ideas.

a year-long Jewish adult education course ("Bible for Adults" or "B4A"), which is part of an intensive two-year cycle of study.

A Brief Sketch of the Two Classes

How does one introduce the Bible within the Contextual Orientation? In the university introduction to Bible, Bible 101, Moshe sits at a desk, dressed in a dark cotton sweater worn over a blue button-down shirt, with a knitted *kippah* on his head, in front of an open laptop connected to a projector that generates slides on a screen behind him. The class has about 40 students. The university, located in the northeast US, is a research institution that also emphasizes undergraduate teaching. It is non-sectarian, with a large population of Jews. In Bible 101, Moshe estimates that at least ¾ of the students are Jewish, with a quarter of them traditionally observant (either Conservative or Orthodox).

Moshe begins with some warm-up welcoming sentences, and then opens his argument—the session is framed as a series of arguments, with evidence to support the theses—with a statement about the relevance of the Bible. "I honestly believe," Moshe declares to the students, "that the Bible is an extremely profound text that deals with a set of issues that are still relevant." Developing his argument, Moshe then proceeds to show (on slides projected behind him) particular passages that relate to a series of supposedly relevant issues: first texts that depict God, then texts that discuss death, then texts that are in some sense about gender. After working through these texts for approximately 10 minutes, he then transitions to a methodological discussion about how the Bible will be studied in this course. Finally, after pausing for questions, he shifts his tone and begins to discuss some practical aspects of the course, regarding the syllabus, preparation for class, assessments, and the like.

In the adult education setting, Bible for Adults, Moshe also sits at a desk in a classroom, dressed in a grey button-down shirt and maroon tie, wearing his *kippah* visible on his head, but without a laptop; instead, he has before him a Tanakh and his notes. Instead of a screen behind him, he has a whiteboard off to his left, on which he writes once or twice during his introduction. While the classroom is located in a synagogue, the course itself is communal; in this particular version of the course, almost all of the 20 adult students come from Conservative backgrounds. In this setting, after his warm-up welcome, he explains that the purpose of this first class session is to provide "four contexts" for the course as a whole: the geographical context of the Bible, the historical context, the context of the structures of the Bible, and what he calls the "contexts of interpretation." He then proceeds to work through each of these contexts.

First, the geographical context is actually not just about the location of ancient Israel between the great powers of Mesopotamia and Egypt but, more specifically, about the significance of that geographical location for the self-understanding of ancient Israelites and impact of that self-understanding on their culture and its product, the Bible. Second, in order to provide the historical context, Moshe focuses especially on the standard periodization of ancient Israelite history, i.e., how to sub-divide the overall biblical narrative into units, which he notes is important for the purpose of explaining biblical texts in terms of the historical events to which the author is responding. Third, he explains the "context of the structures of the Bible" by opening up his Tanakh and describing its component parts and their order. And finally, Moshe concludes by tackling the "contexts of interpretation." He describes the traditional interpretive approach to the Bible, which assumes that the text is "privileged," and then proceeds to describe the contrasting, critical interpretive approach that de-privileges the text. Spinoza serves as a model, here, of the interpreter who uses reason rather than tradition as the criterion of meaning. Moshe makes it clear that this course, B4A, will follow Spinoza's lead.

Commonalities Between the Two Settings

The preceding cursory sketch begins to reveal some important differences between the two courses, most dramatically in terms of the basic structure of the sessions. But before proceeding with a more detailed analysis, I will first spell out the commonalities. First, of course, the instructor is the same person, with the same intellectual background, and presumably, the same core commitments.

In addition, three pedagogic values[8] appear in each. In each setting, Moshe is *aware of the potentially problematic nature of the subject,* or rather, of his approach to the subject, and he acknowledges this difficulty in both settings. In each setting, Moshe is not satisfied talking *about* texts, but instead quickly turns to texts themselves in order to show them to the students. We might call this pedagogic value *the centrality of text.* And in each setting, Moshe is not afraid to express his own voice in the classroom, making his presence felt as a student of the text, and as a person. We might call this his *use of personal voice.*

Alongside these three pedagogic values, there are four distinct (but related) pedagogical objectives that are common to both settings as well. First, Moshe wants students to appreciate the *internal diversity* of the text. Second, Moshe sees his role as *subverting preconceptions* that students bring to the text.[9] Third, Moshe wants his students to establish some *critical distance* from the text. But fourth, surprisingly, there is evidence in each setting that Moshe explicitly *preserves the possibility of personal meaning*; that is, he finds ways to make room for students to establish or maintain personal connections to the text, despite the obvious tension between this kind of connection and the Contextual Orientation within which he teaches.

---

[8] I am using "values" somewhat loosely, to signal a sphere that is distinct from Moshe's subject matter knowledge on the one hand and from his objectives on the other (addressed below). Within this sphere, I am identifying three pedagogic practices that are not mere techniques or strategies but that seem to represent some deeper convictions about teaching this specific subject.

[9] There are a number of possible reasons for this. It may be that the subversion of preconceptions functions as a feature of the Contextual Orientation, given the role that the Bible plays in the religious lives of some students. It may be that subverting preconceptions is a helpful technique to use in an introductory session, when a teacher is trying to engage his students in the course of study ahead of them (in other words, subverting preconceptions is a strategy for hooking students on the subject and for getting them to return to the course). Finally, it may be that subverting preconceptions is a productive pedagogic technique to use *in general,* perhaps because real learning only occurs when one's prior expectations are disrupted (in which case subverting preconceptions is not a specific feature of the Contextual Orientation, nor is it a technique especially helpful for introductory sessions, but instead is always the goal of good teaching in general).

The following chart (figure 1) recapitulates the commonalities between the two settings.

Moshe's subject matter knowledge and beliefs	• Knowledge of and about Bible • Commitment to Contextual Orientation
Moshe's pedagogic values	A. Awareness of problematic nature of the subject B. Centrality of text C. Use of personal voice
Moshe's pedagogical objectives	1. Fostering appreciation of internal diversity of the text 2. Subverting preconceptions about the text 3. Establishing critical distance from the text 4. Preserving the possibility of personal meaning

Figure 1: Commonalities between the two settings

The first category, regarding the instructor's knowledge and commitments, is straightforward (and I have only marked it by bullets in the chart above, as we will not be referring back to it directly). But in order to supply evidence for the commonalities in the second and third categories ("values" and "objectives"), in particular to demonstrate how Moshe strives to accomplish the four key objectives, and most generally to provide the kind of thick description that can help the reader understand Moshe's teaching in greater depth, I will now turn to a closer analysis of selected moments in each of the two sessions.

Introducing the Bible in Bible 101: A Closer Analysis

Moshe begins Bible 101 with a statement about the Bible as a source of answers to important questions.

> The real reason that interests me, and will interest us throughout this class, is that I honestly believe that the Bible is an extremely profound text, that deals with a set of issues that are still relevant. Issues such as: how and why should one bother living? How should

one die? What's the proper way to treat other people? What is the Other? ... [The Bible] almost never has a single answer.

Thus, he begins with an emphasis on profundity and relevance: the issues that he raises are profound ones, i.e., they are fundamental human-existential questions that are eternally relevant. Moshe suggests, although he doesn't actually say it here, that the answers that one finds in the Bible to these questions may be equally profound.

Three analytical points are important here. First, it seems particularly significant that Moshe opens by introducing the idea that students of the Bible may find personal meaning in the text—*preserving the possibility of personal meaning*—not necessarily religious meaning, but certainly personal existential meaning. As if to anticipate the challenge that the Contextual Orientation robs the text of meaning, Moshe affirms the opposite right at the outset. Second, this emphasis on profundity and relevance is a difference between the university class and the adult education class. While he does preserve the possibility of personal meaning in other ways in B4A (about which more below), he does not suggest that the biblical text deals with profound or relevant issues; that claim is entirely absent. (Perhaps Moshe believes that the students in Bible 101 have to be enticed to stick with the class, in a way that the adult students in B4A do not.) Third, and most importantly, Moshe moves almost immediately from his initial argument about the relevance of the text—an argument about *why* students ought to study the text—to an argument about *how* they ought to study it: namely, with an eye towards the internal variation within it.

Thus, the conclusion to the paragraph just quoted—"It almost never has a single answer"—serves as a transition to the next stage, in which Moshe presents passages on God, death, and sex/gender. Each provides Moshe with the opportunity to move from talking about the text to introducing actual texts into the discussion, just a few minutes into the very first class session. As noted above, the *centrality of text* is clearly important to Moshe's teaching, and each brief set of texts provides an opportunity to demonstrate *internal diversity* in the Bible.

However, the discussion of the themes of God, death, and gender does more than just foster an appreciation of internal diversity. In the course of discussing the biblical view of God, Moshe displays passages from Deuteronomy and Exodus,[10] and then says:

> So when you take the very first text up here, which comes from the book of Deuteronomy, where you have the notion that there is no perceived shape of God—had I given you a pop quiz at the beginning and said, "What does God look like according to the Hebrew Bible?," the odds are relatively good that that is, if not the text, the conception or the preconception that many people might have had.... But compare that text to the second text, from the book of Exodus, where a bunch of people ... see God. It can't be any clearer: "And they saw the God of Israel."

Moshe is promoting the idea, here, of the internal diversity within the Bible on a central theological topic. But he is also implicitly promoting the idea of reading the text in its plain sense, like any other text, without the overlay of (later) theological assumptions. In addition, this passage is an example of the phenomenon to which I referred above, namely, *subverting preconceptions:* Moshe transitions from describing the diversity of the text to explicitly questioning the preconceptions of the students.

Pausing here to consider this phenomenon, it is possible to identify three distinct ways in which that subversion occurs. First, implicitly, Moshe begins by subverting a possible preconception that the text is irrelevant or antiquated, instead affirming that its issues are profound ones. Second, Moshe then subverts a more significant preconception, namely that the text is unified, by demonstrating the diversity within the text. But third, and most explicitly, he moves towards subverting assumptions about its content—not just about what the Bible is but about what it actually says—by showing passages that contradict those assumptions.

---

[10] The passages are as follows (JPS translation). From Deuteronomy: "The LORD spoke to you out of the fire; you heard the sound of words but perceived no shape—nothing but a voice.... For your own sake, therefore, be most careful—since you saw no shape when the LORD your God spoke to you at Horeb out of the fire—not to act wickedly and make for yourselves a sculptured image in any likeness whatsoever" (Deut. 4:12-18). From Exodus: "And they saw the God of Israel: under His feet there was the likeness of a pavement of sapphire, like the very sky for purity. Yet He did not raise His hand against the leaders of the Israelites; they beheld God, and they ate and drank" (Exod. 24: 9-11).

Moshe continues his presentation of passages, but when he gets to the topic of gender, he pauses to acknowledge that some of the passages may be offensive. He then offers a signature line, a line he repeats word for word in B4A: "I *teach* the Bible; I did not *write* the Bible. I am not *responsible* for all of the thoughts that the Bible contains."[11] The line elicits laughter from the students, and diminishes much of the discomfort in encountering these texts. It accomplishes this by setting up the Bible as a text from which Moshe is able to *establish some critical distance*. And, of course, he's recommending that the students establish some critical distance as well. Moshe is passionate about the text, and has committed his life to the study of it; he hopes that the students will be able to see that such a life of study is a legitimate option. But he is not responsible for it (or, he is not responsible for all of it). He reserves the right to disavow the text or some aspect of the text. The students should be able to see that that, too, is a legitimate option.

This establishment of critical distance is a central objective of Moshe's teaching. In an interview,[12] he called it "normalizing the Bible," and said that it is "something that Bible professors need to be doing." It is an aspect of the Contextual Orientation that Holtz does not make explicit, and one that most academics would not think to mention as a hallmark of their methodology because it goes unnoticed, like the air that we breathe.

But how does Moshe actually teach this critical distance? First, he teaches it by calling attention to it. He does not use the term "critical distance" here, but the invocation of limited responsibility for the text is no less powerful. Beyond this, however, note that his formulation is constructed in the first person: "I *teach* the Bible; I did not *write* the Bible. I am not *responsible* for all the thoughts that the Bible contains." In this way, Moshe presents himself as a potential role model for the students. He never says anything as explicit as, "I am not responsible for the all the thoughts that the Bible contains – *and neither are you.*" But the implication is that he, Moshe, is a living model of what it means to relate to the text in this way, to hold it at some critical distance even as one is passionately invested in it and devoted to it. This person standing before you, says Moshe, did not write the Bible—but he does teach it.

---

[11] The italics here represent Moshe's own emphasis.
[12] See note 8 above.

And you students, therefore, should be able to envisage, perhaps for the first time, holding the text at some critical distance even as you commit yourselves to its study, perhaps with a rigor you never imagined possible.[13]

Immediately after offering this signature line, Moshe segues back to his argument about the internal diversity of the text, and then transitions to the final arguments of his introduction. This is an extraordinarily rich passage, so I will quote it at length.

> I *teach* the Bible; I did not *write* the Bible. I am not *responsible* for all of the thoughts that the Bible contains.
>
> And the point is, really: *all* the thoughts that the Bible contains. Because the Bible is a very complex book. And the way in which we are going to explain this complexity in class is the way that complexity would be explained in any class that deals with history or any class that deals with history of religion, namely, to realize that the Bible as a complex text is written over a one thousand year period, in a variety of places, by a variety of people coming from different social settings … and as such, even though it is included between two covers, there is no reason to assume that there is a fundamental unity to this text.
>
> I want to briefly say something that perhaps I'll come back to later in the semester and that I'm happy to discuss in more detail out of class. It might seem to some of you that the particular position that I am taking concerning the Bible and its origin is an anti-religious position. That is not something that I am intending to do. Rather, I am interested in reading biblical texts closely, within the context, or contexts, of ancient Israel that engendered these particular texts, and using this ancient history, and these ancient backgrounds, to help us explain what the Bible meant.
>
> Thus, if you are listening to me carefully … one might make a distinction between what the Bible *meant* and … what the Bible *means*. What the Bible *means* is an issue which is up to every individual; that is a highly personal issue, and in fact the Bible might mean nothing! What the Bible *meant* is a different issue, and is connected to the fact that this was produced by a particular culture in antiquity. And my interest in this particular class is, by and large, understanding what it meant to that particular culture.

---

[13] "Look," Moshe says in the interview (see note 8), "I hope that they will take the text as seriously as I take it.... I try to convince my students that this is an interesting text and an important text and a dangerous text."

Having discussed the intellectual issues that he had intended to address in this session, Moshe next turns to procedural issues regarding student responsibilities and so on. These lines, therefore, serve as a conclusion to his substantive introduction to the course.

Four themes emerge from this passage. First, Moshe makes explicit that the point of showing the internal diversity within the biblical texts is to introduce the multiple authorship of the Bible. Second, Moshe inserts a comparison of Bible to other fields, claiming that the method of the course will be just like that of other historical inquiries. This rhetorical move legitimates the study of Bible within the university. The third point of analysis, on the other hand, is a reaction against that very message. The idea of Bible as a field like any other, with no particular special features, is belied by Moshe's attention to the question of whether his approach is "anti-religious." Again, we see Moshe's *awareness of the problematic nature of the subject*. We also see his *use of personal voice*. Being anti-religious "is not something I am intending to do," he claims. "Rather," he continues, "I am interested in reading biblical texts closely." The prominence of Moshe's own persona here is striking. Implicitly, Moshe is telling his students that he, Moshe, represents not only a legitimate and religiously neutral pedagogic approach but an approach that they can consider adopting for themselves—that is, a critical position that is not anti-religious.

The fourth and final point of analysis regarding this passage has to do with Moshe's distinction between what the Bible *means* and what it *meant*. In a personal communication, Moshe observes that he borrows the distinction from Krister Stendahl.[14] However, it does not withstand close scrutiny. Consider the fact that "what the Bible meant" is inextricably bound up with "what the Bible means," in part, for at least one person in that room—namely, Moshe himself! This suggests that we cannot neatly demarcate the historical inquiry from the personal search for present (perhaps existential) meaning. Every claim advanced by a historian about the past meaning of the text is also, inevitably, at least in part a claim about the present meaning of the text. Conversely, many claims about what a text means, in the present, that seek to be

---

14 Personal communication on May 16, 2006, i.e., the day preceding the interview that is cited elsewhere in this chapter. The Stendahl reference is to Krister Stendahl, "Biblical Theology: A Program" [1962], the second chapter in his *Meanings: The Bible as Document and as Guide* (Philadelphia: Fortress, 1984).

compelling or persuasive incorporate implicit claims about what it has meant (or could have meant) in the past, at least to some of its hearers and readers.[15] Moshe himself, it would seem, isn't in fact committed to the meant-means distinction. "The contextual method," he says, "allows ancient meanings to come out with which people can connect in a wide variety of ways." In other words, people will derive contemporary personal meaning from a deeper understanding of what the Bible meant.[16]

But the preceding paragraph is, in the end, a quarrel about hermeneutics. What's important here is that Moshe offers the distinction as an attempt to preserve the possibility of personal meaning, opening the door for those who want to participate in the course but who are worried about the loss of a personal or existential relationship to the text. He is, in other words, attempting to *preserve the possibility of personal meaning*, even as he explains the commitment to the Contextual Orientation that will guide their study together.

Introducing the Bible in B4A: A Closer Analysis

The preceding section of this paper offered an analysis of Moshe's teaching in Bible 101, focusing in particular on the data that provides evidence for the common features of Moshe's teaching mentioned above: (A) his awareness of the problematic nature of the subject, (B) his emphasis on the centrality of the text, and (C) his use of personal voice. It also discussed his four pedagogical objectives: (1) fostering an appreciation of internal diversity of the text, (2) subverting preconceptions about the text, (3) establishing critical distance from the text, and (4) preserving the possibility of personal meaning. This section will focus on the same themes in the second setting, Bible for Adults (B4A).

---

[15] Moshe's suggestion that "what the Bible *means* is an issue which is up to every individual"—as if there were a realm of personal meaning-making that is unconstrained by any demands for arguments and evidence—is well-intentioned but misguided. Of course people do discern idiosyncratic meanings, but those meanings are no more justified than equally idiosyncratic claims about historical meaning.

[16] Compare Holtz's characterization of the Contextual Orientation, that it "hopes to make that [ancient] world intelligible to students of today" (Holtz, *Textual Knowledge*, 92). In Moshe's view, the Contextual Orientation aspires to far more than intelligibility; it provides some of the grounds for personal connection.

As noted in the brief overview of this class above, Moshe adopts a different approach to the introduction of the Bible in B4A than he does in Bible 101. He does not entice these students with the promise that the Bible deals with profound and relevant issues as he did for the college students; he does not address their preconceptions directly as he did by sharing various texts about God; he does not introduce and emphasize the internal diversity within the Bible here as he did there. Instead, he opens by offering a clear and explicit outline of the session, in which he will discuss "four contexts" for the course as a whole. These contexts are the geographical context, the historical context, the context of the structure of the Bible, and what he calls "the contexts of interpretation."

The structure of the opening session may seem rather dry and academic, apparently ignoring the pedagogic values and objectives emphasized above. But this is not the case. In fact, the very first element—the Geographical Context—turns out to be crucially important for Moshe's purposes in teaching within the Contextual Orientation. He does offer a clear-cut description of the geographical location of ancient Israel, but he quickly moves from geographical facts to the *significance* of those facts.

As he begins to explain that significance, he calls attention to what he is about to say in an extraordinary way. "I'm going to make a claim which is going to sound a little odd," he says, "but it is true." He then calls even further attention to his claim: "Unless you remember that it is true, you're not going to be able to appreciate the Bible." So this claim is not only odd, and not only true, but crucially important! What is this claim?

> The claim is very simple: Israel is a small hick country, a latecomer into the world of antiquity, and it is stuck between the two great imperial powers, the power of Mesopotamia and the power of Egypt.

Thus, the important but simple claim is a claim about what ancient Israel was, as a political and cultural entity, from an objective perspective, independent of how it conceived of itself or how those with some familial or religious connections to ancient Israel (in this case, Jews) might conceive of it today.

Why is this claim so important? Why does Moshe emphasize it to such a degree? The claim is important because it represents the kind of objectivity that is a hallmark of Contextualism, which is attuned not only to the objective value of the text but also strives for an objective characterization of the historical periods that the text depicts. Thus, it serves one of his main pedagogic objectives, namely, *establishing critical distance*. It does so in a less subtle way than by declaring "I am not responsible for all the thoughts that the Bible contains." And indeed, the critical distance that it establishes here in B4A is not precisely identical with the critical distance established by Moshe's signature line in Bible 101. In the latter case, the denial of responsibility for the entirety of the text opens up the possibility that some aspects of the texts—some laws or some moral positions or perspectives—are or ought to be subject to critique. In B4A, on the other hand, the critical distance is rather a matter of calling into question the self-representation of the text, of beginning to develop a hermeneutics of suspicion.[17]

How does this work? The ideas of Israel as "hick" and a "latecomer," ideas that Moshe clearly assumes are new to the students, are not of course present in the biblical text. These are not the kind of characterizations that a nation declares about itself: they are too negative, and more importantly, they are characterizations that place the subject on the periphery rather than at the center. However, once one begins to think more objectively about ancient Israel, one is now open to the possibility of asking the all-important question, "Why would the biblical author have written (or believed) this?" The naiveté of accepting the biblical account and the biblical perspective at face value is undermined, if not immediately shattered. The text now becomes a political document, a text that bolsters certain ideological positions in ancient Israel and undermines others, a text that is *doing* something, not merely *saying* something.

But Moshe does not merely emphasize the importance of this claim; he prefaces it by acknowledging that it is going to sound odd to the stu-

---

[17] The phrase "hermeneutics of suspicion" first appears in Paul Ricoeur, *Freud and Philosophy*, trans. Denis Savage (New Haven: Yale University Press, 1970), 32, who used it to refer to a mode of interpretation represented especially by Nietzsche, Marx, and Freud, in which the interpreter assumes that the surface or naïve meaning of a text (or a person's utterances) mask a deeper political or sexual meaning. This mode of interpretation has its excesses, to be sure, but fundamentally, the stance of suspicion about the self-representation of a text is a hallmark of any critical inquiry.

dents. He recognizes the *problematic nature of the subject matter*. The students may not realize, at first, the implications of the innocuous statement, "Israel is a latecomer nation," but Moshe knows its significance: he knows that this will be a new idea for them, one which will not fit with their prior understanding of the place of Israel in the Ancient Near East. In other words, he is also engaged here in *subverting preconceptions*. To be more precise, he is subverting a specific preconception about the centrality of Israel on the world stage as well as a general preconception about the reliability of the self-presentation of biblical texts.

And as he continues, a third preconception emerges, this time quite explicitly.

> If anyone grew up with the idea that Israel is the first great society, or ... the first great writing society, or that there is nothing comparable to Israelite literature, Israelite philosophy, Israelite religious notions in the ancient Near East, the function of the next 10 to 15 minutes is to disabuse you of any of those notions.

The specific preconception here is the notion of Israel's unique cultural creativity or religious genius. Preconceptions such as these may have been part of the students' childhood, parochial notions instilled through Jewish education or worship.

Moshe then pauses, trying to help the students see what they're supposed to be learning.

> And really, what ... this class is about, is not proving that Israel is better ... but rather to help you focus on what the Bible meant in its original context.

Moshe thus declares his allegiance to Contextualism, at the same time echoing the distinction that he offered in Bible 101 by invoking the idea of "what the Bible meant" as the goal of the class. This course, B4A, has a goal that stands in opposition to what might typically be considered appropriate for a Jewish educational setting. Moshe is not interested in claims of the literary or religious superiority of the Bible or of ancient Israel; he is apparently not interested in promoting personal connections to the text (although I will have more to say about this below). He is simply interested in original meanings.

But how does a teacher actually subvert preconceptions about the uniqueness of ancient Israel? Moshe's technique is to introduce students to other sources, demonstrating his commitment to the *centrality of texts*—not just talking about texts but engaging with texts directly. He introduces some Ancient Near Eastern prayers in order to show similarities to and differences from concepts that are familiar to his students from the Jewish tradition, concepts such as food taboos and sacred space. He then concludes this section by reiterating his argument: "Literarily, technologically—to say it one last time—Israel was a latecomer into a world dominated by the two great civilizations of Mesopotamia and Egypt." Geographical context, it turns out, is much more than reading the map.

Moshe's discussion of the second and third contexts (the historical context and the context of the structure of the Bible) does not add to the present analysis, with the exception of one moment that is worth describing carefully. It's a moment that does not, at first, seem particularly notable. How, he asks, should the word "Torah" be translated?

> Torah … should not be translated as "law" but should be translated as "instruction." This might sound overly pedantic, but I think this is actually quite important. Obviously, the Torah is not all law; look at the book of Genesis! … Understanding Torah as law by and large is a Protestant notion which Jews should not adopt. And "instruction," which has law as a subset within it, is probably a better and more accurate understanding of Torah, because narratives … can instruct in the same way as laws can instruct.

As above, with the claim about Israel as a latecomer nation, so too here he calls attention to his point, signaling that it not merely pedantic. But why is it so important?

When viewed through the lens of the analysis of Moshe's Contextualism, what's important about this point is its normativity, the way in which he is advancing a particular norm of behavior. He is not just presenting a sound scholarly argument about a point of translation (although his point about the Genesis narratives is clear); he is *advocating* for the usage of the translation "instruction," and against the translation "law." And the normativity passes over from the exclusively intellectual to the moral or religious. "Jews *should not* adopt [this notion]," he declares. It's not just that it's false. There's something here that is central to the way that Jews should read and relate to this text.

Why should Jews conceive of Torah as instruction rather than law? Moshe likely has in mind the Christian conception of Judaism as a religion of law (as opposed to Christianity, a religion of love). Jews, he is saying, ought not to internalize this canard. But there is a deeper point here, and a more positive one: namely, that Jews ought to relate to the Bible as book of instruction in a broader and more subtle sense than merely a set of laws to be followed. "Narratives ... can instruct in the same way as laws can instruct." Moshe is saying here that this is a text from which one can learn. And furthermore, in some sense, the students *ought* to learn from it, or at least, they ought to know that they can learn from it. Moshe, standing at the front of the room with a *kippah* on his head, is making a case that the Torah not only *was* a book of instruction but indeed can still be so.[18]

This is only a brief moment in the class, but it doesn't take much for a teacher to set a tone, to establish norms, to communicate values. The norm in this case has to do with an attitude toward the Bible that seems to contradict the conventional wisdom about critical biblical scholarship and the teaching of it, according to which it is committed not merely to objectivity or neutrality, but rather to a kind of cynicism about personal meaning. For academic scholars, it is sometimes said, the Bible is just another Ancient Near Eastern text. But here we glimpse an attitude of reverence, a shortening of critical distance, an erosion of cool objectivity. Biblical texts, according to this norm, are texts with which the students ought to engage from a stance of commitment—not necessarily texts to which they should be subservient, but nevertheless texts from which the students ought to learn or to which they ought to be connected. The establishment of this norm surely *preserves the possibility of personal meaning*.[19]

---

[18] In a personal communication (May 16, 2006), Moshe affirms the interpretation offered here, and expands on the point: "Part of the point of Torah as instruction ... reflects an interest in getting away from Torah as history, and planting the seed of an idea that fiction can instruct as effectively as, or more effectively than, non-fiction."

[19] In the interview (see note 8), Moshe makes the point explicitly, in terms of the establishment of a relationship: "The whole point of ... a lot of my teaching is to show that the contextual method is useful ... for creating a relationship between the text and the life of today."

Finally, Moshe turns to what he has called the "context of interpretation." Here he discusses the traditional idea of Bible as "privileged literature," that is, literature that is exempt from standard interpretive techniques according to which the plain sense of the text is assumed to be its meaning. He illustrates the idea by sharing examples of contradictions in the biblical text that are harmonized by midrashic interpretation. Thus, this section represents again Moshe's commitment to the pedagogical objective of fostering an *appreciation of the diversity of the text*. But the rabbis, Moshe explains, who are committed to Bible as privileged literature, are compelled to abandon plain-sense readings. (Of course, what exactly constitutes the "plain sense" or "privileging" in any particular case is surely a complicated issue, which we cannot pursue here.)

Having explained the idea of the Bible as privileged literature, Moshe's next step is to indicate what happened to that idea, by turning to Spinoza. Why Spinoza rather than, say, Wellhausen or perhaps Hobbes?[20] In part, this is because he is not trying to explain the Documentary Hypothesis in particular, but rather the more general approach of interpreting Bible as one would interpret any text (that is, of de-privileging the text). But aside from that, Moshe is calling on Spinoza as a Jew—not the most successful Jew, perhaps, but a fellow Jew nonetheless, and one whom these adult Jewish learners ought to embrace. He makes a point of calling Spinoza by his Hebrew name, "Baruch."

The key line from Spinoza's *Theological-Political Treatise* is the following: "I hold that the method of interpreting scripture is no different than the method of interpreting nature." Moshe does not focus on what "interpreting nature" meant within Spinoza's philosophical system; neither will I. Instead, I will merely note that the comparison of the study of Bible to the study of nature recalls a rhetorical move that he made in Bible 101, when he compared his approach to "any class that deals with history or any class that deals with history of religion." At least in

---

[20] Benedict Spinoza (1632-1677) argued, in his *Tractatus Theologico-Politicus* (1670), against the Mosaic authorship of the Bible, as had Thomas Hobbes (1588-1675) a bit earlier in his *Leviathan* (1651). Both of these books are not primarily works of biblical scholarship, however, but rather political philosophy. Julius Wellhausen (1844-1918) is generally credited with the development of the Documentary Hypothesis in his *Prolegomenon to the History of Israel* (1886).

certain respects, the study of Bible within the Contextual Orientation is no different than the academic study of anything else.

However, Moshe moves immediately from rejecting the idea that the study of Bible is special, to a dramatic *use of personal voice* that attenuates that very point.

> What Spinoza is insisting on, almost for the first time, is that for interpreting the Bible, we don't use outside sources.... The Bible is sufficient for helping us understand the Bible. No one else is going to tell us what something means. If someone says to us that "forever" [in the verse that describe the conditions for retaining a slave] means "until the jubilee year," you say to them, "That's ridiculous!" and "Why would you say that?"[21]

Note the use of the first-person-plural in every sentence of this passage! He continues:

> And thus, Spinoza [insisted] that the Bible is not privileged language, an insistence that I am going to carry through ... in this class, where authoritative interpretations from others will not hold weight. We will use, as Spinoza would say, scripture for interpreting scripture.

With these sentences, Moshe concludes his introduction as a whole.

Now, strictly speaking, Moshe's claim that he and his students will only use "scripture for interpreting scripture" is false. In fact, Moshe used extra-biblical Ancient Near Eastern sources himself, in this very class.[22] More importantly, setting aside the comparisons to other Ancient Near Eastern texts, the language of "we" and "us" is misleading because Moshe knows that his students do not have the capacity to in-

---

21 Moshe is referring here to Exodus 21:2-6, which describes the conditions under which a slave may be retained beyond the standard six years of servitude. According to a plain-sense reading of that passage (v. 6), such a slave is retained "forever." However, Leviticus 25:40 seems to indicate that a slave is freed at the jubilee year. These two contradictory passages are reconciled by the midrashic claim (*Mekilta De-Rabbi Ishmael* 3.17) that "forever" in the first passage means until the jubilee year.

22 It is also worth noting that scholarship always builds on a tradition of inquiry by others, even as it constructs new understandings, so it is never simply a matter of using "scripture for interpreting scripture."

terpret biblical texts independently. The idea that "the Bible is sufficient for helping us understand the Bible" is all well and good, but of course it requires deep background knowledge of Bible and about Bible to even imagine doing so.

So the idea of the Bible as a self-interpreting text is somewhat disingenuous. But setting this claim aside, we ought to focus our attention on other arguments in these passages, arguments just under the surface. First, of course, there is the argument about the internal diversity of the text, in pursuit of the pedagogic objective of *fostering appreciation of diversity*. The specific target against which Spinoza is being wielded, the specific "outside sources" that Moshe rejects, are those midrashic sources that harmonize disparate texts, as in his example of the meaning of the word "forever." The second argument, then, concerns the very concept of "privileged language" which is being rejected. The opposite of privileged language is language that is *not* privileged, language that is mundane, language that is merely human. But human language is open to criticism by other humans. In other words, the second argument reinforces the pedagogical objective of *establishing critical distance from the text*.

But the third implicit argument in this concluding passage is the most intriguing. Earlier I noted Moshe's use of personal voice. But by using the plural here, he is not only introducing his own persona into the discussion but the personae of his students as well. It doesn't really matter whether Moshe uses extra-biblical material. In fact, it doesn't really matter whether the students can interpret it, on their own, without outside sources. What matters is that Moshe is sending a message about self-reliance, about autonomy. When he talks about "we" here, he draws the students into a worldview in which one trusts one's own reading of a text and one does not blindly accept the authority of other interpreters—a worldview, Moshe believes, that should be embraced by modern Jews.

And Moshe is communicating a message about the journey that they are about to undertake. In case any of them is worried about this class—feeling insecure, doubting the wisdom of doing something that they might think is religiously questionable—Moshe is reassuring them, encouraging them. He tells them, in effect, "We can do this, together!" We can access this text. We can use our minds to interpret this text. Indeed, we can make meaning of this text—not the same meaning that traditional interpreters have made, perhaps, but meaning, even *personal meaning*, nonetheless.

Conclusion: Differences within commonalities

The preceding close analyses corroborate my claim about seven features common to Moshe's teaching in both settings. These seven features are specifically related to the study of Bible—not necessarily exclusive to this subject but not generic either. In other words, they are features of subject-specific (and indeed orientation-specific) pedagogy, and the analysis has been enriched by close attention to the subject and the orientational context. But along the way, it has also become apparent that there are some subtle differences within the commonalities. Only via the comparison do we begin to achieve a richer understanding of some of the possibilities inherent in teaching Bible within the Contextual Orientation, some of the choices available. Consider, first, the three features of Moshe's teaching that I called "pedagogic values."

Awareness of the Problematic Nature of the Subject

In Bible 101, Moshe expresses this awareness when he acknowledges that some students might believe that his approach to the text is "anti-religious," before proceeding to deny that it is so. In B4A, this awareness is expressed more subtly, in his acknowledgement that his central claim, about Israel as a latecomer nation, is "odd," but nonetheless true. To be sure, in referring to Spinoza, Moshe calls attention to Spinoza's status as an excommunicated heretic, implicitly acknowledging that this approach is problematic. But he does not feel the need to explicitly deny any destructive intentions. Perhaps the setting of adult Jewish education changes the dynamic. Perhaps, that is, Moshe does not feel the need to head off misunderstandings of his supposed anti-religiosity in a setting in which he is teaching adult members of his own community, on his own time.

Promotion of the Centrality of Text

In Bible 101, Moshe turns to biblical texts very early in the class, asking the students to consider them as evidence for the diversity of voices within the text on "profound" issues. In B4A, on the other hand, he does *not* actually ask the students to study any biblical texts. Instead, this value is expressed through his use of other, non-biblical texts from the Ancient Near East.

Use of Personal Voice

Moshe's use of personal voice emerges most dramatically in his signature line, "I *teach* the Bible; I did not *write* the Bible. I am not *responsible* for all the thoughts that the Bible contains." In addition, in B4A we saw a different example of his use of personal voice, in which he encourages the students to join him on his path by using the first-person plural: "no one else is going to tell us what something means."

Next, consider the four features that I described as Moshe's "pedagogical objectives."

Fostering Appreciation of the Internal Diversity of the Text

In Bible 101, the examples used to demonstrate internal diversity are the "profound" or "relevant" issues of God, death, and gender. In B4A, on the other hand, Moshe uses the more typical (because historically significant) examples of the two versions of the Decalogue and the contradictory slave laws.

Subverting Preconceptions about the Text

In both classes, it is clear that this objective is centrally important to Moshe's teaching, but the specific preconceptions in question are different. In Bible 101, he subverts the preconception, first and only implicitly, of the Bible's irrelevance; second, of the Bible's unity; and third, moving from the nature of the Bible to its thematic contents, of the Bible's conception of God. In B4A, on the other hand, he subverts the preconception that the Bible's presentation of the history of ancient Israel is trustworthy—not on specific events but more globally, in terms of Israel's significance on the ancient stage. He also explicitly and quite pointedly subverts the preconception of the uniqueness of ancient Israel.

Establishing Critical Distance from the Text

In Bible 101, Moshe's signature line ("I *teach* the Bible, I did not *write* the Bible...") implicitly encourages the students to consider the possibility that they might disavow some elements in the Bible, thus establishing critical distance from the text. The key idea here is *responsibility*: students need not feel responsible for the text, at least not in its entirety. In B4A, Moshe accomplishes this pedagogical objective by calling attention to the claim that Israel is a latecomer nation. He thus calls into question the self-representation of the text, opening the door toward reading the text with an awareness of its political agenda.

Preserving the Possibility of Personal Meaning

In Bible 101, Moshe addresses this objective at the very outset, by organizing his presentation around profound, relevant questions, the very questions on which students might hope to find personal guidance. Later on, he introduces his distinction between "what the Bible meant" and "what the Bible means." In B4A, the moments in which Moshe addresses this objective are subtler. He does so at the very end, in his implicit invitation to his students to join him on the journey that, while untraditional, might still be meaningful. But more dramatically, he advises the students to translate the word Torah as "instruction," and thus implicitly preserves the possibility that they might relate to it as a book of instruction as well.

* * *

Some of these differences are the result of conscious choices that Moshe makes in his pedagogy, and others are not (and the reasons behind them are therefore more speculative). But the purpose of the present investigation is not to explore a particular teacher's rationales, or explain the variations by recourse to one or more variables (e.g., the age and life position of his students). Rather, the purpose is to develop a richer and more nuanced account of the Contextual Orientation, of its pedagogical features, and of the choices that teachers do—and might—make within it. I have not attempted to identify the best way to teach Bible, but hopefully I have enriched our sense of the possibilities within one pedagogic orientation to it.

A teacher may strive to foster an appreciation for the internal diversity within the text—but she may now see that there are at least two different kinds of diversity between which she may choose. A teacher may be committed to subverting the preconceptions of her students—but she may now see a number of different possible preconceptions that she might want to think about. A teacher might believe that it's imperative to establish some critical distance from the text—but she may now see two different models for establishing that distance. And, perhaps most interestingly, a teacher who is committed to the Contextual Orientation may still wish to preserve the possibility of personal meaning—but she may now see two strategies for doing so, and there are surely more.

This chapter is an inquiry into the way one teacher introduces his students to the study of the Bible in two different settings. At the same time, it also introduces (or reintroduces) *us* to the Contextual Orientation, offering a closer look at something we may have thought we already knew well enough. While this empirical study was not, as I have stated, intended as an argument for or against the use of the Contextual Orientation, it may help others develop their own arguments with greater attention to the particulars of practice. More broadly, I hope that it will serve to make space for other inquiries—for example, about what teachers who are committed to promoting the centrality of the text actually do with texts in their classrooms, or about the different modes of critical distance and committed engagement that teachers of classical Jewish texts strive to establish and how they do so. While new questions about the Contextual Orientation to the Bible have hopefully become visible because of the analysis offered here, this chapter also suggests paths forward for the serious and careful study of numerous orientations in use in the teaching of Bible.

PART 3

FOCUS ON LEARNING AND LEARNERS

9 Teaching Ancient Jewish History: An Experiment in Engaged Learning

Michael L. Satlow

For a little over fifteen years, I have been teaching (and writing about) rabbinic literature and its historical context to college undergraduates and graduate students, as well as to adults in (mostly Jewish) formal and informal contexts. It was, quite predictably, my own experiences as a student of Jewish history that drew me into the field; the experience of encountering a past that was so much more complex, foreign, and human than the one I learned about in my own Jewish education was thrilling. It is an excitement that remains with me and continues to invigorate me as a human being and a Jew[1]—and that I earnestly want to convey to my students.

Yet while I would be delighted to have my college students leave my classes excited and stimulated by the material, that cannot be the sole or even primary goal of an introductory level college class. In such a class, my primary goal is to get students to think historically about the Jews of antiquity. This means overcoming the general challenges presented by widespread unfamiliarity with both historical thinking and antiquity itself, while at the same time training students to make sense of scattered and discrete primary documents in relationship to each other and their wider context. Ultimately, my goal is also to help students develop critical thinking skills that they might then apply more generally, both to their own personal lives and their academic ones.

For most of my career, I have believed that I have been reasonably good at this. I have generally arranged my introductory class to early

---

[1] For a fuller discussion of how the academic study of Jews and Judaism can enrich one's Jewish life, see Michael L. Satlow, *Creating Judaism: History, Tradition, Practice* (New York: Columbia University Press, 2006), 288-96.

Jewish history as a chronological narrative, moving from the building of the Second Temple around 520 BCE to its destruction in 70 CE. Prior to most classes, students would read a selection of primary and secondary texts and complete a short writing assignment that they would email to me. Class time would be split between lecture and discussion. The level of discussion was generally high, students seemed prepared and engaged, and course evaluations were very good.

But over the past few years I have had gnawing doubts about the success of this course. My primary goal was to have the students master not a single synthetic narrative, but a set of intellectual skills that they could apply to other (previously unseen) data. Historical thinking, as Sam Wineburg felicitously puts it, is an "unnatural act."[2] Through primary and secondary school, to say nothing of popular books and culture, most of us come to understand history as a simple narrative of the past. Yet for most historians, the core of the historical enterprise is less the narrative than it is the interpretive encounter between the reader and her documents. The goal of historical thinking—as practiced by professional historians and teachers—is not a single narrative but the opening of multiple perspectives onto a distant and perhaps ultimately unknowable past. History, Wineburg claims, is used best to teach not single, coherent, and "definitive" narratives, but rather "humility in the face of our limited ability to know, and awe in the face of the expanse of human history."[3]

Was I succeeding? If the measure of my teaching effectiveness was the quality of student work at the end of the semester, I was falling short of my self-expectations. Their final exams were designed to measure not simply student recall but also their ability to synthesize the material in new ways, and I was often largely disappointed by their answers. My prepared, engaged, and smart students could recall material with ease, but had much more difficulty applying what they learned in class to new data.

Perhaps, though, I was not teaching them how to do this. I have long been aware of the research arguing for the effectiveness of active

---

[2] Sam Wineburg, *Historical Thinking and Other Unnatural Acts: Charting the Future of Teaching the Past, Critical Perspectives on the Past* (Philadelphia: Temple University Press, 2001).

[3] Ibid., 24.

over passive learning. As summarized by Derek Bok, "students recall only 42 percent of the information in a lecture by the time it ends and only 20 percent one week later."[4] Lecturing might inspire and in some sense "model" critical thinking, but as a pedagogical technique for conveying both information and critical thinking skills, it fares rather poorly. Rather, the empirical studies suggest, active learning techniques produce better learning outcomes. Over the years, I have attempted to integrate more active and collaborative learning into my classes in order to improve my learning outcomes.

To my surprise, though, I have found that many of my students, both in the university and in adult education classes, are wary of and occasionally even hostile to active learning techniques. In my more cynical moments the term "edutainment" comes to mind, the product of a consumerist culture in which education is seen as a commodity to be purchased. This is not entirely fair; active teaching forces students out of their comfort zones, and is attended by a certain level of the indeterminacy that accompanies such activities and their assessment. The issue is further complicated by the methods of teaching evaluation. In both the university and adult education contexts with which I am most familiar, professional teaching evaluation is based almost entirely on student evaluations, with some consideration given to the design of the course as demonstrated in the syllabus. After receiving one particularly scathing set of course evaluations, I turned the next year to a much more heavily lecture-based format to find my evaluations rise (and student learning fall), much to the relief of my colleagues.

With these concerns in mind, I set out to conduct a more radical experiment in active learning. I was primarily interested in exploring two clusters of questions. First, *how* were my undergraduate students learning, or not? Could I better identify the factors that led to final work that I often found disappointing? The second set of questions was more practical: would more active learning increase the quality of student learning, to the extent that I am able to make such judgments? This last qualifier, of course, also raises the issue of assessment in the humanities. What are we measuring, and how do we measure it?

---

[4] Derek Bok, *Our Underachieving Colleges: A Candid Look at How Much Students Learn and Why They Should be Learning More* (Princeton: Princeton University Press, 2006), 123.

Teaching Ancient Jewish History: An Experiment in Engaged Learning

This paper will begin with a description of the experiment, continue with my interpretation of the data, and end with what I think I have learned, in general as a teacher and specifically as relates to the teaching of rabbinic literature and ancient Jewish history.

The Experiment and the Results

The course that I chose for this experiment was one of my "bread and butter" courses, a historical survey of the Jews from the Persian to early rabbinic periods. This has always been a standard historical survey, focusing on political, social, and economic conditions, while at the same time foregrounding the development of "rabbinic Judaism." The class is designed to develop the historical context necessary for the later academic and historical study of rabbinic literature; in the class itself we read only a few rabbinic texts. One of the primary goals of this course, as I assume is the case with most historical surveys, is to give a broad-brush narrative of the period that will allow students to navigate the period and its data, to develop a frame of reference for historical thinking, so that in more advanced courses, when students encounter relevant data, they will better be able to put it within a context.

Yet in previous renditions of the course, students seemed not quite able to develop this frame of reference to the extent of being able to apply it to unfamiliar texts. When in final projects students were asked to interpret new data, very few would do so in relationship to the models and data presented in class. It seemed unlikely to me that students did not understand what we were covering in class; their ability to summarize, paraphrase, and critically engage materials covered in class was quite good. So I set out to discover what was not "taking" and why.

Toward this end, I radically redesigned the course. What if I no longer gave students an explicit frame of reference, but moved so radically toward an "active learning" model that they were forced to create one for themselves? Could I do this in a way that documented their learning, so at the same time I could analyze how students learned?

To answer these questions, I put a collaborative project at the heart of the course. The class, as a whole, would develop a "wiki" of early Jewish history. A wiki is an online collaboratively-written set of documents (it is the environment used, for example, by Wikipedia). I settled on a wiki for three reasons. First, it would allow students to work together without always having to coordinate their schedules. Second, by allowing peer editing and revision, it would open a window onto how students change their minds as the semester—and learning—progresses. Finally, every change is logged, providing a written record of the entire process.

I had no expectations concerning how this wiki would develop; I was genuinely curious and open to all possibilities. I did, though, have a hypothesis about its pedagogical effectiveness: the hands-on and intensively active approach of the course would raise the level of student learning, which in turn would be reflected in their final, individual exams. It turns out that I was wrong: their final essays did not appear to me to be any better than those in the past. Yet despite this failure, this experiment did give me some insight into the problems with which I have been struggling.

The Experiment

The class was titled "The Beginning of Judaism," and was taught during the fall of 2006 at Brown University. Nine undergraduate students, of different levels, classes, and "concentrations" (Brown's term for majors) finished the course (another two dropped the course during the semester). Both the enrollment and the drop numbers are consistent with the previous times the course was offered. We met twice a week for 80 minutes, in a room that was a bit too large for us but was set up with four tables forming a square; there were also moveable desks in the room, which we sometimes used during in-class group work. My usual place was the side of the table closest to the blackboard; I was the only person sitting on this side. The room had technology hook-ups that we occasionally used to present images and to review progress on the wiki.

At the beginning of the semester, students received a syllabus that included a detailed description of the substantive content of the course as well the structure of the class.[5] The substantive course description at the beginning of the syllabus read:

> Prior to 586 BCE, the Israelites worshipped a warrior God who, they said, had forged them into a nation and continued to protect

---

[5] Five evaluations comprised their final grade: Preparation and attendance (10% of final grade); reading journal entries (20%); midterm essay (15%); the wiki (30%); final take-home exam (25%).

them: He was their king, and they were His subjects. In allegiance to this God, whom they called YHWH, they regularly offered sacrifices at their Temple in Jerusalem. When the Babylonians razed the Jerusalem Temple in 586 BCE, resettling part of the population in Babylonia, they also unintentionally sparked the transformation of the religion of the Israelites.

About a century later a "remnant" of this people returned to Jerusalem, this time as Jews. Now bringing a book they called the Torah, they began to construct a religion fundamentally different from that of their Israelite ancestors. This course is the story of how the religion of ancient Israel was transformed into Judaism. Our story starts with the building of the Second Temple and ends about 1,000 years later, with the beginning of the rabbinic movement and the creation of the patterns of thought and rituals that have lasted to the present day.

In the section on organization and structure, I wrote (in part):

The structure of this class will most likely differ from many of the historical surveys you may have taken. The first part of the class will involve becoming familiar with a narrative that attempts to make sense of the entire period and the different kinds of sources available to historians of the Jews in antiquity.

After the winter break things get more interesting, exciting, and maybe even a little scary. In the second part of the course we as a class will construct our own, possibly alternative, historical narrative. We will work on a wiki; by the end of the semester we should have a history that we can then make publicly accessible. Work on the wiki will be ongoing.

In preparation for most classes, you will do the assigned reading and write a (usually short) entry in your reading journal on Mycourses [Brown's online course management system]. We will then discuss the readings in class, and afterwards you—or the class as a whole or your group, as appropriate—will add to the wiki (also drawing, if appropriate, from your reading journal). For many classes, smaller groups will read related but different materials, and we will use class time to integrate and synthesize these readings.

This is the first time I have tried to teach this way, and I anticipate some messiness in the process. In recognition of this, I have worked into our schedule time for class discussions of the process.

At our first class meeting I emphasized the experimental nature of the course. Then, and throughout the course, I also explicitly stated the learning goals of the course. I told them much of what I have written above, that I had redesigned the class to emphasize active learning so that they might better be able to develop and apply a historical framework for the period.

From the first class meeting on I also explicitly emphasized that there was a "process" goal for the class. Learning to collaborate on projects is an increasingly necessary skill today, and it is hardly an innate one. Some students had prior experience completing group projects, although these were generally limited in scope and highly structured. For all of these students, the lack of structure or clear hierarchy would prove challenging.

The goal of the first three weeks was to provide students with models for what they were about to do. For 4.5 classes we discussed Shaye Cohen's book, *The Maccabees to the Mishnah*.[6] Before each class, students would post in their on-line reading journals their reactions to the assigned reading; only I could see them. Class would consist primarily of discussion, during which I would provide some contextual lecturing but would mainly prod them with questions (e.g., What is his thesis? What evidence does he use? What exactly is the Book of Jubilees—if your mother asks, what will you tell her?). My goal here was twofold: (1) to expose students to the range of data and the methods commonly used to make sense of it, and (2) to help students internalize *a method* for reading scholarly, historical narratives. They had to learn, that is, a particular set of critical reading skills. We used 1.5 class meetings to go the library for an introduction to the resources available there, and to a computing classroom for hands-on training in using the wiki.

These sessions ended on February 15, and February 20 was a holiday. During this week they were to complete their midterm assignment: they read, on their own, an overlapping but alternative historical narrative, Martin Jaffee's *Early Judaism*.[7] The assignment was to write a 5-page pa-

---

[6] Shaya Cohen, *The Maccabees to the Mishnah*, second edition (Louisville, KY: Westminster John Knox Press, 1987).
[7] Martin Jaffee, *Early Judaism*, second edition (Baltimore, MD: University Press of Maryland, 2005).

per comparing Cohen's and Jaffee's books, focusing on how two scholars using the same material can create, structurally and substantively, different narratives. I also wanted to see if they could apply the same questions that we asked of Cohen to Jaffee's book, without my prodding. We spent class on February 22 discussing their papers and introducing the wiki.

The rest of the course was structured chronologically, and the readings were predominantly primary sources. The next three classes focused on the Persian period, during which work on the wiki began. Before each class the students were to write a response to the readings in their journals and make a contribution to the wiki. They were allowed to (but did not have to) "double dip" and use their reading journal entry as their wiki contribution. I explicitly left open the structure of the wiki as well as the nature and scope of their contributions. We spent our time in class much as we had in our discussions of the Cohen book: I would pose questions of the material, and we would discuss. Some of each class was also spent reading together through selected primary texts. I would ask and explain as we went along. I suggested to students that they use what they learned in class to go back to correct and modify what they wrote on the wiki.

We devoted the next seven classes to the Hellenistic and early Roman period. Two of these classes were structured like the earlier classes (e.g., one reading with one class discussion), but five used a different format. For these classes, all of the students did one common reading, but each student was also assigned to one of three "reading groups" that had its own additional reading selection. Our class-time would be divided between three activities. Usually I would give a short lecture or lead discussion about the common reading. Then students broke up into their groups to discuss their readings. Finally, students taught their readings to the class. (In the next section of this paper, I will describe the styles of these presentations and how they changed.) These classes brought us to the spring break in late March, and then some interruptions for Passover in early April.

The week after our discussion of the Dead Sea scrolls we had a "sectarian summit." Students did not post to the wiki that week, but instead each was assigned to a sectarian group: Pharisees, Sadducees, Essenes, authors of the Dead Sea scrolls (as distinct from the Essenes, primarily for pedagogical reasons),[8] and early followers of Jesus. Prior to class on April 17, students were expected to research their sect, both in our previously assigned readings and at the library. They were expected to consult with members of their team during this process in order to ensure broad coverage. During our April 17 class, they worked with their team, all in our classroom. I circulated among them, answered questions, and provoked them by posing arguments that I heard against them from other groups. April 19 was the summit, in which students spoke "in character." The last part of that class was a discussion and evaluation of what had happened. I then asked the teams to make appropriate postings on the wiki.

The last few classes were spent looking at the emergence of rabbinic Judaism. We returned to a single common reading and lecture/discussion format. We then had a class devoted entirely to discussing the wiki, where it was, and what needed to be done in order to finish it. The wiki was "closed" on May 10, and the students completed take-home essays a few days later. The final essay assignment was as follows.

> You must answer the first question, and then you have a choice of answering **either** 2a **or** 2b.
>
> 1. In the periods that we have discussed this semester, we have returned repeatedly to the issue of religious authority and the experts who claimed it. Compare, contrast, and discuss these different forms of religious authority as demonstrated by such experts as priests, prophets, kings, scribes, and rabbis. Can you trace a line of development?
>
> 2. Answer **one** of the following questions:
>
>   2a. The sectarian documents from Qumran provide an internal historical narrative, albeit one that is sometimes difficult to penetrate. Primarily using the selections from the Damascus Document and Habakkuk Pesher found in

---

[8] Our knowledge of the "Essenes" derives only from classical literary sources (e.g., Josephus, Philo, Pliny), whereas the Dead Sea scrolls never use the term "Essene". Many scholars do think that the Essenes described in the classical sources were the authors of the Dead Sea scrolls, but the identification is far from certain and I wanted the students to wrestle with the data itself.

Texts and Traditions (on, respectively, pages 292-299 and 354-356), reconstruct the history of the sect. Your narrative need not be "correct" in the sense that it conforms to modern scholarly accounts, but it should attempt to clarify who, in the eyes of the sect, did what to whom, and when.

2b. Compare the causes of the Maccabean revolt to those of the "Great Revolt" of 66–70 CE. In what ways were they similar, and in what ways different? How do you explain the similarities and differences that you found?

The Results

This essay is a revision of a working paper that I wrote less than two months after the course had ended. In addition to drawing on my recollection, I also consulted private written notes that I kept during most of the course, as well as my entries in the contemporaneous class blog that I maintained (which students could see and were expected to read). Due to time pressure, I curtailed my entries in both media during the last third of the course. Finally, I have a record of every change made in the wiki.

The first part of the course went more or less as I have come to expect. Students would come to class having read the assigned section of the book (usually ranging from 50-100 pages), but most were unable to answer basic critical questions, such as, "What is he trying to prove, and how is he proving it?" Nevertheless, the discussions were good and interesting, with students wrestling with some of Cohen's more provocative ideas. It was clear that students either had either little prior knowledge in which to anchor this reading, or they resisted Cohen's assertions as going against some narrative to which they were already committed; many students had some unpredictable combination of the two. Students were particularly interested in his discussion of canonicity.

My blog entry for February 13 reads:

> We spent most of class discussing issues of canonicity. More specifically, we discussed two levels of fluidity, in (1) establishing a

sacred text and (2) establishing that particular text as authoritative within a given community. This brought us also to a consideration of what a "text" was in antiquity considering the high rate of illiteracy, and whether it was the text itself (i.e., the "words of God") or the ideas in that text that were primary.

There was general class interest in Cohen's argument that the establishment of scripture led to creativity. This is perhaps a thesis that we might want to consider further later in the course.

We also went over the taxonomy of the literary genres presumably "unleashed" through the canonization of Scripture, translation, paraphrase, and commentary, and considered how these forms might have supplemented, replaced, or modified understandings of the biblical text.

The quality of the midterm papers, comparing Cohen's and Jaffee's books, was relatively predictable. Students had a hard time applying the discussions of Cohen's book to Jaffee, and many of the papers remained too superficial, comparing organization and style rather than substance. They told me that they found the assignment extremely difficult.

The discussion of the papers on February 22 was followed by a general discussion of strategy in approaching the wiki. I wrote in my notes for that day:

> Toward the end of class we began to discuss the wiki. I told them that this was their project, that I was not committed to any one process, and that I would step back from the conversation and listen as they decided how to proceed. The discussion was interesting, productive, and inconclusive—they demonstrated a real reluctance to come to clear decisions about "the next (first!) step." At the end of this discussion I stepped in and summarized what I thought I heard and suggested that they organize the wiki into three categories, "Religious," "Political," and "Social." At the moment, these were to serve primarily as heuristics, not as hard categories that will need to be maintained throughout.

I thought at the time that their reluctance to make decisions was due primarily to the novelty of the project, but it turned out to set the tone for the semester. They did grow more comfortable with each other throughout the semester, but they had great difficulty in moving away from ultimately turning to me.

Teaching Ancient Jewish History: An Experiment in Engaged Learning

The class after the first wiki entry illustrates this attitude. According to my notes for February 27:

> About half of the students made entries to the wiki prior to this class. For the most part, these were good, although they took a variety of formats. We had our first anxiety attack at the beginning of class, with one student saying he needs to know what I want him to do. In response I told them an anecdote about my experience working at an investment bank right after college, how I was given responsibilities that required me to put together a team without being told how, whom to approach, or what resources were available to me—and, of course, having no authority over anybody. I had no idea how to do this. One of the goals of our project, then, also involves process, helping students to acquire skills that could be used for future collaborative projects, although unlike many work environments I would be offering more guidance, and the ramifications are far less severe. I think that they heard that, although I predict that this will not be the last panic attack. We then went relatively carefully through the book of Haggai.

Over the next several class meetings students continued to add, somewhat helter-skelter, notes and entries to the wiki. Two things began to strike me about these entries. First, there was almost no revision of previous entries. I suggested in our class blog for March 1 that students revise some entries in light of our class discussion (although I did not tell them what to revise). This suggestion went entirely unheeded. By March 13 I was growing concerned.

I wrote (in part) in my notes after class that day:

> Before class I was growing concerned about the wiki. They were adding to it, but they were not editing mistakes nor at all integrating their contributions. I opened class by saying that we would talk for the first 20 minutes about the wiki—how did they think it was going? I stayed out of this conversation as they very quickly voiced to each other the same concerns that I had, and I was very pleased to see them quickly come to an agreement that they needed to meet in teams outside of class to work through some of the problems.

I made a class blog entry that day that summarized our discussion.

In the classroom, the small group discussions tended to go well. Although this was a small class to begin with, breaking the group down into smaller groups of three to four students really did help them to discuss and engage the readings. For the first two such classes, after group discussions I would reconvene the entire class and give each group 10 minutes to teach their text to the rest of the class. These presentations did not go very well; the presenters had a hard time summarizing and conveying their texts in a way comprehensible to someone who had not read them. After these two classes, I shifted the nature of these presentations to a "jigsaw" format. After the group discussions of their texts, I would mix the groups so that each student would be responsible for teaching his or her text to two or three other students. Almost all the students thought that this worked much better.

By mid-March the wiki had a single access page that had links to three categories, "Religious," "Political," and "Social." Each of these three categories linked to a page with a list of further links. They were:

- **Religious**: Prophecy; Genealogy; God's Relationship to Man; God (Proofs); Ritual; Holidays and Festivals; Values; Religious Courage; Temple; Text; ECCLESIASTES (sic); Nationality and Religion; Synagogue; Special Laws 1, Philo; Circumcision.

- **Political**: The Role of the Priests in Haggai and Zechariah; The Attitude of Cyrus, King of Persia, towards the Judeans: Perspectives in Ezra; The People of Israel and Surrounding Cultures; The Relationship of Artazerxes (sic) to Nehemiah: Perspectives in Nehemiah; Treaty Law in Jubilees; Political and Military Strategy of the Maccabees; Foreign Rulers and Treatment of Jews; Roman Revolutions.

- **Social**: Conversion; Foreign Rule (Social); Ethnic Continuity; Marriage; Samaritans.

There was no order or reasoning behind this list of topics. Several of these links led to pages with more links. Students had continued to add entries (and modify a few) that interested them. Predictably, the entries were stylistically, qualitatively, and quantitatively diverse. One student enjoyed writing on political aspects, and many of those entries were mini-essays on specialized topics. Others wrote outlines or very brief, dictionary-style entries.

Before spring break, on March 22, we had a long discussion in class about the wiki, with several students wanting to work on cleaning up its organization. One of the more significant organizational changes was made on the "Social" page. The new categories were: Conversion and Community; Jews and Gentiles in the Persian Period; Jews and Gentiles in the Early Hellenistic Period; Jews and Gentiles in the Roman Period; Jews and Early Christianity; Race, Ethnicity, Lineage, and Heritage; Marriage, Gender, and Sexuality; Institutions, Groups, and Organizations; and Law and Customs. I will return to this recategorization below, because it seems to me to mark a critical transition from *thinking in topics* to *thinking in themes*.

During that same class, I asked how I could be most useful. Students asked me to go through the wiki and comment on individual essays. During spring break I did so, usually phrasing my brief comments on each entry in terms of questions or resources for further exploration, but occasionally pointing out factual errors. The students did not address or explore the bulk of my suggestions and directions for further exploration.

Work on the wiki stalled through most of April, due to Passover and the "sectarian summit." The latter went extremely well. It turned out to be the only class activity that drove them voluntarily into the library—which previously they seemed very hesitant to use for their projects—and they were engaged in both the preparation and the actual event.

We devoted class on April 26 to a fuller discussion of the wiki. Now students were getting more anxious; they still could not develop a clear organizational or work plan on their own. At this point I intervened strongly. We decided that there should be a looser, rather than hierarchical, system of entry to the wiki for which I would be responsible. We then created lists of what we called "Contextual Essays," "Thematic Essays," and "Names, Texts, and Other Important Things," and created teams of students to work in each category. I left it up to the team to divide the actual workload. As they finished each entry, they added it to the home page. They then were supposed to each take one final look through the entire wiki, adding cross-links and revising as they thought fit.

The "final" version of the home page of the wiki is found at the end of this document (Exhibit A). The entries themselves are inconsistent. The essay on the Hellenistic period, for example, leads to a timeline and a brief paragraph with no cross links; the essay on the Roman period has a fuller section entitled "Historical Trajectory"; and some of the entries attempt to wrestle previously-written material into a new, and not particularly well-fitting, organization. Some, however, are truly excellent examples of synthesis. Unfortunately there were few such entries, and even they exhibit another weakness that ran through all of the entries: although I repeatedly encouraged them to, students rarely consulted non-course materials in the library, and when they did it was almost always the online version of *Encyclopedia Judaica*.

The class concluded with a take-home final exam. As I noted above, I was disappointed with the exams. They were not bad, but they were also no better than what I had received during previous versions of the class, which were taught more conventionally.

Discussion

In one sense, this course could be considered a benign failure. Students learned no less than in previous years, and perhaps, in ways I am unable to measure, they took away more from it. It entailed, however, a tremendous amount of work on my part and theirs, with the uncertainty and social issues involved in group work raising student anxiety levels. I know that I would not repeat the course in exactly the same format.

Yet I learned much from teaching this course, and suspect that I will learn even more over the years as I reflect further on the experience and the data. Below are some preliminary reflections on both broad pedagogical issues and more practical and applied ramifications.

Narratives vs. Data

For most students, "history" means a narrative. One of the primary goals of any history class at the college level is to show that "history" is in fact many narratives, each of which is the human product of the interaction of the historian with data. To do history, then, is not to learn a single narrative but to participate in an ongoing and dynamic encounter with the past. Rather than developing a single narrative, the teacher of an introductory historical survey might better establish a series of frames of reference, both factual and methodological.

For ancient Jewish history in particular (but not uniquely), students arrive with a very incomplete and often misguided set of frames of reference. The issue and the challenges that it presents might be highlighted by comparison to the study of American history. In one experiment, Sam Wineburg put a series of primary historical documents dealing with Abraham Lincoln in front of several students and teachers and asked them to think aloud about these documents.[9] The results were illuminating, primarily in revealing the ways that prior education shapes the contexts we develop to make sense of new data. Yet while these documents frequently challenged prior understandings (e.g., by suggesting that Lincoln believed that blacks were inferior to whites), all of the participants in this experiment had a rich (if sometimes incorrect) frame of reference for making sense of the documents: they all knew the name Abraham Lincoln, had heard of the Civil War, and knew something of the issue of slavery and emancipation. Compare this to documents that mention or deal with Haggai, Qumran, Bar Kochba, or even the Talmud—for most students, these exist unmoored from any time or space.

My experience in this course helped me articulate what I had inchoately suspected. On the one hand, students had no context for the data, so they could make no sense out of these historical texts and artifacts. On the other hand, providing a context through reading and lectures is largely passive learning that rarely enables students to apply it to new data. I was most struck by the fact that despite reading, discussing, and writing on two narrative histories, students were unable—the very next day—to fit primary data into the contexts provided by the histories. Instead, they approached the material from the ground up, thinking in discrete topics and struggling to find the right tools for interpreting the ancient data. That is, when confronting an ancient text, even one that was discussed in the secondary work they had previously read, students rarely would say something like, "This is an example of what Jaffee refers to as...." Instead, they might read a text for the central message or

---

[9] Wineburg, *Historical Thinking*, 89-112.

thesis and in the process ignore the text's most important aspects, at least to the historian.

It was in the move from topical to thematic thinking that I began to see a deepening understanding. I was intrigued by this shift and what it might indicate about student learning. If the progress of the wiki can serve as any indication of student learning more generally, it suggests that the passive learning of frames of reference—even when discussed and written about—is not very effective. This, then, leads me to a hypothesis: students begin to build their understanding from wrestling with data with the tools that they already have. They begin to abandon these tools and try others as they see them fail. Here the classroom discussions were vital *primarily for giving students an opportunity to be wrong*, and thus learning how their existing critical tools are not good for answering certain questions. Only then do they more easily try new approaches, and even then slowly.

Critical Thinking

This experience has also helped me to articulate what I meant by my notions of "critical thinking," which is of course a notoriously vague concept. What I really wanted was not for students merely to be able to regurgitate what they were told, but for them to internalize some frame of reference to the point that they would be able to *apply* it to develop a context for new data; *expand* it to fit to new situations; *explain* how and why it works; and *critique* its weaknesses. As most college teachers in the humanities know, designing not only a course but also tools that accurately assess achievement of these goals is extraordinarily challenging. As Derek Bok notes from his survey of the empirical literature,[10] in actuality few teachers even try.

It is precisely this issue that might account for differences in grade distributions between the sciences and the humanities. The thrust of many courses in the sciences is applying methods to new data to achieve results. These results are often quantitative, giving instructors an easy way to ascertain a student's ability to correctly apply the new tools. That is, the intellectual process—learning new tools and acquiring the ability to apply them correctly—is the same in the humanities and the quanti-

---

[10] Bok, *Our Underachieving Colleges*, 110-127.

tative sciences, but its success is easier to judge in the sciences. Hence, it is not surprising that grade distributions in the sciences tend to be lower than in the humanities, not because there is something intrinsically harder about the sciences, but because there is a more accurate measure of achievement.

In light of my last reflection, though, I wonder if striving for this level of mastery and application in an introductory humanities class is not too ambitious. One of the problems with the wiki assignment, I now realize, was that it involved not only application of critical tools but the actual creation of new knowledge, and this was beyond what most students at this level were capable of doing. Even striving for application might be unrealistic, especially given student expectations of workload (at Brown, students expect to spend at most 4-6 hours a week on workload in a humanities class, and quite a bit more in their science classes). Perhaps a more realistic goal would be to strengthen general historical reasoning skills while providing a broad familiarity with and context for the artifacts of early Jewish history. Further development of this context into causal narratives, then, could largely wait for more advanced courses.

Collaborative Work

If I remember correctly, over my four years of college I was not assigned a single collaborative project. Nor did my teachers even once break a class into smaller discussion groups. As I told my students one day in class, only after college and upon entering the workforce, when I was immediately plunged into collaborative projects at which I was expected to succeed, did it begin to occur to me that I was entirely unprepared for it.

There is wide agreement among educators, especially outside of the universities, that collaborative work is pedagogically effective. Even studies at the college level, particularly in the sciences, have shown dramatic improvements in learning in classes that require collaborative work. Equally important, outside of academic life there are few careers in which one's success does not depend on successful collaboration. Yet although group work is more common today in colleges than when I was student (most, but not all, of my students had previously participated in one or two other collaborative experiences), it is still far from widespread.

The reasons for this are not hard to discern and all reflect legitimate concerns. Group work can be logistically complicated (sometimes by the complexity of student schedules, or something as mundane as the bolted chairs in a lecture hall); it involves the loss of faculty control over the classroom, which in turn leads both to the fear that students are chatting or replicating mistakes rather than learning and to a degree of faculty guilt at not being more active in the classroom; groups proceed at different paces, with some finishing sooner than others; and perhaps most importantly, there is the looming issue of assessment and fairness to individual students.

At the end of this class I was particularly struck by which group assignments succeeded, and which did not. Small group discussions of the readings were almost always successful. The room and class were small enough that I could remain aware of all the groups, and most of them at most times were genuinely working. When these individual discussions sometimes stalled I stepped in to provide a provocative question, which would reignite them. Class discussions after group work, as well as the remixing of groups, were also far more successful than either a class discussion after my lecture or student presentations to the class. The most successful collaborative project was the sectarian summit, and the least was the wiki.

Now, it is this last observation that requires explanation. The summit was not actually a graded assignment per se (except as a part of overall class participation), whereas the wiki counted for a good deal of their final grade. As I had made clear to the students, the class grade on the wiki was also going to be their individual final grades on it (counting for 30% of their overall final grades), although based on their individual contributions (which I could track and document) I reserved the right to adjust their individual grades. This, however, was not incentive enough for them to organize and work well together. Two or three times students did raise in class the issue of assessment for their work on the wiki, but most students did not appear very concerned by this.

There are several possible explanations for why student collaboration on this project was not better. Comparing the wiki to the summit, though, highlights what I think are the two most salient explanations. First, I laid out well-defined criteria for the summit; I told them what I wanted from them, when I wanted it, and how to do it. I gave them means, a vision of the outcome, and a deadline. The wiki was far more open, as I was asking them to develop these things on their own. Such project indeterminacy is of course common in the "real world," sometimes by design and sometimes due to poor management, and some of my students were excited by it. Most, however, found it too overwhelming. Similarly, the small group discussions always improved when I posed sharper questions. This might seem rather obvious, but it emphasizes for me the importance of the teacher's (and manager's) role in setting the most advantageous conditions for collaboration.

The second, more surprising, difference was in the area of presentation and assessment. I might be pushing the data a little, but it seems to me that students were less concerned with their grade on the wiki than they were with performing well in direct competition with their classmates. Perhaps the fear of being shamed before their own peers (or, phrased positively, the desire to best them "on the field") was more of an incentive than a grade, even when they knew that the wiki was a public document. I noticed no differences between genders either. Obviously, different incentives work better for different students, and I am not yet sure what the practical "take away" message of this explanation is, but at least it suggests that issues of assessment do not play as important a role for students in their attitude toward group work as is sometimes thought.

Practical Conclusions

This experiment, although not the success for which I had hoped, still left me with two clusters of insights: the first is more broadly pedagogical, and the second has to do with the use of technology in the classroom.

First, I continue to struggle with the problem of teaching students with little prior knowledge a context for interpretation, while doing so in a way that sticks. In my own courses as an undergraduate and graduate student, history classes that provided a (usually strong) narrative delivered through lecture and reading and then supplemented with discussions of primary texts largely "worked" for me; as a teacher, though, I find that the students for whom this continues to work are relatively few. I have no reason to doubt the research that indicates that active learning provides far better teaching outcomes.

But how is active learning to be incorporated effectively into such learning environments, on whatever topic or level? That is, the issue that I face in this class is almost identical to the one present in my adult education classes, my other history classes, and my classes on rabbinic texts. While I do not yet have an answer to this question, I have learned that active learning still requires intensive teacher intervention. Finding the right balance of student empowerment and faculty guidance remains the challenge.

I suspect that a better approach incorporates the elements of the class that were successful (e.g. small group discussions, role play) with what might be called guided, active modeling. Even with discussions and writing assignments, the Cohen and Jaffee books passively modeled for my students the historical enterprise. This, I think, is the reason that it did not stick; students did not have an opportunity to work through the intellectual operations (that become innate to scholars and many teachers) for themselves. Students need to be shown how to do things (e.g., compare two texts; identify differences; models for explaining those differences) and then given the opportunity to do them, one by one and hands-on.

One practical way that this might be achieved in at least a somewhat formal educational setting might look something like this: students have a reading assignment that they are to complete while consulting a set of guiding questions and explanations. They are asked, as part of their home preparation, to complete a short written assignment that explicitly asks them to relate a primary text to a secondary one. The kind of assignment changes in order to emphasize different intellectual operations, and the operations build in complexity throughout the semester. These written assignments might then be circulated in advance. The beginning of the next class is spent discussing these assignments; they will also be collected and graded. Students then break up into small groups in order to work on a new assignment that uses different data in the same intellectual process. We then reconvene for a discussion of this exercise.

With such a model, the teacher intervenes at three points. First, there is a heavy burden of preparation. The success of the course is largely dependent on the quality and clarity of the guides and assignments. Second, the teacher is leader of class discussions, not only guiding and refereeing but also providing a learning environment in which students feel that it is safe to be wrong. Finally, the teacher serves as an individual coach, grading and commenting on many written assignments in order to help individual students progress according to their own needs and abilities. Supplementing a course like this with an occasional lecture, multi-media presentation (or trip to a museum), or role-playing experience like the sectarian summit could result in a fun (if labor-intensive) class both to take and to teach.

Second, an issue that emerges from this experiment more broadly deals with the effectiveness of technology. Although this class used technology extensively (e.g., online reading journals; class blog; wiki), these technologies are not ends in themselves. Technology may work best to facilitate class exercises rather than transform them. The wiki, for example, is a tool that I had hoped would facilitate collaborative work outside of class to a degree that it did not. The same exercise could have had a traditional written product with more or less the same learning outcome.

Despite my disappointment in this particular case, I remain optimistic about the ability of these technologies to facilitate both out-of-class communication and collaborative work. I suspect that with a bit more thought on my part and the proper incentives, I could better integrate this tool into my courses, providing another forum for informal writing, communication, and engagement. While I will not soon have my students again create their own wiki, I may—as suggested to me by my colleague Jordan Rosenblum—turn them loose on Wikipedia, whose entries on matters dealing with ancient Judaism and rabbinics are by and large execrable. (I would, however, use a wiki again if I were to assign collaboratively authored assignments.) The key, of course, is not to let the promise of the technology get ahead of well-considered educational goals.

I do not yet have more confidence in my success as a teacher—specifically, in having my students absorb and be able to apply a usable historical narrative—than I did when I began this experiment. Yet I am more confident than ever that a sustained focus on learning outcomes and active and engaged learning methods will ultimately lead to greater success in meeting that specific goal—which is, in some sense, my most single most important goal in teaching this survey course. It is that focus which remains at the core of my ongoing reflection on and investigation of my own pedagogy and my students' learning.

Exhibit A: Final Wiki Home Page

Welcome to the Class Wiki of "The Beginning of Judaism" (JS53/RS63). This is a collaborative project undertaken (under compulsion) by the students of the class during spring 2007.

The Babylonian destruction of the Jerusalem temple in 587/6 BCE may have only temporarily suspended sacrifices to the God of Israel, but it also began a more fundamental transformation of ancient Israelite religion and identity. The foundations of the second Jerusalem temple were laid only 46 years after the destruction of the first, but this time by Judeans, "Jews," rather than Israelites, who increasingly relied for authority on a book—the newly redacted Pentateuch or Torah—rather than on the word of the priests. Over the following millennium this transformation would spawn an astounding diversity of groups that claimed to be the true inheritors of the covenant of Israel. Most of these groups, such as the Sadducees, Pharisees, and the authors of at least some of the Dead Sea scrolls, would ultimately wither away. But by 640 CE two of these groups began to crystallize into the religions that we now somewhat roughly label as "Christianity" and "Rabbinic Judaism."

This wiki does not claim to tell a coherent story of this transformation. It instead offers three kinds of resources for exploring the fascinating history of this period. First are three contextual essays that attempt to integrate into a concise narrative the history of the three major political periods. Second is a collection of important themes, and finally many shorter entries on names, texts, topics, etc. The entries are linked extensively to each other, providing many ways to browse and navigate the wiki.

This is a work in progress! Enjoy and, in the democratic although frightening spirit of the wiki, feel free to comment and provide feedback.

Contextual Essays
- Persian Period: 539 to 334 BCE
- Hellenistic Period: 334 to 63 BCE
- Roman Period: 63 BCE to 4th century CE

Thematic Essays
- Conversion
- Ethnicity
- Jews and Gentiles

Teaching Ancient Jewish History: An Experiment in Engaged Learning

- Priests
- Religious Authority
- Revolts
- Rituals
- Sects
- Temple
- Texts
- Women
- Prophecy

Names, Texts, and Other Important Things
- Ezra
- Haggai
- Nehemiah
- Zechariah
- Mishnah
- Philo
- Josephus
- Rabbi Judah
- Enoch
- Jesus
- Samaritans
- Septuagint
- Tanakh
- Maccabees
- Herod
- Pseudepigrapha
- Apocrypha
- Wisdom of Solomon
- Alexander the Great
- Ecclesiastes
- Jubilees
- Hasmoneans
- Pharisees
- Saducees
- Essenes
- Qumran/Dead Sea Scroll Community

10 "A Judaism That Does Not Hide": Curricular Warrants for the Teaching of the Documentary Hypothesis in Community Jewish High Schools

Susan E. Tanchel

Introduction

Delving into students' hearts and minds is not only a teacher's prerogative—it is her obligation. It is essential that teachers find ways to determine whether or not they are, in fact, challenging their students and opening their minds to new content, and to varied possibilities for interpreting the material which the students can consider while developing their own understandings. An important part of the complex educational process involves thoughtfully planning the curriculum through which to work toward these goals, and continually evaluating its impact. Any analysis of the impact of a particular curricular approach depends on a rich understanding of the actual experience of students.

In this chapter, I examine and analyze the experiences of students at a pluralistic Jewish high school studying the documentary hypothesis in biblical scholarship as an approach to reading the biblical text. Because this is a subject area that is laden with theological and emotional weight, and because my students are exposed to the documentary hypothesis more extensively than their peers at other schools, I wanted to understand more intensively—and more intentionally—their experience of learning it. In what follows, I examine selected student writings in order to understand their experience—and especially the challenges they face—in learning and applying the documentary hypothesis. I locate my teaching of the documentary hypothesis in the context of the particular institution in which I work. I classify student experience in terms of different student types, and argue that for all of the kinds of students I encounter, this curricular choice is ultimately not only defensible but indeed beneficial to their theological and intellectual growth.

I conclude by addressing many of the challenges other educators might and do raise—whether or not this is a "Jewish approach," whether it is wise to raise so many intergroup tensions in a high school environment, and how much time to devote to this aspect of the curriculum—and outline how a developmental perspective, too, supports this curricular and pedagogic choice.

Challenges in Exposing Students to the Documentary Hypothesis

As part of the twelfth-grade curriculum at Gann Academy-The New Jewish High School of Greater Boston in Waltham, MA, we teach the reigning scholarly theory of the Bible's authorship, the documentary hypothesis, which posits that several individuals or authorial schools wrote the Torah over a period of several hundred years. This year of study follows three years in which students have focused on literary aspects of biblical texts and have studied a variety of texts with traditional Jewish commentaries. The skills that are taught in successive years are designed to build on one another, with the goal of students interpreting texts themselves through a variety of methods, guided by insights from medieval and modern Jewish interpreters.

More specifically, in ninth grade, students are taught basic literary skills, including biblical Hebrew grammar. They also develop the intellectual habit of critically evaluating interpretations, which prepares them to assess the different methods and interpretations they will explore in the coming years. In tenth and eleventh grades, students study the works of medieval Jewish commentators (specifically Rashi, Rashbam, and Ibn Ezra), learning about each commentator's methodology through selected examples and gaining skills for interpreting the commentator's interpretations. Twelfth-grade Tanakh classes begin with students talking and writing about their beliefs about the historicity, sacredness, and authority of biblical texts. Then they learn about the identifying characteristics, interests, and vocabulary of each of the five ancient sources and practice assigning particular sections of narrative and legal texts to one of them. Additionally, they learn different scholarly theories about the stages of composition of the Torah and critically assess these theories.

Previous research on teaching the documentary hypothesis highlights the potentially significant impact of studying source criticism (which assumes the existence of multiple, human authors of the biblical text and attempts to tease them out) on our students' developing Jewish identities. During the 1960s, the Jewish Theological Seminary began to train prospective teachers who would be using their new curriculum. Ruth Zielenziger, the director of the Melton Curriculum Project at JTS, described how problematic it was for these teachers who had long been teaching in Conservative schools to accept the conclusions of the historical-critical method, despite the fact that this method is at the core of the Conservative movement's approach to the Bible. Her main purpose, she recalls, was "to move people from a literal reading of the Bible to an understanding of the Bible as the myth of Israel."[1] She found, in retrospect, that this was "a tall order" for the students, as they felt as if she "had pulled the rug from under their feet."[2] Similarly, Gail Dorph introduces her study of fifteen prospective educators in Conservative Jewish institutions with a vignette about a young woman who finds coming to terms with the idea that the Torah is a human product challenging.[3] This perspective is confirmed by Dorph's in-depth interviews, in which each of the interviewees rejected the critical understanding of the composition of the text in favor of a more traditional view, seemingly as their only option for retaining their strong emotional relationship with the text.

This tension has not only been evident in programs within the Conservative movement. Many students in the DeLeT (Day School Leadership Through Teaching) Program, a thirteen-month MAT program at Brandeis University that prepares day school teachers for the elementary grades, wrestle with this issue. I have also had similar experiences as a teacher in numerous adult education classes, such as Hebrew College's Me'ah program. Based on these studies and my own teaching experiences, when I initially set out to teach the documentary

---

[1] Ruth Zielenziger, *A History of the Bible Program of Melton Research Center* (New York: Jewish Theological Seminary, 1989), 112.
[2] Ibid., 114.
[3] Gail Z. Dorph, "Conceptions and Preconceptions: A Study of Prospective Jewish Educators' Knowledge and Beliefs about Torah" (Ph.D. dissertation, Jewish Theological Seminary, 1993), 1-5.

hypothesis to high school students, I had every reason to believe that these students would have a similar response to that of their older counterparts.

In my high school teaching experience, almost all students, regardless of denomination, have internalized some version of a belief in the Torah's divine authorship at the core of their religious worldview. Consequently, learning source criticism can initially be controversial, provocative, even threatening to students' religious beliefs and practices. It requires them to confront the possibility that the Torah is the product of human writers, which frequently leads to their questioning the continuing sacredness, veracity, and authority of the text. But it can also help students feel a stronger connection to the text, as they find support for their long-held intuitive beliefs of human authorship, learn about the early history and development of their religion for the first time, find it easier to connect to the text as a whole when objectionable parts can be contextualized historically, and/or find their traditionalist religious commitments stronger after having engaged with theories of human authorship.

Methodology

I collected data during the 2002–2003 academic year from my twelfth grade Tanakh classes at Gann Academy, chiefly during the first four months of the school year, when I taught Genesis 1–2 and introduced students to the documentary hypothesis and the source critical method. In addition to videotaping my class and keeping a teacher's journal, I copied students' weekly journals, short and long academic papers, and reflective papers, and kept copies of all my assignments.

The main data sources were two final assignments: a paper consisting of applying the documentary hypothesis to a "new" text, Numbers 16 (students had studied this text with me in their ninth-grade course using a literary approach), and a short (one- to two-page), less academic assignment: "Please describe your thoughts, your feelings, and your reactions about having learned the documentary hypothesis."

The data analysis was an iterative process. Upon my first reading, I was struck by how troubled every student still was by the material, even at the end of the unit. As I continued to examine the papers, I found that despite their struggles, all of the students (across denominations and religious perspectives) still argued that learning the material was a beneficial experience.

I then formulated five different student types and looked for patterns among the students' writings. I ultimately discovered that I only had evidence for four of the five types: I did not find any students who were halakhically observant, but did not maintain a traditional belief. In what follows I present the four remaining student types.

In the two years immediately following this class's graduation from Gann, my database spontaneously increased as I received six unsolicited e-mails from former students who had been in my class in different years reflecting on their experiences in twelfth-grade Tanakh class; near the end of this chapter, I highlight two that were particularly instructive in their specificity and detail.

Student Voices

Two quick anecdotes illustrate the spiritual landmines that the documentary hypothesis and its implications can set off for students. A few years ago, one student got up in my class and declared, "Ms. Tanchel, you are taking away my God." Another student less dramatically, but equally emphatically, quietly asked me on another occasion why she should still bother to observe Shabbat if God did not write the Torah.

These are two somewhat extreme examples taken from many conversations with students during our immersion in studying the documentary hypothesis. Student writing demonstrates the wider and more nuanced (though sometimes equally agonized) range of student expression as the students processed their experience of learning about and applying the documentary hypothesis.

A traditionally observant young woman, Ayelet, writes:

> It is difficult to come to terms with the ideas of the documentary hypothesis. The documentary hypothesis looks at the Tanach as a history book.... There is no sacredness to the biblical text, but rather it is just like any other book. How can I use a history book to create a spiritual and religious connection to G-d? ... Yet, sometimes the documentary hypothesis is very compelling.... The explanations for the varied writing styles, repetition, and chrono-

logical errors are clarified by the acceptance of the documentary hypothesis. However, I still have not fully come to terms with the idea of a non-God crafted Torah. How can I use the writings of five random guys compiled together by another random person in my religious practice? There must be something more sacred and more holy in the Torah.

Ayelet is torn, trying to reconcile her new knowledge of the documentary hypothesis with her earlier understanding of the Torah as a unique book composed by God. Understanding the Torah as a book of human origin for now diminishes her sense of its sacredness. She had thought of the Torah as a religious document facilitating her connection to God, but basing this viewpoint on divine authorship alone is no longer possible. Learning about the characteristics, interests, biases, and agendas of the different sources has in a sense reduced the Torah to a history book, written by average, "random" people, without a unique qualification or a special connection to God. This is disturbing to her, and for now undermines the place of the Torah text in her religious practice.

Ayelet is looking for a way to simultaneously hold the compelling parts of the documentary hypothesis and the holiness of the text, repeatedly going back and forth between the merits and the disadvantages of the new material, and ending with a statement of her certain belief—perhaps a wish to believe—that the Torah is more sacred and more holy than the documentary hypothesis has led her to believe. Since the documentary hypothesis clearly offers her compelling explanations of textual phenomena that she names specifically, we might say that the problem she has is not that she does not accept the explanations it offers, but that she does.

Another student, David, offers an articulate and thoughtful summary of the documentary hypothesis and how he imagines the passing on of oral traditions and the evolution of the stories and laws over time. He then writes:

> Here's the funny part: despite all my reasoning, there is still part of me that's tugging in the other direction. I know I will never give a d'var Torah basing my ideas on this premise, I know I will never teach this hypothesis, and I know that when I teach my children the Torah, I will tell them all of the stories that I learned as a child

> about Torah Misinai and the authority of the Torah. As much as the logical side of me disagrees, my practice and my belief in how to lead a Jewish life will remain unchanged. It will be sort of weird believing one thing and teaching another, but it's the only way I can make it work for me.

This student, like others, seems to believe that the authority of the text stems from God's authorship of it. That is to say, were the Torah to be a human composition, it would lose its authority. Despite what he knows and accepts logically, there is a strong emotional reason for him to reject or ignore this new information, to compartmentalize it in an effort to maintain his religious practice. David is adamant that he will never use this knowledge when teaching Torah texts to others. The intellectual value of the information is overshadowed and outweighed by the way it threatens his and others' religious lives. He acknowledges the conflict he is facing—"believing one thing and teaching another"—but he knows of no other acceptable solution.

Josh, a student who is self-identified as science-oriented, also grapples with this material:

> To me this experience was definitely worth it.... The use of the documentary hypothesis integrated the science part of my brain with the Torah part of my brain. These past few weeks have showed me a method of interpreting the Torah that is almost refreshing.... For me, this provided the Torah with a whole new dimension which I had not yet explored. Nonetheless, at this point I do not actually believe that the Torah was written by the five different schools. I have separated my theological beliefs from the study in class because I realize that more than anything else, the work in class is a learning process. It is meant to make us think in a different way and not to force us to believe in a certain philosophy. So while I thoroughly enjoy using the documentary hypothesis as a tool, the theological implications of it do not sit well with me. I am not at all upset by the use of this method; I am merely choosing to distinguish between the logical procedures used to analyze the text and the religious consequences that come with it.

Even this student, who is unabashed about the experience being worthwhile, has no desire at this point to embrace any religious consequences of the documentary hypothesis. It is difficult enough for him to have to compartmentalize this newly acquired knowledge. Josh repeatedly states in different words that the material itself does not upset him, but one wonders if he doth protest too much. What is clear, though, is that his experience of learning this material necessitates that he render it an intellectual exercise, rather than allowing it to have an impact on his theological beliefs. He takes refuge in the idea that he is not being told what to believe.

Samantha, a vociferous opponent to the hypothesis, ponders her experience:

> Obviously from my reactions in class, I completely disagree with Wellhausen's opinion. I am, however, glad we learned about it in class. Next year, in college, I am certain that the documentary hypothesis will confront me again—whether it be by a friend or in a biblical studies class—and I am glad that I learned about it before in a comfortable environment.... I don't think I ever actually believed that G-d wrote the Torah and I think this was at the root of my problem with the documentary hypothesis—it gave me an alternative. A couple of days ago someone asked me what I was learning about in my Tanach class. I told him that I was learning about a hypothesis that I didn't believe in. When he asked me what I did believe in, I couldn't answer. I just said, "Not this." But what I would have said a month ago no longer came out of my mouth. I learned what I don't believe in and realize that what I did believe is no longer what I do believe.

Given Samantha's frequent objections to the material, it is surprising to learn that what was fueling her distress was not a deeply held belief in the Torah's divine authorship, but something quite different: her newfound clarity that neither the documentary hypothesis *nor* divine authorship captures her beliefs about the Torah's origin. Yet despite the difficulty of the experience, she is clearly grateful to have confronted this material in high school (if for no other reason than to be prepared for confronting it in a less "comfortable" environment). Moreover, while she remains unclear on what she does actually believe about the authorship and authority of the Torah, she is now working on serious theological questions that were previously hidden from consciousness.

Even the rare student who comes into class believing that human beings wrote the Torah can find the experience of learning the documentary hypothesis uncomfortable. Steven reflects on his experience of finding compelling evidence to support the theory:

> I can't remember a time when I believed that God wrote the Torah.... One might think that I would have been elated when I thought I found more evidence that God didn't write the Torah. After all, it was simply proving my hypothesis. Yet, I didn't feel happy or proud.... It was almost as if I didn't really want to definitely prove that it was definitely humans who wrote the Torah....

It is striking that even for a student who has consistently believed that the Torah is a human product, learning evidence to support this claim—an occurrence that might be expected to inspire feelings of pride and satisfaction—in this instance evokes only regret.

Finally, even for the student who accepts the documentary hypothesis, the matter is not a simple one. Amy writes:

> I have grown up with the idea that the Torah is from Sinai and that God/Moshe wrote it, but if someone proves this to be otherwise so be it.... I also don't think that the documentary hypothesis makes the Torah any less valuable and meaningful. Just because there were different authors of the Torah doesn't mean that our morals or the ideas behind the Torah aren't still there. We exist as a people and with our tradition even if God did not write the Torah. My problem is that I feel like I should have a problem with the documentary hypothesis. The fact that I don't makes me think that my faith in tradition and religion isn't strong enough so I am willing to change my ideas without a second thought. I know this sounds silly, but it's true.... The documentary hypothesis is not a theological problem for me, and that does not mean that my faith is weaker. I believe in both because that is the only thing that can work for me. I believe that logic applies to text, even if it is a religious text.

Amy is a very rare student because she grew up believing in the Torah's divine authorship, but in light of having learned this new material has shifted her position. She makes very clear that this has not reduced the importance or meaning of the Torah for her and that it remains a repository of morals and ideas. Yet she still feels that accepting the documentary hypothesis—not "[having] a problem" with it—somehow reflects badly on the strength of her religious faith. She seems to be trying to determine for herself just how strong she considers her own faith. She wants to persuade herself of its strength, for then she will be able to justify her stance toward the subject matter.

From these students' writings, it is apparent that teaching the documentary hypothesis is a potentially provocative and daunting learning experience. Many students are comfortable with learning the material as an intellectual exercise, but find it challenging to maintain a plausible understanding of the Torah's sacredness that can coexist with viewing it through the eyes of source criticism. Their writings demonstrate a range of preliminary responses to that challenge and the internal conflicts that it raises.

Teaching the Documentary Hypothesis at Gann Academy

The students' voices in the preceding section sharpen the question of whether to teach the documentary hypothesis in Jewish day schools. But we are not trying to answer the question in general here. Instead, we also have to attend to the specific context or milieu in which this teaching took place, namely, Gann Academy. A core part of Gann's mission is to be a pluralistic community—that is, to be a place in which different beliefs and opinions are not only actively valued, respected, and celebrated, but are also challenged and questioned. Applying the method of source criticism to the biblical text helps students to discover the multi-vocal and layered nature of the Torah itself. This underscores the existence of diversity in ancient Israel and thereby illuminates a historical precedent for the pluralism that surrounds the students in their current educational setting.

Gann's mission statement also states that the school strives to create "an atmosphere of mutual respect [that] provides a welcome forum for grappling with fundamental religious questions and strengthening individual Jewish identities." Given these goals, the school could not properly shy away from teaching critical ideas that provide a ripe opportunity and fertile ground for realizing the pluralism of the school and grappling with fundamental religious questions.

What follows are some of the commitments that underlie Gann Academy's academic program,[4] which I will then discuss as they apply specifically to the choice to teach source criticism. (I do not intend to present here a full-blown argument for each of Gann's commitments, but rather to show that the rhetorical positions the school takes align with the teaching of source criticism in a straightforward fashion.)

> 1. Students are nurtured and challenged to develop the capacity of cognitive pluralism. From our perspective, cognitive pluralism means the ability to understand, hold, and grapple with multiple, even contradictory, interpretations and perspectives.

Learning the method of source criticism strengthens students' capacity for cognitive pluralism. When students participate in class discussions on topics such as the sacredness, history, authority, and authorship of the Torah, they have to consider multiple and contradictory perspectives on these issues. In addition, when learning about the documentary hypothesis, they have to wrestle to integrate their new understandings of the origin of the Torah, which likely contradicts their pre-existing knowledge.

> 2. Learning is most effective when it engages students' present passions, connects them with fundamental questions and concerns, challenges them to develop new interests, and pushes them to take advantage of new opportunities and possibilities.

Discussing the origin and authority of the text taps into some of the students' basic questions about their religious past, engages (or arouses) students' love for Torah study, and challenges them to reflect on their beliefs and relationship to Jewish sacred texts. This can all lead to a new interest in biblical studies.

---

[4] This is from Gann Academy's self-study, composed by Gann faculty members as part of its accreditation process.

> 3. In educating our students we are aware that we need to engage the whole student, and thus our curriculum takes into account the intellectual, emotional, physical, and spiritual aspects of our learners.

Learning the documentary hypothesis and source criticism involves more than just the student's intellect. It is an educational endeavor that as we have seen simultaneously engages the student's intellect, emotions, and spirituality. When the student discusses the history of the Torah, it is not simply an intellectual issue; it connects with the student's beliefs about God and Judaism to which she is likely emotionally attached.

> 4. We respect our students as interpreters and thinkers and encourage an environment of dialectical thinking and discussion. We desire our students to become critical enquirers of truth. The skill of logical disputation in the uncovering of truth between seemingly contradictory ideas creates a strong community of learners who come to appreciate the ideas of the past and the challenges of the present.

Learning the documentary hypothesis develops students' repertoire for interpretation and inquiry. In addition, conversations about the history of the composition of the Torah exposes students to people's diverse beliefs about their shared Jewish heritage. Through this public and communal struggling, the learners build a stronger classroom community in which students do not simply tolerate one another's views, but also respectfully challenge them.

> 5. Text-based learning is a central and crucial part of our curriculum. It is important that students appreciate primary and secondary sources not merely as being depositories of information, but as issuing challenges that must be met through disciplined study. Our goal is to teach students to enter into a dialogue with the texts, that is, to ask different sorts of questions of the texts, to interpret them through a variety of methods, and to critically assess the opinions they contain.

By learning the source critical method, students are prepared to engage with a broad scholarly conversation about the meaning of the texts.

And more generally, the engagement with source criticism broadens the range of questions that they can bring to bear, by acknowledging and welcoming questions that assume human authorship, that reflect genuine interest in the history of the text, and that are attuned to potential contradictions within the text. Source criticism provides a new method for making meaning of the texts, while also cultivating the capacity for critical assessment.

Student Types and the Documentary Hypothesis

Gann Academy's student body comprises students from all the major denominations—Orthodox, Conservative, Reform, and Reconstructionist—as well as unaffiliated students. Yet when it comes to considering the idea that human beings wrote the Torah, denomination does not seem to be a predictor for how a given student will initially react. In a classification of the different types of students, it is more fruitful to create a map of student types with respect to the categories of belief and practice as below. I will offer curricular warrants for the teaching of the documentary hypothesis for each of these student types in turn (beyond those warrants that, as we saw above, emerge from the general mission of Gann Academy).

1. *Alienated student:* One might think that (almost) all students innately care about Jewish texts, but this is far from the case. This type of student is alienated and disconnected from the study of Torah. He does not feel compelled by the traditional methods he has learned thus far and feels that there is no value in learning biblical texts. Having rejected them, he knows no way of relating to the sacred texts of his community.

   The source critical approach can provide a way to engage this type of student. Offering him a new way to study and find meaning in texts can make the process intriguing and exciting for him. With this approach, students can derive additional meanings from the text, and explain textual discrepancies in a more persuasive manner. Additionally, this method can provide students with a possible explanation for passages that are offensive to a modern person's sensibilities. In short, learning this method can make the Bible more palatable or easier to connect with. Jeff writes as follows:

> The documentary hypothesis has rekindled my interest in the study of Tanakh. It had died down during the last couple of years for various reasons...but being taught the documentary hypothesis has once again opened my mind to Tanakh, and now, I cannot seem to get enough of it. I haven't been able to quench my desire to know more....

2. *Student who is not halakhically observant, but maintains traditional beliefs:* There is a disconnect for this type of student between beliefs and practices. She maintains traditional beliefs about the origin and composition of the text, but does not observe any traditional practices. Any time a teacher sees a learner believing one thing and doing another, it is a ripe opportunity for conversation and an examination of the student's beliefs. Perhaps the student is holding onto beliefs she thinks she is supposed to have, or maybe the student simply has not questioned or reflected upon the beliefs she formed in her early years. The critical approach may alleviate this dissonance, as it offers the student a new way to make meaning of Torah texts. But the goal is not necessarily to make the student more consistent, but rather to compel her to begin to reflect on her unquestioned, potentially ossified beliefs. Studying the documentary hypothesis affords an opportunity for this student to get clearer on the reasons behind her belief. One student, Ariel, writes:

> This Tanach class has affected me, and my ideas and beliefs have been challenged—something that I had never expected because I am not a religious or observant Jew. I couldn't understand why I would be so annoyed with the idea that God didn't write the Torah. And then it finally it hit me. The fact that God might not have written the Torah did not bother me—but the implication that this could have on the way that I viewed Judaism bothered me a lot. I had never really thought about the authorship of the Torah.... Even though I have my doubts about the documentary hypothesis, I am also excited to see the new way that we can understand the Torah by studying it with the documentary hypothesis. It is going to be a new way to look at the text and I am

looking forward to seeing what new information can be learned. This is the first time that I think I will be treating the Torah as a historical document....

3. *Student who is not halakhically observant and does not hold traditional beliefs:* Most likely this student has come from a public school and/or an unaffiliated home and has already considered that God did not write the Torah. Studying the documentary hypothesis offers this type of student an opportunity to find support for their understandings and to discover that it is an acceptable and accepted Jewish position. The new knowledge and method that this student will acquire can also make the study of biblical texts more interesting. Sarah writes:

> Surprisingly enough, my theological beliefs matched with the idea of the documentary hypothesis before I had even learned about it. It had always been hard for me to believe that the Torah was given at Sinai because of scientific evidence and the like, but I do believe in divine intervention. Just because the Torah wasn't given at Sinai doesn't mean that it is not holy. The fact that it has survived for this long, is the basis of religious life for the Jews, and is such an amazing piece of work is enough for me to consider it holy above all other texts.... The Tanach in relation to the rest of the world just makes more sense when seen through the eyes of the documentary hypothesis. Belief in the documentary hypothesis, or ideas like it, does not diminish my faith and awe of God. In fact, it makes me understand God's role in Judaism more comprehensively. It would be one thing if God were just to give people the Torah, but if he were to enthuse them to write it, then his power and inspiration would have been extremely supreme. The idea that people would have written the Tanach would also teach me about the importance of people in the Jewish religion, and that I, too, can make a difference.

Steven writes:

> I don't even know if God exists and I cannot remember a time when I believed that God wrote the Torah. I didn't experience a blow to my beliefs, therefore, by learning about the documentary hypothesis. What did occur was, my learning the specifics of the writing of the Torah clarified a theory that was previously

somewhat vague in my mind. Previously I could say that I didn't think God wrote the Torah, but I wasn't sure how, when and why humans wrote it. Now that the process of the writing of the Torah is so visible, I am forced to grapple with what it means that the writers of the Torah differed in era, beliefs, and purpose.

4. *Student who is traditional in observance and belief:* Studying the documentary hypothesis affords the observant and traditional student, like all others, a chance to get clearer on what he believes in the context of other academic and cultural ideas about the composition, origin, and authority of Torah. Being challenged to think about and grapple with these ideas ultimately strengthens their religious identities and faith. No longer relying on pat answers, students go beyond stock and simplistic answers and develop more nuanced ones. Anna, an observant young woman, writes:

> I am very uncertain in my opinion of the documentary hypothesis…. Despite my doubts, uncertainties, and questions I still think that learning about the documentary hypothesis was a very, very beneficial experience. I would be very offended if someone rejected the possibility of Torah misinai without studying it thoroughly…. I still strongly disagree with the people who said that teaching things like the documentary hypothesis to "good Jewish kids" is dangerous. My religious beliefs are strongly grounded and I wouldn't start changing them on a spur of the moment decision. I think that learning opposing views can only help us better understand our own. Besides, I'm sure the possibility of something like the documentary hypothesis occurs to everyone at some point, for most people by the time they are seniors in high school. No one is pressuring us to change our beliefs, only to learn about the beliefs of others.

Source Criticism as a Jewish Approach

While my argument to this point has been grounded in the particular experience of teaching at Gann Academy, and has relied on Gann's particular mission and responses from Gann students, I would like to argue that the teaching of source criticism ought to be a part of all community, especially explicitly pluralistic, Jewish high schools. At present, I am aware of no other community high school that invests the necessary time to teaching the history of the five different schools of thought that produced the Pentateuch, as well as some of the actual methods of source criticism.[5] Some choose instead "to examine the assumptions that are brought to the biblical text by traditional commentaries and comparing/contrasting these assumptions to those of modern academic scholars."[6] When discussing modern methods of interpretation, these schools chiefly focus their energies on literary criticism, which does not involve the same potential theological pitfalls.

One of the more frequent objections to teaching this material in any real depth, or at all, is that the conclusions of source criticism do not align with a traditional Jewish position and thus it is "somewhat irrelevant to a traditional Jewish understanding of the text."[7] Students, the argument goes, would be better served by making sense of the text as a whole, in accordance with traditional Jewish interpretation. Students do not need to learn source criticism, for Jews have been learning Torah, without this knowledge, in a variety of settings quite successfully for thousands of years.

However, teaching source criticism does not preclude the possibility of learning more traditional methods of Jewish interpretation; students should have many opportunities to read texts with each of these approaches. But one of our goals should be to excite as many students as possible about the study of the biblical texts, and traditional Jewish interpretation does not grab every student's interest. By offering many different methods to interpret texts, we can make biblical studies "the property"[8] of as many learners as possible, so that they actively engage

---

[5] This is based on phone interviews and e-mail correspondences with heads of Judaic Studies or Bible teachers in eight community high schools in North America. While most of these schools do not teach the documentary hypothesis or source criticism at all, two of them study the assumptions of source criticism, but do not ask their students to practice applying them to texts.

[6] Part of a letter from a head of Judaic Studies at a pluralistic high school in the northeastern US.

[7] This is from a conversation with the aforementioned head of Judaic Studies.

[8] Israel Scheffler, "The Concept of the Educated Person," in *Visions of Jewish Education*, eds. S. Fox, I. Scheffler, and D. Marom (Cambridge: Cambridge University Press, 2003), 229.

with the texts and offer their own interpretive contributions. In the words of William Ayers,

> one of the main purposes of school is to open doors, open worlds, and open possibilities for each person to live life fully and well. Schools must provide students access to all the important literacies of our place and time, and it must help them develop the dispositions of mind that will allow them to be powerful in shaping and reshaping the future.[9]

Given the fraught nature of this material, there is almost no way for a student to maintain a passive relationship to the text. Thus, learning source criticism and processing its implications compel students to confront and think about texts in a new way. Students learn about concepts such as myth and how a myth is different from a historical report. This makes it possible for them to determine the "truths" of the text beyond historical fact, and what these "truths" might mean to them. Students are thereby "emancipated from the simple positivistic appreciation of the historical narratives as either truth or fabrication."[10] At Gann Academy, until twelfth grade students might have been able to maintain child-like attitudes with regard to the Bible, God, and Judaism, but as a result of being exposed to this source critical curriculum, they are more likely to begin developing adult versions of their beliefs.

In addition, while it is accurate that Jews have not historically read texts in this way, it is also true that certain commentators were already moving in this direction. Ibn Ezra is the most well known example of this, as he hinted in various places (see, for example, his comments on Deuteronomy 1:2; 34:1) that Moses did not write the Pentateuch.[11] Moreover, Jewish textual commentators have a history of bringing their

---

[9] William Ayers, *To Teach: The Journey of a Teacher* (New York: Teachers College Press, 2001), 61.

[10] Moshe Greenberg, "On Teaching the Bible in Religious Schools," *Jewish Education* 29 (1959): 238.

[11] Ibn Ezra, seemingly purposely, did not express his belief in a straightforward fashion. Nahum Sarna states, in "Ibn Ezra as Exegete," in *Studies in Biblical Interpretation* (Philadelphia: Jewish Publication Society, 2000), 153, that the commentator thought this information should stay in the hands of the elite. Ibn Ezra believed that those who knew it should remain silent; anyone who publicly doubted the Mosaic authorship of the Torah should be burned.

knowledge from the secular world to bear on their study of religious texts.[12] Two noteworthy examples are the Rashbam, who was unafraid to interpret the biblical text literally, as he would any other text, even if the meaning contradicted halakha,[13] and the Rambam, who sought to reconcile the Bible with current scientific knowledge.[14]

But what is most significant to note is that what gets classified as "a Jewish position" is always changing, as old traditions evolve and new traditions emerge. Most of the students at Gann, as at other pluralistic Jewish high schools, come from movements other than Orthodoxy, and the Reconstructionist, Reform, and Conservative movements all embrace the notion that human beings wrote or participated in the writing of the Torah as a core theological position, and accept the basic conclusions of the documentary hypothesis. It is part of the sacred responsibility of pluralistic Jewish high schools to represent and validate the positions of all the Jewish movements and thereby help as many students as possible feel connected to the material. Teaching only traditional understandings of the origins of the Torah risks isolating students from the philosophy of their movements, as well as rendering them without a framework to read and understand many ideas expressed in books that are found in the pews and libraries of the synagogues they attend.

Embracing Tensions in the Classroom

Even if teaching source criticism can be justified by the nature of the school's mission, the goal of religious growth for different types of students, and the evolution of what constitutes a Jewish approach, some educators legitimately worry about the effect of introducing volatile material into their school environment. More specifically, they are concerned that teaching this material might create tensions between Orthodox and non-Orthodox students and foster a contentious class-

---

[12] In Hellenistic times, Jews used methods of establishing and interpreting texts that were parallel to the Greek ways of reading classic texts. For a discussion of this see Saul Lieberman, *Hellenism and Jewish Palestine* (New York: Jewish Theological Seminary, 1950), 47-82.
[13] See Rashbam's comments to Gen. 1:5 and Exod. 21:1 and 22:6.
[14] Moses Maimonides, *The Guide of the Perplexed*, translated by Shlomo Pines (Chicago: University of Chicago Press, 1963), 327-328.

room environment, which is difficult for a teacher to handle and often unproductive pedagogically. Teaching is already a complex practice, and teaching provocative material that touches on students' basic beliefs makes it all the more so.

But while this content does create tensions in the classroom between students, and thus makes the teacher's job more challenging, these lively, tension-filled discussions are one of the marks of a pluralistic day school—and more generally, of an intellectual learning community. Negotiating differences and living with these tensions are part of the fabric of a pluralistic school; differences are to be acknowledged, challenged, and dealt with rather than ignored. A healthy amount and healthy type of tension leads to growth. By listening to and challenging one another, students become more aware of their own assumptions and beliefs, and begin to realize in what way those beliefs are satisfying, and in what ways they are not.

In addition, this same concern about the creation of tension could be raised in relation to any matter of belief or practice. Students trying to figure out together how they will observe the Sabbath will likely experience tension, yet in a community high school students learn how to create a Sabbath experience in which there is room for contrasting beliefs and practices. This same habit of mind should find its way into the classroom.

Extensive Exposure to the Documentary Hypothesis

Finally, there are some educators who are not concerned about the untraditional character of the material, and who recognize the value of surfacing different views rather than trying to conceal them, but who would suggest that even if it is important to teach students about the documentary hypothesis, their exposure need not be as extensive as it is at Gann. At one school, for example, twelfth-grade students are expected as part of independent research papers to read selected modern critical commentaries, so that they will have some experience reading and critiquing scholars' ideas. The hope behind this approach is that later in life, when students hear comments about how human beings wrote the Torah, they will not be caught totally unprepared. In addition, they will have had the opportunity, at least implicitly, to think about their reactions to the documentary hypothesis and to see, through the work of certain scholars, how source criticism works as a method for interpreting texts.

The potential implications of studying the documentary hypothesis are, however, far too religiously threatening to be treated so lightly. Learning this material can be a destabilizing religious experience for students. Teachers need to dedicate a significant amount of class time to providing students with opportunities to explicitly wrestle with the religious issues caused by studying the material. Students, for example, can explore their feelings through writing journal entries or short papers, as well as by discussing their ideas and personal conflicts in class. Without these opportunities to process their experience, students are left with some potentially disturbing new information, and are given no assistance with handling the consequences of it. While this might be easier for teachers, as they do not have to deal with the potentially destabilizing consequences of the material, the students are not well served by this approach.

Moreover, the documentary hypothesis and its conclusions can leave students quite confused if they are not given sufficient time to understand and evaluate both the method of source criticism as a tool for biblical interpretation and the claims of scholars about a particular text. A significant investment of time is required in order for students to understand the scholars' arguments sufficiently to apply the source critical method themselves.

Jewish community high schools that choose not to teach the documentary hypothesis run the risk of teaching "sacred texts without a philosophical attitude"—that is, teaching in a way that does not provide their students with the opportunity to appreciate the non-literal nature of the texts.[15] When they do so, Israel Scheffler argues, beliefs about the Bible are

> in danger of being received either as literal but incredible dogma, or as mere fairy tale, or as nonsense to be repeated with a pious

---

[15] Israel Scheffler, "Supplement to the Concept of the Educated Person: With Some Application to Jewish Education," in *Visions of Jewish Education*, eds. S. Fox, I. Scheffler, and D. Marom (Cambridge: Cambridge University Press, 2003), 234.

incomprehension that will not survive adult reflection. Certainly there are degrees of sophistication that must be apportioned suitably to the levels of maturity of the pupils. But adult teachers need to be philosophically prepared to provide at least tentative explanations upon demand, to respond to serious questions as to how this or that text is to be taken, even if such response consists only in further questions. Philosophy is in this sense no luxury but a vital necessity for cultural survival.[16]

Scheffler's argument suggests that teachers who do not provide their students with developmentally appropriate opportunities to interpret biblical texts with the aid of modern methods, including source criticism, run the risks of their students either interpreting texts literally or dismissing them as irrelevant, as simple stories that cannot withstand adult analysis.

Developmental Issues

It is of course still important to take into account the age of the learners to ensure that the material is taught in developmentally appropriate ways.[17] Teachers have to be aware of what students at this age are in a position to learn, what ideas will be easy for them to learn, what will be more challenging for them, and what goals and anxieties will get in the way of their learning. Bruner's contention that "intellectual activity anywhere is the same"[18] does not take into account the qualitative differences between the cognitive processes of the child and the adult; children are not simply miniature adults. Piaget, by contrast, has described the different stages that children go through as they mature. By early adolescence, children begin to develop formal operational thinking in which they can generate methods of verifying and testing hypotheses.[19] According to Erikson, they are also situated in the pe-

---

[16] Ibid.
[17] Ralph Tyler, *Basic Principles of Curriculum and Instruction* (Chicago: University of Chicago Press,1949), 37-38.
[18] Jerome Bruner, *The Process of Education* (Cambridge, MA: Harvard University Press, 1977), 14.
[19] Jean Piaget, *The Psychology of Intelligence* (New York: Harcourt Brace Jovanovich, 1950), 87-158.

riod of social development in which they are dealing with questions of identity.[20]

During early adolescence (ages 11-14), the authority for a teenager's beliefs resides principally with the authority figures, particularly parents, in her life (though in many cases they have been internalized to such an extent that they have become the learners' own beliefs).[21] At this stage, their beliefs are part of a tacit, unexamined system.[22] While some adults remain forever at this stage of religious development, most experience a disruption in late adolescence when they begin to realize the limits of literalism and/or they experience inconsistency between authority figures or a clash between an authority's beliefs and their own experiences.[23] The precipitation of this next stage is disorienting, as the learner can no longer rely on external sources of authority.

Learning the documentary hypothesis and the method of source criticism in twelfth grade is part of a larger process that pushes the students to the next stage of religious development. As students are transitioning to the next stage, a process of demythologization occurs as symbols lose some of their original meaning. There are, however, some gains as part of this process as well, for having reflected upon the symbols students develop and clarify new meanings.[24] It is thus a productive time for students to learn the documentary hypothesis. In addition, in this stage the locus of faith switches from being externally motivated to being internally motivated, and is thereby strengthened. Here again, learning the documentary hypothesis can help facilitate this switch, as students are compelled to figure out what they themselves believe. This learning is then part of what moves them onto the next stage of religious development.

Fowler describes the power of this movement, representing "a widening of vision and valuing, correlated with a parallel increase in the certainty and depth of selfhood, making for qualitative increases in intimacy with self-others-world."[25] In his opinion, this move is optimally

---

[20] Erik Erikson, *Identity: Youth and Crisis* (New York: W.W. Norton & Company, 1968), 128-135.
[21] James Fowler, *Stages of Faith* (San Francisco: HarperCollins, 1995), 157.
[22] Ibid., 161, 167.
[23] Ibid., 173.
[24] Ibid., 181.
[25] Ibid., 274.

made in young adulthood—precisely the age of twelfth graders—as it involves the person individuating and differentiating her self (identity) and worldview from those of others.[26]

It is invaluable for this faith questioning to happen when students are still in a supportive Jewish environment. Even if schools and families were able to shelter students during their high school years from learning about the documentary hypothesis, they will inevitably confront it elsewhere. The vast majority of the current and future communities in which these students participate accept the notion that the Torah is a compendium of writings from different schools of thoughts over a period of approximately four hundred years. Thus, they will soon encounter this approach either in a religious or a secular setting, in their synagogues or universities.

In addition, source criticism has been and continues to be an important interpretive tool for a substantial group of serious Jewish scholars. Since the conclusions of the documentary hypothesis are a part of academic discourse, a student's ability to understand these issues influences and increases his/her ability to participate in this discourse. The universities that the vast majority of our students attend often offer thriving academic Jewish studies programs in which the acceptance of the documentary hypothesis is commonplace. It is, ultimately, not only unrealistic but also counterproductive to shield students from this theory. More positively, teaching the documentary hypothesis can open up for community Jewish high school students—on the cusp of their graduation—the scholarly world of Jewish studies, which they can continue to explore during their college years.

Samantha, now a junior in college, writes:

> Learning the documentary hypothesis in 12th grade, discussing who wrote the Torah, and perhaps the entire approach of Bible study at The New Jewish High School [the previous name for Gann Academy] prepared me for the secular world and the bible classes I have taken and will take on a college level. I have found that I am more open to new ideas and understandings of biblical texts and constantly questioning it. I am never afraid to suggest an interpretation that may go against traditional and/or my own religious belief. I have the ability to study the text not only as a

---

[26] Ibid., 182.

religious and holy document, but also as a historical text. In a class about Ancient Israel, I was one of the only students who had even heard of the documentary hypothesis. Not only did it prepare me, but it has also sparked such a strong interest in my studies. I am double majoring in Religion and Politics and will be taking two bible classes next semester.

I am not suggesting, however, that a twelfth-grade Tanakh class at a Jewish community high school, which teaches the documentary hypothesis and the method of source criticism, should resemble an introductory course to biblical literature in a secular university; quite the contrary. Though the Hebrew texts are the same in each setting,[27] the pedagogical strategies are different, as is the surrounding context. Thus, a former student reflected on what the opportunities to grapple with this material meant to him:

> Our 12th grade class had a two-fold mission: to teach biblical criticism, but also to teach knowledgeable and passionate Jews how to understand and relate to biblical criticism. This second aspect is missing in a university course. Anyone can teach biblical criticism, but only Jewish day schools have the opportunity to teach young Jewish adults how to make such methods fit into their Jewish lives. The environment of our 12th grade class was a safe place where I was able to ask questions of the instructor, my peers and myself. I was confronted with very difficult material but was provided a forum in which to discuss how I felt about the material. I would say that we spent just as much time discussing how we felt about biblical criticism as actually learning what it was. And I can confidently say that these discussions are what helped me come to terms with what it is.

---

[27] This similarity, though, is not as meaningful as it might initially seem. After all, the lenses through which the texts are interpreted can be very different. For example, studying Exodus 3 through the lens of medieval Jewish exegesis versus the lens of form criticism will yield different foci and therefore different possible meanings of the text. While a Jewish exegete might focus on why God chose to appear in a burning bush, the form critic will compare Moses' call to prophecy with those of other prophets, such as Isaiah, Jeremiah, and Ezekiel. In addition, while the masoretic text is shared in the university and high school setting, in a college class the professor might suggest some textual emendations based on other textual witnesses, for example, the Septuagint. This would most likely not occur in a high school Tanakh class.

Jewish high schools, unlike universities, are institutions responsible for nurturing students' intellectual *and* spiritual lives, and are interested in and dedicated to supporting students' continued serious Jewish commitment. The high school setting affords each student the opportunity to wrestle with this theory and its implications and to talk about her reactions with teachers and peers, some of whom function as role models for grappling with important issues in sophisticated ways, and with whom she enjoys longstanding and potentially "safe" relationships. For these reasons, a Jewish high school is the ideal environment for first encountering this challenging information. It is educators' responsibility to help students tackle these questions and process the inevitable challenges in the midst of supportive Jewish communities.

An e-mail from another former student, Jason, now a junior in college, highlights some of the benefits of teaching the documentary hypothesis while students are still in high school:

> In our twelfth-grade Tanakh class at the New Jewish High School, we studied the Tanakh from an historical-critical perspective. I came to fully appreciate that experience only later on when I took a biblical studies course in college. During that course, my college friends struggled with the material far more than I did. I am confident in attributing my high level of comfort to the fact that I had previously been able to explore and learn about biblical authorship and related issues in the comfortable setting of a Jewish day school, when I was in high school.... My college classmates were quite confused by the material we were learning and found no place within the class to discuss how they felt; the content of the class raised many personal religious issues for them, but there was no forum in which to discuss them.

Conclusion

It is readily apparent why teaching the documentary hypothesis, and thereby often challenging long-held and/or traditional beliefs, is such a charged topic, and why students can experience discomfort with it. This discomfort is justifiable and even important. The teaching of the documentary hypothesis and the method of source criticism offers Tanakh teachers a profound curricular opportunity to engage their students in a dialogue around key biblical and religious issues, including the authorship and origin of the Torah. These conversations will elevate biblical texts, in the words of Israel Scheffler, beyond dogma or mere fairy tales. Without confronting the documentary hypothesis or source criticism more generally, students are easily left with naïve conceptions—or worse, discard Jewish sacred texts and find them irrelevant, unable to withstand serious intellectual inquiry. There is little long-term benefit to sheltering students and leaving them unprepared to deal with some of the religious issues they will continue to confront as they mature into adult members of the Jewish community.

Given all this, it is far riskier for Jewish high schools *not* to teach this material. Students naturally question the historicity, authorship, and authority of the text.[28] If these questions are met with defensive silence or inattention, the curricular material that students learn may not be incorporated into their thinking but instead kept segregated in their minds, useful for the purposes of a ceremonial occasion or the classroom. They too easily learn implicitly that the material is not worthy of serious thought.[29] Instead students' questions should be nurtured, entertained—even provoked—and responded to meaningfully.[30] Students should have the opportunity to consider the status and authority of biblical texts in an environment that encourages and values their questions and treats them seriously, so that the knowledge will not be inert, learned only for the purpose of an examination, but will enter actively into the student's perceptual engagement with the world.[31]

Jason, reflecting on his experience studying the documentary hypothesis at Gann Academy, writes:

> I have actually become more observant since I first learned about biblical criticism. I would not go as far as saying that I have become more observant specifically because of learning biblical criticism,

---

[28] Greenberg, "On Teaching the Bible in Religious Schools," 46, and my years of teaching experience.

[29] Scheffler, "Supplement to the Concept of the Educated Person," 230. In addition, if, in their twelve years of Jewish education students do not confront the idea that the Torah is a human product, once they are exposed to this idea, they might feel that they have been lied to.

[30] An example of a relevant question might be: if God did not write the text, what is the source of its continued value for the student?

[31] Scheffler, "Supplement to the Concept of the Educated Person," 223.

but I will say that reconciling biblical criticism with traditional Judaism has helped me build a stronger Judaism for myself. My new Judaism is a Judaism that does not hide from theories which could undermine it. Rather, it is a fearless and intellectually honest Judaism which accepts the realities we see as an intrinsic part of the overall Jewish experience and our overall human experience with God.

Despite the complexities involved, teaching the documentary hypothesis is, for all different types of students, a beneficial and even necessary part of the curriculum at a pluralistic Jewish high school. It offers students openings to continue crafting their own theologies, establishing their own relationship to Jewish sacred texts, and envisioning their own Jewish lives.

11 Developing Student Awareness of the Talmud as an Edited Document: A Pedagogy for the Pluralistic Jewish Day School

Jeffrey Spitzer

Talmud is a unique literature, and in many ways it takes the novice student by surprise. I have often initiated students into the study of Talmud by asking them, "What do you think the Talmud does when two rabbis contradict each other?" The first answer is usually, "It says which one's right." More sophisticated students say, "It says why that one's right." The most sophisticated students suggest, "They try to find a compromise." The responses to the answer I give—"It shows why both are right"—are varied. Again, the less sophisticated students ask, "Why doesn't it tell you what to do?" and the more sophisticated students ask, "If the rabbis are contradicting each other, how can they both be right?" Only once did I have a student simply ask, "Why would it do that?"

I assume that most teachers of Talmud have come across this kind of response from beginning students. For some students it is because they think of the Talmud work as "the great classical work of Jewish law"; others come to Talmud study with a preconception based on their previous study of or exposure to halakha or *dinim*, decided Jewish law. Talmud, however, is decidedly not a law code.

When students are exposed to the *shaqla ve-tarya*, the dialogical give and take of talmudic discussion, they frequently assume that it is like a screenplay. I've even heard experienced teachers present this model to their students: "It's like you're being transported back to the yeshiva in Pumbedisa!" It is true that generations of studying Talmud have created cultures in which discussions like those in the gemara get acted out in real time; in some ways, those discussions are extensions of the talmudic process. But the Talmud itself is a highly edited document with a very serious and subtle editorial agenda.

My goal as a teacher is to introduce my students to Talmud in a way that is engaging, so that they want to continue studying—and the most engaging approach that I have discovered is by not hiding or glossing over but by highlighting the sophistication and complexity of the text. I want my students to live in conversation with our sages of blessed memory, but also in conversation with the editors of the Talmud, who inherited a tradition and reshaped it for the generations to come. The challenges facing the editors of the Talmud are comparable to the challenges facing us as teachers of rabbinic literature, and comparable to the challenges which our students will face as future members and leaders of the Jewish community. Our curriculum pushes students to address those challenges—setting priorities for the distribution of limited communal funds, our relationship with Israel, the shape of Jewish identity—by engaging classical texts in a spirit of conversation. As we teachers struggle with decisions about which texts to select, our students struggle with decisions about which texts to privilege in conversations about big Jewish issues; we all emulate the editors of the Talmud by engaging in a creative process of selection and reshaping the conversational Torah for the next generation.

Trusting My Students as Readers

My ninth-grade introduction to Talmud class at Gann Academy, which I have taught for several years, is generally composed of strong students from a variety of backgrounds: most of the students come from two local Conservative day schools, a community day school, and an Orthodox day school. Occasionally some students are from a Reform day school. They have reasonably good Hebrew translation skills, some background in Mishnah,[1] and a little exposure to isolated passages from the Talmud. (The minority of students from Orthodox day schools have more exposure to Talmud than the others.) We study from Tractate Berakhot, using the "Vilna Shas" (the standard printed edition of the Babylonian Talmud, a.k.a. "the Bavli") and a coursepack that I've prepared which includes some vocabulary, questions for guided study, and additional

---

[1] In accord with accepted usage, I capitalize "Mishnah" when referring to the larger work in its entirety, and use "mishnah" when referring to a single unit of the larger work.

talmudic sources. Although I place a strong emphasis on developing text skills, my focus here will be on how students develop a conception of Talmud as a literature—specifically, as an edited text.

I begin our study of Berakhot with the first mishnah. In this famous mishnah, the children of Rabban Gamliel return home late from a party and report to their father that, in apparent violation of the ruling of the sages, they neglected to recite the Shema by midnight. When the students reach this point, I ask them whether the children knew their father's opinion that one is obligated to recite until dawn, or that the opinion of the sages is simply a "fence around the Torah" (*siyag la-torah*). With the one exception of a group of students who had already studied the gemara on this mishnah, I have never had a student who assumed that the children knew their father's opinion. Indeed, I believe the *peshat*, the plain and obvious meaning of this mishnah in its own context, is that the children did not know their father's opinion.

We then proceed to two related questions: why had Rabban Gamliel not told them his opinion prior to this, and why does he choose to tell them now? After a lot of discussion, I usually share with them my own reading; they don't come to this position on their own. My reading is that the *siyag la-torah*, a fence around the Torah, is a very dangerous concept. Once you find out that what you thought was the law was simply a fence around the Torah, you open up the possibility that people will begin questioning any and all aspects of Jewish law. Maybe four sets of dishes is only a *siyag*? If the halakha lets me have a second chance, why can't I just do that in the first place? Knowing about this basic aspect of rabbinic activity is dangerous and potentially subversive, so it is quite reasonable that Rabban Gamliel might want to hold off on letting people in on this secret.

So why does he let them in on it now? I speculate that it is because his children demonstrated that they were mature. Coming home late from a party, they could have sneaked up the back stairs and gone to bed, or they could have greeted their father with a, "Great party, Dad, but we're zonked. See you in the morning." But what they do is say, "We didn't recite the Shema," apparently unprompted and without any apparent motivation other than to be honest. At this point, Rabban Gamliel realizes his children are mature and responsible, and he tells them about *siyag latorah*, and *le-khat'chilah* and *b'di'avad* (ideal and sufficient—that

Developing Student Awareness of the Talmud as an Edited Document

is, respectively, the articulated standard before the fact and the minimal standard that fulfills the requirement after the fact).

What is more, the editor of the Mishnah chooses not to start this particular mishnah with the basics of what the Shema is, but (implicitly) with this potentially subversive concept, and with this tale of how teachers are transformed by the awareness that their students can be trusted with dangerous knowledge. The Mishnah recognizes that some people are not necessarily ready to study rabbinic law from the inside, but it welcomes those who are studying this mishnah as part of the "in crowd," with an assertion of trust that the students will indeed treat rabbinic law with care and not abuse the knowledge that comes from understanding the sources of the law. As we study this text, I in turn tell my students directly and without ambiguity, "You are in this class, and it will change how you understand Jewish law, and it will give you powerful tools, and I trust you enough to let you inside, and let you read for yourselves."

Exposing students to this level of complexity in the first mishnah in Berakhot introduces many of the skills that students will be asked to apply to talmudic texts throughout the year. This reading of the mishnah highlights the way rabbinic texts combine legal statements with narratives. Reading the mishnah with a sense of the drama of Rabban Gamaliel's decision to let his children "inside" raises questions about who knows what, and it assumes that, like a drama, the text is carefully composed in order to create a particular kind of reaction in its readers. This approach assumes an active and creative editor of the Mishnah. These assumptions inform how students understand the talmudic texts they study later in the year. In addition, the extension of my trust in the students raises an expectation that their readings of talmudic texts are significant and important, and demand a level of seriousness that they may not have previously considered.

Berakhot 19a: Excommunication for an Affront to the Dignity of a Rabbi

We then continue our study of Berakhot with the end of the second chapter on 17b, dealing with exceptionalism and the concept of *yohara*, pious arrogance, and then the third chapter, which deals with the topic of *kavod*, dignity, in a variety of different ways. The latter chapter begins with *k'vod ha-met*, the dignity of the dead body, and *k'vod ha-avel*, the dignity of the mourner. By February, we arrive at a fascinating *sugya* on Berakhot 19a dealing with *niddui al k'vod ha-rav*, excommunication for an affront to the dignity of a rabbi.

Rabbi Yehoshua ben Levi asserts that there are 24 cases in the Mishnah of excommunication for an affront to a rabbi, and R. Elazar asks where these cases are, and suggests three cases. Then the anonymous voice of the Gemara, the *stam* (the editorial level of the gemara), presents selected versions of the alleged cases of excommunication and then suggests two additional cases.

By the time we study this *sugya*, the students have already become accustomed to identifying the four historical layers of the Talmud. Whether they use markers or highlight the text on their computers using Word, the students routinely use the method I've taught them in class (coordinating colors with different strata, and using the initial sounds as mnemonic devices): marking *pesukim* (biblical verses) with pink, *baraitot* (non-mishnaic tannaitic sources) and mishnayot with blue, the Gemara of the amoraim in green, and the *stam* with (sunshine) yellow. They know to look for technical terms as keys for the flow of the argument. In this case, the highlighting looks easy. R. Yehoshua ben Levi already announced that we were looking for cases in the Mishnah.

When they study this *sugya*, I have them compare how our Gemara on 19a presents the case (what I call "the front story") with the source for the case (what I call "the back story").[2] When students compare and contrast the front and back stories, they come to some interesting conclusions.

According to the front story, Akavia ben Mehalalel is excommunicated for having made some kind of negative posthumous aspersions about Shemaiah and Avtalion. According to the back story, Akavia is excommunicated for his intransigence concerning his four traditions. Ironically, according to the back story in Mishnah Eduyot, Akavia is excommunicated because he shows exceptional deference to the rabbi who taught him his traditions; he has too much *kavod ha-rav*, not too little. When I ask the students to explain what happened, they quickly

---

[2] The "back stories" are found in Mishnah Eduyot, Mishnah Ta'anit, Tosefta Betzah, Mishnah Kelim, and Babylonian Talmud Bava Metzia 59b.

determine that selective citation of the mishnah changes the focus from Akavia's stubborn fidelity to tradition to his apparent disrespect toward Shemaiah and Avtalion.

According to the front story of Honi haM'agel, he is threatened with excommunication for being obnoxious toward God, which Rashi glosses with the comment that God's dignity is like a rabbi's dignity. In the back story, my students come up with all kinds of reasons for his threatened excommunication, like his flooding Jerusalem, or his lack of consideration for the consequences of his actions, none of which appear in the front story. But they also point out that even in the front story, the claim that Honi acts petulantly toward God is part of Shimon ben Shetach's explanation of why the rabbis don't dare excommunicate him, not a reason for his excommunication.

In the case of Todos, the students are first struck by the repeated appearance of Shimon ben Shetach and his use of almost identical language with Todos as he used with Honi.[3] When they look up the back story from Tosefta Betzah, they are usually stunned to see that the material that so closely resembles the mishnah about Honi from tractate Ta'anit doesn't actually appear anywhere in Tosefta Betzah. In fact, in the Tosefta, no rabbi ever interacts with Todos; he is cited as a support for Rabban Gamliel's minority position concerning roasting a *gedi mekulas* (a whole lamb) for Passover, and the rabbis critique his position, but it makes no reference whatsoever to excommunication. When faced with this case, each time I teach this class, the students rapidly arrive at the obvious conclusion: the editor has manipulated his source and imported the language from the Honi story into the Todos story.

After studying these texts for about two weeks, we pause to process. It is one thing to selectively cite a source, my students assert. It is quite another thing to radically manipulate a source and make it say something that it doesn't. Students frequently find this confusing; some students find it disturbing.

---

[3] Manuscripts (which I display to the class) exclude the reference to Shimon ben Shetach but still repeat the language from Mishnah Taanit. I don't show my students the Jerusalem Talmud's version (which is closer to the Bavli's), but does not solve the underlying question of how the Tosefta's tradition is transformed.

The processing session forces students to reflect on what they think they know about rabbinic literature. Earlier in the year, students study Mishnah Eduyot, chapter 1, including the claim that "one must speak in the language of his teacher" (1:3), and they usually raise this as well as other claims from Mishnah Avot 1:1 about the idea of *mesorah*—the ongoing, accurate transmission of tradition. They have also studied the *sugya* at the end of chapter 2 of Berakhot on *yohara*, where R. Yochanan suggests that the attribution of positions in a mishnah have been accidentally switched.[4] Students usually raise this example, but just as quickly dismiss it. Students realize that there is a big difference between errors in transmission and conscious manipulation. Some students express a kind of diffuse anger at the editor, some are simply puzzled, and others seem to take it in stride. Most years, someone remarks, "How could he do this? Wouldn't he get caught?" This serves as a perfect introduction to the topic of the paper that they write on this *sugya*:

> Did the editor of this *sugya* believe that his readers knew the back stories or did not know the back stories, and how does that affect what you think the point of this *sugya* is?

Although this short-circuits the emotional response of the students who are upset, I prefer to have students attempt to identify the editor's intent with regard to the *sugya* as a whole rather than respond to this one particular case. I want each student to grapple with the challenge of what appears to be an intentional change of the tradition; to expand their conceptions of the rabbinic enterprise in order to enter into the mind of the editor and think about what might motivate someone to manipulate a source; and to be prepared to reconstruct a vision of what tradition means. Writing a paper gives them that opportunity. (Developmentally, ninth graders are still close to middle-school conceptions of honesty and dishonesty, and asking them this larger question helps them confront the editor with a somewhat more sympathetic eye.)

---

[4] R. Yohanan's response to the double, internal contradiction is to suggest that the transmission of the tannaitic tradition is faulty. The typical response, present in the *sugya* by R. Shisha, rejects R. Yohanan's text-criticism and suggests reinterpretation instead. Both approaches provide models for student interpretation of the *niddui sugya*.

The expansion of their concept of the rabbinic enterprise comes with the study of the fifth and final case, the excommunication of Rabbi Eliezer over the *tanuro shel Akhnai* (the Akhnai Oven, Babylonian Talmud Bava Metzia 59b). This case is particularly complex, since the front story, which simply refers to the excommunication of Rabbi Eliezer, is hard to understand as a case of *niddui al k'vod ha-rav* without knowledge of the back story, which describes Rabbi Eliezer calling down miracles and even God's voice to defend his intransigent defiance of the other sages on an issue of purity law. This story presents a rabbinic self-conception even more radical than the revision of the Todos story. Rabbi Joshua asserts the independence of the rabbis from God's direct intervention by radically misquoting Deuteronomy 30:12, "It is not in heaven," and Rabbi Jeremiah glosses Rabbi Joshua's comment by claiming that the rabbis are empowered to determine the law according to majority rule based on his misquotation of Exodus 23:2 as "follow after the majority."[5] Furthermore, the conclusion of the back story seems to argue against excommunication, since Rabban Gamaliel is struck down by heaven at the conclusion of the story for his ruthless treatment of Rabbi Eliezer. Both the radical claim of autonomy and the tragic conclusion of the aggada in the back story shape how students read the *sugya*. When we finish it, students have about two more weeks to sort through all of the evidence and write their papers.

The Students and the Editor

Having looked at how the learning generally proceeds, I will now focus on the experience and work product of a particular ninth-grade class, during the 2006-2007 academic year. All of the following citations are from papers produced by those students.

For those of us with training in reading classical Jewish texts, some assumption of rabbinic intertextuality or at least talmudic intertextuality is usually a given. But by adopting a pedagogy that trusts a student to compare and contrast without imposing the assumption that the

---

[5] This reading of Bava Metzia 59b follows Daniel Boyarin, *Intertextuality and the Reading of Midrash* (Indianapolis: Indiana University Press, 1990), 34-36. Students are asked to prepare the biblical verses as homework preceding the class when they read Rabbi Joshua's emphatic claim of rabbinic autonomy.

texts need to be harmonized, students are forced to confront the editor as a creator of meaning through the sometimes radical reworking of tannaitic texts. In her paper on whether the editor assumed his readers did or did not know the back stories and how that affects our understanding of the *sugya*, Leah[6] wrote:

> Much of the Gemara is devoted to finding the "truths" that govern our lives. In the case of Todos, the editor makes a clear choice to willfully corrupt the "truth," in order to maintain the principle of *k'vod harav*. I think that this shows how important a concept *k'vod harav* is, even if it does not lead to *nidui*.

This comment needs unpacking. We can presume that Leah's first step is to recognize that in some way, the manipulation and reformulation of the *baraita* from Tosefta Betzah was a "corruption" of the truth. It is not clear whether she assumes that the Tosefta's version was historically true or not; even the introduction of the language from Mishnah Ta'anit into the Bavli's version of the Todos *baraita* would have been a corruption. But then Leah tries to integrate her awareness into a larger conception of the traditionality of the editor. In her construction, the editor's willingness to "corrupt" the source is a "choice" that "shows how important a concept *k'vod harav* is." Finally, Leah makes a judgment about the nature of the Gemara itself, which she highlights as the introduction to her paragraph: "Much of the Gemara is devoted to finding the 'truths' that govern our lives."[7] This use

---

[6] All of the names of students are pseudonyms. The student authors of the papers cited have all provided consent for the use of their work in this study. Spelling errors and ungrammatical usage have also been preserved.

[7] David also argued that the editor's manipulation of the Todos *baraita* shows the seriousness with which he held the concept of *kvod ha-rav*, although he did not go as far in making a global judgment about the gemara:

> I think that the editor thinks that cvod harav is very important, thus is viable grounds for excommunication. To emphasize this, the editor brings many cases for *nidui al kvod harav* that simply do not exist. This shows that he thinks it important enough to try to bring cases that prove its seriousness and importance, too, even if they are fabricated or selectively quoted.

Against Leah, David concludes that the editor believes that *nidui al k'vod ha-rav* is justified.

Developing Student Awareness of the Talmud as an Edited Document

of the possessive plural "our" clearly indicates that Leah sees herself and her classmates as the intended readers of the text who are meant to learn great truths.

Other students more directly assess the editor's assumption about his readers. A striking claim by Dov reveals somewhat less reverence for the Gemara, but his insight is quite astute:

> Although, making such obvious changes to text may seem stupid, the editor is actually quiet [sic] clever. He knew that even without any historical or even seemingly real evidence supporting his statements, they would still be accepted as true, simply because of the attitude towards mishna like materials.... The editor counted on this faith in religious text to use false evidence and prove his points in this *sugyah*. He knew that instead of disproving the piece he wrote, rabbis would either ignore or do whatever possible to explain the inconsistencies in the Talmud.

Dov sees the editor as clever and manipulative, relying on his readers' assumptions about authority and traditionality.[8] (In class, Dov went further, arguing that the editor has a personal interest in manipulating the sources that emphasize coercive social power in order to support his own demand for respect.)[9]

For Ariana, even the front stories as they appear in Babylonian Talmud Berakhot 19a are weak, in that they don't actually present cases of excommunication from the Mishnah.[10]

> The way he compiled it makes it so that even if you have never read any of the back stories before, you could see how weak the

---

[8] Interestingly, Dov's primary argument about this kind of traditional harmonization comes from his reaction to Rashi's comment about the *baraita* on Honi—that Honi's petulance toward God is actually a case of *k'vod harav*.

[9] Similarly, Nehemiah (another student) wrote:
> This makes me think, if I am right, then the editor is willing to do whatever is needed to prove his point, so what if he did this in other parts of the Talmud, and if he did, should we always be wary of the editors influence's on the text?

[10] Of the mishnaic cases, only one of the first two cases can be true, and Honi is threatened with *nidui*. Of the non-mishnaic cases, Todos is threatened (repeating the language from the Honi text), and Eliezer is excommunicated.

cases of *k'vod harav* are. Then, if you were compelled to investigate the direct sources or had studied them in the past, you would truly recognize and understand that Rav Yehoshua ben Levi's statement was false, and that *nidui al k'vod harav* is not at all a common occurrence.

That is, although the back stories support her claim that the editor is opposed to excommunication, one could already come to that conclusion just based on the paucity of evidence of supporting Rabbi Yehoshua ben Levi's claim that there are twenty-four cases in the Mishnah.

Faced with evidence that R. Yehoshua ben Levi's contention is contradicted by the evidence of the back stories, several students come to a very talmudic conclusion: *La kashya*, there is no contradiction—the editor intended both to support *k'vod harav* and to delegitimize excommunication. When considering whether the readers would know the back stories, these students came to the conclusion that some would and some would not. Alex wrote:

> My theory is that the editor is trying to reach the beginning students to the Talmud and the great scholars who have been learning the texts for years in different ways.[11] ... The new students to the Talmud would just see these front stories and take from them that *niddui al k'vod harav* is extremely necessary and that it should be top priority for them. They would never know that these cases are not exactly what they seem.... However, the great scholars would look at the whole story and come to the same conclusion I came to and say that there really is no basis to the niddui al K'vod harav cases, so it must not be so important.

---

[11] Akiva (another student) also argues that only the learned may be aware of the back stories:

> By looking at the front stories it appears that *nidui* is a practiced realty and a just rabbinical punishment. However by bringing in the back-story the editor is hinting to us that there are very few cases of actual *nidui*. The editor was aware of both stories and fashioned them two [sic.] show the learned that even though by law *nidui* [is] an OK thing it is not implemented very often.

Akiva does not explicitly claim that the front stories are intended for new students, as Alex, Michael, and Joseph do.

Developing Student Awareness of the Talmud as an Edited Document

That is, by design, the editor wrote for two audiences: younger students, who need to learn the value of *k'vod ha-rav* and would be convinced by the *sugya* in Berakhot that *k'vod harav* is of paramount importance, and more experienced talmudists who, according to Alex, would conclude that *nidui al k'vod ha-rav* has "no basis." It is worth noting that Alex understood that our methodology in class was something different than what beginning students do. He saw himself in the company of the great scholars of Talmud, and saw this kind of study as authentic.

Joseph came to a similar reading but drew a more general conclusion:

> I think that [the editor's] choice to show the severity of *nidui al k'vod harav* to those new to stud[y]ing Talmud and those who don't know the back stories was to send them the message that *k'vod harav* is one of the most important concepts in our religion. On the other hand, it seems like the editor could have been trying to tell the more learned individuals that one of the great things about our religion is to speak up, and go against the authorities, provided it is in a polite and mannered way.

For Joseph, new students should be compliant, but the goal of learning is to be able to speak up in dissent. In this, he has gone farther than Alex; not only should one learn that excommunication is illegitimate, but one should also learn that the goal of Talmud study is to empower one to speak up for truth even against the authority of a rabbi, as long as it is done with *kavod*. It is probably not too much of a leap to say that Joseph identifies with the values of the editor, struggling to navigate between faithfulness to tradition and individual expression.

For all of these students, the meaning of this *sugya* extended beyond the typical question of what makes one liable for excommunication, or how it is that R. Yehoshua b. Levi could make his claim about twenty-four cases. The process question about editorial intent, and the exercise of looking at how the editor of the gemara uses and manipulates sources, expanded their sense of the relevance of the text. With this approach, this *sugya*—in both content and process—is understood as being engaged with issues of authority and community and respect for learning, and the responsibility that comes with learning.

Jeffrey Spitzer

The *Sugya* on Human Dignity

Turning to the next *sugya* (Berakhot 19b-20a), we began our study of *k'vod ha-briyot*, human dignity. This *sugya* presents Rav's claim that preventing a *hillul Hashem*, a desecration of God's name, overrides concerns of *kavod*. Rav's claim is challenged five times with five *baraitot*, each of which at face level claims that *kavod* overrides some Torah law. In the first three cases, the *baraitot* are reinterpreted with *okimtot*, limiting or narrowing readings, which state that what is described only puts *kavod* over rabbinic legislation, not law considered *d'oraita* (law which the rabbis consider having the authority of Torah). The last two cases narrow the definition of *hillul Hashem* to progressively narrower areas of violation of Torah law.

As the students studied this *sugya*, they marked up the text according to its historical layers. Then, as a paper topic, I asked them to assess whether the editor of the *sugya* agrees with Rav's claim that preventing a *hillul Hashem* overrides *kavod* or not. Students used a variety of different strategies to assess the editor's intention:

- They looked at the literary structure of the *sugya* and the sequencing of the arguments.

- They made comparisons with parallel treatments in the Jerusalem Talmud.

- They made judgments concerning which materials they assume might have existed in an earlier version of the Talmud and what the editor must have added.

- They contrasted the *sugya* with their reading of the *aggadot*, the narratives which follow the *sugya*.

- They compared their assumptions about the editor to what they knew of talmudic literature in general.

My analysis of the students' papers here will focus on how they imagined the work of the editor.

Some students made arguments about the perceived weakness of the *okimtot* of the *baraitot* that ostensibly remove the challenges to Rav's statement. Leah wrote:

Developing Student Awareness of the Talmud as an Edited Document

> The *okimta* comes to the conclusion, that the place that the *baraita* stated was impure, is only *tameh derabanan* [rabbinically impure]. This makes sense. However, the *okimta* then continues with "beit hapras shenidash tahor" [a *beit hapras* which is trodden down is pure].[12] ... Adding that the area is actually pure undermines the baraita, because there is no dispute in the first place. This is because a Cohen is able to walk through a pure area from the start.... [The] amoraic treatment of the *baraita*, before this problematic comment about a trodden graveyard being pure, is indirectly in support of Rav.... If the Stam agreed with Rav, then the *baraita* would end with the *okimta* that was consistent with the [Rav's] statement. But because the Stam chooses to leave the comment of "beit hapras shenidash tahor," we can figure that the Stam does not agree with Rav.

Leah's argument is complex; essentially, she claims that the amoraic *okimta* to the first *baraita* is adequate, but that the stam's imported support for the amoraic comment actually weakens the *okimta* by reducing the *baraita* to a meaningless claim. In this, and in other cases of what she perceives to be "weak" *okimtot*, Leah finds evidence that the editor does not actually agree with Rav.

Alex, whom we recall identified two audiences in the excommunication *sugya*, suggests the same approach in this *sugya*:

> In this *sugya*, the editor brings in a lot of evidence going against the *baraitot*, so the inexperienced reader would see all of this evidence and believe that the editor agrees with Rav and that *hillul Hashem* is more important the (sic.) *kavod*. However, the experienced Talmud learner would recognize that the editor brings in weak evidence so they might believe that the editor really does not agree with Rav.

---

12 That is, the Talmud is trying to show why a kohen going through an impure place is not a *hillul Hashem*; all R. Abba had to do was identify the *baraita* as referring to a *bet hapras*, which is only rabbinically impure. If one needs to demonstrate that a *bet hapras* is only rabbinically impure, the first editorial gloss (that one may blow pieces of impurity away) is adequate. Leah realized that the second editorial gloss (that a trodden *bet hapras* is pure) actually weakens the *okimta*. If the path through which the kohen is following the mourner is pure, what has the *baraita* taught?!

Michael is more explicit about how the aggadic text presents a voice counter to the halakhic *sugya*:

> A student of Rav, [Ada bar] Ahava acted on what he thought was Hillul Hashem, as he saw a woman wearing shatnez.... [H]e ripped off her clothes in public, causing her unbelievable embarrassment. [Ada bar] Ahava thought he was acting correctly as that is what his teacher, Rav, had taught him. Unfortunately for Ada, the woman whose clothes he ripped off was not Jewish. Instead of acting in the name of G-d, he grossly violated a woman's dignity. [Ada bar] Ahava was fined a great amount and the whole situation was very costly to him. This story puts Rav in a very negative light, as by following him, his student got into serious trouble.... The editor must have known this story while creating the *sugya*, thus causing him not to agree with Rav's statement completely.

Ariana also read the story of Ada bar Ahava as an indictment of Rav's position and as an indication of the editor's true opinion:

> Ada bar Ahava followed Rav's principle, and the result was the humiliation of a woman as well as being fined 400 zuz. Once again this seems to be the editor's subtle way of communicating his true feelings. At first glance Rav's student is portrayed in a good light, being faithful and dutiful to God's will, however, upon a closer examination, one realizes how important *kavod* truly is.

The editor's motivation in not stating directly his opposition and allowing the *baraitot* to overturn Rav's claim was clear to Ariana:

> In order to guard the Torah commandments and to keep people from using *kavod* as an excuse, the editor chooses not to reveal the fact that some cases of *kavod* supersede even negative Torah commandments.

Ariana, who was not convinced by her classmate's conception that there may have been two potential audiences in the *nidui sugya*, went to great lengths to find an analogue for her claim that the editor did not want to be open about his "true opinion." She cited Mishnah Berakhot

1:1, where Rabban Gamliel did not reveal the concept of *siyag la-Torah* to his children: [13]

> Just as in this case [concerning the time for reciting the Shema], the editor of Berakhot 19b 20a is choosing not to reveal all of the information. Instead, he is pushing the limit back a little further than he knows it is, so that generally people put their d'orraita obligations as first priority. Then, should they recognize an extenuating circumstance, perhaps they could be informed of what the true rule is.

Ariana's comparisons to other rabbinic texts are used to find support for her claim that the editor wanted to conceal his true intentions.

What limits the editor's creativity and power? David imagines some sense of tradition that binds the editor; most of the *baraitot*, he claims, were already collected around the theme of death and mourning. He does not create the *sugya* out of whole cloth.

> Which *baraitot* are chosen reflects on the editor's perspective in several ways. Firstly, four of the *baraitot* relate to death, the topic of the preceding mishnah.... This tells how the editor probably did not bring in these statements, [and] ... brings attention to the third baraita, "Gadol Cavod Ha-briyot," which was obviously added.

Since the third *baraita*, "So great is human dignity that it overrides a negative Torah commandment," is the only *baraita* that does not include

---

[13] She also found a passage from BB 89b in Michael Katz and Gershon Schwartz, *Swimming in the Sea of Talmud* (Philadelphia: Jewish Publication Society, 1997), which is used in the class as outside reading:

> Rabban Yohanan ben Zakkai said, "Woe to me if I speak, woe to me if I don't speak. If I speak, perhaps deceivers will learn; if I don't speak, perhaps the deceivers will say, 'The scholars are not experts in what we do!'" (*Swimming in the Sea of Talmud*, p. 253) Rabban Yohanan ben Zakkai did not want to forbid using the leveling rod unfairly, for he feared that in doing so, he would bring the idea out into the open, and give people ideas of how to cheat their customers. Similarly, the editor would not have wanted to give people the idea that they could easily disregard their d'orraita obligation. By saying that kavod takes precedence, the editor would be opening a possibility for people who did not want to perform their obligations to make excuses in the name of kavod.

a reference to death, David argues, it was brought by the editor into this context of *baraitot* on the theme of death and mourning. Since the issue of *kavod* defines this *sugya* and death does not, David imagines that the editor can create meaning by recontextualizing the materials which had been gathered initially to expand the mishnah's discourse on death.

Joseph draws a much larger methodological point about the limits upon the editor.

> But, we know that the Stam's views must also fit with those of the Rabbis before him, HaZal. Our definitions of *hillul Hashem* also must fit the realms of practicality. The Editor's goal must be to create an understanding of *hillul Hashem* that is reasonable for the community to act upon, but also one that fits within the guidelines of our Rabbis.

From Joseph's perspective, the editor is bound not just by the texts of the tradition, but by his expectations about the community and by his responsibility to rabbinic culture, or, as he describes it, "the guidelines of our Rabbis."

These students used a wide range of approaches to determine what the editor of this *sugya* intended. Although they all had different degrees of reservation about a straight, traditional reading of this *sugya*, the practical conclusions that they drew from their analysis varied widely. What is apparent from all of their papers, however, is an appreciation of the artistry of the editing of the Talmud, a sensitivity to the multivocality of the tradition in both its halakhic and aggadic voices, an awareness that the text of the Talmud reveals hints about its own history, a self-assurance in their own ability to make judgments about what they read, and an eagerness to engage in an authentic conversation with the text of the Talmud about issues that matter.

An Awareness of the Editing of the Talmud and the Pluralistic Day School

The readings that these students develop are startling, and from some perspectives, they are probably disturbing. In many (probably most) educational contexts in which Talmud is studied, such readings would not be allowed. I do not merely "allow" such readings; I foster them, and revel in their creativity and complexity. It is precisely by encouraging my students to see themselves as creative and competent readers of Talmud that they come to see engagement with rabbinic texts as challenging and worthwhile. As a practical matter, I am not concerned that students who otherwise would not violate *d'oraita* law will begin to do so, or that they will start showing disrespect to rabbis simply because they realize that they will not be excommunicated. Rather, because they have been forced to confront an editor who takes both *hillul Hashem* and *k'vod harav* very seriously, students at Gann are perhaps more capable of understanding and valuing those concepts.

Gann Academy's mission statement includes the claim that the school "challenges our students to understand and interpret Judaism as a source of religious obligation." A traditionalist conception of that religious obligation is usually expressed in terms of a claim that the *mesorah*, the textual materials of our tradition, are passed along faithfully and accurately and therefore make a claim of authority. While students in my class frequently conclude that the editor of the Bavli manipulates his sources, they have also been exposed to rabbinic claims of traditionality, such as the chain of tradition in Avot 1:1, Mishnah Eduyot's claim that materials need to be transmitted accurately, and the story of Akavia's stubborn adherence to tradition. By introducing the Talmud as an edited document, and by encouraging students to analyze the motives of the editor, this class challenges my students to confront the claims of the *mesorah* in a very real way.

In my classroom, student interpretation is seen as the medium through which students confront that claim of religious obligation. At the same time, a pluralistic Jewish learning community requires nurturing so that the authentic voices of all students can emerge. Their voices, expressed in class discussion, provide a valuable social context in which they process these talmudic texts. Confronting the interpretations of their peers operates both at the level of what we might refer to as "what the text meant" in its original context as shaped by the *stam*, as well as "what the text means" to contemporary readers. In a pluralistic school, they are trained to hear both traditional claims and not-so-traditional claims with a sense of respect.

This conception of *mesorah*—valuing both reverence in receiving tradition and creativity in conversation with it—is not the only model that my students experience. My colleagues can, and sometimes actively do, try to unteach what they perceive to be the erroneous approach that students learn in my class. I do not mind this at all; we're a team, and none of my colleagues are out to eliminate the sense of ownership and engagement that my students develop. My colleagues may disagree on the contour of the conversation, but we all agree that nothing happens without the conversation.

What brings a school community like ours together is not agreements about halakhic norms or Jewish philosophy, but a commitment to argue passionately and respectfully about the great ideas, and with the great ideas, that come out of our classical texts. All members of our community must feel that they can be part of that passionate and respectful conversation, and that participation in the conversation matters—which can only happen when people learn to read responsibly, using all of their acquired skills, and to trust in their ability, individually and collectively, to read.

These exercises in thinking about the editor of the Talmud also force students to confront the many contradictory voices in rabbinic tradition. For the halakhist, the goal is to find a single voice in the pandemonium of the Talmud. But my students are not halakhists, and mine is a text class; their task is to learn to listen for nuance and subtlety in the text, and to argue for their understanding of the text with nuance and subtlety. They learn to receive tradition, interpret tradition, and communicate creatively and contribute to the ongoing conversation of *torah she'b'al peh*, of what is often called "the Oral Torah"—that is, the rabbinic tradition. These are, of course, key underlying goals, and an important part of the not-so-hidden curriculum of a pluralistic day school.

Finally, the students in my class identify with the editor of the Talmud. This is natural, because their tasks are quite similar. The editor of the Talmud created a world of meaning for his community, and if we take seriously the claims of some of my students, he recognized that different segments of his community would read the texts differently. Similarly, all of our students are engaged in the process of constructing meaning out of a complex and multivocal tradition. But in pluralistic day schools, our students are challenged by the awareness that different segments of the community will interpret our classical texts in radically different ways. When coupled with the ambiguities inherent in rabbinic texts and the diversity of historical readings of those rabbinic texts, the challenges grow. Learning to be attuned to the nuance of how arguments are made and not just to what is said requires great skill. Developing these skills and meeting these challenges are, however, essential for participating in genuine pluralistic dialogue, and establishes a warrant for introducing this level of complexity into a ninth-grade Talmud curriculum.

Conclusion: Similarities and Differences Between Rabbinic Literature and Bible

After completing my research and preparing this paper, it seemed obvious that my work in teaching rabbinic literature at Gann Academy should be seen in the context of the larger Jewish studies curriculum at Gann, and in particular, in the context of Dr. Susan E. Tanchel's work on teaching biblical criticism. Her work is summarized in chapter 10 of the present volume. Tanchel writes:

> A core part of Gann Academy's mission is to be a pluralistic community–that is, to be a place in which different beliefs and opinions are not only actively valued, respected, and celebrated, but are also challenged and questioned. (p. 245)

On this, as I have noted above, there is no difference between my approach to Talmud study and Tanchel's approach to Tanakh study. Tanchel continues,

> Applying the method of source criticism to the biblical text helps students to discover the multi-vocal and layered nature of the Torah itself. This underscores the existence of diversity in ancient Israel and thereby illuminates a historical precedent for the pluralism that surrounds the students in their current educational setting. (p. 245)

Indeed, in the context of the rabbinic reading of Tanakh, one does not need the study of "higher criticism" to support the school's commitment to pluralism. The tenth- and eleventh-grade Tanakh curricula at Gann are dedicated to the analysis of how the various medieval exegetes interpret the biblical text in different ways. Tanchel would claim, and I would agree with her, that the significance of a critical perspective is that the multivocality is located inside the Tanakh (and "the diversity [of] ancient Israel") and not just in the diversity of the minds of the readers, whether classical or modern.

In the context of Talmud study, multivocality is a given. The text explicitly incorporates multiple voices from different periods and locales that are seen as supports or challenges to the other voices preserved in the text. An awareness of the biblical, tannaitic, and amoraic layers is necessary in any kind of study of Talmud. An awareness of the anonymous material as a later, editorial level complicates the study, but the text presents a vibrant conversation even without separating out the *stam*. For scholars like David Weiss Halivni,[14] much of the critical enterprise is defined by an attempt to recapture the original version(s) of traditions that then shaped the later discussions of the Talmud. In my class, however, the critical enterprise is to imagine the intention of the editor in constructing a literary document that preserves a great deal of tradition but is also strikingly creative. The goal is to make sense of the whole, given a fairly clear awareness of the parts.

The contrast with critical study of the Torah seems obvious. The Torah does not mark out its sources, we have no separate documents that preserve different forms of the traditions, and the gaps in the biblical text and the language of biblical Hebrew are not nearly as drastic as the radical spareness of talmudic Aramaic. Although some modern redaction critics focus on the text's composition, the enterprise of biblical criticism at Gann is, as Tanchel put it, to help "students ... discover the multi-vocal and layered nature of the Torah itself." The goal of Talmud criticism is to explore the nature of the conversation that is manifestly constructed between well-articulated sources.[15]

A second point of comparison between Tanchel's work and my own lies in her concern about the risks involved in teaching—or not teaching—biblical criticism. Tanchel stresses how learning the documentary hypothesis can "be a destabilizing religious experience for students" (p. 256). Given a student's own questions about the text and the experience of many students who are exposed to critical approaches in colleges that pay no attention to the religious implications of a critical approach,

---

[14] David Weiss Halivni, *Meqorot u-Mesorot—Nashim [Sources and Traditions: A Source-Critical Commentary on Seder Nashim]* (Tel Aviv: 1968), 7 and 13-15, et passim.

[15] It would be interesting to compare the experiences of students who begin Talmud criticism in ninth grade with their experiences of Bible criticism in twelfth grade.

she concludes that "it is far riskier for Jewish high schools not to teach this material" (p. 262).

The risks faced by the student of Talmud criticism are real but perhaps not as obvious. It is possible to study a great deal of Gemara critically, with an awareness that the discursive anonymous layer is something quite distinct from the earlier materials, without facing questions about what the editor has done to fashion a *sugya*. Yet the particular texts which ninth graders study in my class raise a wide range of questions about how the editor related to the materials of the tradition. Some students who come to Gann with a traditionalist perspective find the idea of sources selectively quoted and even manipulated quite disturbing to their conception of the *mesorah*. On the other hand, many students imagine the editor of the Talmud in their own image, struggling to engage the tradition and to make sense out it. Much of the discussion of Talmud pedagogy in community high schools is about how to make Talmud relevant. By forcing my students to confront the editor's own efforts to make tradition speak, they are given models that make the entire endeavor of *torah she'b'al peh* an ongoing conversation in which they are meaningful participants.

12 A Theory of *Havruta* Learning
Orit Kent

Part I: Introduction

As a form of study that originated in the traditional *beit midrash*,[1] *havruta* (Jewish text study in pairs)[2] has been appropriated in many modern contexts, such as adult Jewish learning, day school and supplementary school settings, Hillel gatherings, and Jewish professional development programs, in which people study a range of texts. The pairs sit with one another, read the text together, discuss its meaning and, perhaps, explore broader questions about life that the text raises. As a form of text study, *havruta* offers learners opportunities to foster interpretive, social, and ethical engagement and thus has great potential for a range of people in different contexts with different learning goals.

Some who study in *havruta* report enjoying the process, noting, for example, that it gives them space to think about the text in the company of someone else, fostering a sense of ownership of the text itself, and of

---

[1] *Beit midrash* literally means "house of study" and refers to a place where Jews study texts, often in pairs or *havruta*. Traditionally, the *beit midrash* was a place where Jewish men studied Talmud out loud.

[2] The Aramaic term *havruta* means friendship or companionship and is commonly used to refer to two people studying Jewish texts together. In this article, the term *havruta* refers to both the learning pair and the practice of paired learning. The history of *havruta* as a widespread learning practice is subject to scholarly debate. (See Orit Kent, "Interactive Text Study and the Co-Construction of Meaning : Havruta in the DeLeT Beit Midrash," doctoral dissertation, Brandeis University, 2008," for a discussion of this issue.) The reason for my focus on *havruta* is that, in our historical context, it has come to be seen and used by many Jewish teachers and learners as a core mode of text learning and as such is worthy of investigation.

being in conversation with the text. Others, or the same people at other times, find the process frustrating: *havruta* partners may not work well together, or get stuck and not know what to do next, or spend most of their time digressing from the topic at hand. However, whether the experiences are meaningful or disappointing, there is generally little critical understanding of the specifics of the process that took place leading to the particular outcome, and thus little knowledge about how to recreate or avoid such outcomes in the future.[3]

Perhaps because *havruta* has generally been used in traditional Jewish contexts such as yeshivot, modern educational scholarship has not taken a close look at this learning practice in order to unpack it and explore what makes for better or worse *havruta* experiences.[4] In my own research, I have used the lens of educational and learning theories to analyze real-life *havruta* interactions in all their specificity, asking: what can we learn about text study and students' meaning-making through a close examination of adults studying classical Jewish texts in one particular *beit midrash* setting?

In the early phases of my research, I conducted a pilot study in order to illuminate some of the rhythms and complexities of *havruta* learning. I identified *havruta* as a complex and potentially powerful Jewish

---

[3] These examples of satisfying and unsatisfying experiences are drawn from discussions over several years with my students in the DeLeT Beit Midrash for Teachers as well as from their written reflections.

[4] This has begun to change in recent years. See, for example, Elie Holzer and Orit Kent, "Havruta: What Do We Know and What Can We Hope to Learn from Studying in Havruta?", in *International Handbook of Jewish Education* 5 (New York: Springer, 2011): 407-417; Miriam Raider-Roth and Elie Holzer, "Learning to be Present: How Hevruta Learning Can Activate Teachers' Relationships to Self, Other and Text," *Journal of Jewish Education* 75: 3 (2009): 216-239; Steven Brown and Mitchell Malkus, "Hevruta as a Form of Cooperative Learning," *Journal of Jewish Education* 73: 3 (2007): 209-26; Sharon Feiman-Nemser, "Beit Midrash for Teachers: An Experiment in Teacher Preparation," *Journal of Jewish Education* 72: 3 (2006): 161-83; Elie Holzer, "What Connects 'Good' Teaching, Text Study and Hevruta Learning? A Conceptual Argument," *Journal of Jewish Education* 72: 3 (2006): 183-205; Orit Kent, "Interactive Text Study: A Case of Hevruta Learning," *Journal of Jewish Education* 72: 3 (2006): 205-232; Aliza Segal, *Havruta Study: History, Benefits, and Enhancements* (Jerusalem: ATID, 2003).

interpretive social learning practice involving norms, phases, moves, and stances, involving social interaction between two human partners, and meaning-making efforts involving three partners—two people and the text.

In my next study of many more *havruta* interactions, I developed a theory[5] of *havruta* in one context, reflecting a set of three dynamic pairs for a total of six core practices. In this chapter, I present that theory through a close look at one *havruta* session. It is not meant to be the definitive theory, but one important frame for helping practitioners and scholars better understand this complex learning experience and make it as fruitful as possible. This theory may also be a helpful lens for both studying and elucidating text-based discussions of other kinds of texts in small and large group settings.

Methodology and Background Literature

My research took place in the Beit Midrash for Teachers[6] in the DeLeT/M.A.T. program at Brandeis University, and was part of the Beit Midrash Research Project[7] at the Mandel Center for Studies in Jewish Education. This *beit midrash* was part of DeLeT's summer program and included women and men studying a range of Jewish texts in *havruta* over a five-week period. For four summers, I collected audio- and videotapes of nine *havruta* pairs in 51 *havruta* sessions. I analyzed the data using a

---

[5] In my use of the term "theory," I draw on Magdalene Lampert's discussion of developing theories of teaching and learning. For Lampert, theory develops from studying the rich particulars of practice and creating language for understanding and talking about practice. See Magdalene Lampert, "Knowing Teaching from the Inside Out: Implications of Inquiry in Practice for Teacher Education," in *The Education of Teachers, Ninety-Eighth Yearbook of the National Society for the Study of Education*, ed. Gary A. Griffin (Chicago: University of Chicago Press, 1999), and Magdalene Lampert, *Teaching Problems and the Problems of Teaching* (New Haven: Yale University Press, 2001).

[6] I wish to acknowledge Elie Holzer for his partnership in developing and guiding the work of the DeLeT Beit Midrash for Teachers from 2003-2007.

[7] See http://www.brandeis.edu/mandel/projects/beitmidrashresearch/index.html for more details.

A Theory of Havruta Learning

grounded theory[8] approach to identify some of the central practices in which these *havruta* partners engage, and used the tools of discourse analysis[9] to further probe the contours of those practices and the ways in which they shape a *havruta*'s meaning-making process.

My work in identifying and shaping a theory of *havruta* is informed by an eclectic group of educational researchers interested in learning and teaching and peer learning, in addition to scholars in the fields of sociocognitive psychology and studies of interpretive discussion and text-based learning. I integrate scholarship from three areas: research on text-based learning; research on peer learning; and research on classroom discourse.

I am particularly indebted to Sophie Haroutunian-Gordon's work.[10] Haroutunian-Gordon, a philosopher and teacher educator, is interested in the conversational aspect of meaning-making, or what she calls "interpretive discussion." In her research, she identifies elements that enable rich interpretive discussion and factors that hinder it. While Haroutunian-Gordon studies whole-class discussions of literature, I view *havruta* discussions of classical Jewish texts as another kind of interpretive discussion.

Within the field of peer and cooperative learning, I draw on Elizabeth Cohen[11] and David and Roger Johnson.[12] Cohen's argument about

---

[8] See Barney G. Glaser and Anselm L. Strauss, *The Discovery of Grounded Theory: Strategies for Qualitative Research* (New York: Aldine Transaction, 1967), and Aldine de Gruyter and John R. Cutcliffe, "Methodological Issues in Grounded Theory," *Journal of Advanced Nursing* 31: 6 (2000): 1476-1484.

[9] See James Paul Gee, *An Introduction to Discourse Analysis, Theory and Method* (New York: Routledge, 2005), and Charles Goodwin, "Conversation Analysis," *Annual Review of Anthropology* 19 (1990): 283-307.

[10] Sophie Haroutunian-Gordon, *Learning to Teach Through Discussion: The Art of Turning the Soul* (New Haven: Yale University Press, 2009), and Haroutunian-Gordon, *Turning the Soul, Teaching through Conversations in the High School* (Chicago: University of Chicago Press, 1991).

[11] Elizabeth G. Cohen, "Restructuring the Classroom: Conditions for Productive Small Groups," *Review of Educational Research* 64: 1 (1994): 1-35, Elizabeth G. Cohen, et al.,"Can Groups Learn?" *Teachers College Record* 104: 6 (2002): 1045-68.

[12] David W. Johnson and Roger T. Johnson, *Learning Together and Alone: Cooperative, Competitive, and Individualistic Learning*, 5th ed. (Boston: Alyn and Bacon, 1999).

group knowledge—that with the proper support, groups can construct knowledge beyond the capacity of any single individual—is especially important; her work also identifies a positive correlation between open-ended conceptual tasks and the amount of interaction among participants in the task. My research is also informed by the work of linguists and scholars of classroom discourse such as Sarah Michaels,[13] Courtney Cazden[14], and Douglas Barnes and Frankie Todd.[15]

Underlying my work are assumptions drawn from sociocultural theories of knowledge based on Lev Vygotsky's work, such as that of Jean Lave and Etienne Wenger, who argue that learning happens through co-participation, not merely in an individual's head, and that learning happens in practice, not by exposure to abstract knowledge out of context and then internalization.[16] Since learning is socially produced and situated, it becomes impossible to separate social processes (how we interact with people) from intellectual processes (how we make sense of particular subject matter); together, they comprise the basis of human learning. This lays the groundwork for understanding the symbiotic and mutually supportive relationship in *havruta* between a pair's working relationship and the development of its participants' thinking and learning.

---

[13] Sarah Michaels, Catherine O'Connor, and Lauren B. Resnick, "Reasoned Participation: Accountable Talk in the Classroom and in Civic Life," *Studies in Philosophy and Education* 27: 4 (2008): 283-297; Mary Catherine O'Connor and Sarah Michaels, "Shifting Participant Frameworks: Orchestrating Thinking Practices in Group Discussion," in *Discourse, Learning and Schooling*, ed. D. Hicks (New York: Cambridge University Press, 1996), 63-103.

[14] Courtney B. Cazden, *Classroom Discourse, The Language of Teaching and Learning* (Portsmouth: Heinemann, 1988), and Courtney B. Cazden, *Classroom Discourse, The Language of Teaching and Learning*, 2nd ed. (Portsmouth: Heinemann, 2001).

[15] Barnes, D. and F. Todd, *Communication and Learning Revisited, Making Meaning Through Talk* (Portsmouth: Heinemann, 1995).

[16] Jean Lave and Etienne Wenger, *Situated Learning, Legitimate Peripheral Participation* (New York: Cambridge University Press, 1991), and Jean Lave, "The Practice of Learning," in *Understanding Practice, Perspectives on Activity and Context*, ed. S. Chalkin and Jean Lave (Cambridge: Cambridge University Press, 1993), 3-32.

A Theory of Havruta Learning: Six Practices

When I use the term *havruta*, I am referring to more than a simple strategy for students to brainstorm together for a few minutes, or what is known in language arts classrooms as "pair and share."[17] *Havruta* here refers to two people working together for some period of time to together make sense of a text, requiring them to draw on a variety of skills for interpreting a text and working with someone else independent of a teacher's direct guidance. Effort is directed at constructing ideas and working relationships, and the ways in which these processes influence each other. Ideally, the two people involved in the *havruta* are responsible for both their own learning and each other's learning; their success is viewed as interdependent. And since there are not only two partners but three–the two people and the text—for meaning-making to occur, there must be interaction not only between the people but also between each and both of them and the text.

During a *havruta* encounter, participants construct and reconstruct the meaning of the text through their moment-to-moment interactions. While these interactions are highly complex and, in their particularity, may be highly varied, key elements emerge. Through a fine-grained microanalysis of audio and video recordings of *havruta* sessions and informed by a prescriptive understanding of good *havruta*, I have identified three pairs of core practices in which *havruta* learners engage: (1) listening and articulating; (2) wondering and focusing; and (3) supporting and challenging.

In many ways, listening and articulating together are the engine that starts the *havruta* and keeps it going—the building blocks of both idea and relationship development in *havruta*. By both listening and articulating, *havruta* partners create space for each human partner and the text to be heard and be part of the *havruta* learning process. This back-and-forth opens up room for new ideas to emerge and for the shaping and refining of ideas already on the table.

The second pair of practices is focusing and wondering: concentrating attention and exploring multiple possibilities. A *havruta* pair needs

---

[17] Lucy McCormick Calkins, *The Art of Teaching Reading* (New York: Longman, 2001).

to wonder in order to generate creative ideas; at the same time, it needs to focus in order to deepen a given interpretation and come to some conclusion (however provisional) about the meaning of the text. While listening and articulating are the engine, wondering and focusing are part of the steering wheel—they help determine the direction that the conversation will take.

Finally, there is the third pair of practices—supporting and challenging—that also serve to steer the conversation. In different ways, they help a *havruta* further shape their ideas. Supporting consists of providing encouragement for the ideas on the table and helping further shape them by clarifying them, strengthening them with further evidence, and/or sometimes extending them. Challenging consists of raising problems with ideas on the table, questioning what's missing from them, and drawing attention to contradictions and opposing ideas. Both of these practices are also part of the steering wheel, contributing to the direction of the conversation and helping the *havruta* partners sharpen their ideas.

In order to have a *havruta* conversation of any kind that is more than just parallel monologues, these practices must take place in some kind of balance, one that will differ from pair to pair, interaction to interaction, and even moment to moment. On the surface, the practices in each pair are mutually exclusive. For example, to focus on an idea, one must for the moment put aside wonderings about other ideas. However, a tension inheres within each pair of practices in trying to strike some sort of balance and relationship between them—a tension that can make *havruta* interactions dynamic, undetermined, challenging, and engaging. These practices are best supported in a learning environment that fosters collaboration. This does not mean that everyone needs to agree. A collaborative environment is one in which students understand that their success as a havruta is interdependent and that they are therefore responsible to and for one another. Furthermore, such a context places a high value on participants working together to develop the most compelling ideas and interpretation possible, and not simply sticking with their own original ideas.[18]

---

[18] "Collaboration" and "collaborative environment" are further discussed later in this article.

A Close Look at One Havruta Session

In what follows, I closely examine one *havruta* session in order to illustrate the practices described above. This case is not an ideal type or an illustration of a "perfect" *havruta*, but instead a close look at one rich *havruta* session, providing images of what *havruta* can look like (especially with particular kinds of framing and support).

The pair in the session below are two DeLeT fellows studying in the DeLeT Beit Midrash for Teachers. This is the fourth time they are studying together in *havruta*. Debbie and Laurie are young women in their twenties.[19] Debbie is entering her second summer of the program, having spent the past year working in a first-grade classroom. Laurie just started the program two weeks earlier. Both women come to the DeLeT Beit Midrash with experience studying Jewish texts: Debbie attended Hebrew schools and Hebrew high school, majored in Jewish studies in college, and studied in Israel for three months before entering the DeLeT program, and Laurie attended Jewish day school for nine years and took Jewish studies courses in college. However, neither has spent significant time studying talmudic texts in the original or studying in *havruta*.

The text that Debbie and Laurie are studying—a very short narrative about two rabbis—is from the Babylonian Talmud (Tractate Ta'anit 9b). They have been given the text, reproduced line by line in the original Aramaic, as well as English and Hebrew translations. The English (based on the Soncino Talmud translation) of the text handout reads as follows:

1. R. Shimi b. Ashi used to attend [the lessons] of R. Papa and used to ask him many questions

2. One day he observed that R. Papa fell on his face [in prayer] and he heard him saying:

3. May God preserve me from the insolence of Shimi

4. The latter thereupon vowed silence and questioned him no more[20]

---

[19] Debbie and Laurie are pseudonyms.
[20] Elie Holzer designed the presentation of this text.

The *havruta* assignment reads:

> Together with your *havruta*, study this text very carefully.... Offer a compelling interpretation of the story of R. Shimi and R. Papa. Then insert 2 sentences (not more!) to help a potential reader better understand your interpretation of the story. This interpretation needs to be an outcome of your *havruta* study. You may offer a second interpretation on a separate sheet.

They have 45 minutes to work on this in *havruta*.

Debbie and Laurie begin their *havruta* by agreeing on a process for reading the text together out loud. In this first phase of their *havruta*, they read the text four different times and clarify the basic plot of the narrative. In the second phase of their *havruta*, they begin an interpretive discussion, which is focused on exploring the motivations of the characters in the text: why would R. Shimi ask so many questions? Why does R. Papa have a problem with the question asking? During the third phase of their *havruta*, they step back to clarify their overall theory about the text's message about the teacher-student relationship. They discuss a number of different big ideas that they learn from the text (e.g., that one should always be careful of what one says no matter where one is, and that one must always be aware of the potential impact of one's words). Finally, in the fourth phase of their *havruta*, they move from their interpretive discussion of the text to focusing on completing their written assignment.

In each of the sections that follows, I will focus on a different pair of *havruta* practices, looking at excerpts from Debbie and Laurie's *havruta* and then analyzing the excerpts through the lens of each set of practices. In an actual *havruta*, the practices are often interwoven, and all six of the practices apply to this interaction between the two people in the *havruta* and between the people and the text, but for the purposes of illustrating them clearly, I artificially separate them in order to elucidate one pair of practices at a time, and at different points focus more heavily on one or another aspect of the interaction.

Part II: The Practices of Listening and Articulating

What is the Text About?

After Debbie and Laurie clarify the meaning of the words in the text and which lines in the text seem to refer to R. Papa and R. Shimi, Debbie suggests that they read the text in full for a fourth time, this time making clear as they read which line is being said by whom. Here they are both working hard to make sense of the text—to listen to what it has to say. As before, they take turns reading each line.

Upon completing the reading, Debbie opens up the conversation by turning to look directly at Laurie and asking: "What do you think this is about?" This is typical of their *havruta*—they read the text to hear what it has to say and then look to each other and explicitly invite the other person's articulation of meaning.

DEBBIE: What do you think this is about?

LAURIE: Oh, my gosh. Well, okay, so it seems, I mean the first thing that stands out the most is this insolence thing, because there's something that Rabbi Papa really, really doesn't like about the fact that he's asking him so many questions, or I think, at least I'm connecting the rudeness with the question asking. It doesn't say that specifically, but do you think, what do you think? What connection would you make between—

DEBBIE: The rudeness—

LAURIE: —rudeness and what's already happened?

Instead of merely making a pronouncement about what she thinks the text must mean, Laurie uses the word "seem" to articulate her idea. Her interpretation is exploratory and not definitive. Laurie invites Debbie into her thinking by explaining how she arrives at this idea—she is connecting rudeness with question asking. She makes it clear that this isn't an idea said explicitly in the text, but is her inference based on what she has learned from listening to the text. Laurie concludes her articulation by inviting Debbie's response, inviting Debbie to begin to articulate, and making clear she's ready to listen to Debbie.

Debbie agrees that there's a connection between rudeness and question asking.

DEBBIE: Well, it's funny because I do think there's a connection, but the connection is so ambiguous and it's weird because you would think asking questions is a positive thing we want students to do.

LAURIE: Ya.

DEBBIE: So it must have been, the insolence must have been in the kinds of questions.

LAURIE: Hmm.

DEBBIE: I'm guessing. Maybe he was asking questions that were either not appropriate or maybe of ways to make, maybe, the teacher look bad—

LAURIE: Hmm. Ya.

DEBBIE: —or that were condescending, or something that was inappropriate so that Rabbi Papa would say "may God preserve me" from taking action on this student, beating him into the ground. ((laughter)) But it seems to seem it has something to do with definitely the questions.

LAURIE: Ya.

DEBBIE: And then what's funny is something, an action has to happen right here for Shimi the student, well, actually, not the action because Shimi did see him—

LAURIE: Ya.

DEBBIE: —observed him, so then Shimi learned his lesson, "lesson,"—

LAURIE: Ya.

DEBBIE: —and decided not to question him "no more."

As Debbie starts to talk, one sees from her articulation that Debbie is actually listening to a number of things: she is listening to what Laurie said about there being a connection between the questions and insolence and responding to it; she is listening to the text stating that R. Papa prayed to God to "preserve him" from R. Shimi's questions; and she is listening to her own notion that asking questions is generally a good thing for students to do. Building off of the ideas she has gathered through listening in different directions, Debbie determines that R. Shimi's questions must have been insolent and then gets more specific in articulating her interpretation, providing examples of the types of rude questions that R. Shimi may have asked.

The conversation continues as follows:

LAURIE: Yes. So I wonder if there's some kind of internal thing maybe going on with Shimi here, like he feels something. Maybe he's embarrassed or maybe he's ashamed or he—

DEBBIE: What do you mean ... by that?

LAURIE: Well, no, because I liked what you were saying about how there's an action that takes place here or something, or then you said oh, no, wait, he did see him, so he knew what he said. I think that's what you were—

DEBBIE: Hmhm.

LAURIE: —that's how I heard it.

DEBBIE: Right.

LAURIE: But I agree with you that there's still some kind of transition that occurs here where he changes his attitude and he vows silence. So there's just some, the way I see it, there's some internal change or something, like he's no longer inquisitive. He's silent for whatever reason, whether, and I'm curious what you think, whether, I mean maybe there's not a person who's right and wrong, but is it, was he really asking rude questions or was he just, or was the teacher just overreacting and he's now silenced his student, who is just curious and is trying to inquire? So I don't know. Maybe we can talk about that in a minute, but—

Laurie listens closely to Debbie's articulation of a question about an internal shift that takes place with R. Shimi, closely enough to repeat the point back to her, and wants to have listened well enough that she makes sure she understood correctly. Laurie then expresses agreement with Debbie's idea that there's something that happens that is missing from the text that makes R. Shimi vow silence. The gap that Laurie has noticed in the text prompts her to re-listen to and reconsider their idea that R. Shimi is asking rude questions. She begins to think about the meaning of the text from another perspective and to question R. Papa's reaction—was he perhaps overreacting? As happened with Debbie before, Laurie's close listening sparks new, deeper ideas for her to articulate.

Types of Listening

Debbie and Laurie's exchange calls attention to a number of different ways that *havruta* partners listen to one another: listening to follow along, listening to understand, and listening to figure something out.[21] Debbie and Laurie both listen in order to follow the other's ideas. Listening to follow along means that one focuses on hearing the other's words in order to keep up and not lose the place. (Sometimes the objective in listening to follow along is to gear up for one's own turn, though that runs the risk of not really listening while one mostly waits out the other person until one can articulate.) Debbie and Laurie provide each other with many listening cues to demonstrate that they are following along, as will be discussed shortly.

Listening to understand is different from listening to follow along. When one *havruta* partner tries to understand the other's ideas, the

---

[21] For slightly different categories, see Sophie Haroutunian-Gordon, "Listening in a Democratic Society," *Philosophy of Education Yearbook* (2003): 1-18.

partner moves the other from an object of attention to a subject in his or her own right. To understand the other, one needs to practice both outer and inner silence—creating an outer space for the other to articulate and also silencing the many internal voices that arise in one's own heads so that s/he can truly pay attention to what the other is trying to say.[22] In order to grasp another's meaning and/or draw it out further, some listeners find they must ask both clarifying and critical questions. Laurie indicates her listening to understand when she makes reference to Debbie's earlier statement, checks in to make sure she heard it correctly, and makes space for Debbie to correct her.

> **LAURIE:** Yes. So I wonder if there's some kind of internal thing maybe going on with Shimi here, like he feels something. Maybe he's embarrassed or maybe he's ashamed or he—
>
> **DEBBIE:** What do you mean … by that?
>
> **LAURIE:** Well, no, because I liked what you were saying about how there's an action that takes place here or something, or then you said oh, no, wait, he did see him, so he knew what he said. I think that's what you were—
>
> **DEBBIE:** Hmhm.
>
> **LAURIE:** —that's how I heard it.
>
> **DEBBIE:** Right.

Debbie indicates this type of listening when she responds to and builds off of Laurie's statement and question about the connection between rudeness and questions.

> **LAURIE:** What connection would you make between … rudeness and what's already happened?

---

22 Leonard J. Waks, "Listening from Silence: Inner Composure and Engagement," *Paideusis* 17: 2 (2008): 65-74. For a similar idea, see William Isaacs, *Dialogue And The Art of Thinking Together* (New York: Doubleday, 1999).

DEBBIE: Well, it's funny because I do think there's a connection, but the connection is so ambiguous and it's weird because you would think asking questions is a positive thing we want students to do.... So it must have been, the insolence must have been in the kinds of questions.

Listening to understand goes a long way to helping *havruta* members feel respected and also to making sure that different perspectives and questions get raised and responded to.

Debbie and Laurie also listen for the purpose of figuring something out. That is, as they are engaged in trying to figure out the motivations of the characters in the text, they listen both to one another and the text, to figure out the puzzle before them.

Listening Cues

It is not necessarily always clear to one *havruta* partner that the other partner is listening to her, and Laurie and Debbie provide each other with many cues to indicate listening and their interest in hearing each other's articulations. They demonstrate that they are following along when they fill in each other's words, with their many "hms" and "ya's" after each other's comments, and by their attentive demeanors. They look at each other and the text a lot, they nod their head as the other one is speaking, they say "yes" over and over again in response to what the other one says, and they invite the other to speak by saying: "What do you think?" or stating an interpretive idea as a question. They also paraphrase or "revoice" the other's words.[23] All of these cues indicate that each partner takes the other person's ideas seriously and listens to them, encouraging further articulations. These listening cues are very important because they can encourage the articulator to keep working at his or her articulation and not stop thinking about the particular idea before she has tried to fully work it out. The listening and articulating dance thus continues.

---

[23] Mary Catherine O'Connor and Sarah Michaels, "Shifting Participant Frameworks: Orchestrating Thinking Practices in Group Discussion," in *Discourse, Learning and Schooling*, ed. Deborah Hicks (New York: Cambridge University Press, 1996), 63-103.

A Theory of Havruta Learning

Types of Articulations

Laurie and Debbie's exchange also call attention to two types of articulations: exploratory articulations and definitive articulations. Much of the early parts of Laurie and Debbie's *havruta* is full of exploratory articulations, articulations that have the quality of thinking out loud. For example, at the very beginning of the transcript excerpt, Laurie thinks out loud about the sense of the text and tries to elicit a response from Debbie. Again:

> **LAURIE**: Well, okay, so it seems, I mean the first thing that stands out the most is this insolence thing, because there's something that Rabbi Papa really, really doesn't like about the fact that he's asking him so many questions, or I think, at least I'm connecting the rudeness with the question asking. It doesn't say that specifically, but do you think, what do you think? What connection would you make between … rudeness and what's already happened?

She has not yet arrived at a conclusive understanding of why R. Shimi's questions were so troubling to R. Papa. Rather than simply thinking about this issue in her head, she invites her *havruta* partner into her thinking by articulating it out loud and specifically asks for a response to her ideas. In addition to inviting one's partner into one's thinking, this kind of articulating can also help people work through their own ideas. The more they talk, the more they get clearer on what they are actually thinking and wanting to say.

The second type of articulating, definitive articulation, is stating one's idea. At first Debbie articulates to think out loud, suggesting different ways that the questions may have been insolent.

> **DEBBIE:** Well, it's funny because I do think there's a connection, but the connection is so ambiguous and it's weird because you would think asking questions is a positive thing we want students to do … I'm guessing. Maybe he was asking questions that were either not appropriate or maybe of ways to make, maybe, the teacher look bad—

As she continues to talk, her articulation becomes less exploratory and more definitive.

DEBBIE: —or that were condescending, or something that was inappropriate so that Rabbi Papa would say "may God preserve me" from taking action on this student, beating him into the ground. ((laughter)) But it seems to seem like it has something to do with definitely the questions.

She says that there's "definitely" a connection between insolence and questions. However, even as she becomes more definitive, she still uses language like "it seems," leaving space for Laurie to offer other alternatives. In this way, she creates a context for their *havruta* work to keep drawing on the interpretive resources they both bring to the table, even as their conversation progresses and begins to focus on certain interpretive ideas.

Holding Three Voices

In addition to the tensions inherent in figuring out how to take turns in these roles of articulator and listener, *havruta* partners need to be able to listen to multiple things at the same time: the text, their partner's ideas, and their own ideas. Throughout their *havruta*, there are many examples of Laurie and Debbie trying to juggle these multiple foci of their attention. As discussed earlier, Laurie listens to Debbie wondering whether R. Shimi has an emotional reaction to hearing R. Papa and listens to the text well enough to notice that it leaves that information out, which then gives her the help she needs to come to a more nuanced interpretation of what is happening in the text. (While the larger focus is on hearing the voices of all three partners, as a practical matter at any given moment it may only be possible for people studying in *havruta* to focus on two out of three voices, with one falling temporarily into the background.)

Taking Turns Listening and Articulating

Debbie and Laurie take turns listening and articulating, which allows them to build a respectful working relationship, to draw on both of their ideas, and to move the conversation productively forward. Taking turns listening and articulating is slow and hard work—it entails focusing on the other person and the text, restating the other's ideas, and building on those ideas further. However, by taking turns in this way, *havruta* partners bring each other and the text into the conversation and can create a sense of respectful dialogue in which all parties' ideas have space to be articulated and heard.

Besides building a sense of respect, this kind of turn-taking takes advantage of both people's thinking in order to synergistically enhance the pair's overall ideas. Ultimately, for *havruta* to be not a monologue in which one person uses the other to bounce off ideas, but an interpretive discussion that draws on the collective wisdom of all parties, each partner must have time to articulate and listen. In this way, it is a partnership with all parties contributing as subjects in their own right and responding to one another.

Consider the following exchange:

LAURIE: [T]here's something R. Papa really, really doesn't like about the fact that he's asking him so many questions....

DEBBIE: So ... the insolence must have been in the kinds of questions.... Maybe he was asking questions that were either not appropriate or maybe made the teacher look bad ... or something that was inappropriate.... Shimi ... observed him [R. Papa praying], so then Shimi learned his lesson and decided not to question him any more.

LAURIE: I wonder if there's some kind of internal thing going on with Shimi ... maybe he's embarrassed or maybe he's ashamed ... maybe there's not a person who's right and wrong ... was he really asking rude questions ... or was the teacher just overreacting?

By taking turns listening and articulating, Debbie and Laurie avoid getting stuck on only one reading or on one or two details, examine multiple dimensions and multiple readings of the text, and keep building on and developing their ideas. If they had just stopped with Debbie's initial articulation, the idea of whether the questions actually were insolent and the uncertainty about R. Shimi and R. Papa's motivations would have gone unexplored. However, as Debbie has been honing her interpretation, Laurie has been listening to understand Debbie and to figure out the connection between questions and rudeness and R. Shimi and R. Papa's motivations for their actions. Based on her listening, Laurie reexamines the ideas that the questions were insolent and suggests an alternative reading.

Through their back-and-forth between listening and articulating, Laurie and Debbie develop a respectful working relationship, while increasing the "interactivity"[24] of their various ideas. And in the space of interactivity—a space in which ideas get bounced about, elaborated on, or discarded—there is the potential for fresh insights. Because they not only articulate but also listen in various ways, they are able to build on each other's ideas, incorporating pieces of each other's ideas and developing them further, drawing on their collective thinking potential.

Part III: The Practices of Wondering and Focusing

To Explore or to Move On?

In the early minutes of Debbie and Laurie's *havruta* session, there are many examples of their initial wondering, about both their partner's ideas and the text. They finish reading the text for the fourth time and immediately turn toward one another with open-ended questions about what the other person thinks about the text. They also wonder a lot about the meaning of the text, raising a long list of questions.

Their partner questions are all open-ended, encouraging the other person to freely talk through her ideas. For example, Debbie asks, "What do you think this is about?" and "What do you mean by that?" Laurie asks, "What do you think? What connection would you make between the rudeness and what's already happened?" and "What do you think? Was he really asking rude questions or was the teacher overreacting?" Laurie's partner questions are often followed by more specific questions that help her partner focus her response.

Debbie and Laurie's text-oriented wondering questions are sometime generated when they look again at the text, and sometimes it is the questions themselves that generate another look. For example, Laurie asks, "Was he really asking rude questions or was ... the teacher just overreacting ..." and "If Shimi only had good intentions ... then what does this say about the teacher? Is he misinterpreting his student ..." and "Who is overreacting?" Debbie asks, "What is the nature of this kid?" and "What is [R. Shimi's] intention?" and "Is he misinterpreting

---

[24] Peter Elbow, *Embracing Contraries* (New York: Oxford University Press, 1986).

his student ... is the teacher the one overreacting ... or is it the teacher who is not overreacting and the student is being mischievous and inappropriate in some way?" The text questions indicate that Debbie and Laurie continue to entertain different possibilities about what this story is about. They consider many of the details of the text and work hard to figure out how they fit together in this short narrative. Their text questions also point to a focus of their wondering: they are both trying to figure out who is at fault in this story. While they do not specifically articulate it as such, this question hovers over most of their interpretive discussion.

As the early wondering phase of their *havruta* continues, Debbie and Laurie focus on details of the text and interpretive ideas *and* wonder about these things. Their wondering leads to focusing, which in turn leads to further wondering.

LAURIE: ... Maybe there's not a person who's right and wrong, but is it, was he really asking rude questions or was he just, or was the teacher just overreacting and he's now silenced his student, who is just curious and is trying to inquire....

DEBBIE: ... One of the things that I think you also touched upon is what is the nature of this kid.—

LAURIE: Ya.

DEBBIE:—Is this kid doing something that is, you know, not appropriate or is the teacher overreacting, or is the child, you know ?

LAURIE: Because there are definitely kids who say "teacher, teacher," all the time, but—

DEBBIE: Right. But what is the intention. I think what's important is the intention behind that—

LAURIE: Ya.

DEBBIE: —Because what's interesting is I would think if let's say there were only three lines, I would say oh, wow, so Shimi must have been asking questions that were inappropriate and this and that, but think about a kid in the classroom who specifically wants to make a stir. Just by hearing the teacher saying, you know, "may God preserve me from the insolence of" the student, I don't think necessarily that child would make a change if their intent was to be mischievous in their questions,—

LAURIE: Hm.

DEBBIE: —but it seems that Shimi, it's almost as if maybe he was asking, maybe he over-asked questions, but maybe his intention was positive because that was such a change. I mean hearing those words made such an effect and I would say a negative effect....

Following their discussion about the connection between rudeness and questions, Laurie asks whether R. Shimi was really asking rude questions or whether the teacher was overreacting. Laurie's question enacts wondering, and the result is that it focuses Debbie's attention on R. Shimi's nature. Earlier in the conversation, Debbie had proposed that R. Shimi was merely asking rude questions. This time, her focus on R. Shimi's nature leads her to wonder more about what type of person Shimi is. She specifically wonders: "What is [Shimi's] intention?" This question shifts the conversation to consider the intentions behind R. Shimi's actions and not just the actions themselves. Debbie's new focus leads her to wonder about R. Shimi's intentions, and she then spends a few minutes building a compelling case based on the idea that R. Shimi may well have had very good intentions.

As they develop their ideas and also become aware of the passage of time, they shift their discussion from an exploration of characters' motivations. Debbie becomes more focused on the task and Laurie helps them step back to consider their interpretation of the overall text.

DEBBIE: So how about we start? Okay. ((Reading out loud from the text:)) "Rabbi Shimi b. Ashi used to attend the lessons of Rabbi Papa." Okay, so—

LAURIE: "and used to ask him many questions."

A Theory of Havruta Learning

DEBBIE: "Two lines."[25]

LAURIE: So. Okay, wait. First, sorry. Before we make our sentences, I'm just trying to go back to the bigger picture.

DEBBIE: Okay.

LAURIE: Do we want to talk about that because maybe it will help us clarify our theory about—

DEBBIE: Oh, okay, you're right.

LAURIE: So what do we think this is saying or could be saying about the teacher-student relationship maybe. Or, I mean I guess that also depends on how we interpret it, but what do you think, just your gut feeling, when you?

DEBBIE: Oh, gosh. You know, the first thing is that any discouragement a student gets, you could really shut them off and really, it makes a big impact on their willingness to be open just based on the tiniest thing.... What do you think?

LAURIE: ... I guess it's you have to be really, really careful because you don't know who can hear you or if your students are there, they might misinterpret what you're saying.

While Debbie has started to focus on the task, Laurie pulls them back to consider "our theory" and consider the Big Idea behind the narrative. Debbie at this point has an interpretation with which she is satisfied and hence is interested in shifting gears. She feels that she has answered the question of "who is at fault"—R. Shimi was overly inquisitive and R. Papa overreacted, so both R. Papa and R. Shimi are at fault in some way. Laurie is not satisfied with this as an answer; there are still issues she is trying to figure out.

Laurie's question about what this text says about the teacher-student relationship reframes their discussion from being just about R. Shimi and

---

[25] She is saying out loud two words from their assignment.

R. Papa to being about a much larger concept. Because Debbie maintains a sense of wondering toward the text and Laurie's ideas (even though she has arrived at one explanation), she engages Laurie's question. In the process of going back to the text to respond to the question, Debbie clarifies her larger understanding of the meaning of the story—that this text is a warning about what discouragement can do to students—and also clarifies her understanding of a detail in the text—that R. Papa's intentions were not malicious and that he did not mean for R. Shimi to overhear him. Laurie extends Debbie's articulation, qualifying it to say that the text is about the need to be "really, really careful" when you speak, because you don't know who can hear you or what the impact of your words might be.

To recap the interplay between wondering and focusing in Laurie and Debbie's *havruta*, then, we can say the following.

1. Laurie and Debbie engage in early **wondering**, exploring many aspects of the text. Their wondering is **focused** by an overarching question: Who is at fault?

2. Laurie notices the time; Debbie begins to **focus** on the task and **focuses** on a particular interpretation (R. Shimi overasked questions and R. Papa overreacted).

3. Laurie continues to **wonder** about the meaning of the text and how to resolve the question, "Who is at fault?" She raises various alternative ideas (e.g., Shimi was questioning R. Papa as a person). Debbie considers Laurie's ideas.

4. Debbie **focuses** on the assignment. Laurie stops her to **wonder** about the "big picture" and what this text says about the teacher-student relationship.

To Wonder or to Focus?

In the case of Laurie and Debbie, wondering often takes the form of working on different ways of understanding a text. This occurs when the *havruta* is curious about the meaning of the text and considers different alternatives in an attempt to figure out the best way to make sense of the text. Wondering entails asking many questions, most basically, "What does this mean?" Debbie and Laurie also focus on particular ideas or ways to understand the text. They keep those ideas at the center of their attention for a given period of time. This kind of focusing gives *havrutot* an opportunity to deepen an initial idea and try to work it through. In generative *havruta* discussion, focusing on a way of understanding the text occurs in dynamic relationship with wondering about the meaning of the text.

When *havrutot* initially read a text, they often respond in one of two ways in their effort to make sense of the text: (a) They very quickly come up with an interpretation about the meaning of the text, focusing on that one approach; (b) they leave things more open and wonder about the meaning of the text, returning to it multiple times in order to figure it out. In this example, Debbie and Laurie use the second strategy. This phase of their discussion is a time to immerse themselves in the text and wonder out loud about its meaning, coming up with many creative ideas about how to read the text. The unstated and even unconscious dilemma is that if the *havruta* wonders in too many directions, it will end up *wandering* and not move forward with any one idea. At the same time, if *havrutot* do not wonder, they often get carried away by unexplored and underdeveloped first impressions. In addition, the act of wondering allows partners to take hold of the text in their own ways, sparking a certain level of creative energy that helps fuel and refuel the *havruta* interaction. While Debbie and Laurie engage in this kind of immersive wondering in the early phase of their *havruta*, as time passes they become more focused on their emerging ideas and also on completing the task at hand.

Wondering Driven By a Gap in the Text

Debbie and Laurie's wondering is motivated by the fact that the text does not explain R. Papa and R. Shimi's actions in full. There is a space or gap in the text that engages them in wondering and theorizing about Shimi's questions. Wolfgang Iser[26] writes that textual gaps engage readers, since the reader is driven to try and fill the gaps in order to make sense of the text. In this way, wondering about gaps pulls the conversation forward. And their overarching question (or what Sophie Haroutunian-Gordon calls their "genuine issue"), which emerges through their wondering,

---

[26] Wolfgang Iser, *The Act of Reading: A Theory of Aesthetic Response* (Baltimore: John Hopkins University Press, 1978).

keeps them engaged with each other and the text. It creates a purpose to their conversation—to figure out whether R. Shimi is at fault because somehow his questions were rude, or whether R. Papa overreacted to R. Shimi. The result is that the wondering is not wandering, but allows them to build a more and more comprehensive interpretation. This is a kind of focused wondering, with a focus that is sustained over time. Their conversation will conclude when they have satisfactorily addressed their genuine issue.

Wondering and Focusing In Multiple Directions

Havrutot such as Debbie and Laurie's can wonder about and focus on a number of things. Debbie and Laurie first focus on the text, reading it and trying to listen to it to discern its meaning, before intentionally bringing in their own ideas. If, as *havruta* partners try to understand the text, they focus too narrowly, they may miss important details in the text; if they focus too broadly and try to tackle the entire text all at once, they may become overwhelmed and not have an opportunity to probe particular details. Debbie and Laurie's focus on the text leads them to wonder about particular parts of it. Through this wondering, they generate interpretive ideas, some of which they focus on in order to deepen the idea and their understanding of it.

Debbie and Laurie also focus on the assignment given to them for this *havruta* session. *Havrutot* at times find themselves vacillating between focusing on the assigned task and letting it fall into the background as they get carried away by a particular idea or part of the text.

In addition to directing their wondering and focusing on the text, its interpretation, and the assigned interpretive tasks, Debbie and Laurie also very explicitly wonder about and focus on each other's thinking. The beginning of each part of their interpretive discussions is framed in the following way. One of them starts by saying: "What do you think this is about?," proactively drawing out her partner's thinking. This question puts a focus on the partner and clearly indicates that the first person is wondering about her partner's ideas. The partner responds by thinking out loud and then asks the first one what she thinks about what she just said. This pattern of "what do you think?"—motivated in part by their wondering about and focusing on each other—helps Debbie and Laurie engage with the material together and get inside each other's thinking.

The Interplay between Wondering and Focusing

There is a more dynamic and iterative relationship between wondering and focusing than simply that the pair wonders about the meaning of the text and then focuses its attention on an interpretation and then is done. Each practice is enacted against the backdrop of the other and keeps leading to the other. Neither Debbie nor Laurie (nor the pair as a unit) at any point engages in one practice to the exclusion of the other. For example, when Laurie wonders about their larger theory, this question is connected to trying to complete the assignment and work out an interpretation of the full text. Her wondering is focused on helping them answer an important question. This is focused wondering—wondering that is targeted to one area. And while Debbie is focused on her interpretive idea that R. Papa overreacted, she still engages with Laurie's wondering and continues to think through her interpretation and entertain other possibilities. She demonstrates wondering focus—a focus that has room for new questions, ideas, and foci.

Laurie and Debbie's example suggests that, in order for there to be a productive tension between wondering and focusing, *havruta* participants must be willing to engage in both practices and move back and forth between them. In concert with this, productive tension also seems to entail being respectful of one's partner and being genuinely open to and interested in her approach, even when it is different from one's own. This is crucial to Laurie and Debbie's success. In this way, the partners are able to complement each other, learn from the different approach each may take, and build something together, rather then simply aggravating each other, with each going in a different direction.

Part IV: The Practices of Supporting and Challenging

Supporting to Develop Ideas and Create a Collaborative Spirit

Returning for a final close look at the case of Laurie and Debbie through the lenses of supporting and challenging, we see many examples of how they support one another in their *havruta* discussion and how this support helps them build and expand on each other's ideas.

Laurie and Debbie each make supportive moves to explicitly help the other develop her ideas.

LAURIE: So what do we think this is saying or could be saying about the teacher-student relationship maybe. Or, I mean I guess that also depends on how we interpret it, but what do you think, just your gut feeling, when you?

DEBBIE: Oh, gosh. You know, the first thing is that any discouragement a student gets, you could really shut them off and really, it makes a big impact on their willingness to be open just based on the tiniest thing, but what's hard about what I just said and hearing myself saying it is that this was not meant to be heard, it seems because "one day he observed that," you know, it seems that this was supposed to be private. So I don't know if this was, if it wasn't intentional. I wish I knew what happened afterwards with Rabbi Shimi and Rabbi Papa, their interaction and, and ya. What do you think?

LAURIE: Ya, I agree. I think... [Long pause.] Sorry. I got distracted [unclear]. I definitely, I agree that I think, I agree with you that this wasn't meant to be overheard. So it's not necessarily, it wasn't necessarily meant to lead to him being silent. That's the interesting thing is he's not asking for him to be silent. He's not going directly to him and saying please don't ask me any more questions, so I don't know that it was meant to make him be silent, but then why would he. But I guess it's like you have to be really, really careful because you don't know who can hear you or if your students are there, they might misinterpret what you're saying.

Laurie asks a question: "What do *we* think this is saying ... about the teacher student relationship?" This question, asked in the plural, further emphasizes the collaborative nature of their work—figuring out the lesson of the text is not an individual endeavor. The question is a supportive move since it is meant to help them flesh out their larger understanding of the text together—supportive of not any particular idea or question but of her partner's thinking process. It is representative of many of the questions that they ask each other, questions that are open ended, that do not have a right answer but support their joint work.

Laurie's supporting move creates space for Debbie to think through her ideas. Debbie points out that the text teaches that discouragement can shut a student off. At the same time, she poses a challenge to her idea—that what R. Papa said was not meant to be overheard. In the context of a collaborative *havruta* in which both partners continuously draw attention to alternative understandings of the text, challenging oneself makes perfect sense.

After Debbie has finished articulating her idea, Laurie offers supportive language to Debbie. She starts out with general support—"Ya, I agree." And she then gets more specific: "I definitely, I agree with you that this wasn't mean to be overheard...." She then builds on Debbie's idea that R. Papa's prayer was not meant to be overheard by extending it to mean that the prayer was not meant to make R. Shimi become silent. The lesson she draws from this is that "you have to be really, really careful of what you say because you don't know who can hear you," or if your students will misinterpret your words.

Up until this point, they have maintained a strong collaborative spirit through the different forms of support they provide to one another. They seem to be completely on the same page and instead of directly challenging one another, allow the text itself to challenge their thinking.

Challenging to Help, not to Argue

This sense of total agreement comes to an end when Laurie extends her idea a little bit further.

> **LAURIE:** I think it's going to the extreme and it's saying even when you're alone and you don't think anyone's listening, it can still filter out and, your students can still pick up on it.

> **DEBBIE:** But then doesn't that go against the whole notion of being able to pray and open up to God? Let's say you're, you know, it's during the lunchtime and he's doing the *minchah* service and he did this as he's praying. He said this, hoping, maybe to get strength, you know, like you said before, to preserve him from lashing out at this child. And then Shimi heard that. So I wonder: Is it saying to not open up your feelings even alone because somebody might hear you

because if you don't, you know, it seems like he's calling out to God to help him. You know, "Please preserve me from this rude child so I won't kill him." But Shimi, I mean I think it's, line four is a pivotal point because it shows the outcome of hearing such a prayer.

Debbie challenges Laurie's interpretation, suggesting Laurie's idea could be interpreted to mean that one should not open up to God in prayer, which logically does not make sense. She draws out the scene in which R. Papa was praying to God in order to help make her case. She then poses a challenging question to Laurie: "Is it saying to not open up your feelings even alone because somebody might hear you ..." However, she starts out by saying "I wonder," making clear that the question is not just a question to challenge Laurie but is a question that she too is wondering about. Debbie then shifts the focus of the conversation back to line four of the text, "The latter thereupon vowed silence and questioned him no more," which to her is the key to understanding the lesson of the text.

Laurie responds to the challenge by at first seeming to agree with Debbie. However, she does not simply acquiesce to Debbie's challenge and retreat, as she might have done if she either felt threatened by the challenge and/or was not particularly invested in her own idea. Debbie's gentle challenge has pushed Laurie to clarify her idea further. As Laurie talks, it becomes clear that she has another point she is trying to make.

LAURIE: Yah. And I think the other thing is that Shimi, I think there's, I agree. I think that there's sort of a disconnect here, where this [Shimi becoming silent] shows what happened, but Shimi could have also gone to him and said "I heard you. What's that about?" instead of just becoming silent, and he, Rabbi Papa, could have talked to him instead of, I don't think it's saying don't open up to God but it seems like—

Laurie is suggesting that the story could have been played out differently—that it might have had a different ending if R. Shimi had talked directly to R. Papa or if R. Papa had talked directly to R. Shimi. She is not trying to say that the lesson is not to open up to God, but that saying things when you are alone doesn't help you avoid negative consequences and so perhaps it is better to think about speaking to people directly. In this example, Debbie's challenge is the catalyst which pushes Laurie to begin to think through a clearer version of her alternative interpretation of the main point of the text.

Types of Supporting Moves

We can see in Debbie and Laurie's *havruta* examples of three different types of supporting moves. One kind of supporting move that they make quite frequently is to offer each other "supporting language." For example, when Debbie speaks, Laurie often says "hmm" in response to Laurie's articulations. The "hmm" doesn't necessarily indicate that Laurie agrees with Debbie's idea but signals to Debbie that Laurie is paying attention to Debbie's idea and that the idea may be worthy of further consideration. This kind of supporting move is not inconsequential. During the course of any one *havruta* session, partners come up with a great number of ideas. Many of those ideas die off seconds after being first uttered, while a few continue to be worked on as part of the discussion. Supporting language, however subtle or vague, can help keep an idea in play that might otherwise meet an untimely demise and can provide needed encouragement to a partner to continue to engage with the idea even when it seems hard.

Another level of supporting is implicit supporting. It occurs when partners build on each other's ideas. By building on one's partner's ideas, one sends a signal that these are good ideas and worth working on together. Laurie and Debbie engage in a great deal of this kind of implicit supporting, an aspect of interpretive discussion that I call co-building.[27] For example, as seen in the excerpts of their discussion above, Debbie suggests that the big idea of the talmudic text is that "any discouragement a student gets ... [can] really shut them off."[28] She then

---

[27] See the definition of and discussion about co-building in Orit Kent, "Interactive Text Study: A Case of Hevruta Learning," and Kent, "Interactive Text Study and the Co-Construction of Meaning."

[28] It is worth noting that in both the text as understood here by Debbie and in the *havruta* pair itself, encouragement and support keeps questions and ideas in play and people engaged, and discouragement and lack of support serve to shut off the development of questions and ideas, and also possibly the person him- or herself.

notes that R. Papa's prayer was not meant to be overheard. Laurie takes this latter idea and develops it further, stating that since it wasn't meant to be overheard and R. Papa didn't directly go to R. Shimi and ask him to be quiet, R. Shimi's silence can be understood as an unintended and unfortunate outcome of R. Shimi overhearing something not intended for his ears. Laurie's extension of Debbie's idea allows her to suggest a slightly different big idea, which is focused less on the interaction between teacher and student and more on the unintended consequences of one's actions. As Laurie says, "You have to be really careful because you don't know who can hear you...." This is an idea that Debbie further extends in the latter part of their *havruta*.

A third level of supporting comes in the form of making explicit moves to help one's partner develop her idea. This comes in the form of asking questions about one's partner's interpretation or the text that creates space for her to think some more, clarify her ideas, and flesh them out further. For example, Laurie asks Debbie, "So what do we think this is saying or could be saying about the teacher-student relationship maybe?"[29] and then pauses so that Debbie can think out loud. Explicit supporting moves also come in the form of offering supporting evidence for one's partner's idea. For example, as Laurie builds on Debbie's idea, she points to what is missing from the text to support their idea that R. Papa didn't intentionally silence R. Shimi. She notes that the text doesn't tell them that R. Papa went to R. Shimi to ask him to be quiet. "He's not going directly to him and saying please don't ask me any more questions." This extra bit of support for the idea seems to give the idea staying power for this *havruta*. Both Debbie and Laurie continue to be in agreement through the rest of the *havruta* that R. Papa didn't intend for R. Shimi to overhear him.

In these examples, all three types of supporting moves are focused on the ideas and the thinking, and not the person. This is important. The point of offering support is not that one likes or dislikes one's partner, or even necessarily likes or dislikes her idea, but that one is committed to helping develop the richest interpretations possible. Even if one

---

[29] This question also signifies the practices of both listening and wondering. It is useful to notice that in just one move a learner can engage in more than one *havruta* practice.

doesn't agree with one's partner (at least at first), one can still support her in making her ideas stronger. In the process of doing so, one may gain insight into one's partner's ideas, or even one's own. All three types of supporting moves are directed at the ideas on the table and are a means to encourage them forward.

Types of Challenging Moves

There are two main types of challenging that we see in this *havruta*. First, there is a direct form of challenging in which the partners say things like: "Is this idea supported by the text?" "What are the limitations of this idea?" Or, "How would this idea stand up under this particular hypothetical situation?" When Debbie challenges Laurie's idea in the excerpt above, she is suggesting a hypothetical situation in which Laurie's idea would not stand up. Laurie has said that the text is possibly suggesting that "even when you are alone and you don't think anyone's listening," you have to watch what you say. Debbie challenges this suggestion first with a principle: "But then doesn't that go against the whole notion of being able to pray to God and open up to God?" Debbie then brings a hypothetical scene to illustrate the principle and thereby calls attention to a limitation in Laurie's idea. Debbie's challenge helps Laurie step back and clarify her thinking. By helping one's partner entertain alternative evidence and ideas, this kind of challenging can help with the refinement of the *havruta's* thinking. It forces the partners to try to reconcile differences and in the process to get clearer on the limitations of a particular idea.

There is another type of challenging, a more implicit type of challenging in which the *havruta* partner simply suggests an alternative reading. Laurie does just that when she responds to Debbie's challenge. She suggests a third way to read the story—that the story could be read as being about a fundamental communication gap between the characters, since neither rabbi talks directly to the other. The weakness of implicit challenges is that they can go unnoticed and therefore not have an impact on the larger discussion. This is in fact what happens with Debbie and Laurie. Debbie doesn't pick up on Laurie's larger point and (in a later part of the transcript) simply takes the conversation back to an earlier idea she is still holding on to.

As with the supporting moves, when a *havruta* makes a challenging move, the challenge is not to the other person but to the idea, and the challenger does not need to disagree with the idea in order to challenge it or wonder about a possible weakness in it. The point of the challenging is to be able to help each other step back and think through one's ideas: are these ideas supported by the text? How does this interpretation stand in the face of alternative interpretations? In this way, *havruta* partners can help one another develop the strongest possible interpretations.

The Importance of Constructive Challenging

In their book *Academic Controversy*,[30] Johnson, Johnson, and Smith talk about the need for a "supportive climate" and a cooperative mode of working together for people to feel safe enough to challenge one another and to do so effectively. In the context in which Laurie and Debbie are learning together, the DeLeT Beit Midrash for Teachers, teachers spend time helping students create a spirit of collaboration, which focuses on the idea that *havruta* is a mutual undertaking—that both parties need each other in order to maximize their learning, augmenting each other's individual learning and doing things collectively that we cannot do as individuals—and that a successful *havruta* relies on each party being willing to take responsibility not only for her own learning but for her partner's learning as well.

Even before DeLeT students begin to study with each other, *havruta* partners meet to discuss their strengths and weaknesses as teachers and learners and how they might best be able to support one another through the course of the *beit midrash*. They continue to pay attention to their working relationship, reflecting on it and giving each other feedback about it, throughout their time in the *beit midrash*. In fact, in the middle of the course, each pair tape records itself so that pair members can look for evidence of ways that they are helping their partners' learn-

---

[30] David W. Johnson, Roger Johnson, and Karl A. Smith, *Academic Controversy: Enriching College Instruction through Intellectual Conflict*, ASHE-ERIC Higher Education Reports 25: 3 (Washington, DC: Jossey Bass, 1996).

ing and also examine instances when they make moves that get in their partners' way. For example, some students have pointed to the fact that they cut their partners off, not fully listening to their partners' ideas and helping them develop them further. The ongoing development of a sense of collaboration can, among other things, help *havrutot* successfully engage in challenging one another's ideas.[31]

Part of building a collaborative environment entails helping students develop a commitment to working together to develop the most compelling ideas possible, not simply sticking with an idea at the expense of all else. It is this commitment that can motivate them to put their own ideas aside for a moment, and stop to think about someone else's idea and how to make it stronger through supporting moves as well as investigate its weak points through challenging moves. In this way, constructive challenging is very different than debating, in which the goal is to win by making points that are often at the expense of one's colleagues. The goal of constructive challenging within *havruta* is to work with one's partner to notice the limitations of the ideas on the table (whatever their origins) and refine them. When effective, challenging can help a *havruta* come up with a better articulated interpretation, a more all-encompassing idea, or a new idea altogether.

The Interplay Between Supporting and Challenging in Debbie and Laurie's Havruta

Looking across the entire *havruta* session, Debbie and Laurie evince a great deal of support for one another's ideas and their challenges are very gentle—so gentle that they could go unnoticed. While it is important for a *havruta* to engage in supporting, too much supporting and too little challenging can lead to uncritical affirmation. Debbie and Laurie's *havruta* is at times at risk of moving into "affirmation" territory. While they generally steer clear of simply affirming one another,

---

[31] A commitment to and sense of collaboration is an important basis for all of the *havruta* practices, and engagement in the practices can also serve to reinforce this sense of collaboration. I specifically highlight collaboration here because there is more risk associated with challenging, and it is therefore even more important that the *havruta*'s work be based in a sense of collaboration to help make the challenging constructive.

if they were to continue to work together, it would likely be useful for them to focus on increasing the amount of challenging and making it more explicit.

Too much challenging with little support also has its risks. In such a case, a *havruta* can easily enter a never-ending cycle of debating, in which they simply take stands rather than exploring ideas. Finally, little challenging with little supporting can lend itself to a static discussion, in which each person puts forth her ideas without benefiting from interplay with her partner's thinking. As scholar of education Laurent Daloz posits,[32] the ideal condition for growth is to have a high degree of supporting along with a high degree of challenging. In such a situation, the *havruta* can work on strengthening the ideas on the table, while also examining them with a critical eye and grappling with alternatives.

Part V: Conclusion

> "It's important to learn with and from others so as to widen your perspective and think about things in new ways.... It's also good to be able to ask questions of another person and also to be able to voice your ideas out loud in order to clarify them for yourself."
> -Laurie's reflections

In Laurie's words we hear some of the potential benefits of *havruta* learning: working with a partner can expand one's perspective. One can learn new ideas and strategies from one's partner. One is helped by the questions that one's partner asks. Simply articulating ideas out loud to someone else provides an opportunity for clarifying one's thinking. Reading Laurie's remarks leaves the impression that not only did she have a productive *havruta*, and not only did learning with another positively affect her learning experience and the ideas she and her partner produced, but also that she had a sense of *how and why* she learned in a way that could continue to buttress her future learning.

---

[32] Laurent A. Daloz, *Mentor, Guiding the Journey of Adult Learners* (San Francisco: Jossey-Bass, 1999).

Obviously, it is important for every teacher to consider her learning goals and whether or not *havruta* is an appropriate way to help meet them. *Havruta* is not a panacea for teaching challenges or the right strategy to be used in every learning situation. *Havruta* is being used more frequently in a variety of contexts, but often without a plan to assure that students learn, and without pedagogic attention to its use, and with the implicit assumption that if we simply put two people together, they will have a generative discussion centered on the text. Even when learners do have productive *havruta* interactions, there is still a great deal of room for teachers to consider the greater learning potentials offered by deliberately and carefully framing *havruta* study, asking themselves not only "Why study in *havruta*?" but "What must I know or be able to do to make *havruta* an 'educative'[33] learning experience?" To maximize *havruta*'s potential, we must step back to consider the practices that create the opportunity for generative learning, what can get in the way of such learning, and—most significantly—what teachers can do to maximize *havruta's* learning potential.

Finally, a few words about meaning. In speaking of how teachers can locate meaning in students' work, Patricia Carini writes:

> What is meaning? Meaning arises through the relationship among things or persons: that mutual reciprocity that occurs in the act of truly "seeing" something.... Meaning designates the experience of relatedness which enhances and makes more vivid each of the events or persons it joins. For meaning to arise, there must be recognition.[34]

For Carini, there is something important about the quality of attention we have for another that affects the meaning we are able to make. It is through relating that true seeing arises, and through such powerful seeing of others and ourselves that we construct new meaning. Carini's description of what can occur between a teacher and student—the true

---

[33] John Dewey, *Experience and Education* (New York: Simon & Schuster, 1938/1997).

[34] Patricia F. Carini, ed., *Observation and Description: An Alternative Methodology for the Investigation of Human Phenomena*, North Dakota Study Group on Evaluation (North Dakota: University of North Dakota Press, 1975), 15.

seeing that leads to meaning-making and understanding—is no less applicable to what can occur between two *havruta* partners, and between the *havruta* partners and the text that they study.

At the heart of Laurie and Debbie's *havruta* relationship is the responsive space that each helps create in reaction to her partner and the text—that they create together through their listening and articulating, their wondering and focusing, their supporting and challenging—and through which they together find and make meaning. It is perhaps the power of this responsive space to which the Talmud alludes when it tells us that when two people listen to each other when studying halakha, the Shekhinah—God's presence on earth—listens to them as well.[35]

---

[35] Babylonian Talmud, Shabbat 63a.

PART 4

FOCUS ON CONTEXT

13 "Torah Talk": Teaching *Parashat Ha-shavua* to Young Children

Shira Horowitz

Introduction:
Listening to children's voices and "Torah Talk"

Young children have so much to say about the world. Listening to their comments and observations fascinates me; listening to their questions challenges me and reminds me that children are filled with wonder and wondering, and that I need to continually find ways to provide opportunities for their questions, which are at the heart of their learning.

In my classroom, I teach *Parashat Ha-shavua*, the weekly Torah portion, to kindergartners and first graders in a way that shares my passion for reading and studying the Torah[1] and also allows me to hear my students' voices. We take stories in the Torah and make them come alive as I guide children through a process of connecting to biblical text as they begin to see themselves as part of the Jewish people's textual tradition. It is a text that I love reading and studying, part of a tradition that I care about deeply and want to share in an authentic way, but I feel an equally strong responsibility to listen to my students, to help them find their own connections and their own voices with which to respond to the Torah text.

My students' comments and questions during Torah study reinforce my belief that young children are capable of thinking about big ideas, and give me insight into their spiritual development and into how they think about God and the Jewish people. Their interactions with each other allow me to create a community of learners with shared language

---

[1] This chapter is entirely about my teaching of *Parashat Ha-shavua*, the weekly portion of the Torah. When I speak about "teaching Torah" or just "Torah" without a definite article, I am locating my teaching—and my students' learning—in the entire body of Jewish learning. When I refer to "the Torah," with the definite article, I am specifically referring to the first five books of the Hebrew Bible and its weekly Torah-reading cycle.

and experiences discussing Torah together. Each fall, I begin again with a group of students who are relatively new to talking about Torah. As the year goes on, they build content knowledge as well as skills for listening and responding to the Torah text; as we create a culture of shared Torah learning, the students change as a class, learning to listen to each other and respond in respectful ways. "Talking Torah," listening to each other's ideas, and reflecting together all become part of our classroom culture.

This does not all happen magically at the beginning. But every year, a time comes when I step back and listen to the conversation and find the change has occurred: children are sharing ideas, reflecting, questioning and challenging each other, and referring back to other sections of Torah. Suddenly, I think, this is what sophisticated Torah discussions sound like. These students know how to study Torah. This is a community of Torah learners.

In this chapter, I will explore the context in which my particular approach to teaching *Parashat Ha-shavua* to young children has developed, and then focus on my goals in teaching Torah in this context. At the core of my method is its consistent, predictable structure and schedule. Like a writing or reading workshop in which children come to expect certain beginnings, time to do certain kinds of work, and certain kinds of endings, "Torah Talk" is based on a particular structure with four major components. I will explain each of them in detail, and illustrate one lesson from planning through implementation.

Background and Assumptions

When I began teaching *Parashat Ha-shavua* to kindergartners and first graders at the South Area Solomon Schechter Day School,[2] there were very few resources for teaching it to young children (*First Steps in Learning Torah with Young Children,* published by the BJE of Greater New York,[3] was a notable exception). Most early childhood resources seemed

---

[2] The school is now located in Norwood, MA, and has been renamed Kehillah Schechter Academy (KSA).
[3] Rivka Behar, Floreva Cohen, and Ruth Musnikow, *First Steps in Learning Torah with Young Children* (New York: Bureau of Jewish Education of Greater New York, 1993).

to suggest that we could use the Torah only as a source for "Bible stories," emphasizing creation and Noah's ark while skipping non-narrative sections entirely. I had come to teaching with a strong background in early literacy as well as a personal interest in and connection to learning and teaching Torah. With the support of our Head of School at the time, Jane Taubenfeld Cohen, I decided to take all that I knew about good early literacy teaching and apply it to teaching Torah. I never imagined at the time that the routines I was introducing to that group of kindergartners would develop into a structure for teaching Torah that I would continue to use for 15 years.

I started with several assumptions about literacy. First, oral language is an important skill for young children. Long before they can express their ideas through writing, children have much to say aloud. As teachers, we need to make sure that children have the opportunity to express themselves through talk, both for the sake of oral language development and as a rehearsal for their writing.

The second assumption is that children need to learn to respond to texts that they hear or read. Reading (or listening to a story) is a process of making meaning, in which the reader (or listener) interacts with the text. When children hear or read a text, they should be able to retell it, to respond to parts they like, to make a personal connection. They should be able to ask questions of the text. These kinds of responses can happen in oral discussions or in response journals. Both talk and writing are useful tools for making sense of the text.

Third, children just learning to write can begin to learn to use written expression as a way to record their ideas. When we offer them a journal, we broaden our ideas about their "writing" to include talk, drawing, and writing. Often this writing can offer us a window into children's thinking beyond what they might tell us orally or directly.

Finally, speaking, listening, reading and writing are all important literacy skills that children can use across the curriculum. If children spend time writing in a Torah journal, they will practice important writing skills that will transfer to other times of the day. If children practice responding to stories in the context of Torah, this will enhance their ability to understand and respond to other books. Therefore, a literacy-based Torah curriculum would not "take away" from time spent on other areas; in fact, it would enhance it.

"Torah Talk": Teaching Parashat Ha-shavua to Young Children

In addition to these assumptions about literacy, I also began with some assumptions about children and Torah. Children wonder about their world and often think about big, difficult ideas. Given the opportunity, children will ask questions that are often deep and philosophical. The Torah is filled with stories and ideas about many of the same questions that children wonder about: How was the world created? What is a family? What are right and wrong ways to act with other people? What do we know about God? I also brought to this project the assumption that, given the right support and structures, Torah learning at the earliest ages can be the beginning of lifelong learning.

Context: My School, My Students, My Classroom

I began teaching Torah to kindergartners and first graders at the South Area Solomon Schechter Day School in 1995. SASSDS (now KSA) is a Conservative Jewish day school in the greater Boston area with an integrated curriculum. As the classroom teacher, I am responsible for teaching both the Judaic and the secular curricula. Whenever possible, I try to find ways to connect the two, through either content or skills. A unit on the moon, for example, includes observations and discussions of its phases, as well as an introduction to the Jewish calendar. Although my schedule does include self-contained lessons in Torah, reading, writing, and math, the lines between subjects are often blurred, as we illustrate Torah stories we have read, or compare a character from literature to a biblical character.

The students in my first grade classes are 6 and 7 years old. Some can read English quite well, while others are just learning. All are just beginning to read and write in Hebrew. Some come from homes where *Parashat Ha-shavua* is a common, familiar topic of discussion, while others come with little or no familiarity with Torah study. Students also come with a variety of abilities and learning styles: some learn well by listening, while others need to move, or need visual cues; some are able to express their ideas easily, while others need additional support to succeed. Any methods I choose to teach Torah must have room for all of these different kinds of learners.

Well before we begin to study *Parashat Ha-shavua*, we look at the *Sefer Torah*, stored inside the *aron kodesh* (ark), which holds a central place in our classroom. We notice how beautifully it is decorated and discuss why the Torah would be stored in such a special place, and we open up the Torah scroll so students can look inside and observe what they see. All of this is done in an atmosphere of seriousness and awe. From the beginning, I establish the fact that if the *Sefer Torah* is out, we must pay attention to it, not start talking with our friends about their clothes or arguing about who was first in line. Similarly, holding a *Sefer Torah* is a privilege in my classroom, one that carries with it the responsibility to behave appropriately.

We begin each day with a morning service. Each Monday and Thursday, during first grade *Tefillot*, we take the Torah out of the *aron* and have a small Torah service. A student walks around with the Torah as we sing "*Torah tziva lanu Moshe*," and everyone has a chance to kiss it. We then open up the Torah and I chant one or two lines from the week's *parashah* in Hebrew. We do not have our full study of Torah at that moment, but we name the week's *parashah* and we make very explicit links to the Torah discussion we will have later.

As the students get used to hearing the words of Torah chanted aloud each week, they begin to notice familiar names and words. At first I might call their attention to a specific word ("See if you can hear a name of someone you recognize..."), and later, they begin to do this on their own. As their spoken Hebrew vocabulary develops, they often notice words that they know, linking their modern Hebrew learning with their study of the ancient words of the Torah. After I am done reading from the Torah, we usually go around the room so that everyone can say a word they heard and recognized. All of this teaches students to listen closely to the Torah reading, to focus and notice that there are words they know and may even be able to understand long before they are fluent in Hebrew.

Every Monday and Thursday, when it is time for "Torah Talk", the routine is this: (1) I tell the story of the weekly *parashah*, (2) students act it out or do some other interactive activity, and (3) we sit in a circle and each student has a chance to share a comment or question that they are thinking about (something they like, something that confuses them, or something they wonder about). On Thursdays we repeat this routine and add one step, (4) the students write and draw a page in their Torah journals.

"Torah Talk": Teaching *Parashat Ha-shavua* to Young Children

Choices and Challenges

The text of the Torah is challenging for children at this age. The written text itself is not yet accessible to them because of their reading level. Even when read aloud, whether in Hebrew or in translation, the language is often above their comprehension level. Beyond the difficult language, the themes and concepts are also sometimes quite challenging for young children. The text deals with difficult questions involving personal relationships, abstract ideas about time and history, and complicated concepts such as an understanding of God. Children who are still at an age where they understand things quite literally may struggle to understand these aspects.

Another challenge to teachers of *Parashat Ha-shavua* is that there are many places in the Torah where the text moves very quickly—for example, during the many powerful stories packed into the first few *parashiot* of *Bereishit*. By studying *Parashat Ha-shavua*, we are forced to choose selections from each *parashah*, inevitably rushing through or skipping sections on which, in another context, we might have chosen to spend more time. Yet other weeks it can feel challenging to find something appropriate for or relevant to young children—for examples, in the *parashiot* devoted to the laws of sacrifices or sexual purity.

The school calendar also presents its difficulties. When holidays, vacations, and other events interrupt our schedule, we can put our studies of math and science on hold and return to them when we next meet. But the cycle of *Parashat Ha-shavua* marches on whether we are there or not. When we "miss" a *parashah*, do we try to catch up or just skip it? In theory, since we are focusing on the portion for each week during that week, there is no need to "catch up" and fill in, but we sometimes need to fill in the story line of a missed *parashah* or *parashiot* so that the subsequent story makes sense, or occasionally to make sure that we don't miss an important component of early Jewish literacy such as, for example, the Ten Commandments.

What we gain by staying linked to the reading for any given week (rather than focusing on certain texts for longer periods of times) is the ability to convey a sense of continuity, a commitment to the wider Jewish community, and an attachment to the place of Torah within the Jewish world. Just as students learn about holidays and come to realize that Jews all over the world are celebrating the same holiday at the same time, they learn that this week's *parashah* in our classroom is the same as this week's *parashah* throughout our school, in their synagogues, in Israel, and throughout the world. Those who come from families where the *parashah* is discussed at home can bring in information they learn there. Those who go to synagogue on Shabbat can carry with them the information they learn at school and find it echoed there. When they cycle back through these *parashiot* for a second and third time in successive grades, the students learn to place themselves in a cycle of time that is marked by stories as much as by holidays, and by revisiting these stories each year, remembering the pieces we've learned before and looking for new details and new meanings.

Torah as Both a Literary and a Religious Text

I have many goals for my kindergarten and first-grade students in our Torah curriculum. I want them to: appreciate that for Jews, learning Torah is not just like reading or studying any other book; understand the sense of *kedusha* (sanctity) with which Jews approach the Torah; hear it as a special story about our people and land, a text that connects them to the Jewish people throughout time; and regard it with a sense of ownership and pride. At the same time, I want them to learn to approach and interact with the Torah text like they would any text: to be able to listen to the stories and the non-narrative sections and retell the plot or other details, summarize what is important, and talk about a character's motivations or surprising plot twists.

In many ways, the literacy skills that children develop as they study Torah each week are the same as the reading comprehension strategies they learn to use when reading picture books or hearing fairy tales, such as retelling, summarizing, inferring characters' feelings, and visualizing images to match the words. They learn to make connections between their own experiences and those in the text, as well as between different stories or different parts of text. They learn to make characters "come alive" as they place themselves in the shoes of the characters and imagine what they might say or how they might act. They learn to use speech and writing to make sense of their reading. In choosing a favorite part of the story to talk or write about, they learn to respond to the text in a very personal way and interact with it, asking questions of the text

"Torah Talk": Teaching *Parashat Ha-shavua* to Young Children

and even challenging it at times when it doesn't make sense to them. Developing all of these skills in Torah study helps them not only in their study of Torah, but as they encounter any literature.

While I encourage children to respond in many different ways to each *parashah*, I particularly encourage them to ask questions of the text, to find parts of the text that they do not understand or that they wonder about. They can and do use the Torah text as a context for asking many of their big questions, including many of the things they wonder about God. So it goes both ways: challenging the text and asking questions of it are not only good generic reading skills, but traditional ways for Jews to respond to Torah. For both reasons, I want children to know that questions are worth asking even when they don't have simple answers, and to value the very process of wondering and thinking about difficult questions.

However, when I am teaching *Parashat Ha-shavua*, I am not only helping children build the basic foundations of reading literacy both generally and with respect to the Torah but also building Jewish cultural literacy as they get to know the Torah text as both narrative and law, learning the plot and characters of key stories and exploring passages that contain rules and directions relevant to contemporary behavior. Additionally, I want children to connect to the Torah text at a more personal level than they would to any other single piece of literature. I want the Torah's stories to come alive for them as they think about the people in Torah as real people with emotions, thoughts, and interactions. By asking my students to put themselves into Avraham's shoes as they act out moving to a new land, or imagine what Noah was thinking when God asked him to build an ark, I encourage them to take these stories and make them their own, and to see these characters—especially the *avot* and *imahot*, the original matriarchs and patriarchs—as part of their family. We spend a lot of time understanding the family relationships between Avraham and Sarah; Yitzchak and Rivkah; and Yaakov, Rachel, and Leah. When Yaakov's name is changed to Yisrael, we talk about the term *b'nei yisrael* (the children of Israel) and its use today. I encourage my students to see themselves as the children's children's children, placing themselves on the larger Jewish family tree. Similarly, I make many explicit connections between the land of Israel as the place of Torah stories and the modern state of Israel.

Beyond developing literary skills (both general and Jewish) and engaging with the content of the Torah text, I want my students to develop a love and respect for the Torah itself, and to place it in the greater communal context outside of our classroom. The sections of Torah we talk about are not just the chapter we happen to be up to, but are for the most part being read by Jews all over the world that day or week. I encourage my students to look at this ongoing return to the Torah text as a privilege. I want them to feel emotionally connected to the Torah itself, to be excited when they hear a piece of the Torah that they've heard before, to love hearing Torah stories and discussing ideas from Torah—and to share this love of Torah with each other, with their families, and with others in the school.

Finally, it is also important that the students make connections between Torah and their own lives. When we study creation, we relate it to the practices of Shabbat. Biblical characters become models for teaching values (e.g. Rivkah is a model for the value of kindness to animals when she offers water to the camels). When we study laws given to Moshe at Sinai, I focus particularly on those that my students can follow in their own lives. When the connections are less obvious, I make them more explicit (e.g., relating sacrifices to the ways we pray to God today).

Components of "Torah Talk"

The depth of conversation, the connections my students are able to make, and the ways in which they are able to respond to the Torah text by the end of the year are all supported by the structure that we build and use throughout the year. As Lucy Calkins says about writing workshops:

> It is significant to realize that the most creative environments in our society are not the ever-changing ones. The artist's studio, the researcher's laboratory, the scholar's library are each deliberately kept simple so as to support the complexities of the work-in-progress. They are deliberately kept predictable so the unpredictable can happen.[4]

---

[4] Lucy M. Calkins, *Lessons From a Child: On the Teaching and Learning of Writing* (Portsmouth, NH: Heinemann, 1983).

"Torah Talk": Teaching *Parashat Ha-shavua* to Young Children

"Torah Talk" has four main components:

1. Telling/retelling
2. Acting out
3. "Torah Talk" (after which the larger framework is named): sharing comments and questions
4. Torah Journals

Telling/Retelling

Each Monday and Thursday, I begin by telling and retelling the story or parts of the *parashah*. I present the story orally, though I often have a text in front of me. I usually have the *Humash* open so that I can refer to specific phrases in Hebrew, and so that the children make the connection that this story is in the written text, even though they are hearing it orally.

Clearly, any oral retelling involves making choices about what to tell and what to focus on. I usually prepare by reading through the whole *parashah* myself so that I have the overall context. Often I choose the most familiar stories in the *parashah*, the key narrative parts, or a part that I think has a relevant lesson that my students can apply to their own lives. As I make each of these choices, I focus on my larger goals for teaching Torah: teaching general and Jewish textual literacy skills; fostering Jewish cultural literacy; developing in my students a love of and respect for the Torah as a whole; and encouraging a sense of Torah's relevance for contemporary behavior. (I explore this in greater detail in the section of this chapter entitled "Choosing Which Parts to Tell," below.)

Acting and Role-Playing

Either during the retelling or after I am done, when the *parashah* is primarily narrative, I have the students act out parts of the story they have just heard. I quickly assign parts, set the scene, and then let them re-enact the scene as they imagine it. When necessary, I even suggest what each character should say.

Part of the reason for doing this is simply to get students up and moving after a long time of sitting still and listening. For some students, this movement and active involvement is essential to being able to take in the story and remember it. While oral storytelling and referring to the written text are essential to Torah study, they are not the ideal modes of learning for all students. For some students, this activity allows them to put themselves in the shoes of the character and bring the story alive. While they often re-enact just what they heard from the text, there are many times when the "actor" elaborates on the story. They fill in lines that they think the character might have said, or show with their movements and facial expressions how they think the character might have felt. At some level, they are interpreting the text, making their own midrash.

Because this active engagement is so important, there are times when I have everyone stand up and act out a certain part of the *parashah* together. For example, when learning about *b'nei yisrael* being slaves in Egypt, I might have everyone act out working hard as slaves and not being able to take a break. When we learn about the special clothes that the *kohanim* (priests) wore, I often assign half the class to be *kohanim* and the other half to make the special clothes and dress the *kohanim*. This activity takes only about two minutes, but everyone is actively involved and the text is made more real.

Acting out these stories also helps the children to imagine and understand the world of the past, keeping the text in its historical context. When they act out "walking through the desert with the camels," the activity helps them to understand that people in the times of the Torah used different forms of transportation than we use today. At the same time, re-enacting the stories may help the child bring the text into the present in some way. When they act out Avraham inviting guests into his tent, they can, for example, connect that experience to their own experiences welcoming guests into their homes or our classroom.

"Torah Talk" (Comments and Questions)

After we are done retelling the story and acting it out, my students know to return to the rug, sitting in a circle, to get ready for "Torah Talk." We then go around the circle, and each person has a chance to give a personal response by making a comment about the *parashah*, mentioning something they remember or especially liked about the *parashah*, or asking a question. Often we use a "talking stick" to mark whose turn it is and to remind each other that only the person holding the stick should be talking while others are listening. I go around and give each person a turn. I find that this takes away some of the pressure that children often feel when they are wondering when they will be called on and trying to remember what they want to say. It also helps them to be able to listen to others' comments and questions as they build their discussion skills.

At first, particularly with the youngest children, this activity can be challenging. Some children have trouble thinking of anything to say. Some need to be prompted with sentence starters ("I remember when ..." or "I liked the part when ..."). Some children will only repeat what students before them have said. Still, each child has a chance to say something aloud, and this often helps them to rehearse what they will later write or draw in their Torah journals. At this early stage, when most children do not say more than one line, I find it helpful to write down what each child says so that we can refer back to it. Sometimes I type up these responses at the end of each week and send them home to share with families.

Over time, these very structured routines develop into sophisticated discussions about the *parashah*. Students begin to ask questions and wonder aloud about things they hear. They question each other and challenge each other's comments, or offer their own answers to their friends' questions. As they get better at listening to each other and responding appropriately, we can often let go of the "one turn each" structure, and they begin to talk to each other in a more natural way. By the end of a year of practice "talking Torah" with each other, they can sound like a group of much older students, having deep, thoughtful discussions.

"Torah Talk" is another critical way in which the students develop a relationship with the text. They learn that the way to listen to Torah stories is not only to listen passively, but also to interact and respond. Even a child's simple retelling of a part that they remember helps that child to make the text personal, as the words come from his or her mouth. By choosing one part of the story that they like, students learn to bring their attention to different parts of the text or story and select a detail. They also learn that it is okay, even encouraged, to have an opinion about the text.

As they learn to give reasons for why they like a certain part of the story, some students are interested in sections that feel familiar (like stories about people getting married or having babies), others are excited by characters who do extraordinary things (such as the brothers throwing Yosef in the pit), and still others are fascinated by learning about God's power (creating the world, for example, or making the flood). By sharing these out loud in a group, they also get to hear what other people choose as "favorite" parts, which can stretch children to think about something they might not have thought of on their own.

The structure of "Torah Talk" allows everyone to participate from the beginning, while allowing for responses to become more varied and sophisticated as the year progresses. At first, most of what the students do during "Torah Talk" is either retelling parts of the *parashah* or choosing parts that they like:

> "I liked it when Avraham moved to a different place."
> "I liked it when Avraham listened to God."
> "I liked when God promised them that they would have children."

Throughout the year, children continue to retell parts of the *parashah* and choose their favorite sections. But they also begin to think about characters' feelings and wonder why people act in certain ways in these stories:

> "I like when his [Yosef's] dad chose him for his favorite son."
> "I don't like it when they took the coat and put animal blood on it, because that made their dad really sad."
> "Why did the brothers lie to their own father?"
> "Why did they throw him in a pit?"

When learning non-narrative sections of Torah, children focus on a variety of aspects of the text and respond in a variety of ways. After learning about some of the rules presented in *Parashat Mishpatim*, some students restate the rules they have learned. Some wonder why there are so many rules. Others use this *parashah* to add to their growing understandings of God:

> "Don't steal."
> "If you dig a hole, you should bury it up so nobody falls in."
> "The rules are to keep people safe."
> "Without rules, we wouldn't know that there would be a God, that there would be a thing called Shabbat or the Jewish religion. We wouldn't know anything about being Jewish."

Sometimes they challenge the text or challenge God with their questions:

> "Why did Yaakov give Yosef a colorful jacket if that wasn't fair to the other brothers?"
> "Why did the brothers want to trick the father that he was dead?"
> "Why did Par'oh keep changing his mind?"
> "Why did God make all the plagues?"
> "If God said don't murder, why did God kill Par'oh's son?"
> "How could God have made all those people die if God is supposed to be good?!"

Their questions can be literary, about the text itself, or theological, about the view of God raised by the text. Once they begin to ask questions, the children are not only responding to the text but interacting with it. They are practicing a good general literacy skill—asking questions as you read (or hear) a text—as well as engaging in a very Jewish way of reading Torah.

From the beginning, I encourage children to ask questions and give a lot of positive feedback each time they ask a question rather than just saying, "I like the part when...." Some years, when these "big" questions seem to come up throughout the week and not just during "Torah Talk", I keep a notebook labeled "Questions about God and Torah" near the *aron kodesh* in our classroom, in which children can write (or dictate) their questions as they arise.

Other teachers often ask me how I answer the harder questions, whether they are questions about God or about whether the stories in the Torah are "real." In fact, I rarely answer any of the questions at all, unless they are basic factual ones from the story that can be easily explained. I often respond with, "That's a great question." Sometimes, I turn it back to the child who asked, saying "What do you think?," or ask if another student would like to try to answer. When it is a question that often comes up in traditional commentaries or other Jewish thought, I might say, "Many adults ask that question, too." Depending on our time constraints, we may or may not have a discussion about the question, or we may return to the question at another time. Or I may simply say, "Great question. Let's not answer that right now.... Keep thinking about it."

The time constraints of our classroom setting combined with the limits on children's ability to sit through long discussions make it impossible to return to every child's question. However, a consistent message to the students is: questions are worth asking even when we don't get an answer right away. Asking questions is a valid way of thinking in its own right. Not all questions have easy answers; some are the kind that we keep thinking about for a long time.

Torah Journals: Dictating, Drawing, Writing

If we conceive of young children's "writing" as their talk, drawings, and print combined, even those who are not yet proficient readers and writers can "write" and express their thoughts. In my classroom, as in most, children write from the very first day of school, in an ongoing writing workshop as well as in particular subject areas like Torah. They quickly get used to the idea that they can use the sounds they hear to write before they know conventional spellings, and learn to copy unusual words like people's names from lists posted around the room.

In this context, Torah journals have flowed very naturally. From the opening weeks of school, students have a place where they record what they learn from each *parashah* and their personal responses to them. Children who are not yet independent writers often draw or have teachers act as their scribes. For those who are beginning to write, Torah journals can be a place for them to experiment with new words and ideas. As with reading comprehension strategies, the integration of these literacy skills and Judaic content comes naturally, with each providing support for the other.

After each Thursday's "Torah Talk" discussion, students work on their Torah journals. This sequence is important because in many ways the oral talk works as a rehearsal before the children do the more challenging task of writing. I encourage them to draw a picture, to write, or to dictate something from the *parashah*: a part they particularly liked, something they wondered about, a question they had. Although reading response logs are often used in classrooms with older children, this is an adaptation that works even with kindergartners. (I use blank white paper for their journal pages.)

I use similar techniques with first graders, except that I provide paper with some lines and expect them to write more independently along with their illustrations. In addition, I try to stretch the first graders' thinking about the *parashah* by providing pages with specific questions for them to answer, often questions which link the *parashah* to their own lives explicitly.

Choosing Which Parts to Tell

Most *parashiot* in the Torah are complex, long, and filled with far more than I could possibly teach in one or two lessons. How do I decide what to tell and what to emphasize each week?

I begin by reading the original Torah text myself. If it is chiefly a narrative section, I sketch out the main narrative points. Sometimes these fall easily into a short outline of several important events. Other weeks, there are too many different parts of the story with many important details, and I have to make decisions about which parts I will include.

Some stories I identify as basic to Jewish cultural literacy even for children—for example, Avraham welcoming the guests to his tent, and Moshe at the burning bush. Others involve narrative details without which the larger story does not flow. I cannot skip the section about Yosef being thrown into the pit if I want the later stories about his reunification with his brothers to make sense. Finally, some sections in the Torah reflect larger themes that I want to emphasize as part of the students' Jewish education, because the themes are connected to Jewish identity and/or because they teach values or practices that I want to encourage students to incorporate into their own lives.

After I read the *parashah* itself, one of my favorite resources to use is *First Steps in Learning Torah with Young Children*, which was mentioned briefly above. For each *parashah*, the authors choose a few passages and suggest a way to present the narrative. They usually connect the passages to a Jewish concept that relates to children's lives, and also provide suggested activities for early childhood classrooms. While I often choose to include more details from a given *parashah*, I find that this series' authors provide an excellent starting point as well as wonderful extension activities.

Planning: Organizing for Me and for My Students

Just as I need this outline of the main narrative points I want to tell, to help me organize the information I have chosen in a given *parashah*, my students also benefit from organizers that help them pay attention to the most important information. As I plan my telling, I know that some children will listen and remember every detail while others would not possibly be able to hold onto all the information. I need to decide ahead of time which are the most basic elements that I want to be sure every child will remember. This might include, for example, the names and places I want them to remember, as well as the two or three main points. As I tell the story, I try to emphasize these key elements through repetition, and highlight them so the students know they are important to remember. Sometimes I list them on a chart, stop and ask review questions as I come to these parts, and/or stop and say, "This part is *really* important," before continuing with the story. With my own list of narrative points to highlight, as well as basic names, facts and important "big ideas," I am better able to teach in a way that conveys to every student the essence of the lesson on that *parashah*.

As I plan, I also look for points of connection that I want to emphasize. If I notice that a character in the *parashah* has the same name as a child in my class, I know from experience that this will generate excitement. If a child in the class has a new baby sibling, the appearance in the *parashah* of a child being born will also be very exciting. Sometimes their general experience and background knowledge serves as a connection that helps children understand a story—for example, thinking about their own experiences with brothers and sisters can help them connect to the jealousy among siblings that comes through in so many of the stories in *Bereishit*.

While I want children to connect the stories of the Torah to their own lives and use that information to help them understand what they're learning, I also want them to be able to think about the ways in which these stories are unfamiliar and take place in another time and context. In my planning, I look for places in the text that will not make sense to the children without some clarification. People lived in tents, not modern houses. They got water from a well, not a faucet in the sink.

"Torah Talk": Teaching *Parashat Ha-shavua* to Young Children

They were traveling in a desert, not through a forest or city. Emphasizing these points over and over helps young children understand how life was different "back in the Torah times" and to visualize the narrative in a different way.

While I want my students to relate to the Torah as a narrative text filled with wonderful, exciting, and interesting stories, I also consider the elements of Jewish identity and values I plan to emphasize over the course of the year, and which if any are found in a particular *parashah*. For example, our connection to the land of Israel is rooted in the Torah. When I teach sections of Torah in which this idea comes up, I plan an explicit connection to what they are also learning about the modern state of Israel. First-graders in my class also learn about prayer as a way of communicating our thanks, our wants, and our needs to God. When I identify an example in *Parashat Ha-shavua* of someone using prayer in one of these ways, I plan to emphasize it and connect it explicitly with our own experiences during *tefillot*. Later in the year, when we arrive at *parashiot* that are filled not with stories but with rules and laws, I look for examples that my students can relate to and apply to their own lives. Thus, the study of Torah is about both "far away and long ago" and our lives as Jews in the here and now.

I also do my planning with an eye toward which parts will make sense for students to act out. I may include the larger narrative or focus on a small section. Sometimes there will be only three or four actors, and everyone else will be the audience. Other times, I assign several individual roles but ask everyone else to play a group part (e.g., the Egyptians suffering from the plagues, while Moshe goes to talk to Pharaoh). Occasionally, I will pair everyone up and everyone acts out a scene simultaneously as I narrate—for example, the situation I described above, in which one person in the pair is the *kohen* and the other dresses him in the appropriate clothing.

I rarely plan the exact dialogue or casting. I expect the acting out to be rough improvisation, not a polished performance. Ideally, I want students to think about the story and imagine the words a character might have said, or use the words that I have told them from the text. If a child cannot think of what to say, however, I do not hesitate to suggest ideas or even give them the specific words to say. By the end of the year, most students are able to improvise successfully without much prompting.

Implementation: *Parashat Lech Lecha*

What does each of these components look like in practice? To provide a more complete picture, I will describe in detail one lesson on *Parashat Lech Lecha* that I taught on a Monday in the fall of 2004, from planning through implementation.[5]

Like many of the *parashiot* in *Sefer Bereishit*, *Lech Lecha* is full of stories and details and is in many ways a foundational section for children to learn. The first of our Jewish ancestors, Avraham and Sarah, are introduced in this *parashah*, and the rest of this biblical book will tell the stories of their family. Children must become familiar with them for the purposes of the narrative and as part of their basic Jewish cultural literacy. This *parashah* also introduces the idea of the *brit*, the covenant between God and Avraham. With its two focal points, an emphasis on children and on the land of Israel, the *brit* becomes a central theme throughout the rest of *Bereishit*.

Because this lesson took place early in the year, I needed to limit how many narrative points I included; the more details I told the children, the less likely it was that they would remember the ones I thought were the most important. I knew I would be most successful if I identified parts of the story to which the children could relate. Finally, I knew that I was still establishing their connection to the people and families in the Torah. Avraham and Sarah were not characters that my students already knew well, cared about, or whose actions they were able to predict, but they would be hearing about them and "living with them" for a number of weeks. The choices I made for this *parashah* would carry over into the following several lessons.

The way the *parashah* starts out, with God telling Avram *"lech lecha"*—to leave his home and go to a new place—is essential to understanding the *parashah*. After that, the children would need to know that Avraham did what God told him to do and went to this new place, and to understand the idea of the *brit*, the promise that God made to Avraham, and the components of that promise. The only other plot line that I chose to include was the argument between Avraham and Lot's herdsmen over the land, so the children would begin to understand the importance of

---

[5] My intern videotaped this lesson while I was teaching.

land in that time and place. In addition, I felt that Avraham's behavior in choosing not to fight with his nephew, instead allowing Lot to choose which direction to go, provided a model that my students could consider emulating in their own conflicts. "You could act like Avraham," I imagined, might become part of the language of the classroom in coming weeks when I wanted to suggest the value of avoiding conflict when possible by offering a compromise.

I chose not to include the story of Avraham going to Egypt during the famine and pretending Sarah was his sister rather than his wife, the episode in chapter 14 about the war between the kings, or chapter 15's covenant. While these will be interesting texts for these children to learn later in their Torah study, I need to make reasonable choices based on time constraints and the students' developmental abilities. The stories of Hagar and Yishmael being sent away, and even of Avraham's circumcision, are texts that would be difficult but interesting to teach, and if there were more time I could imagine including them at this age, but knowing that the narrative could move forward without these plot points I reserved these, too, for later study.

Telling

The first thing I want my students to know is the name of the *parashah*. Since they are introduced to it when we take out the Torah and read from it first thing Monday morning during *tefillot*, I usually begin our "Torah Talk" session with two review questions: Does anyone remember the name of last week's *parashah* (implicitly reminding them that we are reading a section of a continuous text that links from one week to the next, much like a new chapter of a long book)? Does anyone remember the name of this week's *parashah* from this morning?

I then introduce two important people who I want the children to recognize: Avram and Sarai.

> This *parashah* tells us about two very important people. One is named Avram, and the other is his wife named Sarai. You might have heard about Avraham and Sarah. They're the same people, but their names are going to be changed.

I emphasize these names several times, asking the children to repeat them and making sure they say the names correctly. Many of them recognize the names Avraham and Sarah from their previous exposure to Torah. I introduce them this way to connect to what the children already know.

> When this *parashah* starts out, the *parashah* tells us that God is talking. God comes to Avram and says, "*lech lecha.*" What does that mean?

Since we went over the name of the *parashah* earlier that morning during the Torah service, I want to see how many children remember what the words mean. Several respond right away: "Go."

> Right, go. God says, I want you to go to a new place. I want you to leave here, leave your land, leave your family's house, and go to a new place that I will show you. And when you go to that new place, I will make you a great nation, and I will bless you.

This idea of leaving a familiar place and going to a new place is central to this *parashah*, and will be repeated several times.

For the first time that day, I ask the children to predict what Avram would do. Most of them expect that Avram would do whatever God asked, and I confirm for them that in fact that was what happened. At this point I stop to emphasize a connection that many of the children will be able to make between their own experiences and this story.

> Has anybody here ever moved before? Does anybody remember what it felt like when you had to move? I want you to think about Avram and Sarai, and what they might have felt like when God said, I want you to move to a new place that I will show you.

But I also want to emphasize how different the context was. As they began to visualize Torah stories and make pictures in their minds, they needed to imagine people walking rather than driving, moving through a hot and dry desert rather than along a modern highway.

> They had to walk and travel with their camels, because they were going through the desert. What's it like in the desert?

After a short discussion about the desert, I returned to the story, intentionally emphasizing the connection to the land of Israel.

> ... They started going to the place that God showed them. Do you know the name of that place? In the times of the Torah, it was called *Cana'an*. And *Cana'an* is an old name for what we call today, Israel.

As I describe the argument between Avram's and Lot's shepherds, I emphasize Avram's willingness to compromise in order to avoid a fight.

> When they got to *Cana'an*, they had a little problem. Avram had his own sheep, and his nephew Lot had his own sheep. In the area where they were, there wasn't enough food for the animals. The people helping them started to fight. Avram said, "You know what, I don't want to have a fight, Lot. You're part of my family. So you choose where you want to go. Whichever way you choose, I'll go in the other direction."

Next, I describe for the students the encounter that Avram had with God, in which God made the promise that would be known as the *brit*, which is central to understanding this *parashah* and all the subsequent stories in *Bereishit*. I give them non-verbal cues—my voice gets very quiet and I pause before telling them that this part is very important. Before I add the third element of the promise, I review the first two:

> God starts to talk to Avram. He's in *Cana'an*, which is going to become *Eretz Yisrael*. God starts to talk to Avram—and this is *really, really* important:
> God makes a promise to Avram. A really big promise. God says to Avram, Look around you. All the land that you can see is going to be yours and your family's forever and ever. Your family is going to get so big, you'll have children, and they'll have children, and they'll have children ... and Avram, your family is going to be so big—Look at the dust in the earth. Can you count it? As many pieces as the dust of the earth, that's how many children there will be. And then a little while later, God said, look up at the stars. If you can count how many stars are in the sky, that's how big your family is going to get. And this land, *Eretz Yisrael*, is going to be your family's land forever and ever and ever.

At this point, I am explicit about our own connection to this *brit*; I want my students to see themselves as part of Avram's family, part of God's promise, connected to Avram and Sarai and the children they will have, and connected to the land of Israel. This *parashah* establishes that connection, and we will come back to it throughout our study of Torah all year.

> Does anybody know, if Avram had children, and they had children, and they had children, and they had children … and it went on and on and on, does anybody know who ends up being in Avram's family?

Different children offer some answers: Yitzchak, Leah, Rachel, Yosef.

> What about their children and their children and their children? ("Us.")
>
> Right, us! Because every person in the Jewish family is part of that promise that God is talking about. So, if the Jewish people are all part of this promise, if we're all part of this family, then which land is part of this promise too? ("Israel.")
>
> So God makes this promise forever and ever, about Avram's family and about the land. And this promise is such an important promise, that it has a special name. A promise that lasts forever and ever like that is called a *brit*.

One girl recognizes the word *brit* from *brit milah* and starts to ask, "Oh, like when babies…" This is a wonderful connection, and I am pleased that she made that association. I acknowledge her comment, but choose to move on quickly rather than open up a conversation about *brit milah* at this point.

> Right, when babies have a *brit*, they are becoming part of the Jewish family and becoming part of God's promise.
>
> One more thing, because this is an important part of this story. There's one more part of this *brit*. First tell me the two parts we learned already. God promised what? What's #1? As many children as the stars, and the dust. And what's part two of the promise? You'll have this land of *Eretz Yisrael*. And God will bless you.
>
> And then God says, I'm going to change your name. From now on, Avram, you will be called Avraham. And Sarai, from now on you will be called Sarah. Avraham and Sarah will be your names forever and ever.

After this long telling, I quickly ask everyone to stand up and join in a group stretch before we begin acting out the story.

"Torah Talk": Teaching *Parashat Ha-shavua* to Young Children

Acting

I assign four main roles to begin the acting. Knowing that the Hebrew name of one of my students is Avram, I choose him for that role. I extrapolate from the text and include a role for Sarai as well. (I often choose to expand the female roles in our acting, when the women are present in the story but the text does not tell us what they said.) I quickly assign another child to play Lot, and one more to play God's voice. I let the children know that I will have a part for everyone else, but it will not come at the beginning.

I started the acting by coaching the child playing God. "What are you going to say?" When the child begins in a quiet, shy voice, I remind her to speak in a loud, strong voice: "*Lech lecha!*" She does not seem confident about what her part entails. When that happens, I often prompt children with questions or even give them the specific words to say. "What are you going to tell Avram? And then what's going to happen? 'I will bless you....'"

I then turn to the children playing Avram and Sarai:

> Avram, the Torah doesn't tell us this: What do you think might happen next? Who do you think you might talk to about the plan?
> Sarai, what are you going to say? The Torah doesn't tell us this part, what do you think she said?

Each child has a change to vocalize what his character might do and say.

> OK, and then go get your nephew, Avram—your nephew Lot—and tell him the plan.

Avram walks over to Lot, tells him the plan, and Lot agrees to go.

Just as I provide them with the words they can say when necessary, I also direct the action and let them know where to go and how to transition. When I ask the three students playing Avram, Sarai, and Lot to walk over to the "new place," I assign half the remaining students to be the people taking care of Avram's animals and the other half to be the people taking care of Lot's animals.

I remind them often of the context they are in, such as the hot desert, and ask them to act in the way they think would be appropriate: "You're walking through the desert—do you think you're running?"

Now that all the students are participating in the acting, they need even more stage directions. I direct the shepherds to stand with either Avram or Lot and to start arguing with each other because there is not enough room here for all of the animals. Needless to say, the children love the chance to have a fake argument and they exaggerate beautifully. After a few moments, I stop the scene and let Avram take over: "I don't want to argue. You can go anywhere you want, and I'll take the other."

Then I have everyone except Avram and Sarai sit down. I remind them that God is about to talk to them. They listen attentively, but the child playing God does not know what to say. I look for other students who can help her out, and I stand next to her to help as well. The goal of this acting is, of course, not to test her memory; I want each child to feel successful and to experience the role-playing, even if I have to feed the lines to her directly.

> Let's listen really closely because God's going to talk to you. What are you going to say? (Kathy, playing God, says, "I don't know.") Does anybody remember what God's promise was? Aviva, come help Kathy.

I sit down next to Kathy while Aviva whispers in her ear, and then Kathy says:

> Look all around you. Everywhere you can see will be yours. You will have as many children as there are dust and stars. I promise you that this land will be yours and your family's forever and ever.

I remind Kathy that there was one more part of the promise: "Tell them their new names." "Avraham and Sarah."

We end as I ask all the students to give themselves a big hand. I count down 5-4-3-2-1, as an already familiar cue for everyone to return to their seats in the circle.

Responding: "Torah Talk" and Torah Journals

After the students finish acting out the story, I called them back together for "Torah Talk." As they sit down, I remind them of their options for responding: "You can say something you like, something you remember, maybe something you wonder about or a question you have." While I held the Torah, the children passed around a pretend microphone. This microphone establishes whose turn it is and reminds them to talk one at a time. One by one, we go around the circle. Here are some examples of the children's comments:

- David wants to know whether God had lied. Were there really as many Jews as the dust and the stars?
- Natan wonders, "Why did God want Lot, Avram, and Sarai to move to a new place?"
- Anat first says, "I like the part when they had the baby." When I remind her that no one had actually had a baby in this *parashah*, she clarifies that she liked it when God promised that Avraham and Sarah would have children.
- Aviva wonders, "Why did God have to change Avraham and Sarah's names?"
- Naomi questions, "Why did God say they would have children and then they didn't?"
- Ayelet comments on her role in the acting rather than the story itself, saying, "I liked being one of the helpers."

The range of comments and responses on this particular day is fairly typical of the early part of the year. Some students relate to the *parashah* through the particular role they acted out. Others find connections, however tenuous, to familiar elements from their own lives. Some begin to wonder aloud and ask questions about why things happened in certain ways.

At this point in the year, I rely heavily on the structure to support students' participation. Just as a graphic organizer can help students succeed in a written task, the organizing structure of a partially scripted discussion, in which each child says what he or she likes or asks a question, helps students succeed in this oral task. (Later, they will be more likely to respond to other children's questions or comments, and our discussion will often be less structured and more natural.)

The students' Torah journals reflect their visions of what they imagined when they heard the *parashah*, as well as a particular piece that they choose to write about. Aviva's picture emphasizes the hot sun and the sand of the desert, with a man and a woman standing side by side.

Her words refer to the *brit*: "I like when God made all of the promises to Avraham and Sarai."

Naomi's picture is similar, but it is also filled with stars in the sky, and her words emphasize the connection to Israel: "I liked the part that was my favorite part from this time when we went to Israel."

Unlike these other two, Kathy's picture clearly shows Avraham and Sarah looking very unhappy. She, too, drew a desert sun and sand, but her picture shows hills in the desert and people traveling over this distance. Her picture is labeled, "Avram, Sarai, and Lot walking in the desert with their animals."

The students' responses relate to many of the themes I emphasized, including those that I expected they would connect to in a personal way. They thought about moving, about the desert, about having babies. They were interested in God's promise to Avraham and Sarah and wondered about why God had to change their names. They wondered why God would ask them to move to a new place, and thought about the connection to Israel. In my planning and teaching, I shape their receiving of the Torah text; by listening to their comments, encouraging their questions, reading their journals, and looking closely at their drawings, I then in turn see the Torah through their eyes. In future weeks, I will build on their ideas, clarify their misconceptions, and watch their responses develop and their love of Torah grow. Most of all, I watch them become a community of Torah learners who think and talk about Torah with each other in increasingly sophisticated ways.

Conclusion

Given the right structures, young children can learn *Parashat Ha-shavua* in a way that is developmentally appropriate yet still takes the text—and the children—seriously. When we approach the Torah text each week as both a literary and a religious text, we help students develop their general literacy skills and their basic Jewish literacy while engaging them in the age-old Jewish enterprise of engaged textual interpretation. Children can make connections with their own lives, bringing the Torah text off the page and into their world, and learn to love studying Torah, a love they share with classmates and others in their families and communities.

"Torah Talk": Teaching *Parashat Ha-shavua* to Young Children

In the time since I first wrote the working paper that was the basis for this chapter, I have continued to teach *Parashat Ha-shavua* to first graders using this approach. Just as I find something new each time I return to a familiar section of Torah text, I continue to hear new ideas and new questions each time I teach Torah to a new group of students.

My thinking about my teaching has continued to evolve. I continue to see evidence that a predictable structure like "Torah Talk" helps to scaffold children's success. I remain committed to teaching Torah text in an authentic way that also honors my students' developmental needs. I still find that integrating oral language skills, reading comprehension skills, and early writing skills into my teaching of Torah enhances both my literacy teaching and my Torah teaching.

At the same time, I have developed new questions about my pedagogy. I find myself wondering how I can use more visual cues, including pictures, props, and charts, to tap into the visual learners in my class—how I can use physical props and pictures to hook children's attention without detracting from their ability to create their own mental images. I also wonder about ways to make the children's thinking more public—for example, charting their responses and questions and posting them on a bulletin board. This could allow us to return to the "Torah Talk" comments in future discussions, or to expand on them, though I worry that this might detract from the more interactive discussions that often evolve as the year goes on. I wonder about which other discussion practices I could explicitly teach and then encourage among the students: ways of challenging each other when they disagree, for example, or ways of referring back to previous conversations.

When we finish a cycle of *Parashat Ha-shavua* each year, completing the entire Torah, we return to the beginning and start all over again. The text is the same, but we may read it differently because we are different people this year than last. As I go forward in my teaching of Torah to young children, the essential goals and structure remain the same, but the details inevitably change. My students are different this year than last, and so am I, and my experiences over the years cumulatively influence the choices I make in each subsequent year.

14 Using the Contextual Orientation to Facilitate the Study of Bible with Generation X

Beth Cousens,
Susan P. Fendrick,
and Jeremy S. Morrison

Introduction

Barry Holtz suggests a map of "orientations" for the teaching of Bible in Jewish settings.[1] Holtz establishes an orientation as:

> ... a description not of a teacher's "method" in some technical meaning of the word, but in a deeper sense, of a teacher's most powerful conceptions and beliefs about the field he or she is teaching. It is the living expression of the philosophical questions.... What is my view of the aims of education, and how as a teacher do I attain those aims?[2]

For Holtz, then, an orientation to the Bible is an often-unconscious set of ideas shaping the approach to the biblical text that a teacher takes in his instruction.

Among his orientations, Holtz describes the "contextual orientation," a historical approach informed by biblical scholarship, understanding the component texts of the Hebrew Bible in their own time; he describes it as used primarily in university settings.[3] Below, we will demonstrate that the contextual orientation can, in fact, be used productively in set-

---

[1] See chapter 3 in Barry W. Holtz, *Textual Knowledge: Teaching the Bible in Theory and in Practice* (New York: Jewish Theological Seminary, 2003), revised as chapter 2 of this volume.
[2] Ibid., 48-49
[3] Ibid., 92 , and see pages 33-4 above.

tings in addition to the university, and for purposes other than scholarly exploration.

This chapter investigates the expression of one teacher's "powerful conceptions and beliefs" about the teaching of Bible in a liberal synagogue, examining how the contextual orientation can consciously be used in this setting as a deliberate part of a teacher's overall approach to reaching a particular population. We explore how this approach affects the learning and engagement process for adults in their twenties and thirties, and how the contextual orientation can help young adults develop a deeper and more complex attachment to and understanding of the Bible—and can facilitate that attachment in the first place. We offer an examination of the contextual orientation in use, beginning with the development of the pedagogic orientation of the teacher (one of the authors of this chapter). We focus in particular on one session of a bi-monthly class and present interview data from three participants in this class. Their reactions to the class session illustrate that historical approaches to the biblical text as part of an overall teaching strategy can effectively and meaningfully connect young Jewish adults to the ongoing study of the Bible.

Background

Torah and Tonics on Tuesdays (Tx3) is a bimonthly class for Jews in their twenties and thirties held at Temple Israel of Boston. Now in its fourth year as an ongoing, year-round, adult education offering, Tx3 is a component of a large-scale outreach and engagement initiative for adults called The Riverway Project: Connecting Twenties and Thirties to Judaism (RWP) through Temple Israel. The director of the project, and the teacher of Torah and Tonics, is Jeremy Morrison, a rabbi in his 30s and a member of the synagogue's clergy team who spends 70% of his time working with this demographic group.

RWP, which began in the spring of 2001, is comprised of worship, learning, and social justice activities, and is conducted in a variety of settings both within the Temple Israel building and in various locations throughout the Boston metropolitan area. In an attempt to engage unaffiliated Jews in the creation of Jewish community in both informal and institutional settings, RWP provides a panoply of connecting points, including casual Shabbat experiences in participants' homes, low-cost opportunities to formally join this urban congregation, and the Torah study through Tx3.

A general understanding of RWP's goals and the characteristics of its participants is important background for an examination of the curricular and pedagogic choices that Morrison makes when leading Tx3. Approximately 1000 people have, to varying degrees, connected with RWP programming. Several hundred of them have formally affiliated with Temple Israel. The population of RWP participants is heterogeneous. The majority of them are over the age of 25. The range of professions represented is vast, and includes artists, graduate students, entrepreneurs, architects, teachers, doctors, and lawyers. Approximately 50% of participants are married or in ongoing relationships; about 25% of the participants are in interfaith relationships. Several participants have infants or toddlers.

For many, RWP is either their first encounter with organized Jewish activity or marks a return to Jewish communal life after a hiatus that began when the participant left home for college. If a participant's family was affiliated with a synagogue during his childhood, it was most likely Reform. Roughly 15% of participants describe their Jewish background as Conservative, Reconstructionist, Humanistic, or secular, and an estimated 2% of RWP participants report that they are from Orthodox homes. What unifies most RWP participants is a low level of Jewish knowledge and a beginner's experience of Jewish ritual. Few have engaged in the study of Jewish texts before coming to Tx3; most have only the most rudimentary or no understanding of Hebrew.

Tx3 is designed to fit easily into the life of a busy young adult. The program, supported by a donor, is free for participants. Each session includes dinner along with beer, wine, and soft drinks. It begins at 6:30 p.m., with an initial unstructured 30 minutes of eating and socializing. The instructor arrives at approximately 6:50 and an hour of text study begins at 7:00. On average, there are 25-30 students, although as many as 50 have come for a single session. There is a core group of approximately 40 students who each attend at least once a month.

The setting is casual, with students sitting at circular tables of six to eight people; eating and drinking continue throughout the hour of study. The instructor stands in front of the group with a flip chart and colored markers, leading the group in reading out loud from the Plaut edition of the *Humash*[4] and in an interactive conversation about the Torah portion of the week. Often the instructor brings a handout for students that includes several text-related commentaries from traditional and modern Jewish sources. A given handout might include texts as diverse as a piece of Talmud, a passage from the Hasidic writings of the *S'fas Emes*, a reading from Martin Buber, and an article from an Israeli newspaper.[5] The amount that students speak is usually as much as or more than the instructor speaks. Questions and debate are common.

Methodology

This chapter draws on qualitative research methods to explore its central questions.[6] A close analysis of the interactions among teacher, participants, and subject matter during one evening of text study will illustrate how Morrison employs the contextual orientation and point toward some other characteristics of his pedagogical approach. To

---

[4] Gunther Plaut, ed., *The Torah: A Modern Commentary* (New York: Union of American Hebrew Congregations, 1981), produced by the Reform movement.

[5] While this chapter investigates Morrison's utilization of the contextual orientation, his teaching reflects aspects of several of Holtz's orientations, including *parshanut*; decoding, translation, and comprehension; literary criticism; reader-response; and personalization. (See Holtz, *Textual Knowledge*, 92-95.) Most often, about 75% of the class period attends to direct exploration of the biblical text; Morrison then directs students to one or more commentaries, traditional and/or modern. In this way, he exposes students to multiple types of Jewish texts as well as multiple ways of approaching the Bible.

[6] This chapter's first author, Beth Cousens, has completed an empirical case study of the Riverway Project. Her academic interests focus on the Jewish growth of adults in their twenties and thirties. In studying the Riverway Project, she explored how the various strategies that Morrison uses enable participants to develop strengthened connections to Judaism and new understandings of the role that Jewish traditions and ideas can play in their lives. She relied on a variety of qualitative research methods to construct her study, including participant observation in all Riverway Project-related activities and semi-structured interviews with Morrison and frequent and semi-frequent Riverway Project participants. This work on the contextual orientation was part of her larger study, "Shifting Social Networks: Studying the Jewish Growth of Adults in Their Twenties and Thirties" (Brandeis University, doctoral dissertation, 2008).

investigate how participants experience Morrison's teaching and especially the contextual approach, Cousens conducted a semi-structured interview with three frequent participants in Tx3, who each participated actively in the specific Tx3 session under analysis. Among other demographic factors, the subjects vary in their childhood experiences with Judaism, their levels of education, and the areas of the country in which they were raised.

Each interview focused on the participant's Jewish background and previous ideas about Bible, motivation for participating in Tx3, overall experience in Tx3 and with The Riverway Project, and experience that evening during the class. To help the participants recall their reactions to the class, during each interview Cousens and the subject together examined segments from the class transcript. In each case, the subject was able to bring to mind his general feelings during the class and his response to the ideas that Morrison introduced. As is traditional in qualitative research, we present this dense analysis of one evening's study and three participants' reactions in order to demonstrate and further develop our theory about working with this population—that is, that the contextual approach will draw members of Generation X into the study of Bible—with the assumption that this theory should and will be further tested through additional research with this age group, as well as in various settings and with different populations.[7]

Building An Orientation:
A Teacher's "Powerful Conceptions and Beliefs"

As we stated at the outset of this chapter, our starting point is Holtz's conception of orientations to teaching Bible—the idea that a teacher has an overriding teaching philosophy that encompasses his deepest convictions about the field in which he is engaging and that shapes his goals, teaching and learning activities, responses to questions, and interactions with students. An understanding of how and why Morrison uses the contextual orientation in Tx3, then, benefits from a brief exploration of the evolution of his deepest convictions about the study

---

[7] For a full discussion of the use of cases in education research, see Sharan B. Merriam, *Qualitative Research and Case Study Applications in Education* (San Francisco: Jossey-Bass, 1998).

of Bible and the role that such study can play in one's connection to Judaism.[8]

Born and raised in Brookline, Massachusetts, Morrison grew up in a home in which a liberal arts, secular education was valued. Both of his parents have doctoral degrees. Literature, art, and music were mainstays in his childhood home; striving for academic excellence was prized.

Morrison and his brother were the fifth generation of his family to be affiliated with Temple Israel, the locus of his involvement in Judaism. His family attended Friday night services about once a month, and celebrated Shabbat (with Friday night dinners), Passover, and the High Holy Days. From kindergarten through twelfth grade, he attended the synagogue's religious school, confirmation classes, and post-confirmation program. In high school, he was involved with the synagogue's youth group, served as its president, and developed close relationships with his rabbis, experiencing the synagogue as his "second home." Yet, during college, he was only nominally connected to organized religious activity.

Morrison does not recall having any textual connection to Judaism in the first two decades of his life; his religious school transmitted a sense of permissiveness in asking critical questions about Judaism and its traditions, but not the Jewish value of text study per se. A substantive exploration of Jewish texts and their applicability to his life began for Morrison only after college—in his case, when he entered rabbinical school at Hebrew Union College-Jewish Institute of Religion (HUC) at age twenty-four. For the first time, he engaged in studying biblical and rabbinic texts in their original languages and began learning interpretive skills. His own adult search for religious authenticity, then, has from the beginning been rooted in the study of Jewish texts, the activity with which he and his students engage at Tx3.

The study of Bible was the largest component of the core curriculum in Morrison's program. This emphasis on biblical studies is a reflection of the Reform movement's historic connection to the Bible as its central, defining text.[9] Moreover, as a pre-professional school, HUC seeks to

---

[8] While it is beyond the scope of this chapter, a serious investigation of the development of a teacher's own orientation(s) can help bring those orientation(s) to consciousness for the purpose of the teacher's critical examination of his teaching.

[9] See Michael Meyer, *Response to Modernity: A History of the Reform Movement in Judaism* (New York: Oxford University Press, 1988), 45, 172-3, 268, 362.

emphasize tools relevant to the teaching of Bible over those relevant to teaching rabbinic texts, as Bible remains the primary Jewish text taught in Reform educational settings.

For Morrison, exposure to the contextual orientation in particular (during the first time he undertook serious study of the Bible) was revelatory. He became more engaged with the subject matter as he sought to understand the ideological goals of the writers, their theologies, and the complex web of relationships between the Bible's components. As he learned more about biblical history and life in the ancient Near East, narratives that Morrison had learned in his childhood acquired new meaning and greater complexity.

Morrison describes his pedagogic goal in Tx3 as helping his students, too, to see the biblical text as complex and interesting, and develop a reverence for the text that grows out of understanding its complexity. He sees many adults who enter his community feeling a great gap separating them from Jewish texts and their interpretation. They are eager to learn, yet lack the basic skills and knowledge through which to access Jewish texts on their own. They seek ownership of their heritage, but frequently know neither where to begin nor how to incorporate Jewish learning (and living) into their often hectic lives.

The Use of the Contextual Orientation with Adults in Their Twenties and Thirties

The questions that Morrison encounters in his classroom conversations with Riverway Project participants often include fundamental questions about the Bible: Why was the Bible written? When? Who wrote it? His students' questions begin as a search for information, and the answers they receive generate more complicated queries that express a deep desire to make a coherent framework out of the many fragments of their Jewish knowledge and experiences. How can I believe in something that might not have occurred? How do I find and make meaning for myself in this complex text?

Morrison at first used the contextual orientation in his teaching at Tx3 because it is how he naturally approaches the biblical text—that is, it is a pedagogic approach that he did not initially consciously choose for this setting. As he interacted with students in their twenties and thirties, his reflexive approach was reinforced and made more deliberate as he found that the contextual orientation effectively drew his students into study of the Hebrew Bible and engaged with and responded to their questions.

The contextual orientation to the Bible is appropriate for and potentially highly effective with adults in this age cohort for several reasons. An early 1990s novel named the children of baby boomers "Generation X" for their cynicism and doubt about their futures.[10] Generation X came to look skeptically at society's traditional institutions, to believe and trust what they discover for themselves, and to crave authenticity in relationships.[11] For them, "subjective knowing," or what they know personally, carries greater import than "propositional truth," ideas that others give them as certainties.[12]

Also, more highly educated than any American generation before them,[13] today's adults in their twenties and thirties demand a similar level of intensive, complicated intellectual exploration in their extracurricular learning. In addition, individuals coming of age today can construct their identities from a multiplicity of concepts and beliefs, piecing together attitudes if they wish from any systems they choose.[14] In doing so, they combine their skepticism and distrust of inherited ideologies

---

[10] Douglas Coupland, *Generation X: Tales for an Accelerated Culture* (New York: St. Martins Press, 1991). Writers about Generation X do not agree regarding the birth years that mark this population, each using different cultural events to note the beginning and end of the cohort. Following the birthrate, which decreased significantly in the mid-1960s and then increased in the late 1970s, we understand baby boomers to have been born from 1946 to 1964, and the next generation, Generation X, to have been born 1965 to 1980. Generation X, then, includes 46 million Americans, compared to 80 million baby boomers and 76 million millennials, those who come after Generation X. See Lynne C. Lancaster and David Stillman, *When Generations Collide* (New York: Harper Business, 1972), 20-32.

[11] Douglas Rushkoff, *The GenX Reader* (New York: Ballantine, 1994), 5.

[12] Richard W. Flory and Donald E. Miller, eds., *Gen X Religion* (New York: Routledge, 2000), 9.

[13] Jeffrey Jensen Arnett, *Emerging Adulthood: The Winding Road from the Late Teens through the Twenties* (New York: Oxford University Press, 2004).

[14] Richard R. Osmer and Friedrich Schweitzer, *Religious Education Between Modernization and Globalization: New Perspectives on the United States and Germany* (Grand Rapids, MI: Eerdmans Publishing Company, 2003), 20.

with a respect for information and a desire for guides who can inspire them personally.

The contextual orientation exposes the biblical text as multifaceted and layered, making it easier for students to develop their own textured and varied understandings of the Bible. Rather than inheriting a particular unified reading, with a contextual understanding students can examine the many different biblical ideas available to them, and have the potential to construct their own Jewish identities—and establish what will be emphasized in their own Jewish lives—shaped by this range of ideas. In addition, to the extent to which they bring experience with historical or other scholarly study of other, non-Jewish texts, the contextual orientation makes a connection between their previous studies and their Jewish studies. Use of the contextual orientation in this setting frames as Jewish a scholarly, critical approach to the biblical text, instead of requiring students to give up what they have already learned in other settings,

Portraits of Three Tx3 Students

Brian Ehrlich[15] is thirty and works in a psychiatry fellowship at a local university. Raised on Long Island, his parents are small business owners who created a warm Jewish environment for him and his brother. They spent the High Holidays and Passover with family in New York City and on Long Island, and had an annual Hanukkah party with cousins at their grandparents' home; when they attended synagogue services, they did so at the Conservative congregation that his grandfather helped to establish. "My family has made it—sort of culturally it's a very important aspect of our lives," he explains. At a small liberal arts university in the Northeast, Brian sought out his campus Hillel organization, a "good social scene," where students helped to cook Friday night Shabbat dinners and campus Jews congregated in a tight-knit community. A musician, Brian came together with another student, a "jack of all trades when it came to music," to create a klezmer band, and they played at the campus Hanukkah party every year.

---

[15] Students' names have been changed and certain aspects of their portraits have been altered to mask their identities.

During medical school in Boston, Brian continued to look for a Jewish network. He became friends with several other Jewish students who hosted Shabbat dinners in their homes and gave him a Jewish community in Boston. For Brian, Judaism is about "the value of education, hard work, the sense of family that's involved.... Growing up it wasn't a ... religious household but ... there was this sort of togetherness of family, and all the families we were friends with.... They all seemed—we're all so very different but at the same time we're all so very much the same." In medical school, this feeling was reinforced when he spent time with his Jewish friends and their families—it was all "familiar."

When his community of medical school friends graduated and moved to residencies around the country, Brian found himself without a Jewish community and connection in his life. In New York, it had seemed, "everything is Jewish even when it's not." But Boston came to seem like a "funny Jewish town" where it takes "work to be Jewish." Brian began to feel "lost in everything else," as though he wasn't "connecting with everything here.... I think that comes from lack of Judaism." At the same time that he started to regret his lack of a Jewish connection, Brian began a serious relationship with a non-Jewish woman. As they discussed her learning about Judaism, building a Jewish home together, and her possible conversion, Brian sought out Temple Israel at the recommendation of a college friend who had become a rabbi. He and his fiancée appreciate that they will be welcomed into Temple Israel; they will be married there, and they will rely on Temple Israel and the Riverway Project to orient them to the rhythms and purposes of a Jewish life.

Torah study with the Riverway Project contributes significantly to the sense of Jewish community and connection that Brian craved. He recalls feeling some kind of relationship with Torah at his bar mitzvah: "I remember being thirteen years old and incredibly nervous and I had to have a little extra stand so I could be seen from the bimah.... And I remember thinking, this is really neat. Here's this text that has no vowels and I'm reading from it.... And I think that that 'this is really neat' idea stuck with me." He appreciates that Tx3 allows him to return to the connection to Torah that he began in childhood, and that Morrison's teaching helps the text become "relevant to today." He doesn't remember ever considering the question of authorship of Torah prior to Tx3, but speculates that had anyone asked, he would have answered that it is not the "word of God," but rather the recording of some "fables" by "three Jewish guys with long beards."

Daniel Schwartz is in his early thirties and is a comedy writer. He was raised in the Boston area by his father, a professor of religion at a Boston university, and his mother, a teacher. When he was a child, his family lived for a time in Israel. He spent his elementary school years in Orthodox Jewish schools in Boston and in Israel, went to a public high school, and attended Yeshiva University as an undergraduate. One night in his senior year, he saw a flyer recruiting counselors for a Jewish overnight camp in Russia. He signed up, "became very enamored with Russia [and] with Russian Jews," and stayed for two years working with Jewish communities in Russia. This experience led him to Israel, to a master's degree in diaspora Jewish education at Hebrew University, and to work with diaspora students in Israel. When he came back to the US, he held a variety of jobs in finance and media in New York before he decided to work full-time on his comedic work.

Raised as an Orthodox Jew, Daniel continued to practice traditional Judaism until returning to Boston from New York. Explaining his move away from Jewish ritual observance, he describes how his father's Jewish practice existed alongside his simultaneous lack of belief in God and Torah's divine authorship. His father is a "non-believer," and also a "practicing Jew. Pretty strictly a practicing Jew.... So we grew up with that, [and] I think on the one hand it opens your eyes to different perspectives, on the other hand ... in our home—there were no taboos."

Friday night dinner in the Schwartz home would begin with traditional Shabbat rituals and liturgy. They would sing "Shalom Aleichem," make *kiddush* over the wine and *motzi* over their meal—and then discuss why the Bible "was a man-made ... set of books" or "how *not* wrong homosexuality is." As Daniel reports, "It was all open" in his family. As a result, Daniel felt free to choose his career over Jewish ritual observance, although he continues to understand traditional Judaism as the "right" way to be Jewish. (He does continue to seek out and create communal meals on Shabbat.)

His most significant Jewish communal involvement is Tx3. He began participating in Tx3 in order to meet people when he first returned to Boston, but continued because he appreciates the way that it is taught. While he considers traditional Jewish rituals and approaches to be more authentic than newer rituals and interpretations, he also understands and values Morrison's "critical" approach to the biblical text. It feeds Daniel's "rational side" and his questions about the divine authorship of the Bible. As he puts it, "I was raised in America—man and snake don't talk." He has both a "Jewish perspective on life" and a "western perspective on life," and expresses uncertainty that he ever will—or can—pick just one. He participates in Tx3 exactly because this setting allows him to express uncertainty, and to discuss the encounter between his two perspectives.

Sari Schein is in her late twenties, a doctoral candidate at a prestigious university in the Boston area. She was raised outside of a medium-sized city in the Midwest, her father a professor at a large university and her mother a kindergarten teacher. The second of two children, she was enrolled in the closest non-Catholic private school to their house after her brother's unhappy experience with public school. Because her school had very few Jewish students and her family had no Jewish institutional involvement, Sari came to know very few Jews. Yet, she says, "we definitely felt Jewish—sort of a secular Judaism." She always felt somewhat different than her classmates. Her family celebrated some holidays, with grandparents visiting from their different East Coast locations. She fondly remembers her maternal grandmother, who would "cook all sorts of food like bulkies and homemade soup and knaidlach," and she has "lots of good memories and feelings" from these experiences.

As she continues to describe her own Jewish childhood, she emphasizes her father's upbringing and tells a story that shows how in some sense his memories of his own New York Orthodox Jewish upbringing became her own memories and shaped the core of her attitudes toward Judaism. Her father's father had studied philosophy in college and easily slipped away from his Orthodox beliefs, although not his Orthodox lifestyle. Her father inherited his father's atheism and, while he appreciated the family Jewish experiences of his own childhood and shared those stories with his daughter, he chose to raise his family without active Jewish involvement and without any Jewish learning. Sari remembers "being told as a kid that this [Sunday school] is a waste of time." She remembers thinking "it's so strange" that she had such a "rich educational background growing up," but no Jewish learning. Once handed a Bible by a Christian friend, she remembers how foreign it felt to her, and how confusing religion in general was.

In college, Sari tried to connect to Jewish life through Hillel, participating in meals and some Jewish learning. Her college community, however, felt filled with people who "knew the songs" and had "been to summer camp." Instead of studying at Hillel, Sari learned about Judaism through the religious studies department, taking classes with a renowned historian of American Judaism. She feels "committed" to marrying someone Jewish, and since college has been deliberately spending time in Jewish communities, to learn and also to meet other Jews. In graduate school in Boston, she returned to Hillel, more determined to stick it out despite her discomfort, and this time looked for a class to help her learn more. Her Hillel rabbi helped her find Tx3, and since then she has tried to participate in every class.

A historian, Sari values Judaism deeply because it is her "family's history." Before Tx3, however, she did not think about the Bible itself at all—she laughs even when asked the question—and had read it (the Oxford Study Bible version) only for a college course. She never believed that God wrote the Bible: "If you don't believe there's a God, then a God can't write the Torah."

Teaching and Learning Jewish Texts

Each of these three students participated actively in the Tx3 class on Tuesday evening, April 27, 2004. The session focused on the double Torah portion *Acharei Mot-Kedoshim* (Leviticus 16:1-20:27), specifically on the sacrifices that God directs Aaron to make after the death of his sons. Morrison frames the session by raising the question of the relationship between the two Torah portions and the definition of holiness that they present. He introduces the lesson by asking students to define the word and concept *kadosh* (holy). During the conversation, he also introduces a translation of *hol* as "the mundane." To explore these issues, Morrison asks students to read together and out loud Leviticus 16: 1-22, which describes the scapegoat ritual that Aaron conducts. In the rest of the lesson, Morrison directs students to different biblical texts that expound on the concepts of *kadosh* and *hol*; the delineations of sacred space; the relationship between God, man, and sin; and the roles of the priest. Students raise questions about the texts and these concepts, and discuss their ideas with each other as well as with Morrison.

Contextual Orientation to Facilitate the Study of Bible

By reviewing several of the tools that Morrison employs as part of that night's teaching and learning, we can begin to understand the contextual orientation as part of an overall effective teaching strategy. For Morrison, a primary aspect of the contextual orientation is examining how the biblical writers conceived of their world. During this session, a student observes that different books of the Bible present different notions of God. Commenting on Moses' relationship with God, this student (Brian) says:

> This might almost be a leap, but it's almost as if God is sitting here talking face to face with Moses in Exodus, and then here in Leviticus the sin happens and God is this kind of misty, fiery thing.

To respond, Morrison draws directly on the ways in which the texts' writer(s) understood God's presence in their world:

> Right. I mean there's this notion that in Genesis you can fight, you can physically engage with—I mean anytime you see an angel in the Bible, in the Torah in particular, it's God, as another version, another aspect. They believed, and I think we've spoken of this here, in the Ancient Near East it was like you could turn the corner and bump into God. And they're never surprised. I mean Jacob encounters this angel, and they wrestle, and he's never like, "What the heck are you doing here?!" There's never shock. But Brian is absolutely right. In Leviticus, all of a sudden, if you touch God, you die. There's a whole different notion of what God is.... The priestly writers of Leviticus have a very different conception of what you can do with God and the access you can have. The writers of the earlier stories of, say, Jacob encountering an angel—there's a much different understanding in which you and me and anyone else can bump into God and even, hug Him and not get singed.

Here, the student makes a literary observation: different texts offer different points of view. Morrison validates and expands on this idea, suggesting that different passages or even books represent different writers' understandings of God. Morrison then goes on to suggest that these understandings may have developed over time, introducing a historical perspective, and goes a bit further into what the writers may have actually believed or understood about God. Brian points to a discrepancy that he sees in the text; Morrison offers an explanation for that discrepancy based on his ability to situate the biblical text as a historical document comprised of multiple sources (although without making direct reference to the documentary hypothesis or other hallmarks of critical biblical scholarship). The contextual orientation is reflected in Morrison's identification of different stances towards God that develop over time, creating for his students a sense of the text's complexity.

In another example, Morrison and the students explore the text again from the writers' perspectives, this time examining how they made sense of phenomena that were seemingly incomprehensible. A conversation about *tzara'at*, a set of afflictions and impurities that can occur on the body and also within the walls of a house, raises these questions.

> Morrison: ... So as with the skin, if your home broke out with this thing called *tzara'at*, there's a process, you actually deconstruct your house and you throw the stones ... into the area outside the camp, and that helps purify your house. It also deals with the same thing with clothes. Why do you think with something like a skin ailment, you create all of these processes of purification?
>
> Brian: From a public health perspective though, open sores are bad, are contagious. And so, to maintain health, in this camp here, you need to do something. So these are the instructions for how to get rid of the problem.
>
> Morrison: Good. So that could be said, as a good reason for why or how to deal with the skin ailment. What about the house?
>
> Daniel: You mean why does your house get it?
>
> Morrison: Yes. Why does your house get it? Is that what you just said Daniel? ...
>
> Brian: But even if they didn't understand about germs. Germs don't just live on your skin; they could be elsewhere in the house.
>
> Morrison: But you just said, I think, a telling thing: "If you don't understand about germs." I mean, at some level, I think that all of this ritual, and this applies to what we are about to deal with

Contextual Orientation to Facilitate the Study of Bible

tonight, deals with ... about how do you create a kind of control over something you don't have any control over? How in their world, and it's true in our world as well, to a degree, in which so much cannot be explained, how do you create systems that help explain it? Especially when things are not of your doing.

Sari: I was just thinking that cleaning of a house strikes me as being a very psychological response to purification. So you may be able to rid yourself of it, but you're not going to feel like you've eradicated the problem until you've removed every stone, literally, in your house.

In this exchange, we see another way that the contextual orientation answers students' questions and expands interpretive possibilities for them. Morrison raises a question about the writers' intent, located in the writers' own time: Why would they have created these means of purification? A student, Brian, responds with a pragmatic explanation, thinking about the actual world in which the writers lived and the phenomena they needed to address. Morrison pushes the question: What about the house? Brian again offers a pragmatic explanation—or more specifically, a scientific perspective—bringing in his own professional framework. Sari gives another understanding of the writers' motivations, this time from a psychological perspective. Both students are exploring an idea that Morrison emphasized during their exchange: the writers were trying to comprehend and control a mysterious element of their lives.

Here, the contextual orientation encourages students to think about the extent to which the biblical writers in their time might have reflected some of the same concerns that we have today—about contagion, and more generally about whatever plagues us, physically or psychologically. In other words, it invites them to read the text as reflecting a particularly ancient way of grappling with a timeless problem. This view of the text, while it does not directly engage with biblical scholarship, nevertheless grounds the text in its time by exploring its religious and psychological themes, inviting students to mentally step into the world of the text in order to understand the ancient writers and their context.

In a third example, Morrison focuses on the ideological aspect of the text, using the contextual orientation to demonstrate that the biblical writers might have been making a particular point about their society.

Morrison returns to the subject of Aaron's sons being killed in the previous week's Torah portion, and links this earlier event to the present conversation about impurity and holiness:

> Morrison: Now returning to our piece for today: ... There's a sin on the part of [Aaron's sons]; did that somehow affect the space? These guys make this offering, fire comes out, and zaps them.... They did something wrong and something toasts them. What happens next with Aaron? ... Vis á vis Aaron and this space [the tabernacle]? What does the text say? [Here, a student reads out loud Leviticus 16:2-3: "The Lord said to Moses: Tell your brother Aaron that he is not to come at will into the shrine behind the curtain in front of the cover that is upon the ark lest he die.... Thus only shall Aaron enter the shrine with a bull of the herd for a sin offering and a ram for a burnt offering."]
>
> Brian: Is this an instruction as to who can go in and out of that space?
>
> Morrison: Definitely. We're dealing with priests—meaning the priests can go in and out but you can't ... And there is also, of course, a hierarchy here. God's "contained" in some sort of "box." Certain people in this hierarchy are allowed to go towards that God and others are not.

At first in this interchange, Morrison asks about what the text says. Together, he and the student elucidate the religious hierarchy suggested by the text: only certain individuals can enter the tabernacle, the holy space. The student implies in his question that the instruction is meant not just for Aaron, but also for this entire religious society. Morrison answers the question by alluding to the text's ideological bias in support of the hierarchy that existed at the time this text was likely written and edited—reflecting a positive view of the specialized role of priests not just in the Tabernacle in the wilderness, but also in the ancient Temple in Jerusalem.

Through all of these exchanges, several important aspects of Morrison's approach emerge. First, students' freedom to ask questions should be noted. Brian says about this, "I, sort of tend to try to start at the very ... let's just try to get an idea as to what we're talking about." He "feel[s] comfortable" with Morrison as a teacher, and has noticed that

Morrison's teaching encourages questions. Indeed, Morrison almost always asks immediately and repeatedly after the first reading aloud of text during the session, "Questions? More! Come on, guys," he says, and students respond with probes about various contextual details of the text—setting, objects, words—that seem foreign and complex. They demand information, in part because Morrison has created an environment that allows and encourages them to do so.

Second, we see that the process of the creation of the text is itself an area of focus. Part of complicating the text for students involves demonstrating to them the long evolution of the canonical biblical text, and imbuing them with an appreciation of that process. As Morrison repeatedly refers to the writers, their intent, when and where in time and history they were writing, the text appears not as a monolithic entity emerging in one voice, but as a multi-faceted, layered, and deliberate product of multiple religious voices.

Finally, as should be evident, the contextual orientation operates on the assumption that the text is not simply God's communication to human beings, but was written by human hands and reflects human involvement in its creation. God is often a character in the discussions during Tx3, and the possibility of divine involvement in the authorship of the text is not excluded from conversations, but human composition of the Torah is consistently assumed. At the very least, a human contribution to the text is certain. Perhaps paradoxically, it is precisely Morrison's assumption that the received biblical text is human and not exclusively or even primarily divine that allows him to engage students in Torah study as an emerging sacred activity.

Students and the Contextual Orientation in Use

Interviewing Brian, Daniel, and Sari, and reviewing with them selections from the transcript of this Tx3 session, allowed us to gather their general reactions to Tx3 and their specific reactions to the uses of the contextual orientation reviewed above. All three participants indicated that the way that Morrison approaches and investigates sacred texts allows them to appreciate the issues with which the texts engage, and to begin to understand a place for the study of sacred texts in their lives. In fact, the students' reactions reveal what Morrison found to be true in his own experience: the use of the contextual orientation toward the Bible leads not to a distancing from it, but to a personal connection to the text.

Brian, Daniel, and Sari each reported that they came to Tx3 already believing the Bible to be of human origin. Brian, for example, explains, "I figured it was a bunch of stories that were told ... I never sort of thought that this was a divine piece of work. It's pretty neat, and it's well put together, but ... I never thought like, this is the word of God." He stresses as well that he could already see discrepancies in the text; for example, he saw that "Genesis was so very different from Deuteronomy, just sort of the tone and everything." He appreciates, then, what he calls the "practical level" at which Morrison creates discussion—that is, that he raises issues of the text's writing and context, and questions about the society and environment in which the narratives take place.

Similarly, Sari loves studying with Morrison because "his whole approach to the Bible, to the Torah, is that it's a text that's meant to be torn apart and rearranged—and that's our tradition." She understands this relationship to the text—what some might loosely call deconstructing the text—as part of approaching it as a historical document, and a human one. In one session, she recalls, Morrison "basically was explaining that it's a historical text, that it's pieced together, it's about what people believe God wanted, it wasn't necessarily the word of God." For her, that was "a really interesting moment," in which she identified at a fundamental level with Morrison's description of his approach to the text. Tx3 helped her begin to study sacred Jewish texts because Morrison's approach allowed her to relate to and study them in the same way that she studies other texts.

Both Brian and Sari stress that this approach keeps them "going back" to Tx3. "I've never even approached Judaism this way," Brian says, in a confident, excited tone. The approach to which he refers involves Morrison's uncovering the layers of the text's origins alongside the text's deep relevance. Reading the text as they would any other piece of literature, but one that is both ancient and relevant to his life, has helped him to see the text as "clever"—and to see Judaism as complex and of value for more than just a bar mitzvah boy. Morrison's approach has kept Brian engaged in Tx3 and therefore in Torah study, helping him develop a connection to the Bible and to Judaism.

Similarly, Sari has found the biblical text to be as complicated and rich as those that she studies in her profession. About finding Tx3 and

Morrison's approach to study, she explains, "I think I felt in some sense like I'd arrived." She has come to develop a relationship with Judaism and the Bible that makes sense to her as an adult. She summarizes her newly developed understanding as: "So you have this tradition, and this explains why it influences Jewish beliefs, and Jewish beliefs evolve and change as they're brought into different contexts, different historical time periods. That makes sense to me...." She is developing a stance towards Jewish sacred texts that fits into her understanding of the development of religion: the texts are historical documents, and human understandings of them shift throughout history. Seeing Judaism in its entirety (including its central texts) within a historical context has helped her develop a more comfortable relationship with Judaism.

For Daniel, Morrison's use of the contextual orientation is more complicated, but as important as it is for Brian and Sari. He describes Morrison as a "gifted teacher":

> He tries to get you to think.... You know, use your brain. He tries to get people to think critically.... He tries to get us to analyze. To dig deep, and to, you know, well, here's one thing that five sentences or two chapters here earlier we read x, and this here says y, and it's speaking about a similar thing; why do we have two different perspectives, what do we learn from that.... Also, I think, he tries to get us to take a kind of biblical criticism approach.

Daniel appreciates that Tx3 is intellectually challenging, in that it invites students to examine the text closely and try to understand its discrepancies. Daniel recognizes that, in Tx3, he reads the Torah not only as a traditional commentator might, looking for answers and resolutions in the text itself, but also as a student of biblical criticism, open to the possibility of multiple authors and historical layers in the biblical text.

As described earlier, Daniel understands religion in two ways: he appreciates both the critical approach and the traditional approach that considers the text divine and perfect. He explains, "I appreciate them both for what they are, I've studied them both to some extent or another, and ... I'm not afraid of either one." Moreover, he says, biblical criticism will not "shake" his "faith." He is comfortable with traditional Judaism, but he is also comfortable with an approach to the Bible that understands it as human in origin and rooted in a historical context—

the traditional perspective does not satisfy him. "I mean, I'll be honest with you, it's like, if I were to sit in a class ... any, you know, strictly Orthodox class, and they're teaching me Torah from a Rashi-oriented perspective, I'd come back with [biblical criticism]"—that is, with an academic or analytic approach to the text like Morrison's.

Unlike Brian and Sari, Daniel values studying the Bible with an assumption that it is divinely inspired. Yet, like his peers, he also values approaching the text assuming human authorship. He does not want or need to pick one perspective over the other: "I forever will be somewhere bouncing in the middle," he explains, and has chosen to spend time in Tx3 rather than pursuing Torah study with a more traditional (or more secular, strictly academic) approach. In class, he does sometimes raise the rabbinic understanding of the text when Morrison offers a contextual understanding, but he returns to Tx3, and implicitly to Morrison's historical understanding, again and again.

Daniel spent much of his twenties trying to accept that he would not be able to integrate his American and traditional Jewish identities. He came to believe that he had to choose one or the other, or vacillate between the two, but that they could not be combined into a viable Jewish identity. Morrison's approach works for Daniel because he can incorporate it into the burgeoning American Jewish identity he is developing as an adult. In Morrison's class, he can engage in the study of sacred Jewish texts, a religious activity, from a Western/academic perspective. Daniel has lived both traditional and non-observant Jewish lifestyles. In Tx3, he is testing involvement with a non-traditional Jewish community; his experience in Tx3 gives him a laboratory in which to continue experimentation with developing an adult Jewish identity.

Brian points toward another impact of Tx3. Because it brings him into a closer relationship with the biblical text in all its complexity, Tx3 addresses questions Brian confronts with his patients in psychiatry, "figuring out, how does one live a life." His learning helps him think through these issues when he sees those same questions in a very ancient text. Moreover, he says, "even, for me, sort of figuring out, how do I make the choices in my life, what's a good choice/what's not a good choice, how do I make things work," he says, "I think it's helpful to think about things in this way." Viewing the biblical text in a historical perspective, with all its diverse strands and voices, helps him to reflect on his own life, and to reflect with his patients on theirs.

The contextual orientation also speaks to Sari's professional identity. She approaches texts and intellectual life "as a historian." Morrison's approach to the biblical text is, for her, "very similar to the way I think about text as a historian and someone who studies literature, and it really fascinates me," she says. It helps her practice a way of thinking that she loves and is familiar with, in a Jewish context. Moreover, it speaks to how she understands her personal Jewish identity: "To me, it's my family's history, you know, generations and generations." Approaching the text from within its historical context helps her connect the way she views the Bible not only to her professional studies, but also to the way she understands her family, which sits at the root of her Jewishness.

For all three of these individuals, the contextual orientation in Morrison's teaching supports their emerging Jewish identities. It is arguably the single most important pedagogic element that keeps them coming back to this Jewish learning environment.

Conclusion

Our interviews with Brian, Sari, and Daniel have uncovered examples of how the contextual orientation can have a significant impact on and appeal to students in their twenties and thirties. These individuals have had different levels of Jewish education, different involvement in Jewish ritual, and different amounts of exposure to and immersion in Jewish texts as children, but for all three, the contextual approach became crucial to their participation in and enjoyment of Tx3, and thus in Torah study.

As we described earlier, for Morrison the contextual orientation not only stimulated in him a deep interest in and commitment to the study of Bible, but also served as a way into Judaism more generally; it connected him more deeply to many of the ideas embodied in Jewish ritual and life. His own experience drew him to use the contextual orientation in the classroom, especially as he saw how it helped students develop a connection to the Bible and its study, and also to Jewish communal life. While the reader might be concerned that the contextual orientation contradicts long-held Jewish ideas about the divine authorship of the Bible and therefore would serve to turn students away from Jewish practice and Jewish connections—that is, to promote a scholarly interest in Bible, but not a Jewish interest—our interviews, however, yield evidence of a contrary tendency.

For example, at the time of her interview for this study, Sari indicated an interest in learning Hebrew and reading from the Torah publicly; she had not had a bat mitzvah as a child and wanted to participate in that kind of celebration. In the eighteen months after her interview, she learned to chant Torah and studied biblical Hebrew, and recently celebrated being a bat mitzvah with friends from the Riverway Project. Without the Riverway Project, Sari would not have become interested in or able to pursue this intellectual and spiritual exploration of Jewish tradition. While an investigation of students' Jewish journeys is outside the scope of this chapter, there is evidence of similar change on the part of many additional participants in Torah and Tonics.[16]

The approach to the Bible in Tx3—what Sari called "rearranging the pieces"—and its similarity to the way that students have learned to approach other texts in their lives helps students see both the contextual orientation as a "Jewish" approach and studying the Bible as a comfortable part of their "secular" (or at least, non-traditional) lives. The conversations that they have in Tx3 help open questions about the roles of community and the sacred in their lives. The contextual orientation should be seen, then, as useful in more than academic environments—and not only as a tool with which to study Bible for its own sake, but as a way of investigating sacred Jewish texts that can be personally meaningful and relevant.

Another aspect of this project's contribution lies in a teacher's own reflection. This project required Morrison to ask himself deep questions about his teaching that otherwise would have remained hidden in his work. As Holtz reminds us, an orientation and its particular practices are often largely unconscious—even for someone like Morrison, who has thought a great deal about his pedagogy. It is reflected not just in

---

[16] For example, their participation in Torah and Tonics and in additional learning opportunities that Morrison leads has helped other participants to reformulate their families' holiday celebration (adding to them the study of traditional Jewish texts), to engage in further learning opportunities at the synagogue and elsewhere, and even to consider sending their children to Jewish day school. In sum, a number of participants have become regular students of Judaism.

Contextual Orientation to Facilitate the Study of Bible

the active process of choosing texts, teaching strategies, and responses to students according to consciously held assumptions about how to approach the Bible, but through innumerable instinctive choices and approaches. In this project, we considered the particular pedagogic choices Morrison made only after this Tx3 session took place. But what would happen if each educator considered these choices before each class, if teachers consciously explored the orientations that influence the presentation of subject matter and the many choices they makes as educators? What would be the impact of this kind of reflection on students' learning, and on teachers' ongoing practice?

Since Morrison's involvement in this study, he reports becoming more cognizant of the particular nature of his commitment to, and motivation to use, the contextual orientation. He can now be more deliberate with the introduction of contextual information, and can identify his less intentional uses of the contextual orientation and consider mobilizing them toward specific ends. He can also consciously choose when to use another orientation instead, moving to other areas of his subject-matter knowledge and other approaches to the Bible when he determines it is appropriate.

This study, then, has significance for researchers in their work on Jewish learners in their twenties and thirties, and for practitioners as they consider their own orientations and practices, as well as for one specific practitioner in his ongoing work.

As we constructed and executed this research study, we were aware that a serious examination of pedagogy that uses the contextual orientation would ultimately involve far more than documenting and analyzing students' reactions. However, the notion of orientations in teaching Bible in Jewish settings is still very new, and so far we have little data on how teachers develop their orientations about Jewish subject matter, and how orientations are used in various learning environments and with different populations. This study's additional value, beyond its focus on a successful Jewish educational approach with a relatively disengaged population, then, has been its presentation of an orientation in use, and of a teacher's examination of his own orientation and its expressions. We hope that, among other things, this initial study can provoke other educators to identify the evolution of their own orientations, examine how their orientations influence their teaching practices, and evaluate the effectiveness of those practices.

There are still many basic and essential questions to be explored in research on the use of orientations in the teaching of Jewish texts. What do the various orientations actually look like in different learning environments, as executed by different teachers? Do Holtz's different orientations actually look as distinct in practice as they do in his taxonomy? Empirical studies of Holtz's orientations within Jewish education (similar to Grossman's in general education),[17] looking at the actual use of such orientations in the teaching of Bible, are few and far between. More work is required for us to understand what it means in practice to teach from a given orientation.[18] In terms of the contextual orientation specifically, more research is needed with learners of various ages and backgrounds and in different settings to understand more about their experience of the contextual orientation and the understanding of Bible that emerges from it.

In this study, however, we have seen that three major elements in Morrison's teaching form the beginning of a framework for a contextual orientation to the Bible. The three elements are (a) identifying authorial strands and distinct textual perspectives, (b) considering the writers' intentions and concerns in their own time, and (c) analysis of the ideology reflected in a given passage. These three—in conjunction with learning about the Bible's historical context and the history of its emergence as a finished text—serve not to undermine the positive Jewish identities of the Generation X students that we observed, but to strengthen them.

---

[17] Pamela Grossman, *The Making of a Teacher: Teacher Knowledge and Teacher Education* (New York: Teachers' College Press, 1990).

[18] It is worth noting here that a teaching orientation is not the same as one's personal beliefs, theological or otherwise. That is, teachers may feel more comfortable with some orientations than with others, but in principle, any teacher with the requisite knowledge can employ any orientation. At the same time, teachers can be more coherent, conscientious, and deliberate in their work when they examine their deepest beliefs about their subject matter, when they understand the orientations to which they are naturally inclined (or which they might wish to adopt) and how they teach from these orientations. See Gail Zaiman Dorph, "What Do Teachers Need to Know to Teach Torah?" in *Essays in Education and Judaism in Honor of Joseph S. Lukinsky*, ed. Burton I. Cohen and Adina A. Ofek (New York: The Jewish Theological Seminary of America, 2002).

15 Academic Study of the Talmud as a Spiritual Endeavor in Rabbinic Training: Delights and Dangers

Jonah Chanan Steinberg

Introduction: Academicians and The Spiritual

Academicians today tend to be suspicious of any pedagogy that responds positively to the spiritual motivations students bring to the study of rabbinic sources. Present-day passions and interests might well be expected to distort one's reading of an ages-old literature. Yet scholars of rabbinics have become the primary purveyors of talmudic and midrashic learning to future rabbis, at least in the progressive movements, so those of us who teach in rabbinical schools are, in fact, answerable to much more than the future of an academic discipline. We are responsible also for the ways in which classical rabbinic literature will figure in lived Judaism and in Jewish spirituality.

This is not a role for which all scholars of rabbinics have signed up, and it is not a responsibility that all desire. Many if not most scholars of rabbinic sources did not take up this discipline with the aim of shepherding people on spiritual journeys or training them as Jewish leaders. In the process of working on this chapter, a colleague from another institution reported to me that when certain kinds of questions arise in her classes, she tells her students, "You should really speak with your rabbi about that." That may be an appropriate response in some academic circumstances, but I am training rabbis, so that buck has to stop somewhere.

The conversations that rabbis are meant to be able to have must *start* somewhere—and I would argue that one of the things that actually makes rabbinical students into rabbis is that their training to engage with the thorniest questions of life takes place, in large part, over and around and through these classical texts. Consequently, we who teach the texts need to be prepared to talk about the big questions, and willing to speak about the issues that these religious sources raise.

That same conversation with a colleague led me to jettison my clumsy effort to define the spiritual in an earlier version of this chapter. Instead, for the purposes of this discussion, we can now define the "spiritual" as being all those things about which an instructor might think to say, "You should really talk with your rabbi about that."

The same colleague also said, about the yearnings and searches that sometimes bring students to her university classes on Judaism, "It's not my job to make it nice for them." That is to say, she does not see it as her task to allay doubts, dissipate fears, and facilitate tidy theologies. My response was that I do not often feel that the Babylonian Talmud, for example, is inclined to "make it nice" for my rabbinical students in those ways—and so I do not see that as my job either. Classical rabbinic texts have canny ways of putting us right in the thick—or sometimes in the terrifying thin—of things, and that is exactly where rabbis need to be.

Having taught in several rabbinical schools, I have certainly observed the phenomenon of scholars taking umbrage at the notion—usually pressed upon them by rabbinical school deans—that they should shape their teaching with the spiritual development of rabbinical students in mind. As a rabbinical school associate dean, in a program that seeks to have the study of classical sources also be a living conversation about present experience and a Jewish future, I take delight in seeing insights from the Talmud classroom play out in the real life of our school's community, and experiences from our communal life and from our students' various pursuits being brought to bear in the classroom. While some of my colleagues in academia surely think I have gone over to the dark side—in rabbinic parlance, the *sitra achra*—of anti-intellectual populism or anachronistic pretensions, in this chapter I explore how fostering talmudic learning as a spiritual element of rabbinic training can be a legitimate pedagogic approach for a scholar. I introduce my own pedagogical choices in that regard, and identify the benefits that arise from those choices in my own experience of teaching in our field.

Since this involves a discussion of students' experiences, I include the voices of actual students as an appendix at the end of this paper—excerpts of written responses that a few of my rabbinical students, during the academic year 2007-2008, volunteered when I asked them what might be important for teachers of rabbinic literature to hear from students on the topic of textual study as a spiritual endeavor.

A Scholar's Training and the Teaching of Rabbis

My focus on the interests and concerns of rabbinical students flows from, rather than against, my own schooling as a critical, analytical, and historical reader of rabbinic texts. My training does not come from the world of the yeshiva, but rather from a secular (if sectarian) Labour-Zionist Hebrew day school, from Brown University, from Hebrew University's Talmud and *Mahshevet Yisrael* (Jewish Thought) departments, and from Columbia University, with a good deal of New York University and the Jewish Theological Seminary of America in the mix as well. As a result, my students imbibe a critical sensibility and critical methodologies from me part and parcel with whatever else comes across in my teaching. They come with an eagerness to experience textual study as part of their spiritual journey toward the rabbinate, and I encourage them to consider critical awareness and critical questioning as essential on that journey. Not only should rabbis not be naïve, they should have the spiritual maturity that comes of acknowledging the human element in the teachings and the texts of Jewish tradition.

Guided by my own fascination with religious creativity, I teach my students to appreciate the development of our tradition as a great creative process and as a series of decisions set in history. I was trained by a pioneering scholar of Talmudic textual criticism, David Weiss Halivni (who incidentally also has written about the importance of analytical study in his own spiritual development), so a great deal of what happens in my classrooms has to do with disassembling talmudic expositions into their component pieces; figuring out what the composers of the text had on their workbenches, so to speak, from previous generations; and then discussing what it was they may have been trying to do in their tweaking and elaborating and assembling the discrete parts into something new, to make a previously unheard music.

Rabbinical students can find it tremendously exciting to begin thinking in terms of the *formation* of rabbinic texts. To use a physics metaphor, one might say that a powerful intrinsic energy is released from the sources when the cohesion of their component atoms and molecules is challenged. In seeing the various pieces of a text broken apart from one another, students can become attuned to the creative forces that brought the elements together, which is important for students striving toward their own productive and inventive syntheses of inherited teachings.

The Rabbinical School Context

My own teaching takes place in the larger context of a rabbinical program, at the Hebrew College Rabbinical School, designed with questions of relevance and spirituality very much in mind. As conceived by Arthur Green, the founding dean, the core courses of the rabbinic text program in our rabbinical school are structured thematically, following, in a creative way, the themes of the *Shisha Sidrei Mishnah*, the six orders of the Mishnah:

- First year: *Berakhot*—liturgy, prayer, Siddur and *hilkhot Tefillah* (laws of prayer).
- Second year: *Mo'ed*—the year cycle and Shabbat.
- Third year: *Nashim u-Gevarim*—the life cycle, birth to death and mourning, along with personal status, sex and gender, marriage, and divorce.
- Fourth year: *Nezikin*—personal and social responsibility, communal governance.
- Fifth year: *Kodashim* and *Taharot*—which we somewhat liberally re-interpret to concentrate especially on theology; and, as a halakha course in that final year, *Hullin*, which is to say, *kashrut* (a traditional rite of passage in rabbinic training).

The other major strand of our core text curriculum follows the *Hamishah Humshei Torah*, the five books of the Torah, with students in each year focusing on the interpretive tradition, ancient through contemporary and critical, on each successive book.

The very structure of the textual curriculum at the center of the program signals an orientation toward the concerns of future rabbis.

The curriculum is built to focus on the areas of life in which rabbis will operate, and the cycle of readings—of texts—over which rabbis will meet their communities. (The curriculum also includes a range of other courses, from a sequence of history courses to seminars on other areas of Tanakh, and of course pastoral training.) Our program in the area of traditional textual sources signals to our students, in its very structure, that they *should* expect core textual studies to relate to those things that "you should really ask your rabbi about."

Prayer in a Learning Community and Learning Prayer

I teach primarily in the *Berakhot* year, in the *Nashim u-Gevarim* year, and in the final year of our program—years 1, 3, and 5. Here I will focus on the first year—the *Berakhot* year—not only for the sake of economy in this brief exploration, but also because: (a) this is the year in which our students are initiated into intensive textual study as it is practiced in our program, and (b) the topic of prayer and liturgy is very much related to the day-to-day life of our school's community in ways that our entering students immediately experience and that immediately raise rabbi-worthy questions.

To set the scene, I must say a brief word about the nature of *Tefillot*, of worship, in a trans-denominational rabbinical school. In our very diverse community, we are able to pray together at least once a week as a whole community. *Tefillah* opportunities of differing sorts are available and organized by students throughout the week, but at least once a week we come together as a whole community and allow the prayer leaders of the day to take us through their own traditions or experiments. This means that everyone experiences a certain level of discomfort from time to time, in return for learning, through experience, about what is important to the various members of our community.

Meanwhile, in my first-year Talmud classroom, toward the end of the first semester, we celebrate a *siyyum* (a concluding celebration) at the end of *perek tefilat ha-shahar*, the fourth chapter of the Babylonian Talmud's Tractate *Berakhot*. This means that at the same time as, outside the classroom, my students are acclimating to the experience of prayer in our ritually multifarious community, inside the classroom the issues on the table are issues of *tefilah*: rival accounts of our liturgy's origins, differing opinions concerning practice, questions of structure and spontaneity, rules and compromises, not to mention stories and recommendations about prayer in less than comfortable circumstances. The fourth chapter of *Berakhot* also includes the archetypical narrative of a house of study rocked by a dispute that begins with a difference of liturgical opinion, in the famous story of Rabban Gamaliel and Rabbi Yehoshua (known as *"bo bayom"*).

The chapter itself does not let us get away from the truth that the stakes are high when we meet one another across differences of opinion and custom and try to learn and pray together. As Rabbi Nehunya ben Hakanah's short prayers in the chapter indicate, a *bet midrash* (traditional house of study) should be entered with a healthy apprehension of the all-too-possible *takalot* (mishaps) that can happen there, and care in that regard can increase the chances of exiting the *bet midrash* with a sense of gratitude for the privilege of taking part in the grand conversation of our tradition. When Rabbi Eliezer's students ask him, on his deathbed—as narrated in this same chapter—to teach them "paths of life" by which they can "merit the life of the world to come," the sage's very first admonition is, "Take care to honor your colleagues." Every year, I see my students take that teaching very much to heart as they experience their differences from one another around issues of prayer, as well as in their shared work of studying the tradition.

Pedagogic Dangers

In the title of this chapter, I promised delights *and* dangers. Perhaps analytically-oriented, academic scholars can all too well imagine the dangers when the text on the table is so relevant to present religious experiences in students' lives—relevant to issues with which students are experimenting and sometimes struggling. A cynic might say that I use the energy and fascination that comes from such synergy between text-study and life to trick my students into quickly acquiring technical skills and critical competence, because they want to know what happens next and don't want to miss anything. In fact, their zeal to learn arises quite organically and naturally in this environment, so that my job feels like facilitation far more than manipulation.

The students acutely feel the need for traditional categories and considerations to bring to bear on their activities outside the classroom, and they need to ground their experiences in a conversation that starts somewhere deep within their tradition. I, too, am a participant in this same adventurous community. The themes of the Talmudic chapter, familiar as they may be to me, are also ones that I experience anew, with each new group of students, every time a new cohort becomes a part of our ritual community and begins intensive textual study at the same time.

Another academic danger arises in connection with the following talmudic question, which also appears in the fourth chapter of Berakhot: To what do the eighteen (or nineteen) blessings of the Amida (statutory daily prayer) correspond? Do the blessings correspond to eighteen (or nineteen) mentions of the Divine in the recitation of the *Shema*? Do the blessings correspond to eighteen (or nineteen) mentions of the divine in "*havu l-Adonai b'nei elim*" (Psalm 29)? Or do they perhaps correspond to eighteen (or nineteen) vertebrae in the spinal column? In other words, the questions on the table are these: are the rabbinically ordained blessings of our prayer modeled on a divine pattern revealed through Moses according to the Torah? Does the statutory form of prayer instead correspond to an ancestral example of human worship, modeled by the psalmist? Or might the form of the Amida relate to something deeply encoded in our own bodies and selves?

Why are these questions "dangerous" in a rabbinical school classroom? Let me answer that question with another: how can one stop a class of first-year rabbinical students when they have started in on such a conversation? Do you let the discussion run to yoga—especially considering that the very next talmudic line reads: "*ha-kore tzarikh she-yikra ad she-yitpakeku kol huliot she'ba-shidruh*" ("One must bow so that all the vertebrae of the spinal column stand out")? And, then—if one does let the conversation range in that direction—how far do you let an animated argument about material body and spiritual experience continue into present-day issues of science and religion before you rein students back in to the text on the page?

The pedagogic pay-off for such text-inspired excursions, beyond whatever intrinsic value the conversations have, is a classroom full of first-year rabbinical students who are, again, absolutely committed to the project of acquiring the technical skills to read the next page and the next. The text has entwined with their own personal questions and experiences—as, I believe, it is meant to. The ancient text on the table has become the basis for the conversation that is relevant in the present moment.

I should emphasize at this point that in order to facilitate worthwhile conversations that jump *off* the talmudic pages, one has to be seriously expert in, and consistently mindful of, what is *on* the page. Text-based conversations about meaning and relevance that take place in rabbinical schools are all too often caricatured and dismissed as being of a dilettantish sort, implicitly invoking the authority of talmudic learning but barely skimming the surface of a traditional text before streaking off to someplace else. As a teacher, my pedagogy demands a serious and competent study of each text I teach—its nuts and bolts, in its own particularity and in its historical context—and only then, on that basis (and for a balanced amount of time, so that other texts can be similarly approached) do I make room for the associations and ramifications that the text can generate.

To be sure, there is always yet another kind of danger lurking: the hazard of anachronism and of collapsing critical distance. However, with a minimum of guidance, students can become quite discerning. On the whole, our rabbinical students learn to be scrupulous and careful about identifying and distinguishing what comes from them and what they see on the page itself. Furthermore, as a matter of teaching practice, it is much easier to contend with and contain students' passions and imaginations than to attempt foisting critical interest upon students who are unenthused.

To put it another way, when one forces rabbinical students through a dry, technical text-criticism for its own sake, their passion for learning the skills of reading traditional texts most often withers on the vine, but if the study of sources is intermeshed with the pressing issues that actually confront students' souls in the present moment, the utility of technical skill and critical scrutiny needs no defending or justifying in the classroom. The Babylonian Talmud, arguably more than any other work in the traditional corpus, gives us not just the Jewish but the human condition, forcing us to confront difficult questions and uncertainties. It does so in an almost merciless way that is very appropriate to the training of those who have an impulse to stand with their fellow human beings in life's moments of crisis, large and small, in the midst of life's mysteries and its enduring questions.

Conclusion

I work very hard to ensure that each one of my first-year rabbinical students has a positive experience of hard work that leads to comprehension and real attainment. The work I do as a teacher is based on a love of rabbinic literature, and of its audacity, that I want my students to share. That love can only be shared in the real encounter with text, and that encounter depends on skills. Through internalizing talmudic text—which is to say, through engaging in meaningful conversations that start in technically competent readings of Talmud—my students make the lifeblood of rabbinic Judaism their own. Without a doubt, some of these future rabbis will inspire another generation of students who will want to apprentice themselves to scholars of rabbinic texts. Meanwhile, if and when any of my fellow scholars of rabbinics do find themselves saying to their students, "You should really talk with your rabbi about that," I want the rabbis I am training to be ready—not with pat answers and pabulum theologies, but with the ability to facilitate the next steps of a spiritual journey that is inspired by serious textual encounter.

Appendix: Student Observations

Rabbinical student Sarah Tasman writes:

> If I didn't feel like our academic work was part of my spiritual growth, or integrated somehow, or if I felt as though my teachers could not understand my need for this, I am honestly not sure I would have the constitution for this material and for an environment so intense, if it were purely academic and unfeeling.

Rabbinical student Minna Bromberg, PhD, writes:

> I still find myself coming back to that over-used Thoreau quote from the conclusion of Walden: "If you have built castles in the air, your work need not be lost; that is where they should be. Now put the foundations under them." For those of us who come to serious Jewish learning as adults, and even more so for those of us who come with a background in Judaism *primarily* as a spiritual path, technical skills-building can be as much a labor of love as anything else. One of my favorite occurrences in rabbinical school is when I come upon a text in my studies that I have heard quoted

out of context dozens of times. Suddenly, I turn the corner and a sweet little phrase or story that I had always been told was "from the Talmud" is right there on the page in front of me. This time, though, I encounter it in Aramaic and in its context and it takes on a new richness. More than a deepening in the meaning of the tidbit itself is my own opportunity to approach it with a greater sense of authenticity and ownership. It goes from being an uplifting refrigerator magnet that I repeated with embarrassment to being a sweet fruit on a living tree. And it is technical skill building that makes this possible.

Rabbinical student Margie Klein, paraphrasing the words of Rabbi Ebn Leader, another of the teachers at the rabbinical school, writes:

> I could be anywhere right now. Organizing for fair wages or sailing on a Greenpeace boat. But I'm here because I think this is the most important way I can positively influence the world. I'm here to understand these texts so that these texts can help me transform the world through my teaching and my actions.

Sarah Tasman again:

> I felt I had become so close with *perek revi'i*—there were parts I understood easily, parts I struggled with, parts I tore at and picked apart, parts I settled into comfortably, parts I fought my way into. It was one of the most intense and multifaceted relationships I have ever had. When we finished, it really was a feeling of saying goodbye to the chapter but knowing we would see each other again—and it felt so *viscerally*, not just metaphorically. I would call this feeling "Divine," for lack of a better way to describe something that feels so real, so human, but so entirely something else. For even 1/1000 of a feeling like this, I am grateful.

Rabbinical student Tamar Grimm writes:

> At this point in my studies, the aspect of study that seems most deeply connected to spirituality is learning text in the Beit Midrash. This is especially so when the texts are in some ways *about* dialog and lovingly wrestling with another. So, the pursuit is spiritual for me to the extent that it encourages and guides me in seeing the divine in my study partner and, through that work, in the text. The word that comes most to mind here is "engagement"—with text, with other, with self.

Talmud Study as a Spiritual Endeavor: Delights and Dangers

And she also offers:

> In a women's Rosh Chodesh group I met with this week, we made artistic representations of our sources of growth and spiritual nourishment. One of the first things I included was Talmud study. Learning Gemara is similar to rock climbing or other challenges that when done in pairs require a great deal of trust, communication, self-awareness—and the experience creates a spiritual connection among the people who share it. The way we learn Gemara at Hebrew College gives us a voice in religious conversations that have been going on for centuries. We study Talmud not only as a means of acquiring knowledge or improving our text skills—we study to engage with the big questions of life and challenge ourselves, and the tradition, to figure out how to live on this earth. If that's not a spiritual endeavor I don't know what is.

Finally, rabbinical student Daniel Berman writes:

> Jonah, you probably don't remember, but when I had just started school and we were studying Mishnah Berachot, I went for a run at sunrise and as the sun rose I could start to make out the colors, and I stopped in my tracks and recited the *Shema*. It was completely unanticipated, and one of the most beautiful moments in my life, and I shared this story in our Talmud class and then I asked you the same question that you are asking us now: How is this study a spiritual pursuit? And you answered my question by starting to sing the Mishnah, bringing the words into a radically different realm with melody and emotion, and my deep love for text study was fully born. Text study gives us an opportunity to express a part of the self that has no other means of expression. Text study becomes deeply personal. It allows us to be vulnerable, *and* courageous. It connects us to an historical trajectory *and* opens up possibilities for future identity that we could have never imagined.

16 Teaching Rabbinics as an Ethical Endeavour and Teaching Ethics as a Rabbinic Endeavour

Sarra Lev

Introduction

A colleague recently told me the following story. She was attending a workshop at a conference on "Multifaith Dimensions of Theological Education," studying the well-known aggadic passage about Moshe sitting in the future *beit midrash* of Rabbi Akiva (Babylonian Talmud, Menahot 29b). In this midrash, Moshe sits in the last row—the place of the poorest students—and is frustrated at not understanding the discussion. It is only when R. Akiva explains to his students that the law he is transmitting was given to Moshe at Sinai that Moshe is pacified. Moshe says to God, "Creator of the Universe, you have a man like *that* and you are giving the Torah to *me*?" God replies "Be silent, for this is my decree." When the group read the text aloud, and then proceeded to discuss it, a Christian feminist scholar from North Korea challenged them: "Isn't there an ethical problem in studying this text—which is so steeped in assumptions regarding hierarchy, gender, etc.—without explicitly stating a critique of the text?"

When my colleague told me this story, I was surprised. There may well be ethical criticisms of this text, but compared with other rabbinic texts, which can at times be blatantly sexist, homophobic, and/or xenophobic, this was not one that I necessarily would have problematized.[1] Take, for

---

[1] Perhaps this only strengthens her point, highlighting the pervasive but sometimes veiled nature of the ethical issues in our sacred texts. I imagine her issues were along these lines: the text, mainly through its unstated assumptions, promotes a hierarchy which places the "smarter students" in the front of the room; makes "not knowing" into an activity which elicits shame; and assumes

example, the following passage from Niddah 45a, which follows on the mishnah that tells us that "a girl of the age of three years and one day may be betrothed by intercourse":

> Our Rabbis taught: A story is told of a certain woman who came before R. Akiba and said to him, "Master, intercourse has been forced upon me when I was under three years of age; what is my position regarding [marrying someone in] the priesthood?" "You are fit for the priesthood," he replied. "Master," she continued, "I will give you a comparison; to what may the incident be compared? To a babe whose finger was submerged in honey. The first time and the second time he cries about it, but the third time he sucks it." "If so," he replied, "you are unfit for the priesthood." Observing that the students [who were observing the conversation with the woman] were looking at each other, he said to them, "Why do you find the ruling difficult?" "Because," they replied, "as all the Torah is a tradition that was handed to Moses at Sinai, so is the law that a girl under the age of three years [with whom a man has had intercourse] is fit for the priesthood one that was handed to Moses at Sinai." R. Akiba too made his statement only for the purpose of exercising the wits of the students.

Such obviously problematic texts make the pedagogic questions even more poignant. How can we teach these texts without confronting their problematic ethical stances head-on—and how do we do so while still preserving them as meaning-making texts?

When the Christian scholar raised her concern about the workshop text, the presenter reportedly responded by saying that the *way* in which the group was studying the text—sitting in a room with women and men in a non-hierarchical setting—constituted a implicit critique of the text's assumptions around hierarchy and gender. The implication was that no further discussion of those particular issues was necessary. In practice, in my own teaching of rabbinic texts, I often tacitly fall back on a similar answer—but it is by no means in and of itself an adequate response to the range of ethical challenges presented. While it is true that we do study these texts in a non-hierarchical, non-

---

(and thereby constructs) a reality that excludes women altogether from the room in which the learning takes place.

segregated[2] setting, that does not address the fact that they are taught as holy texts while appearing to hold some values and assumptions that directly conflict with our own. If we ask our students to engage in studying problematic (and even painful) texts like that of Mishnah Yoma, or even less loaded texts, as if they are entirely value-neutral, we miss an opportunity for ethical education.

The challenge to confront and critique these texts matters to me not only because I too am a feminist approaching rabbinic texts as pieces of my own psychospiritual history,[3] but also because I teach at the Recon-

---

[2] I say non-segregated rather than non-sexist because I believe that many of the sexist dynamics reflected in the texts do continue to permeate our own classrooms, even while women and men study together. In a course I took on feminist ethics, for example, I did a short informal experiment in which I recorded for a full session the number of times men spoke versus the number of times women spoke, and timed the length of each comment. The results were astounding, especially given the subject matter of the course. The same can be said of the continued emphasis in our communities on the value of knowing, and the resulting shame which comes with not knowing.

[3] What I refer to here is best articulated by Alasdair MacIntyre in his discussion of moral identity:

> I can only answer the question "What am I to do?" if I can answer the prior question "Of what story or stories do I find myself a part?" We enter human society, that is, with one or more imputed characters—roles into which we have been drafted—and we have to learn what they are in order to be able to understand how others respond to us and how our responses to them are apt to be construed.... Hence there is no way to give us an understanding of any society, including our own, except through the stock of stories which constitute its initial dramatic resources (Alasdair MacIntyre, *After Virtue: A Study in Moral Theory*, Second ed. [London: Duckworth, 1993], 216).

He continues:

> Notice also that the fact that the self has to find its moral identity in and through its membership in communities such as those of the family, the neighborhood, the city and the tribe does not entail that the self has to accept the moral *limitations* of the particularity of theose forms of community.... (Ibid., 221).

If we accept that the "stock of stories" of the Jewish narrative constitutes us psychologically and spiritually as Jews, then the only way to reconstitute what it means to be a Jew is to visit those narratives and understand how they have done that work on us so that we can then move beyond the limitations of our own narrative.

structionist Rabbinical College (RRC), where one of my—and the institution's—goals, among others, is to train rabbinical students to become ethical leaders. But how much do I, in practice, confront the ethics of the texts, and how much do I fall back on the implicit claim that the very fact that we are doing it differently is its own sufficient critique or skip over the ethical issues entirely for "lack of time?"

This paper investigates some of my attempts thus far at dealing with the issue of how, and how much, to address ethics head-on in the teaching of rabbinic texts. In the first half of the paper, I analyze my teaching in two recorded classes in order to understand under what circumstances my students and I engage in conversations about power and ethics, and under what circumstances these conversations are circumvented. In doing this study, I also sent out a questionnaire to a number of students, past and present, asking questions about what they had learned about ethics in studying with me. In the second half of the paper, I discuss the responses of the six students who answered the questionnaire.

In doing this analysis, I was interested not in arriving at solutions but in examining my own patterns of teaching—what facilitates or hampers my goal of using my classes to teach ethics. For the purposes of this paper, by "teaching ethics" I mean employing in our study of sacred texts a lens through which we examine ourselves and our values in a manner that can help us act as spiritual leaders in promoting social justice. The most consistent conclusion that emerged from this study may seem obvious, but was so blatant in its consistency that it seems worthy of mentioning at the outset: when students came into class with ethics as the frame, they were more likely to think about the texts through an ethical lens, and discussions were more likely to lead in that direction—a point to which this paper will continually circle back.

First and foremost, I am trying to teach my students how to sit at the table with the rabbis, and to refrain from employing their own agendas and values systems in initially trying to understand the texts. However, if these are ultimately to be "their" holy texts, which will shape decisions they make about how to be in the world and what they will teach and preach to congregations, is this a valid pedagogic stance? What will such students do with texts they see as being in conflict with their values, both as rabbis and as human beings? No matter what one's particular ethical lens might be, in teaching classical texts we are always faced with this essential pedagogic question.

Two underlying, intertwined questions, then, are at the heart of this paper. The first is what we do when teaching rabbinic texts that clash in some way with our own ethical principles—a question we might ask in all teaching contexts, not just in rabbinical seminaries. The second is the more complex question of how we employ the teaching of these texts to help our students become better ethical leaders—that is, how one uses rabbinic literature in order to help rabbinical students become better people, better leaders, and better at understanding the deeper psychological issues of the history of our people—and how we balance that desire with the goal of teaching skills, making sure that our students know how to properly decipher and understand the texts as they are.[4]

The Context

My classes contain a range of students who represent a wide spectrum of attitudes toward rabbinic texts. Some regard these texts as sacred in a way that requires that we find our spiritual guidance from them while leaving our own ethical standards at the door of the *beit midrash*, forgiving or ignoring those parts that seem unethical. At the other end of the spectrum are those who reject the texts almost entirely for their content and biases, refusing to see them as sources of ethical teaching. As a comprehensive strategy, neither response is sufficient for religious Jewish ethical leaders. My struggle lies in forging a relationship between the texts and these future rabbis in which my students feel compelled to engage the ethics of the texts head on, neither accepting them unquestioningly nor ignoring or rejecting them. It is my assumption that it is their—and our—responsibility to bring an ethical lens to textual learning and interpretation. And it is with this assumption that I began the inquiry represented in this paper.

---

[4] I am dissatisfied with the most common *de facto* pedagogic responses to these questions, which either simply frame the texts in their historical contexts, ignore the ethically problematic parts of the texts for pedagogic purposes, or—as Ed Greenstein seems to suggest we do with respect to the teaching of Bible—choose a methodology to apply to reading and teaching a particular text based on the message we want to derive from it. See Edward Greenstein, "A Pragmatic Pedagogy of Bible," *Journal of Jewish Education* 75:3 (2009): 290-303.

Although I believe that this charge falls upon all readers of these texts, there are qualities of rabbinical training in particular that serve to highlight that responsibility:

1. Rabbinical students see this literature, and/or know that fellow Jews see this literature, as "holy" (whatever that may mean to each of them), and therefore as wielding power over their lives.

2. Rabbinical students are not just studying the literature to know it, or even to live it themselves—but also to teach it to future generations of Jews. The teachings of these rabbis will be the primary exposure to rabbinic literature of many of their congregants and students.

3. Rabbinical students need to learn the tools, as rabbis, to be critical of power relations in the world, because they will be spiritual leaders who will be called upon to confront injustice.

Having outlined the unique issues present in teaching rabbinical students, let me also clearly identify my own subject position as a teacher at RRC in particular, as the pedagogic issues are quite different at different rabbinical colleges. The RRC curriculum, for example, gives equal weight to all the layers of Jewish tradition and civilization, and so spends less mandatory time than many other rabbinical schools on rabbinic texts. It also demands that a great deal of students' time be dedicated to practical rabbinics skills, which places constraints on the time available to teach basic text skills. In addition, the RRC community understands contemporary ethical standards in a way that is shaped to a certain extent by feminist theory, queer theory, and a liberal agenda. While the ethical issues for me and my students may not be the same as those for people who learn and teach elsewhere, the question of what we do as teachers when our personal and communal ethics conflict with those in the texts cuts across denominations and contexts.

The Classes

The two class sessions I recorded and analyzed were both in courses on midrash. One, which met on the RRC campus, consisted of seven students; the other, with only two students, met at my home in the evening, and often ran overtime, allowing us to spend more time on discussion. I introduced each of these class sessions by asking if I could record the class and explaining why.[5] Thus, the students all knew that I was interested in thinking about the place of ethics in our class discussions. I, too, was aware of the issue off and on during the class.

During the class at RRC we examined three texts, beginning with a short series of three- to four-word midrashim on *ben sorer u'moreh*—the stubborn and rebellious son, who is sentenced to be stoned. The verse in the Torah (Deut. 21:18) reads *"Ki yihyeh l'ish ben sorer u'moreh,"* "If a man has a stubborn and rebellious son...", and goes on to explain that the son should be taken out to the elders and stoned. The midrashim we examined prevent this extreme punishment from occurring by limiting its application—claiming that the word *ish* refers only to a father, not a mother, and that the word *ben* limits the subject to a son, not a daughter, and to a child, not an adult. The series of midrashim ends with a halakhic statement that a minor is also exempt from the punishment (because he is, of course, a minor).

This text raises many ethical issues. To name just a few: What does it mean for the Torah to suggest that we kill (some of) our stubborn children? What implications does the rabbis' claim that the law applies only in the case where there is a father and only to sons (and not daughters) have? How does this ruling fit (or not fit) into larger gender questions raised by rabbinic literature? What does it mean for our rabbis to have developed their own set of ethics that seem to disagree with the Torah's? Are there ethical implications to the rabbis' interpretation? Was it unethical for them to have ascribed a meaning to the Torah text that is so antithetical to the *peshat* (the plain meaning of the text)? Does it matter that their decision to do so was itself based on a desire to correct something they saw as unethical?

During the course of the 75-minute discussion on the *ben sorer u'moreh* text, these types of ethical issues came up only six times (if one counts a discussion during the break)—and five of those times, as the transcript reveals, I steered immediately away from the issue of ethics and back to the practical tools of analysis.

---

5   In the class that met at RRC, this was only a brief comment, whereas in the class in my home we spent some time discussing the paper I was planning to present at a conference, which was the first version of this chapter.

Teaching Rabbinics and Teaching Ethics

The first time an opening emerged to discuss ethics was when Dina[6] was asked to explain the text.

> Dina: So the question that I have at this moment is—Ellen's been saying to me that they are minimizing the categories because it's so awful and heinous, what happens, that how can we, how can the rabbis not prevent that from happening often?
>
> Ellen: I only said that's what happens in Gemara.
>
> Dina: So I liked the idea and I went with it, but I have a question about the distinction—so I can understand them talking about a boy and not a girl, but I don't understand why they are talking about … I don't know enough about ages to know at what age does someone become a man, is it thirteen or not, and when does someone become a minor.
>
> SL: So let's first ask: how and where would you find out that information?

From here the discussion delves into one of resources (how to use Steinzaltz's reference guide, Gemara, words they could have looked up, medieval commentaries, etc.) and from there we proceed with a discussion of the actual answer to the question—discussing the different categories of age and their distinctions and characteristics in the halachic system. In the course of this discussion, I left behind entirely the comment that Dina had made about the rabbis' goals, and the potential discussion about the very issues that I am suggesting here are essential to open up in the classroom.

We then moved forward into analyzing the possible midrashic "hooks"[7] for this text, at which point opportunity number two for a discussion on ethics emerged. During this discussion, a student suggested that we are dealing with the gender ambiguity of *ben*—does it mean son, or child? Again, I affirmed that this is indeed the hook, but

---

6   All of the students' names have been changed.
7   The hook for a midrash is the textual basis upon which it is built. Thus, the ambiguity of the word *ben*, which can mean "son" (relational and gendered), "offspring" (relational but un-gendered), "child" (age but not relation), makes it a good "hook" on which to "hang" a midrash.

took no advantage of the comment to discuss feminist issues of gender, gender ambiguity, the question of andro-centric language, or any of the other possible issues that could have emerged from the comment. We continued discussing possible hooks in the text, which then led us into a general discussion about midrashic hooks. At this point, a student brought up the point that *ish*, too, suffers the same problem of gender ambiguity. Again, I divert the discussion to the issue of the hook, and then to a discussion of the hermeneutical principles being used in the midrash.

About a half hour into the class, during a discussion in which we are exploring the question "How does this midrash actually apply?," I raise the question: "Under what circumstances would there be a situation in which a man would have a *ben sorer u'moreh* but a woman would not? Under what real-life circumstances would we be able to apply this midrash so as to not kill the rebellious son?" The suggestion came up that it might be true in the case where there are two mothers—an opening for a discussion of gay and lesbian issues. My response to the student, however, was a pithy "OK, probably not," which generated some laughter and a few more jokes about lesbian mothers in the period of the midrash, lasting about a minute.

Again, I moved the discussion forward with the question, "Ok, so Dina stopped reading at the word *l'isha* [to a woman]. Why?" We began a discussion of exegetical midrash and how one identifies when a midrash ends and begins. During the break, fifteen minutes later, Ellen asked a question about the gender implications of the statement "if a man has a son," as opposed to an alternative formulation, "if a woman has a son." She raises the issue of what it means to say "has a son" and the fact that the woman gives birth to the child, but the man "has" him and how that relates to their reading of the midrash.

> Ellen: To me in biblical land if a man has a son that means something very different than "if a woman has a son"—do you know what I mean?
>
> SL: No, say more.
>
> Ellen: Like, the woman is the birther of the son, but it's really the *man* who has the son. I don't know—I'm just thinking about how important it is for a man to have a son, and [words unclear]—it's

just a different ball of wax. It just seems like if at the rabbinic table we were like—now we're just talking about male single parents, you'd have to say more than *k'she-yihyeh ben l'ish v'lo l'isha*[8]...

My answer to Ellen focused neither on the issue she raised about single parenting, nor on the issue of the androcentric view of progeny (that the text makes the actual birther of the child invisible in writing, stating, "if a *man* has a son"). Instead, I latched onto her comment about syntax, and whether the words, the way they are written, could mean what the students were proposing. Ellen's questions about "ownership" of children, paternity and maternity having different societal weight, etc., were lost in our discussion.

After a break, when we reconvened, we revisited the discussion about age. It was only one hour and five minutes into the discussion that I opened up the discussion of contemporary meaning by asking, "OK, this is a great Reconstructionist text—why?" Even here, I am not so much politicizing the discussion, or offering an ethical lens through which to view the text, but rather focusing on seeing the text through a Reconstructionist lens. While this may, in a roundabout way, prove to be about ethics as well, that is not at all how I framed the question. As a result, we discussed the rabbis changing the Torah text, and the discussion turned to the question of how they fit the Torah into their own social context. Joseph raised a question about whether the midrash is influenced by the fact that the rabbis might not have had any power to enact the death penalty in their own time, and we had a several-minute discussion on that issue as it relates to Mordecai Kaplan and his understanding of the ethical imperative of making change. Ellen said:

> It seems that the way they do this is based on the exegetical principles that they made up, so in order to do the same thing I don't think we could use their same principles, we'd need another set of principles, and is it a chicken and egg thing about the principles and the things that we'd want to do with them?

---

[8] Earlier, another student had proposed that the midrash is about a single parent. It was suggested that if so, the text would have had to read "*k'she-yihyeh ben l'ish v'lo l'isha*" rather than "*k'she-yihyeh ben v'lo k'she-yihyeh ben l'isha*."

This would have been a perfect entry point into a discussion about rabbinic texts and ethics—where our ethics come from and where those of the rabbinic sages come from, how these rabbis related to the ethics of the Torah and how we relate to theirs, how these rabbis solved their own ethical problems with the issues that came before them, and how we can deal with those which come from the rabbinic texts. It seems to me that such a conversation would be a rich beginning to a semester-long examination of ethical issues that arise from rabbinic texts.[9] At that moment, however, I understood that we had two more texts to get through in half an hour, and did not know how to balance the need to get through the material with the value of making the material meaningful to the students' lives. I wanted to get the lesson across, without taking too much time. The result was the following conversation:

> SL: Right. So as Reconstructionists, I think we do use a different set of principles when we do it.... And there's [also] an argument between the people *in* these schools about the principles you're allowed to use. Like we said—R. Akiva drashes [i.e., interprets] an *et* [a word that usually merely indicates a direct object] and R. Yishmael comes along and says, "What are you talking about, how can you drash that *et*?!" So there's not one set of things at all. So for Kaplan, we could have the people who drash the *ets* and the people who dispute that. That's part of it for him.
>
> Ellen: But that's what I'm saying—there is a bigger boundary, but there's a boundary beyond which ...[that is] even if people are disagreeing they're remaining within the boundary.
>
> SL: Yes, so that's the question—where's the boundary? But that's always the question in any society.

The second part of class was devoted to two texts. The first[10] tries to answer the question: "When it says *v'hayah ka-asher yarim Moshe yado v'gavar* ('And it came to pass when Moses lifted his hand that Israel

---

[9] This is only the fourth of thirteen class sessions.
[10] Mekhilta d'Rabbi Yishmael, Beshalach, Masekhta d'Amalek, 1 *s.v. ve'hayah ka'asher yarim Moshe*

prevailed'),[11] how is it possible that the Torah would tell us it was *Moshe* who did this, and not God?!" The midrash spells out that when Moshe raised his hands, the people looked upward (presumably toward God) and believed, and thus God acted on their behalf. We spent fifteen minutes on this much easier text, during which the last four minutes were devoted to the question, "What is their agenda here and what could you do with this text as a rabbi?" The short discussion that followed began by asking about whether or not this was an anti-Christian polemic—are they trying to say the power is not in a person, but in God?—and then moved to a comment on the fact that the Israelites were empowered (i.e., they made God act on their behalf by their belief), thereby creating the victory.

With the final text that we explored for the last ten minutes of the class, there was no discussion whatsoever about implications or meanings. The discussion focused solely on the technical aspects of translation and understanding.

What emerges from the above reprise of the class is that, though it is my goal to bring together the texts with discussions on ethics, at many points when there was an opening to use the texts as a jumping-off point to discuss these very issues, I avoided letting the conversation move in that direction in any way before the basic meaning of the text was fully determined. During the study of the first text, in the first few cases where there were openings, I changed the subject back to understanding either how to analyze this particular midrash, or how to analyze midrashim in general. Only at the end of the discussion on that text did I allow other questions to be raised.

Despite the fact that I knew that this class was being taped for the purpose of this paper, even at the end of examining a particular text, I did not frame the discussion in ethical terms directly, but instead in terms of the question, "What would you do with this as a rabbi?" The fact that the discussion turned to ethics in these cases happened in spite of that framing, rather than because of it.

Additionally, instead of making room for a classroom discussion on the above issues, even when the opportunity came up, my responses seem to have tried to offer "answers" in light of one particular stream

---

[11] Exod. 17:11

of thought—Reconstructionism. That is, when Ellen said, "there's a boundary beyond which ... [that is], even if people are disagreeing they're remaining within the boundary," she opened an opportunity to discuss a number of issues, including how our boundaries are the same as and different from those of the ancient rabbis, whether this teaches us anything about what the limits of our own boundaries are in the Reconstructionist movement, how we determine what is "right," etc. If we are able to see that the rabbis lived within a set of boundaries, it might teach us how to explore our own. Rather than answering "yes, so that's the question—where's the boundary? But that's always the question in any society," and moving onto another text, this too would have been a point at which to engage in a discussion of ethics.

Once again, with the second text, until we had established a good translation and explanation of the textual problem and its solution, I was unwilling to pause and entertain questions on ultimate meaning or significance. At the end of the text, once this had been achieved, I again asked the question, "So what is their agenda here and what could you do with it as a rabbi?"—again, not framing the discussion in terms of ethics directly. I did not ask, for example, "What are the implications of the fact that the rabbis take the power away from Moshe?" or "What are the implications of the fact that they give the power to *bnei yisrael*, the Israelites?"

We did not look at whether there are ways that we as a people still understand ourselves or present ourselves as having sway over God's decision to make us powerful; why we might once have felt this way, or might choose to feel this way or otherwise now; what some of the lingering effects of those midrashic messages are on us as a people today; and whether these effects cause us to see ourselves in ways that may be problematic or to act in ways that may be unethical. And again, not surprisingly, the comments of the students were not focused on the ethical value of the texts, but on their value for us as teachers.

I will now highlight aspects of the class that met at my home more briefly. While some of the same issues arose there, the difference that I noted was that in this smaller class of just two students, my implicit framing of the class at the beginning had a greater effect on the turns the discussion took throughout the session. Because I had opened by explaining why I was recording the class, at one point Naomi, one of the students, actually said, "so speaking of ethics…" which led to an eleven-minute conversation (out of the first 38 minutes of class) about

Teaching Rabbinics and Teaching Ethics

the ethical implications of the use of particular prooftexts in certain manuscripts versus other manuscripts.[12] The conversation began with my attempt to finish up the discussion of a particular text and move onto the next one (I said, "OK, anything else on this?" after having analyzed the basic structure of the midrash), but the student swung it back towards the ethical conversation, referring directly to my framing of the question at the beginning of class.

A second text elicited the same type of conversation. The text in question offered four different opinions on the following question: when the Torah says you must return a bull to your *oyev*, your enemy, to whom—what enemy—is it referring? The first opinion claims that *oyev* refers to the *oved elilim* (one who worships idols); the second, that it refers to a convert who has returned to his original religion; the third, that it refers to a *yisrael m'shumad*, an Israelite who has left the fold; and the fourth, that it refers to a *yisrael* who has personally wronged you. For the first five minutes, we dealt with translation, explanation, and a number of midrashic rules, and then spent about ten minutes discussing the possible messages of both the four individual opinions contained within the midrash, and of the redactor's arrangement of the opinions in this format, from "farthest" to "closest." While my own reading was that the rabbis chose to make it less and less likely that you would have to give back the bull of anyone outside of your immediate circle, one of the students understood it differently. If the text refers to someone who is in the outer circle (her example was a Palestinian), one might never have the opportunity to give back a lost object. This midrash attempts to make sure that we know that we are responsible to those we are immediately in conflict with, as difficult as that might be.

Our different analyses gave us an opportunity to discuss which opinion the redactor privileges, how *kal va-homer* ("if X, then all the more so Y") reasoning might affect our reading, and how we might avoid assuming the agendas of the rabbis and instead deduce from the texts what those agendas are. This meant that we could engage in a conversation both on the ethical level and on the level of technical prowess.

---

12 This was an advanced class in which the use of critical editions was assumed. For this text the critical edition showed that different manuscripts used different prooftexts to support the same midrash.

The Questionnaire

The RRC curriculum is divided historically into five years (Biblical, Rabbinic, Medieval, Modern, and Contemporary). During the Rabbinic year, students study primarily Mishnah, Talmud and midrash. After their Rabbinic year students are required to complete three classes in advanced rabbinics.

I divided the student-respondents into three sets based on which classes they had taken with me. Set 1 consists of Iris, Esther, and Mimi, who are all in the same class and studied two courses in their Rabbinic year with me: a survey course in midrash, and a beginners Talmud course in which we learn the Babylonian Talmud's Sotah (which deals with the suspected adulteress). The latter is particularly challenging from a feminist perspective. Iris was one of the most skilled students I have ever taught, and the material moved smoothly for her. Esther struggled much harder through the material and ultimately prevailed. Mimi took an additional third course the previous semester on false witnesses and the death penalty. All three of these students were in their third or fourth year when they answered the survey.

The other three students were all recent graduates at the time they answered the survey. Of these, Set 2 (Ronit and Caren) took as many rabbinics courses as they could squeeze into their schedule, including the first-year courses mentioned above, and another that features most prominently in their responses on the subject of marriage. This latter course was one of a series that I taught entitled "Reconstructionist Sacred Cows" in which we studied subjects which even in the liberal Reconstructionist movement are considered core "Jewish values"—among them marriage and circumcision.

Set 3 is comprised of only one student, Leah. Leah took only one course with me, having spent her rabbinic year in Israel. The subject of the course was sex ambiguity. Leah disliked rabbinic texts from the beginning, and my course did not convince her otherwise.

The questionnaire consisted of six questions:[13]

---

[13] Several of the students did not keep to the format of the questions, and instead wrote a longer essay addressing the various issues. Thus, I present below specific answers to questions I asked as well as reflections which I believe pertain to the questions.

Teaching Rabbinics and Teaching Ethics

1. Have you felt like classes with me have taught you anything about
    a. ethics
    b. how to think politically on a large scale about the role of Jews in the world, about forms of injustice (specific or not,) etc.
    c. how to be a better person?

2. Have you felt like classes with me have
    a. changed the way you view a subject?
    b. radicalized you?
    c. failed to deal with the "important issues"?

3. Have you felt like classes with me have been missing these elements?

4. Other than simply thinking that good text skills make a better rabbi, is there any other way in which you have felt like classes with me helped you become a better rabbi? How?

5. Do you feel that there is a good enough balance between examining these types of issues and learning skills?

6. Keeping in mind that there are only four required rabbinic text classes at RRC, do you have suggestions on how to improve this aspect without letting go of the skills building?

I divided Question 1 into three slightly different ways of asking about the same pedagogic issue—that is, my desire to use my teaching of Talmud to ultimately teach and empower students to act as spiritual leaders for social change. I wanted to use language that might speak to whatever ways students might frame this for themselves.

The answers from the first group alone vary enough that attention should be drawn to the differences. Mimi answered the question with a basic "No." She drew attention to the fact that the way I managed class dynamics taught her about ethics, but for her this had nothing to do with the material itself or how we studied it. When asked if the classes had changed the way she views a subject, she did state that it had, in that she understood that "the misogyny of the rabbis is real, but such texts can still be worth studying for skills as well as content." Her two other examples in answer to this question were less about ethics and more about the subject in general.

When I asked (in Question 2c) whether my class had failed to deal with the "important issues," however, Mimi answered:

> NO—This is one area where I think your classes excel. We deal with the issues that come out of the text pretty thoroughly—either in terms of what were the issues for the rabbis, what are the issues for us today, how do we teach/use these texts with congregants or other types of audiences.

Mimi's answer points to the fact that she sees a difference between engaging directly and explicitly with ethics, and simply dealing with the "important issues." Upon reflection, I believe this could be a result of two different but intertwined issues:

1. What it means to "learn about ethics": It is possible that the answers to question 1 reveal the very issue I am grappling with—a searching for the texts themselves to embody the ethics we would like to see. When my students were asked if they had learned anything about ethics from the texts, they could not answer positively, even if we had discussed "the important issues" because they felt that the texts had not delivered the ethics they were looking for.[14] I will return to this point further in my analysis.

2. Framing: For each text we study during a semester, once we have finished studying the technical details of the midrash or *sugya*, I ask the students, "How would you use this as a rabbi?" In these discussions we often do what Mimi considered "dealing with the important issues" (relevance to contemporary Jews) without asking questions about ethics in particular. The fact that we do, in fact, have a conversation for each text about relevance allows for different answers to the questions "did you learn about ethics?" and "did we deal with the important issues?" and draws attention to the way in which the framing of the discussion directly affects the discussion itself. Only those students for whom the term "the important issues" is equal to "ethics"

---

[14] This was reflected in the responses of other students to this question as well.

will come away answering these questions identically. Furthermore, since I myself believe that the "important issues" are those that build us into better, more ethical human beings, I myself need to frame the conversation in ways that will lead us to speak about ways in which these texts might do that work.

Iris, who had the easiest time of the three with deciphering the plain meaning of the rabbinic texts themselves, gave a very detailed response in which she referred to the sacred cow curriculum. Here she describes the impact on her of the very fact that I mentioned it in a conversation:

> First, I recalled having a conversation with you … where you talked about the importance of teaching on the "sacred cows" of Judaism…. I think the subject matter alone that you choose to address in class encourages (forces?) students to think about Jewish ethics / power and ethics / power in Jewish contexts in ways that other methods of teaching don't. Simply put, when you approach learning Talmud in order to learn the underpinnings of halakha … you develop a very different kind of relationship with the texts than if you are learning texts specifically with the intention of examining some of these larger ethical / power / political issues (even if the focus is more on learning text skills than an in-depth exploration of these issues themselves). I found that the more you made those intentions explicit, even if we couldn't spend a lot of time on them in class, the more I was thinking about them for myself.

Again, it would seem that the framing of the texts in the context of the issue of ethics—in this case, things we as a Jewish community are not willing to examine carefully for their ethical impact—made Iris's experience of the same courses quite different. Admittedly, in other answers she notes that several of the courses she was taking and the people she was interacting with helped her to think about the material through this lens. In her answer to question 6, regarding suggestions for improving this aspect, she again mentions that

> it would be beneficial for you to be even more explicit about some of your goals in this area as learning the skills of asking some of these questions goes hand in hand with the reading / deciphering skills (if you ask me it's these questions that are the difference between being able to translate and being able to understand).

While Iris felt that she had spent a great deal of time examining the ethical issues of these texts, Esther, who had studied precisely the same courses as Iris, answered the following:

> Ethics via Talmud:—not really. I mean not from the texts themselves. If we learned ethics it was by distinguishing what we would consider acceptable behavior, from what the rabbis considered acceptable. I suppose the text about *mita yafah*—when the rabbis were discussing the best death to give to someone (out of mercy), would be the one example I can think of where I saw them struggling to be ethical in the meting out of capital punishment. But most of the time their ethics seemed to be in the realm of *bein adam l'makom* [between human beings and God], as opposed to *bein adam l'havero* [interpersonal], and therefore I couldn't relate. I frankly did not find the rabbis very ethical at all....

Esther goes on to give examples of the unethical behavior of the rabbis.

> Mostly I came away from Talmud with the thought that my religion had been framed by misogynistic bastards.... The minute I figured out that the ENTIRE *sotah* procedure was moot (due to the nonexistence of the temple, due to the fact that the Mishnah itself tells us that they stopped doing it)—what I was left with was the thought of these sexist assholes dancing on the head of a pin, while imagining the woman naked, how many strips of cloth would she have, how would they expose her breasts. And they framed my religion? If we have ethics as Jews now it is in spite of them, not because of them.

At first the answers of the two students look entirely opposite from one another—Iris claiming that she did learn about ethics, and Esther claiming that she did not. However, in fact the two are remarkably similar. Neither feels that the rabbis of the Talmud are necessarily their ethical predecessors or guides. Both did, in fact, discover lessons about ethics and power in the sources. Esther's lesson was precisely that her ethics and those of the rabbis who composed these texts do not match. What I did not clearly communicate in class is that that, in itself, is a lesson in ethics. What Esther's answer reflects is the fact that I did not teach the students *how* to think about ethics when one is confronted with a text one perceives to be unethical. Iris may have started out not expecting or requiring the sources to be her ethical guides. Alternatively, by her own words, she took my framing of the "sacred cows" curriculum as license to understand the texts in this way. The students' answers both reflect the fact that framing is necessary. For Iris, there was enough of a frame into which to put the rest of the course. For Esther, there was not.[15]

This lesson is further confirmed by the answers of the second group of students, who were writing from a memory which stretches back two years rather than from the more recent experience of study with me. Both of these students took additional courses with me, including one "sacred cows" course on marriage. Caren answered my question on ethics as follows:

> I think that the classes I took with you addressed ethics/larger political issues/being a better person in the way we always took some time to discuss how we would teach these texts, which means we looked at their political impact and what we disagreed with. I don't recall all the details of those discussions, but I generally recall the theme of oppression/objectification of women vis-à-vis the Sota, the inequality of marital laws in Kiddushin.... The overall sense I got was that we could study the texts before us with wholehearted enthusiasm without ignoring the ethical questions they raised.

Caren recalls us discussing these issues in the context of the question that I routinely ask on finishing a particular *sugya* or midrash: "How can we use this as a rabbi?" But in my own experience and memory, even this question rarely elicits a discussion about ethics except insofar as we are often engaged in the discussion of "do we want to bring these problematic texts into our congregations?" Thus, for example, after studying a *sugya* about the power of words and their use and misuse in the tractate of Sotah, someone might just as easily say, "We could use it to teach a class on how to write a Torah scroll" as, "We could use it to think about

---

[15] I wonder also if it is not only the framing of the classes themselves, but the way I asked the questions on the questionnaire that left these answers sounding so different. It would have been possible to ask, for example: "Did the course give you tools to think about ethical issues, even when the ethics of the rabbis were clearly different than your own?" This question would have given Esther the feeling that I was not looking for her to find her ethics in the texts, but rather in the discussions we had *about* the texts.

the ways in which we as a Jewish community sometimes misuse words to protect us from looking at ourselves." The question itself does not direct the class discussion toward the students taking account of either themselves personally, or all of us taking account of ourselves as a Jewish community.

Ronit's answer to this question was somewhat different—she did not feel that the classes had taught her about being a better person, but she did feel that they had taught her about ethics

> ... in the sense that I was challenged to think more critically about issues. For example, I had to think more deeply about what it means to create an equal partnership/covenant between two people. I also think that the Sotah class I took pushed me to think about the ethics behind the Torah text in a deeper way.... The class on Kiddushin made me create a more thoughtful wedding for myself.

Caren, who studied with me a number of times in the past years, answered as follows:

> A way in which my studies with you taught me about ethics has to do with the methodology of Talmud itself (and thus came more from the text discussions than our sidebar discussions about contemporary meaning). That is, I believe the Talmud's dialogical thinking conveys an important ethical teaching about there being more than one way of looking at truth, non-dogmatism and honoring of the process of searching for truth, not just the final result. Of course, this aspect is inherent in the text itself, but your focus on methodology brought that lesson home for me more strongly.

I wondered while reading the responses whether Ronit and Caren, who took the sacred cows course with me, may have felt that by definition we were dealing with the course more politically, and whether that may have affected their reflection on other subjects we studied together. It is my impression that, in fact, during the sacred cows course we spent no more time on ethics than in any other course. We analyzed the *sugyot* in the same way as we did for non-sacred-cow classes—trying to understand the flow of the argument, the historical layers, etc. The difference between this course and the others lay chiefly in the very fact that I framed the curriculum as studying "Sacred Cows." I have no way of confirming the hypothesis generated by my wondering, but given the other evidence regarding the strength of framing, it is worth considering.

If framing is the main factor, however, a question remains. Why is it that despite both my students' and my own awareness that I was working on the question of ethics in teaching rabbinic texts, and despite my general commitment to that aspect of my teaching, the subject of ethics still did not come up explicitly nearly as often as it could have in these class sessions? I believe one answer lies in one of the responses of the sixth student, Leah, to the questionnaire.[16] Leah's answer reflects precisely the concern that I have regarding the balance between the time I spend on ethics and on skills. Leah answered the question about whether my classes had taught her about ethics as follows:

> *You do.*[17] *Your classes* are comprised of Talmudic arguments that confused the pants off me ... there's a very real tension with teaching politics in a class where so much effort has to go into just reading the texts themselves. There's just not time, either in class or outside class. I think for people who are good at this stuff there might be more opportunity.

Thinking of the image of Moshe in the *beit midrash* of R. Akiva, I am very aware that, even as we expose the fragility of the humanness of our predecessors, we too must eventually sit at the back of the room reflecting on how our teaching is understood and used by the students of our students. But in the meantime, we have the opportunity and responsibility to pay deliberate attention to the questions that motivate our teaching, and to be reflective and purposeful about our own pedagogic practice in light of those questions.

16　This issue came up in the responses of Caren, Mimi, and Iris as well.

17　The statement that I, separate from the content of my class, taught ethics is one which is reflected in Mimi's response as well, and is deserving of attention in a different paper devoted solely to that subject. I will say, however, that I believe that we, as educators, often fail to recognize the simple notion that I learned as a youth leader in Hashomer Hatzair—*dugma ishit* (personal example) is our most powerful teaching tool when it comes to the teaching of ethics or character building. It is here that I believe I most fail to recognize my power and potential as an educator.

Conclusion

Several themes emerge from this study and are worthy of our attention.

- **Letting the students find their voices is an element in teaching for ethics.** The transcripts of my two classes, and the class at RRC in particular, revealed that even when the conversation provided a natural opening for a discussion on ethics, I did not take advantage of the opportunity to discuss what I feel is ultimately most important to discuss—largely out of a combination of feeling pressed for time (as Leah pointed out) as well as not being as secure on *how* to do that type of education in this context (see other bullet points below). At the same time, what the questionnaires revealed is that there is an element of the way in which I conduct my classes which allows students to "find their own voices" in the process of discussions on a variety of issues.

    Both Mimi and Esther pointed out that letting students have time to do this, not only with regard to technical skills but also in regard to analysis of the text as a meaning-making source, was essential to them. I want to consider how to make more room in my classes for students to find their voices both when we analyze methodology and when we discuss the "issues," even if time does not seem to permit. That aspect of the learning must be given fair time to develop, perhaps even at the expense of my feeling that we should be learning *just one more* technical skill.

- **The text itself (with a focus on methodology) can teach ethics**. Caren pointed out that "the Talmud's dialogical thinking conveys an important ethical teaching about there being more than one way of looking at truth," which was highlighted by my focus on methodology. This comment introduced the added factor of the form of the Talmud (as opposed to its content) as a source for teaching on ethics. In her estimation, the very nature of the Talmud text itself and the way that I reflect upon that nature is a way that ethics are transmitted in a Talmud class. The fact that less advanced students did not reflect upon this indicates that this is something worth pointing out and discussing, even when I am not making a pointed effort to discuss the ethical *content* of the text.

- **Framing is essential**. It became completely clear through both listening to my classes and reading the questionnaires that I need to frame what I am doing for the students—and for myself—not only once, but continually throughout the semester and perhaps each class. When I spent several minutes talking about this paper at the beginning of the class I conducted at home, it changed the lens through which we were examining the text into one of ethical considerations. The fact that I merely mentioned why I was taping the class that met at RRC did not have the same effect.

    In the questionnaires, the need to frame my intent more carefully was explicit (especially in Iris's response). That need was also implicit in Esther's belief that she *did not* learn ethics because she came away feeling that the rabbis were unethical. On one hand, taking the time to discuss how we would teach troubling texts served to acknowledge their nature, took note of their political impact, and surfaced disagreement with them. On the other, had I framed how we learn about ethics as not merely searching for the ethics we already have in the ancient texts, but rather exploring ethics through the very fact that there are tensions between our beliefs and those of the rabbis, Esther's answers might have been very different.

- **Over and above framing, I need to develop and teach a methodology**. The transcripts of my teaching revealed clearly that (despite my own pedagogic interests) discussions about ethics come up in my class only coincidentally, and that I do not have a particular or deliberate way of dealing with the questions when they emerge. At the same time, the questionnaire revealed that students did feel that they had an opportunity to discuss things that mattered when I asked at the end of each textual study, "How would you use this as a rabbi?" Thus, while the subject was not systematically addressed, neither was it entirely ignored. More importantly, the space for the conversation is already carved out in my classes, as is the potential for a deeper understanding of ethical issues.

    Framing is not the only piece of this puzzle that must be present. It is also necessary to develop a methodology that will actively and methodically introduce the subject of ethics into classroom discussions, and will elicit growth in that area through a discussion of these texts. This methodology must include a discussion of ethics in their social/historical context. However, because historicizing ethics is not enough for rabbinical students who approach these texts as eternal religious sources, the methodology must go beyond simply putting those texts into a historical context, extending into seeking to learn about and understand ourselves in relation to the ethics in the texts, and to help us to grow through that understanding.

In Ronit's case, looking critically at the texts on marriage challenged her to think critically about the issues in them—what it means to create an equal partnership—and affected her own wedding ceremony. For students who cannot access this other level of learning the texts without more explicit instruction, framing might facilitate this level of analysis. This necessitates the following point as well.

- **It is necessary to make "learning ethics" independent of whether our ethics are reflected in the texts we are studying**. It became clear to me as I did this work that it is essential to differentiate between "learning ethics" and the particular ethical content of the texts we are learning. That is to say, we can learn ethics as easily from studying a text which lays out opinions that we consider entirely unethical as we can from a text which promotes ethics with which we agree. The question is how the class discussion of that text evolves, and not what the tradents in the text believe. It is essential, however, to make this distinction clear to students. This has not been immediately obvious to my students, and I need not only to practice this distinction, but also to discuss it conceptually from the beginning of the semester and throughout the course. Again—framing.

- **In some cases, the very fact that I chose subject matter which was *contra* the ethics of the students can achieve this goal better than other subject matter**. This was stated particularly in Iris's answers, but also appeared as a theme in Mimi and Caren's responses. It was also obvious from class that many of the conversations which might have developed emerged from students' differences with the ethical underpinnings of the text. Even Esther, who said "The texts we learned in your class did not really teach us about injustice, other than REPRESENTING injustice," also said "Ethics via Talmud:—not really. I mean not from the texts themselves. *If we learned ethics it* *was by distinguishing what we would consider acceptable behavior, from what the rabbis considered acceptable."* If Esther's eyes had been turned in a different direction, she might have answered that we learned a lot about ethics, through examining what she considered *unethical*. Where I failed was in not turning her eyes in this direction. I needed to make that explicit. Yet again—framing.

In an article based on her own teaching, Marjorie Lehman writes, "I no longer believe, as I once did, that by enabling my students to strengthen their decoding skills I have left them with the most significant tool necessary for examining the texts of the Talmud. My goal is to do more than teach them how to read the texts of the Talmudic corpus in Hebrew/Aramaic. I want to teach them how to read between the lines, to question, to analyze, and ultimately to discover meaning in these texts."[18]

I agree with Lehman, and yet I return to the original challenge of what one does with the sometimes terrible meanings that we might discover. Issues like gender privilege and hierarchy can arguably be sidestepped or overlooked in some cases, as in the story with which we began this paper—that of studying the text depicting Moshe in the *beit midrash* of Rabbi Akiva—but what of the more unavoidably painful issues and texts? These (sometimes shocking) texts provide a window onto the world in which the other "milder" texts are situated, and further extend the range of ethical concerns with which we could theoretically engage—concerns which, for some readers of a given text at a given moment, are unavoidable. I want to take up Lehman's challenge, to discover meaning (or, if we cannot discover meaning, to find a way to instill meaning) even in such texts, and especially in our ethical encounter with them.[19]

---

[18] Marjorie Lehman, "For the Love of Talmud: Reflections on the Study of Bava Metzia, Perek 2," *Journal of Jewish Education* 68:1 (2002): 87-103, esp. 87.

[19] I have been considering how this might happen differently than merely using our own "better" ethical behavior as a corrective, saying, "The context in which we are studying it is different and that is good enough." I believe that we must use these texts as jumping-off points to consider our own ethical choices and beliefs, and to question ourselves through study of the texts. As this is not the subject of this paper, it will remain to be explored in a different venue.

This study has allowed me to begin to tease out the obstacles that have thus far stood in the way of my fully committing to what I understand to be an ethical obligation inherent in Lehman's challenge. If we are to "discover meaning in these texts," that is, we must develop a system with which to engage with their ethics, neither accepting nor rejecting them, but making meaning out of them by exploring our own values through them. We cannot remain content, as Lehman says, with merely decoding. We must ask ourselves, how can we offer our students (be they rabbinical students or others) real discussions of the content of these sources from the perspective of ethics? And more important, how can we give our students tools with which they can disagree with the texts, and yet still bring meaning to the experience of studying them and learning from them? I believe these are the questions that every one of us who is a teacher of rabbinic texts must tackle if we are to make these texts speak to the next generation.

Our students will ultimately leave us and create their own circles of learning and living, and their own methods of teaching. We can be sure that there will be times when, like Moshe, we do not agree with or even understand those methods. If, however, we are able to carefully consider how to teach them the tools to become the leaders and teachers we wish them to become, we will have the satisfaction of knowing that in some measure their teaching is a result of the work we have done in crafting and shaping our own.

List of Contributors

Michael Chernick is Deutsch Professor of Jewish Jurisprudence and Social Justice at HUC-JIR/New York.

Beth Cousens is a consultant to Jewish educational organizations, working in areas of strategy development and evaluation.

Susan P. Fendrick, formerly a Senior Research Associate at the Mandel Center for Studies in Jewish Education at Brandeis University, is an editor and editorial consultant.

Barry W. Holtz, is Dean of the William Davidson Graduate School of Jewish Education and the Theodore and Florence Baumritter Professor of Jewish Education at the Jewish Theological Seminary.

Shira Horowitz taught at the South Area Solomon Schechter Day School until 2012 and is currently a field instructor for the Brandeis DeLeT/MAT Program.

Jane Kanarek is Assistant Professor of Rabbinics at the Hebrew College Rabbinical School.

Orit Kent is a Senior Research Associate at the Mandel Center for Studies in Jewish Education at Brandeis University.

Sarra Lev is Chair of the Department of Rabbinic Civilization and Associate Professor of Rabbinic Literature at the Reconstructionist Rabbinical College.

Jon A. Levisohn is Associate Professor of Jewish Education at Brandeis University.

Jeremy S. Morrison is Rabbi and Director of Education at Temple Israel of Boston, MA.

Carl M. Perkins is Rabbi of Temple Aliyah of Needham, MA.

Daniel Reifman teaches and serves as Mashgiach Ruchani at Midreshet AMIT in Jerusalem.

Michael Satlow is Professor of Religious Studies and Judaic Studies at Brown University.

Jeffrey Spitzer is Chair of the Department of Rabbinic Literature at Gann Academy.

Jonah Chanan Steinberg, formerly Associate Dean at the Hebrew College Rabbinical School, is presently Executive Director of Harvard-Radcliffe Hillel.

Susan E. Tanchel, formerly Associate Head of School at Gann Academy, is presently Head of School of JCDS, Boston's Jewish Community Day School.

Index of Biblical and Rabbinic Sources

1. BIBLE

Gen.
1:5	111, 118, 254
37:28	37
39	31
42	32

Exod.
1:1-6:1	163
3	260n27
3:5	163, 166, 169
17:11	399n11
21:1	254
21:2-6	205n21
22:6	254
23:2	271
24:9-11	194n10

Lev.
16:1-20:27	364
16:1-22	364
25:40	205n21

Num.
16-18	23

Deut.
1:2	253
4:12-18	194n10
6:7	110
21:18	394
24:1	139, 141n21
24:1-4	138, 139
25:5-20	146n23
30:12	271
34:1	253

Josh.
5:15	169

2Sam.
15:30	169

Isa.
20:2-4	169

Jer.
2:25	169

Ps.
29	383

Ruth
4:1-15	146n23

2. MISHNAH

Avodah Zarah
5:2	101

Avot
1:1	270, 281

Berakhot
1:1	278-279
9:5	170

Eduyot
1:3	270

Kiddushin
1:1	130n3, 143, 145, 146
3:1	91
3:5	90
3:7	97, 100

Index of Biblical and Rabbinic Sources

Menahot
10:9	120n8

Pirkei Avot
5:22	13

Yevamot
3:8	93

3. TOSEFTA

Bekhorot
1:14	120n8

Berakhot
1:2	120n7

Hullin
10:7	120n8

Parah
4:6	120n8
12:12	120n8

4. MIDRESHEI HALAKHA

Mekhilta De-Rabbi Ishmael
Beshalach, Masekhta d'Amalek 1	398n10
3:17	205n21

5. BABYLONIAN TALMUD

Avodah Zarah
66a	101n16

Bava Batra
23b	87n7
89b	279n13

Bava Metzia
59b	268n2, 271

Berakhot
2a	110
17b	112, 267
19a	268, 273
19b-20a	276, 279
26a	116
63a	170

Kiddushin
2a-b	148
3a-b	143, 148
40b	11
63a	90
64b-65a	97

Menahot
29b	388

Niddah
45a	389

Shabbat
18b	92n8
63a	322

Zevahim
24a	166

6. JERUSALEM TALMUD

Bava Metzia
2, 9	170

Berakhot
1:2	120n7

7. MISHNEH TORAH

Laws of Yibum and Halitzah
1:1	146n23

General Index

Academic 16, 28, 33, 40, 49, 52, 61, 63, 105, 107, 124, 187, 195, 203, 209, 229, 239, 246, 251, 259, 318, 372, 377
Active learning 214-215, 218, 231-232
Adar, Zvi 45n71
Adult education 20, 60, 76, 105, 161, 186, 189, 214, 232, 238, 286, 353
Aesop 41
Aggadic 59, 60n21, 70, 108, 278, 280, 388
Agudas Yisroel 73n37
Allen, George 167
Alter, Robert 31, 32, 33, 40, 45, 49
Amichai, Yehuda 78n42
Amoraim/Amoraic 62, 90, 99-103, 116, 118n5 and 6, 119, 124, 125n9, 129, 136, 268, 277, 284
Ancient Near East 15, 24, 26, 30n70, 38, 39, 43, 195, 199, 352, 359
Archaeology 30, 49, 62n23, 125n9
Ayers, William 253
Bach, Alice 34
Bal, Mieke 34
Ball, Deborah 18
Bar-Ilan University 177
Barnes, Douglas 290
Bashan, Eliezer 169
Beit midrash 286-288, 318, 388, 392, 409, 413
Beit Midrash Research Project at the Mandel Center 288
Bekiut (Bekius) 73, 74, 76-78, 131, 136
Benderly, Samson 48
Berman, Daniel 387
Berman, Scot 60
Bhutto, Benazir 182, 183
Board of Jewish Education (BJE) of Greater New York 325

Bok, Derek 214, 228
Boyer, Ernest 16
Brisker derekh 107, 108, 112, 114, 122, 123
Brody, Robert 123
Bromberg, Minna 385
Brown University 216, 229, 379
Bruner, Jerome 257
Buber, Martin 42, 43, 355
Bush, George W. 168
Calkins, Lucy 332
Camp 20, 128, 132, 362, 364, 366
Carini, Patricia 321
Cazden, Courtney 290
Character development 46, 68
Christian 62, 68, 136, 170, 171, 176, 203, 225, 234, 363, 388, 389, 399
Close reading 31, 36, 41, 45, 49, 141, 154
Cochran-Smith, Marilyn 17
Cohen, Burton 46, 50
Cohen, Elizabeth 289
Cohen, Shaye 218, 219, 221, 222, 232
Columbia University 379
Commonplaces 19, 249
Community 16n4, 38, 77, 109, 111, 162, 174, 225, 245, 247, 248. 255, 261, 265, 275, 280, 281, 282, 325, 329, 350, 353, 358, 360, 361, 364, 374, 381, 383, 393, 405, 408
Compassion 60, 175
Complexity 14, 15, 26, 40, 41, 62, 64, 70, 86, 196, 230, 232, 265, 267, 280, 283, 358, 366, 372
Content knowledge 15, 325
Contextual approach, orientation 29, 35 42, 44, 61, 62n24, 68, 186, 189, 200, 210, 239, 352, 355, 376
Cosby, Bill 166
Cousens, Beth 355n6, 356

General Index

Critical/critically 23, 24, 28, 31, 32, 49, 55, 59n18, 62n24, 63, 71, 74, 80, 83, 100, 102n17, 109n2, 187, 191, 192, 195, 196, 206, 208, 213n2, 214, 215, 228, 229, 237, 238, 256, 283, 284, 287, 299, 320, 357n8, 360, 363, 371, 379, 384, 401n12

Culture 14, 21, 22, 24, 30, 38, 69, 70, 71, 75, 107, 160, 164, 172, 180, 184, 190, 196, 214, 224, 264, 280, 325, 364n10

Curriculum 18, 19n8, 24, 27n4, 28n11, 39, 44, 45, 48, 50, 60n20, 77, 107, 128n2, 133, 236-238, 253, 257n17, 265, 282, 283, 326, 327, 330, 357, 380, 381, 393, 402, 407

D'var torah 159, 163-165, 167, 168, 172, 178, 180, 181, 241

Daf yomi 67, 67n37, 73

Daloz, Laurent 320

Dante, Alighieri 32

Darshan (pl. darshanim) 160, 161, 180

De Saussure, Ferdinand 84n6, 88

Decoding 48, 50, 78, 84, 129, 355n5, 413, 414

DeLeT (Day School Leadership Through Teaching) Program at Brandeis University 238, 288, 293, 318

Derash (pl. derashot) 21, 159, 162, 163, 165, 168, 172-174, 176, 180-184

Derrida, Jacques 94

Diachronic 29, 68, 102,

Discipline 16, 27, 28, 37, 38n42, 52, 56, 57, 62n23, 65n27, 79, 82, 107, 377

Diversity 20, 52, 57, 64, 67, 191, 194, 207, 245, 282, 283

Division-of-labor model 17, 18

Documentary hypothesis 12, 34, 204, 236-263, 284, 366

Dorph, Gail 238

Dowd, Maureen 178

Duran, Solomon b. Simeon b. Tzemah (Rashbash) 170

Dworkin, Ronald 95n10

Eban, Abba 183n13

Eco, Umberto 84

Egalitarian 129, 156

Erikson, Erik 257

Ethical (practices, development, principles, reasoning) 46, 47, 50, 156, 164, 287, 388n1, 407n15, 413n19, 388-414

Ethics 82, 112 116, 394-414

Exum, J. Cheryl 34

Feminist/feminism 29, 34, 35n32, 44n64, 70, 388, 390, 393, 396, 402

Fendrick, Susan P. 58n16

Fish, Stanley 38, 88

Fishbane, Michael 132, 157

Fonrobert, Charlotte Elisheva 70

Formalism/formalist 88, 89, 90, 100,102

Fowler, James 258

Frank, Yitzhak 135

Frankfurt Lehrhaus 161

Freud, Sigmund 200n17

Frymer-Kensky, Tikvah 34

Gann Academy-The New Jewish High School of Greater Boston in Waltham, MA 237, 239, 245, 246, 248, 251, 253, 255, 259, 262, 265, 283, 284

Gardner, Leonard 44

Gemara 59n27, 104, 138, 142, 258, 260, 262, 266, 266n7, 269, 279, 381, 389

Gender 34, 70, 128n2, 136n15, 189, 193, 195, 208, 225, 231, 380, 388, 389, 394, 395, 396, 413

Gottwald, Norman K. 28, 29

Green, Arthur 380

Greenstein, Edward L. 29, 49, 392n4

Grimm, Tamar 386

Gros Louis, Kenneth 32

Grossman, Pamela 26, 27, 53, 54, 56

Halakha 61n22, 66, 67, 81, 82, 83, 104, 106n1, 116, 129, 254, 264, 266, 322, 380, 405
— halakhic discourse 81
— halakhic discussion 55

— halakhic flexibility 83n2
— halakhic framework 112
— halakhic implications 64, 64n24, 64n26
— halakhic norms 282
— halakhic orientation 63, 63n24, 66, 67
— halakhic reasoning 104
— halakhic rubric 114
— halakhic ruling 14
— halakhic subject 108
— halakhic texts 59, 70
— halakhic voices 280
Halbertal, Moshe 134
Haroutunian-Gordon, Sophie 289
Hartman Halbertal, Tova 134
Hasidic 129, 355
Havruta (Hevruta) 21, 55, 130, 135, 142, 155, 286-295, 298, 300-305, 308-311, 313, 315-322
Hebrew 40, 48, 50, 81n1, 106, 116, 129, 132, 135, 236, 260, 265, 284, 293, 327, 328, 329, 333, 347, 352, 354, 374, 413
Hebrew Union College Jewish Institute of Religion (HUC-JIR) 105, 357, 379, 387
Hebrew University 362, 379
Hermeneutics 29n14, 34, 83, 88, 96, 100, 104
— legal hermeneutics 89, 94
— of suspicion 55, 55n12, 72, 200, 200n18
— of trust 55, 72
Heschel, Abraham Joshua 164
Hiddush (*pl.* hiddushim) 63, 65n26, 73, 109
Hillel (Foundation for Jewish Campus Life) 364
Hirsch, Samson Raphael 37, 166, 167, 169
Historical approach 29, 37, 43
Historical thinking 53n3, 212-213, 213n7, 215

Hobbes, Thomas 204
Holtz, Barry 53, 54, 57, 186, 198n16, 352, 355n6, 374, 376
Holzer, Elie 288n6
Ibn Ezra 237, 253
Ideology/ideological 22, 23, 29, 55, 56, 59, 60, 63, 67, 72, 74n38, 80, 136, 138, 150n29, 151, 154, 156, 200, 358, 359, 367, 368, 376
Individualized learning 33
Informal 60, 60n20, 129, 212, 233, 353, 390n2
Initiative on Bridging Scholarship and Pedagogy in Jewish Studies 15
Inquiry 13, 14, 15, 16, 17, 17n6, 21, 28, 39n48, 52, 69, 75, 146, 159, 188, 197, 200n23, 210, 247, 262, 288n5, 392
Instruction/instructional 19n9, 27, 59, 68, 69, 70, 76, 77, 78, 133, 202, 203, 209, 257n17, 352, 412
Instructional triangle 19, 20
Integration 18, 78, 152
Interpretation 55n12, 200n17, 203n18
— Biblical interpretation 36, 256
— contexts of interpretation 190, 199, 2231
— legal interpretation 90, 96, 100
— literary interpretation 53, 187
— Talmudic interpretation 60, 63, 97
— textual interpretation 22, 38, 68
— tradition of interpretation 66, 109, 187
Interpretive
— interpretive approach 37, 43, 190
— interpretive community 38, 88
— interpretive frames 27
— interpretive orientation 50, 54, 74, 75, 78
— interpretive possibilities 137, 153, 154, 157, 367
— interpretive practices 58
— interpretive process 75
— interpretive questions 72, 136

General Index

— interpretive skills 21, 102
— interpretive stance 27
— interpretive strategies 38, 64
Iser, Wolfgang 309
Israel/Israeli 30, 34, 45n71, 64, 78, 129, 164, 170, 182, 190, 196, 200, 201, 202, 204n20, 207, 208, 209, 224, 234, 238, 245, 265, 293, 330, 331, 341, 342, 344, 346, 350, 355, 362, 402
Iyun 125, 131
Jacob, Benno 37
Jaffee, Martin 218, 222, 232
James, William 187
Jastrow, Marcus 135
Jewish beliefs 126, 164, 371
Jewish studies 15, 15n2, 83n3, 107, 259, 283, 293, 360
Jewish Theological Seminary of America 128, 379
Jewish thought 78, 126, 337, 379
Johnson, David 289, 318
Johnson, Roger 289, 318
Jordan, Michael 166
Josephus, Flavius 220n8
Justice 47, 60, 64, 148
Kalmin, Richard 123
Kaplan, Lawrence 103n18
Kaplan, Mordecai 397
Karaites 107
Katz, Jacob 83
Kennedy, John F. 183
King, Martin Luther, Jr. 164, 166, 167, 176, 182
Klein, Margie 386
Kling, Simcha 183n13
Kraemer, David 70
Kugel, James 36
Lampert, Magdalene 288n5
Lave, Jean 290
Leader, Ebn 386
Learning
— learning community 255, 281, 374n16, 381

— learning environment 159, 232, 292, 373
— learning experience 76, 130, 288, 320, 321
— learning goals 22, 218, 286, 321
— learning outcomes 62, 214, 233
— learning opportunities 62, 72
Lehman, Marjorie 70, 413, 414
Leibowitz, Nehama 35, 36, 37, 43, 50
Lesson plan 16, 45
Levinas, Emmanuel 60
Lewin, Walter H.G. 158, 159, 176n9, 186
Lincoln, Abraham 227
Lishma 14, 47, 47n79, 74
Literary
— literary analysis 31, 33, 61, 68, 76
— literary approach 29, 35, 44, 45, 239
— literary critical approach 31, 187
— literary critics/criticism 32, 34, 36, 38, 49, 54, 88, 252, 355n5
— literary method 40
— literary orientation 41, 42, 44, 60n21, 68, 71, 74n38, 75, 78
— literary texts 26, 63
Liturgical 59, 70, 114, 382
Lund, Nelson 95n10
Lytle, Susan 17
MacIntyre, Alasdair 390n3
Mahloket 63
Maimonides (Rambam) 78n42, 254
Mandel Center for Studies in Jewish Education at Brandeis University 11, 83n3, 288
Marx, Karl 200n17
Massachusetts Institute of Technology 158
Me'ah program of Hebrew College 238
Meaning
— theologically meaningful 56
— personal meaning 42, 44, 191, 192, 193, 198, 198n16, 203, 209, 210

General Index

Melton Curriculum Project of the Jewish Theological Seminary of America 238

Melton Research Center at the Jewish Theological Seminary of America 30, 44, 238

Method of teaching 58, 62n24, 64n25, 214, 405, 414

Methodology/methodological 31n23, 56, 58n17, 88, 109, 109n2, 128n2, 136n15, 188n7, 189, 227, 280, 289, 321n34, 392n4

Meyers, Carol 29, 34

Michaels, Sarah 290

Midrash/midrashic 36n38, 67, 129, 165, 177, 179, 181, 184, 205n21, 206, 271n5, 334, 377, 388, 393, 394, 395, 395n7, 396, 397, 397n8, 400
— midrashic exegesis 100
— midrashic interpretation 204
— midrashic literature 37, 59, 75

Mishnah 13, 22, 62, 66-69, 69n31, 73, 90, 91, 97, 99, 100, 103n18, 110, 111, 132, 143, 144, 146, 218, 265, 266, 268, 268n2, 273, 280, 390, 402

Model of teaching 14, 19, 20, 55n10, 56, 58, 332

Moral/moralistic
— moral attunement 74n38
— moral autonomy 45
— moral behavior 40
— moral decision making 46n75
— moral identity 390, 390n3
— moral insights 160
— moral lessons 40
— moralistic approach 41, 42
— moralistic-didactic orientation 50, 54, 78

Morrison, Jeremy 353-358, 365-375

Moscovitz, Leib 123

Motivation 62, 66, 266, 294, 300, 303, 306, 330, 356

Multivocality 62, 280, 283, 284

National Ramah Commission 128

Neusner, Jacob 107, 108, 109, 110, 122, 123, 124n9

New Critics 29n14, 32

New York University 379

Nietzsche, Friedrich 200n17

Northwoods Kollel of Camp Ramah in Wisconsin 128, 129

Noth, Martin 29

Obama, Barack 166

Orientation 21, 26, 27, 28, 29, 33, 34, 37, 38, 39, 46, 48, 49, 50, 53n7, 54, 58, 58n17, 59, 59n18, 63, 64, 65, 66, 67, 68, 75, 76n40, 77, 78, 186, 186n2, 192, 193, 198, 198n16, 199, 205, 207, 352, 353, 355, 355n6, 356, 357n8, 358, 365, 366, 367, 369, 370, 376, 376n18, 380

Parshanut 29, 31, 35, 37, 44, 48, 50, 54, 72, 78, 355

Pedagogy 14, 15, 15n2, 17, 18, 18n7, 29, 51, 59n18, 64n25, 80n43, 107, 128, 129, 130, 157, 158, 184n15, 207, 209, 233, 264, 271, 285, 374, 375, 377
— pedagogic approaches 29, 40, 51, 116, 122, 197, 355, 378
— pedagogic challenge 16, 126, 159, 160
— pedagogic goals 28, 65, 79, 358
— pedagogic inquiry 15
— pedagogic objectives 191, 192, 198, 200, 204, 206, 209
— pedagogic practices 53, 56, 58, 64, 78, 136, 138, 187, 191n9, 409
— pedagogic purposes 392n4
— pedagogical content knowledge (PCK) 15, 26
— pedagogical methods 54, 105, 188
— pedagogical values 153, 191, 199, 207
— subject-specific pedagogy 15, 16, 17, 53, 80n43, 207

Peirce, Charles Sanders 84n6

Personalization 42-43, 355n5

General Index

Peshat 16, 22, 55, 59n26, 60n32, 61, 116, 122, 136, 142, 266, 388, 394
Philo 220n8
Philosophy 36n35, 38n42, 52, 55n12, 83, 108, 123, 129, 200n17, 201, 242, 254, 257, 282, 356, 363
Piaget, Jean 257
Pitzele, Peter 50
Plaut, Gunther 354-355
Playful 74, 159, 184, 185, 185n16
Pliny 220n8
Pluralistic 21, 57, 74, 245, 255, 281, 283
Post-modern (approaches) 34, 49
Post-structuralism 93, 94
Practical 15, 18, 19n8, 38n44, 46n72, 57n14, 214, 226, 231, 370, 393, 394
Principled eclecticism 75n39, 79, 80, 80n43
Rabbenu Tam (Rabbi Yaakov the son of Meir Tam) 149-153
Rabin, Yitzhak 183n13
Ramban (Rabbi Moses the son of Nahman, Nahmanides) 149
Rashba (Rabbi Solomon the son of Abraham Adret) 130n4
Rashbam 237, 254
Rashi (Rabbi Shlomo the son of Yitzhak) 148, 149, 150, 237
Reagan, Ronald 183n13
Reconstructionist Rabbinical College (RRC) 390-391, 393, 394, 402, 403, 411
Reflective practice 16
Relevance 47, 50, 92, 161, 179, 193, 275, 333, 370, 380, 384, 404
Religious education 38, 45n71, 128n2, 359n14
Richard, Michael 167
Rishonim 102, 108, 118, 124, 131, 137, 142-144, 148-150, 154, 156
Ritva (Rabbi Yom Tov the son of Abraham Ishbili) 148, 149

Riverway Project: Connecting Twenties and Thirties to Judaism (RWP) at Temple Israel of Boston 353, 354, 355, 358, 361
Rosenberg, Joel 32
Rosenblum, Jordan 233
Rosenzweig, Franz 161, 179
Rosenzweig, Michael 64n25
Rossel, Seymour 39, 40, 41
Rothstein, Gidon 70
Sacred 55, 59, 129, 202, 237, 239, 241, 245, 246, 254, 262, 263, 369, 370, 388, 388n1, 391, 402, 405
Sarna, Nahum 30, 31, 37, 43, 44, 45n70
Scheffler, Israel 256, 257, 262
Scholarship of Teaching and Learning (SoTL) movement 8-11, 14, 16, 17
Schreiber, Doniel 66
Schwab, Joseph 19, 28, 46
Sequentiality 77n41
Shakespeare, William 32, 41, 87
Shalom Hartman Institute 60
Shapira, Meir 73n37
Shulman, Lee 15, 16, 17, 26n2
Silberman, Laurence H. 95n10
Skeptical stance 72
Skills 21, 49, 50, 60n19, 61, 65n26, 75, 76, 77, 77n41, 81, 81n1, 102, 106n1, 123, 129, 134, 134n10, 137n17, 155, 156, 212, 213, 218, 229, 237, 265, 266, 282, 291, 325, 326, 338, 350, 357, 358, 382, 383, 392, 393, 403, 404, 409, 410, 413
Smith, Karl A. 318
Soloveitchik, Hayyim 108, 123
Source criticism 29, 34, 238, 239, 245, 246, 247, 248, 262
South Area Solomon Schechter Day School (SASSDS)-Kehillah Schechter Academy (KSA) in Norwood, MA 325, 327
Spinoza, Baruch 190, 204-207
Spira-Savett, Jon 79n42

General Index

Spiritual 44, 44n64, 47, 64n26, 71, 73, 112, 132, 157, 177, 240, 247, 261, 324, 374, 377, 378, 392, 393, 403
Stam 107, 116, 118n6, 119-122, 124, 125n9, 268, 277, 280, 281, 284
Steinzaltz, Adin 395
Stendahl, Krister 197
Subject matter 18, 20, 26, 26n2, 27, 28, 29, 46, 53, 54, 80n43, 159, 184, 191n9, 192, 200, 201, 245, 290, 355, 258, 275, 376n18, 390n2, 405, 412
Sugya 55, 65, 66, 67, 103n18, 107, 111, 112, 115, 116, 119-122, 129, 131, 132, 134-137, 143, 144, 146-152, 154, 155, 268, 270-273, 275-280, 285, 404, 407
Synagogue 20, 21, 30, 48, 74n38, 106n1, 159, 160, 160n2, 163, 164, 169, 170, 184, 184n15, 190, 224, 254, 259, 330, 353, 354, 357, 360, 374n16
Tanchel, Susan 283, 284
Tannaim/Tannaitic 136, 142, 268, 270n4, 284
Tasman, Sarah 385
Taubenfeld Cohen, Jane 326
Teacher's beliefs 27, 28, 54, 58, 352, 353, 356, 378n18
Teacher's research 15, 17, 19, 38n44,
Technique 14, 18, 40, 54, 55, 56, 58, 82, 128, 131, 133, 137n17, 153, 183, 188, 191n9, 202, 204, 214, 339
Technology 216, 231, 233
Tefillah 112, 117, 117n4, 118, 118n6, 119, 121, 122, 380, 381
Textual ambiguity 37
Theology/theological 41, 45, 123, 155n32, , 197n14, 376n18

Theory 16n5, 26n1, 56, 57, 237, 250, 259, 261, 286, 288, 288n5, 289, 289n8, 356
Todd, Frankie 290
Tolstoy, Leo 32
Torah and Tonics on Tuesdays class at Temple Israel of Boston (Tx3) 353, 354, 356-358, 360-364, 369-375
Torah lish'ma 74n38
Tosafot (Tosafists) 130n4
Translation 19n8, 48, 50, 54, 71, 103n18, 106, 131, 135, 136, 137n17, 144, 157, 202, 265, 293, 329, 364, 400, 401
Trible, Phyllis 34
Truth 40, 59, 61, 62, 90, 124, 247, 253, 272, 273, 275, 359, 382, 408, 410
Visotzsky, Burt 50
Vygotsky, Lev 290
Walfish, Avraham 69
Walker, Alice 164
Waskow, Arthur 50
Weiss Halivni, David 284
Wellhausen, Julius 204
Wenger, Etienne 290
White House 168
Wilson, Suzanne 53
Wimpfheimer, Barry 61n22
Wineburg, Sam 52, 213, 227
Wisdom of practice 29, 38
Wissenschaft des Judentums 109
Wood, Chip 133
Woods, Tiger 166
Yehudah Aryeh Leib of Ger (S'fas Emes) 22, 23, 355
Yeshiva 20, 61, 63, 64n25, 65n27, 83, 105, 123, 129, 134, 134n10, 135n11, 264, 379
Yeshiva University 362
Yeshivat Chovevei Torah 83
Zielenziger, Ruth 44, 48, 238

www.ingramcontent.com/pod-product-compliance
Lightning Source LLC
Chambersburg PA
CBHW052054300426
44117CB00013B/2121